EQUALITY AND LEGITIMACY

Equality and Legitimacy

WOJCIECH SADURSKI

OXFORD
UNIVERSITY PRESS

This book has been printed digitally and produced in a standard specification in order to ensure its continuing availability

OXFORD
UNIVERSITY PRESS

Great Clarendon Street, Oxford OX2 6DP

Oxford University Press is a department of the University of Oxford.
It furthers the University's objective of excellence in research, scholarship,
and education by publishing worldwide in

Oxford New York

Auckland Cape Town Dar es Salaam Hong Kong Karachi
Kuala Lumpur Madrid Melbourne Mexico City Nairobi
New Delhi Shanghai Taipei Toronto
With offices in
Argentina Austria Brazil Chile Czech Republic France Greece
Guatemala Hungary Italy Japan South Korea Poland Portugal
Singapore Switzerland Thailand Turkey Ukraine Vietnam

Oxford is a registered trade mark of Oxford University Press
in the UK and in certain other countries

Published in the United States
by Oxford University Press Inc., New York

Reprinted 2011

ISBN 978-0-19-954517-9

Acknowledgments

I have been associated with the European University Institute in Florence and the University of Sydney while writing this book. I owe a big debt of gratitude to my friends, colleagues, staff, and students in these two excellent and friendly academic institutions. I wish, in particular, to thank my secretary Marlies Becker whose help and support has always been invaluable to me.

In the course of writing various earlier versions of some parts of this book I benefited from conversations and discussions with, and comments from, many people. I can list only some of them here: Silvina Alvarez, Zenon Bankowski, Tom Campbell, Adam Czarnota, Duncan Ivison, Martin Krygier, Massimo La Torre, Neil MacCormick, Eric Millard, Gianluigi Palombella, Philip Pettit, Giovanni Sartor, Michael Troper, Neil Walker, Kevin Walton, Jeremy Webber, Lorenzo Zucca, and three anonymous reviewers of the OUP.

I also had an opportunity to present earlier versions of some of the chapters at various seminars and conferences around the world, including at the Universities of Edinburgh, Sevilla, Paris-X (Nanterre), Sydney, New South Wales (Australia), Warsaw, Parma, Catanzaro, and Victoria (Canada).

I was very lucky to be able to collaborate with some extremely gifted doctoral students at the European University Institute who helped me to improve the quality of the manuscript: Mehreen Afzal, Sara Dezaley, and Alun Gibbs.

Early versions of some parts of Chapters 1 and 2 have been published as articles in, respectively, Oxford Journal of Legal Studies and Ratio Juris. I am grateful to the publishers of these journals for their kind permission to include the revised texts of these articles here.

This book is dedicated to Anna, with great affection and gratitude.

November 2007

Acknowledgements

I have been associated with the European University Institute in Florence and the University of Sydney while writing this book. I owe a big debt of gratitude to my friends, colleagues, staff, and students in these two excellent and friendly [illegible] which, in particular to thank my secretary [illegible] [illegible]

Introduction

In the words of arguably the most eminent living legal and political philosopher, 'A legitimate government must treat all those over whom it claims dominion not just with a measure of concern but with *equal* concern'.[1] This contention, hardly controversial, links two major concepts in legal and political philosophy—legitimacy and equality—by making the former dependent on the latter. But what does it mean to say that a government is legitimate? For instance, does it necessarily imply that citizens have a moral duty to comply with all the directives it issues? And what type of government-sponsored equality deserves to be praised as displaying 'equal concern'? These two questions point to a web of interlocking problems and dilemmas, some of which will be addressed in this book.

It is concerned with legitimacy and equality and, more importantly, with the relationship between the two. The stage is set in Chapter 1 where I undertake a twofold inquiry. First of all, I will explore the meaning of law's legitimacy, by positioning it vis-à-vis two contiguous concepts: that of a justification of the law, and that of the duty to obey the law. I argue that legitimacy may be aligned with either of these two concepts but not with both of them at the same time, at least not without introducing some additional non-legitimacy related considerations. The basis of this argument is provided by a discussion of a very influential and important theory of legitimacy, namely that developed by Joseph Raz. It is also particularly relevant to my purpose because Raz has been charged, by various critics, that his conception did not allow the inclusion of the democratic process as *a* criterion of legitimacy—a critique in my view unjustified, but instructive for the study of the relationship between legitimacy and democracy. This, indeed, will be the second aim of this chapter: to clarify the link between legitimacy and democracy, but only in *this* one aspect: is it correct to contend that compliance with the proper democratic procedures is all that is required to endow the law with legitimacy, or does the law also have to comply with some standards as regards its content so as to be endowed with legitimacy? I incline towards the former, but will argue that those 'merely' procedural democratic principles presuppose some quite fundamental moral choices which are themselves not 'procedural' but very substantive indeed.

These substantive moral principles which underlie, as I claim, democratic procedures are identified and discussed in more detail in Chapter 2. The assertion made in Chapter 1, namely that democratic procedures largely presuppose some egalitarian moral conceptions, is explored in Chapter 2, with the purpose

[1] Ronald Dworkin *Is Democracy Possible Here?* (Princeton: Princeton University Press, 2006) 97 (emphasis in original).

of identifying how these egalitarian conceptions contribute to supporting the legitimacy of the outcomes of democratic procedures. This constitutes the central argument of the entire book so I should clarify briefly its structure and its aspiration. In the overall project of the book this argument aims to show that equality plays a crucial role in conferring legitimacy on a democratic process. The structure of the reasoning in Chapter 2 can therefore be presented, in a schematic way, as exploring a triangle formed by three concepts: majority rule (understood, subject to certain qualifications explicated at the beginning of Chapter 2, as an irreducible core of democratic procedures), equality (understood as proposed in the chapter, as that of equal political opportunity), and legitimacy (in the sense clarified earlier in Chapter 1). The relationship between these three concepts is the following: while the connection between majority rule and legitimacy is taken for granted, as a 'fixed point' in our reflective equilibrium, the relationship between majority rule and equality is the focus of the argument developed in the chapter; and the relationship between equality and legitimacy (in the sense that legitimacy is based on a certain conception of equality) is the conclusion.

While Chapter 2 will be dominated by approaches and perspectives brought into the discussion of equality by *political* theory, Chapter 3 will turn to *legal* theory, and will explore the thorny ideal of equality in law. I will try to show exactly why this ideal is thorny. First of all, its proponents usually oscillate between two levels—that of the application and that of the content of the law—without always appreciating the difference between the two. Still, this is perhaps the least problematic issue; what really renders the ideal troublesome is that some, apparently easy, 'value neutral' tests (that is, independent of the overall moral judgments of the scrutinizer) for discrimination are useless in this instance (such as, that legal rules should make no, or as few as possible, distinctions between classes of addressees, or that the law should not draw lines between addressees in terms of characteristics which are immutable, such as race or sex) while, on the other hand, collapsing the assessment of legal equality into an undifferentiated judgment of justice or fairness is counter-intuitive and equally unhelpful. I will propose a half-way solution which aims at overcoming the weaknesses of these two unhelpful positions by reflecting—again, in a reflective-equilibrium mode—upon the moral wrongs which we can discern, with a certain degree of confidence, in various instances of undoubtedly invidious discrimination; this will provide a basis to suggest ways to identify, in a workable manner, this wrong by looking at its external indicia. This would allow us to subject a given legal classification which, owing to the presence of these indicia, warrants our suspicion that invidious discrimination is at work, to a more searching, stricter scrutiny than routine cases of legal classifications.

While Chapter 2 focuses on political equality and Chapter 3 on legal equality, in Chapters 4 and 5, I turn to *social* equality. But what *is* social equality? Is it social in the sense that it describes the properties of society as a whole, such as the absence of domination, hierarchy, structural discrimination, as opposed to a more 'individualized' equality which focuses instead on the specific factors which determine the relative amount of goods (distributional shares of utility, of welfare, of resources etc) enjoyed by one individual as compared with others? In Chapter 4, I explore the general contours of social equality by questioning the status of this distinction between a 'collective' and an 'individualized' interpretation of social equality, and argue that this distinction is unhelpful and, in some of its interpretations, confused. Occasionally this distinction intersects with some interesting problems about social equality, such as whether for someone who values equality per se, 'levelling down' everyone's situation so as to achieve more equality should be an attractive ideal—which, of course, would discredit equality in the eyes of many of us. But, from the point of view of the discussion developed afterwards, what is central is a defence of the 'individualized' approach to equality as perfectly aligned with those values which render 'collective' interpretations of equality so attractive. Indeed, much of the remaining argument is focused on a species of an apparently 'individualized' conception: the conception according to which equality demands that only (and all) of those inequalities which result from various instances of bad luck be removed ('luck egalitarianism'). This is another way of saying, as John Rawls urged, that people's distributive shares should not depend on factors that are arbitrary from a moral point of view, that is 'according to their social fortune or their luck in the natural lottery'.[2] A number of preliminary questions have to be addressed before a more careful analysis of the conception of luck egalitarianism is proposed in Chapter 5. So the remainder of Chapter 4 reflects on whether the very idea of 'natural and social lottery' makes sense, and also whether 'natural' and 'social' contingencies should have equal status in a normative conception of social equality. An argument will be discussed (and eventually, rejected) that, while natural and social contingencies may be equally 'arbitrary from a moral point of view', natural contingencies (such as genetically determined talent) may be so closely related to an individual identity, or individual self, that any 'luck neutralization' aimed at these fortuitous factors may raise some fundamental moral objections.

It is only once these objections are addressed, and these concerns allayed, that we are able to address 'luck egalitarianism', as perhaps the most attractive conception of social equality, in more detail in Chapter 5. The conception is based on the idea that people should be responsible for their choices but not for that which comes to them, or which happens to them, as 'brute luck'—and so the relationship between these two central notions, luck and responsibility, in an overall luck egalitarianism moral framework, will be considered at the outset. I will then review and assess the distinction between two main conceptions which have traditionally informed the main debate within luck egalitarianism: equality of welfare and equality of resources. This distinction, introduced years ago in the seminal article by Ronald Dworkin, which can be seen as foundational to this

[2] John Rawls *A Theory of Justice* (Oxford: Oxford University Press, 1971) 75.

whole conception, allows us to reflect upon the role of individual preferences in luck egalitarianism, and in particular those preferences which are expensive and which place particular pressure on scarce societal resources.

The moral insight underlying luck egalitarianism builds on the distinction between what is a person proper and what are 'merely' circumstances, with the implication that while the attributes of 'circumstances' should be subjected to neutralization under luck egalitarianism, the attributes of a person should not. The status and meaning of this distinction will be reviewed, with particular attention attached to the question of whether this distinction correlates properly with the distinction between that for which we may hold a person responsible and that for which we should compensate a disadvantaged person. Finally, having clarified the meaning and the intellectual resources available to 'luck egalitarianism', I will address the central question: to what extent is this 'egalitarianism' truly *egalitarian*? In other words, on what grounds can we be certain that a systemic attempt to neutralize the effects of bad brute luck will bring about a society which is substantially more equal than contemporary societies as we know them? After all, neutralization of luck must be across the board, so the argument goes, such that we would also have to neutralize the *equalities* which result from luck, and not only *inequalities*. My response will be that 'luck egalitarianism' is not an oxymoron and that neutralizing the incidences of bad luck, as understood in Chapter 5, will have powerful egalitarian consequences, although the reasons for this belief are perhaps more conditional and contingent than many 'luck egalitarians' would have us believe.

How do these three dimensions of equality, political, legal and social, intersect with each other and inform our sense of the legitimacy of law in a democratic state? In the Conclusion, I will try to respond, by bringing the main threads of this book together.

Contents

Table of Cases

AUSTRALIA

EUROPEAN COURT OF HUMAN RIGHTS

US

Table of Legislation

1

Law's Legitimacy and Democracy

It is often said that a democratic state, in order to be fully legitimate, must not only issue its laws in a procedurally correct way but must also ensure that they comply with certain substantive values. Democracy, it is said, not only requires designing and following the correct procedures but its laws must also comply with certain values, such as human dignity, liberty etc, in order to be fully legitimate. In this chapter I will subject this understanding—which I will refer to interchangeably as the 'output democracy', 'value-enhanced' democracy or 'democracy-plus' conception—to critical scrutiny. However, my main purpose will not be so much to refute this view but rather to reflect on what such a call for the alignment of democracy with certain values really means—what plausible interpretations can be given to this claim. A more detailed refutation (based not so much on the head-on attack on output democracy but rather on a claim that some important, substantive, and legitimacy-conferring values are ingrained in procedural requirements of democracy, and in particular in the majority rule) will be attempted in Chapter 2. Here, more specifically, my main concern will be with the links between an output democracy (democracy that is not 'merely' procedural but rather claims to have been infused with the 'right' values) and judgments concerning the legitimacy of democratically enacted laws. Just as the principle of the rule of law can be understood in a purely procedural or in a more substantive way (that is, either that government is subject to *all* laws, whatever they may be, or that it is only subject to those laws that can be viewed as 'right' or 'just'), so the democratic rule can be understood in a similar manner. Can those laws that have procedurally democratic credentials but diverge from our views about the right 'substantive' values still be said to be legitimate? This is a somewhat stylized way of asking the question of central concern in this chapter.

As the above question immediately suggests, a great deal depends on how we understand the concept of law's legitimacy. In trying to prepare the ground for the discussion of the legitimacy of 'output democracy' that will occupy the first half (Parts 1–4) of this chapter, I will first attempt to elucidate the notion of law's legitimacy by disentangling it from two other contiguous concepts: the justification of law and the obligation of citizens to obey it. I will take, as my starting point, a leading (and perhaps currently the most influential) theory in this area, namely Joseph Raz's so-called 'service conception' of legitimate authority

(Part 1). This choice is influenced not merely by the critical resonance that this theory has found in recent jurisprudential writings but, more relevantly from our point of view, by the fact that it has been accused of displaying insufficient respect for the importance of procedurally democratic law-making as a significant factor in assessing the legitimacy of laws, and also of underestimating the importance of promoting a critical, reflective attitude amongst citizens towards the law to which they are subject. The discussion of Raz's conception of legitimacy, therefore, brings us directly into the heart of the relationship between democratic law-making and the legitimacy of law.

Even if, as I will argue, Raz's conception may be unsatisfactory in some regards (Part 2), this is *not* due to its alleged disregard for the importance of democracy nor to the idea, which it allegedly promotes, that citizens should always defer to authority (Part 3). The reason that such a suspicion may have arisen in the first place is related to the ambivalence of the very notion of 'legitimacy', and its position vis-à-vis the justification of the law on one hand and the citizens' obligation to obey on the other (Part 4). I will argue that if legitimacy is understood as relating to the question of a given law's justification, then the objections of Raz's critics are groundless; if, in turn, legitimacy is viewed as creating or supporting the citizens' duty to obey (which is *not* the case in Raz's work), then a different, separate argumentative step is required to show that it is legitimate, in addition to being justified. Therefore, even if a justification-based understanding of legitimacy does not *require* that a law have certain procedural, democratic credentials (although, of course, the two are perfectly compatible), this is not necessarily the case when legitimacy is viewed as obligation-inducing: this, however, is not Raz's concern, at least in terms of his 'service conception' of legitimate authority.

This clears the conceptual ground for a more substantive argument concerning the relationship between legitimacy and democracy and, more specifically, for critical scrutiny of the demand that law, in order to be legitimate, must embody certain substantive values. This will be undertaken in the second half of the chapter, Parts 5–7. First, I will look in detail at the conventional warnings against purely procedural democracy, and suggest that the best way of understanding the calls for supplementing democracy with substantive values, in order to endow it with legitimacy, is to try to imagine what a democracy *devoid* of substantive values might look like, and what the advantages and disadvantages (if any) of such a system might be (Part 5). To the extent that 'democracy without values' is inconceivable (given that the very choice of a democratic design is inevitably and strongly value-based), the warning against value-insensitive democracy is itself meaningless. However, I will argue that, beyond this foundational stage, the infusion of democracy with values may be seen as a meaningful demand, particularly if, as I will seek to demonstrate, a resort to the concept of 'pure procedural democracy', by analogy to Rawlsian 'pure procedural justice', is not readily available to us. We cannot be sure that, once the democratic procedure has been put in place, the values that inform its design will be replicated in the actual functioning of the system.

In what way, then, can we plausibly understand the call for output-based democracy? I will suggest two possible understandings: one 'motivational' (Part 6), the other 'constitutional' (Part 7); and I will show that both exhibit a problematic, troublesome relationship to society's moral pluralism.

1. Legitimacy of Law and the 'Service Conception' of Authority

When is a state *justified* in issuing authoritative directives to its citizens? And if it *is* justified in doing so, does it follow that its directives—its laws—are necessarily *legitimate*, leading to the creation of a *duty to obey* on our part? These three questions—about justification, legitimacy, and the duty to obey—are often merged into one, and this, I will argue, leads to confusion. A good starting point for an attempt to disentangle them is Joseph Raz's so-called 'service conception of authority', if only because it is currently so influential, both among its supporters and its detractors. The 'service conception' consists of three theses: the dependence thesis, the normal justification thesis, and the pre-emption thesis. Here, I will only outline each of these in a simplified manner, and by paraphrasing Raz. According to the first thesis, authoritative directives should only be adopted for reasons which apply to their intended subjects (and not, for example, for reasons relevant to the authorities themselves). The second holds that desired outcomes will most often be achieved if the subjects allow themselves to be guided by the directives of the authority rather than acting on those reasons directly. The third states that the authoritative directives supersede, rather than complement, the reasons for their own adoption (which I will here refer to as 'original reasons', as opposed to the directives which constitute new reasons for action).

This conception is, at first blush, vulnerable to the objection that it cannot be squared with the idea that citizens should display a critical, reflective attitude towards the authorities that govern them; a critical attitude characteristic of a democratic society in which it should be generally accepted that, as HLA Hart famously put it, 'however great the aura of majesty or authority which the official system may have, its demands must in the end be submitted to a moral scrutiny'.[1] Even though Raz had anticipated objections along these lines and protested in advance that '[n]o blind obedience to authority is here implied',[2] nevertheless the charge has been laid. Ronald Dworkin, for one, has observed caustically that '[t]his account of the nature and point of authority insists on a certain attitude

[1] HLA Hart *The Concept of Law* (Oxford: Oxford University Press, 1961) at 206.

[2] Joseph Raz *Ethics in the Public Domain* (Oxford: Oxford University Press, 1994) at 215.

toward authority',[3] namely, 'a degree of deference toward legal authority that almost no one shows in modern democracies'.[4] It is worth looking more closely at Dworkin's argument:

> We do not treat even those laws we regard as perfectly valid and legitimate as excluding and replacing the background reasons the framers of that law rightly considered in adopting it. We rather regard those laws as creating rights and duties that normally trump those other reasons. The reasons remain, and we sometimes need to consult them to decide whether, in particular circumstances, they are so extraordinarily powerful or important that the law's trump should not prevail.[5]

Dworkin then goes on to elaborate this point by giving the example of President Abraham Lincoln who, during the Civil War, suspended the writ of habeas corpus even though the United States Constitution denies such a power to the President acting on his own, instead assigning it to Congress. Dworkin's criticism, however, misses the point, and his Lincoln example actually seems to *confirm* rather than undermine Raz's conception. Raz is not suggesting, in his service conception of authority, that citizens are advised to follow the authority's directives rather than their own reasons for action; rather, he is saying that *if and when they do so*, then the authority is, for them, legitimate. This is a *conceptual* analysis of the notion of legitimate authority rather than a *normative* thesis about the subjection of citizens to the authorities.

This distinction calls for some additional explanation. Raz himself has explained, after his original exposition of the 'service conception of authority', that it is 'a normative-explanatory account' of authority, and that it displays 'an interdependence between conceptual and normative argument'.[6] Therefore, it is important to be clear in what way the conception is indeed normative-conceptual, as opposed to 'normative-only' and 'conceptual-only' and, in addition, whether the special interdependence of the conceptual and the normative in Raz's thesis makes it vulnerable to the charge of undue deference, as expressed by, for example, Dworkin. Raz himself explains the other contrast, between his own and a purely linguistic concept of the authority, in the following way: a 'purely linguistic account of authority claims to yield a simple explanation of what people believe who believe that someone has legitimate authority'.[7] In the context of the broader argument this suggests that the emphasis is on the word 'simple', and the contrast between a 'linguistic' and Raz's own conceptual-normative account is that the latter 'avows that it does not necessarily conform to everyone's notion of authority in all detail'.[8] It is only in this sense

[3] Ronald Dworkin 'Thirty Years On (Book Review of *The Practice of Principle* by Jules Coleman)' Harvard Law Review (2002) 115: 1655 at 1671.

[4] Dworkin 'Thirty Years On' 1672.

[5] ibid.

[6] Joseph Raz *The Morality of Freedom* (Oxford: Oxford University Press, 1986) respectively at 64 and 63.

[7] ibid at 65.

[8] ibid at 65.

that Raz sees his own theory as being also normative: it does not attempt to track the ordinary usage of the concept of legitimate authority in every detail (an admittedly impossible task) but rather stipulates that a right usage of the notion of legitimate authority should necessarily imply the presence of three facts described by the dependence, normal justification, and pre-emption theses. This, Raz suggests, helps us single out important features of our recognition of legitimate authorities, and it helps explain what we 'believe when [we] believe that a person has authority'.[9] This last formulation immediately suggests the other relevant contrast, namely between the conceptual-normative concept (as the one submitted by Raz) and the normative-only, as attributed to Raz (wrongly, in my view) by Dworkin. Raz's concept, in itself, does not tell us anything about the proper moral attitude of citizens towards authority. It does not dictate, per se, the scope and limits of deference towards (legitimate) authority. It only helps us 'explain what they believe in when they believe that a person has authority'[10] rather than announce a moral principle that once the person or an institution is endowed by an addressee of the directives with authority, the addressees should substitute their own reasons with the authoritative directives in their practical action.

The language that Dworkin uses to describe the status of the original reasons after the law has entered into the scene in fact confirms this: rights and duties created by the law 'trump' the original reasons—which is exactly what Raz describes by using the language of 'pre-emption'. 'The reasons remain . . .', Dworkin observes, but this does not mark any difference between the (Razian) pre-emption thesis and his own account, because the reasons 'remain' only in the sense that they inform us whether, under the circumstances, we should comply with the law's directives or consider some extra-legal, even illegal, course of action. This residual role of the original reasons which persist after law has entered the stage is perfectly compatible with—indeed, supports—Raz's pre-emption thesis, because the limits to the pre-emption are at the same time the limits of law's legitimacy. If the law's 'subjects do not guide their actions by its instructions instead of by the reasons on which they are supposed to depend'[11] then the law, at this point, is no longer a legitimate authority for them because it does not fulfil the role of mediating between people and the practical reasons upon which they act. That this 'mediation' is central to Raz's account is confirmed by his proposition that the dependence and the normal justification theses 'regard authorities as *mediating* between people and the right reasons which apply to them, so that the authority judges and pronounces what they ought to do according to right reason'.[12]

Dworkin's example of Lincoln and of his suspension of habeas corpus seems to confirm this: 'Most of us treat the Constitution as both legitimate and

[9] ibid at 66.
[10] ibid at 65–66.
[11] Raz *Ethics in the Public Domain* at 215.
[12] ibid (emphasis in original).

authoritative. But many commentators nevertheless think both that Abraham Lincoln was morally right to suspend habeas corpus during the Civil War and that he acted illegally'.[13] Expressed in Raz's terms, what Lincoln did was to revert to the original reasons for action rather than to act on the Constitution's authority: the perceived emergency inclined him into an illegal but politically and morally preferable solution. Far from questioning Raz's pre-emption thesis, as his intention is, Dworkin actually confirms Raz's account in his own parlance: legal rights normally trump our various extra-legal considerations (eg of utility), but extra-legal considerations may trump the law's authority when compliance with law's directives is morally or politically indefensible. This becomes even clearer when Dworkin adds:

> Lincoln did not deny the Constitution's authority in making his decision; he simply weighed that authority against competing reasons of the kind the Framers had also taken into account which retained their vitality. Lincoln found that the latter were, under the circumstances, strong enough to outweigh the former.[14]

It is somewhat puzzling why Dworkin sees this account of Lincoln's unconstitutional but morally and politically justified action as contrary to Raz's account of what constitutes legitimate authority. The point of Dworkin's account is as follows: the framers of the Constitution had contemplated various reasons that the President and/or Congress might have had for suspending the writ and in the end had decided that the reasons for the President to act alone were not compelling enough to grant him this constitutional power. Those reasons (ultimately discarded by the framers) 'retained their vitality' nevertheless (although in an extra-legal realm, so to speak), and Lincoln acted on them, in contrast to what the Constitution provided; hence, he acted illegally but, in the eyes of Dworkin and 'many commentators' with whom he aligns himself, morally correctly. This is perfectly compatible with Raz's account: in Raz's terminology, on this particular issue, Lincoln decided that it was better to revert to his own original reasons for action (which, we may infer, were related to the most efficient way of avoiding great national disaster in a situation of emergency, and which mandated his unilateral action to suspend the writ) rather than use the authoritative directives contained in the Constitution as the best way of giving effect to those original reasons. So, in this particular case, he denied the legitimacy of the Constitution, which is just another way of saying, as Dworkin himself admits, that Lincoln acted 'illegally' and at the same time in a 'morally right' fashion.

There is one way in which the above defence of Raz's conception *may* be challenged, and its consistency with Dworkin's account of the Lincoln example questioned. It may be argued that the property of legitimacy applies to the authority *across the board* rather than to its *specific* directives, so that a subject may disregard

[13] Dworkin 'Thirty Years On' at 1672.
[14] ibid.

one or another specific directive of an authority (or, in Raz's terminology, act on her own reasons for action rather than allow the authoritative directives to pre-empt them) and still recognize the legitimacy of the authority as a whole. Such an interpretation seems to be offered by Dworkin when he states that, in his example, 'Lincoln did not deny the Constitution's authority in making his decision', and yet that 'he acted illegally'. This, however, seems to be a pedantic gambit. The fact that Lincoln 'acted illegally' on this particular issue means that, *on this particular issue*, he denied the legitimacy of the Constitution as applying to him. The recognition of legitimacy may be a matter of degree: Raz mentions that a legal system's legitimate authority 'may not be as extensive as it claims'.[15] We may, of course, adopt by definitional fiat a convention whereby legitimacy applies only to the authority as a whole rather than to its particular directives but then we would need another idiom to describe the situation in which a subject recognizes the general authority of a given entity but refuses to recognize a specific directive as properly incorporating the right reasons relevant to himself. Nothing is lost by saying that such a specific directive is held to be 'illegitimate' by this subject, and nothing is gained by assigning the notion of legitimacy only to authority in general, and denying it to specific authoritative directives.

2. Authority and Identification of Valid Law

The upshot of the previous part of this chapter is that Raz's pre-emption thesis seems to be a useful enough account of what it means for subjects to treat an authority as legitimate. What is more problematic, however, is the account of the law as necessarily and always identifiable without regard to the original reasons that the law-makers have amalgamated, so to speak, into the legal directives. It is one thing for Raz to insist on the conceptual truth about 'legitimate' authorities pre-empting the citizens' appeal to non-legal reasons insofar as they recognize the legitimacy of a given directive; it is quite another thing to claim that the law must be fully identifiable by its subjects without ascertainment of the original reasons for action that it is now meant to displace. The latter claim is not a necessary condition of the intelligibility of the former.

We can say that, insofar as we recognize the law's legitimacy, we disregard the competing, non-legal reasons for action (in the sense that if those non-legal considerations outweigh the legal directives, then this is just another way of saying that the law's legitimacy has reached its limits), *and also* that in order to ascertain the correct meaning of the legal directives, we must appeal, at times, to the very reasons that the law seeks to translate into the language of legal rules. The latter statement may upset the architectural elegance of Raz's construction in the sense that the original reasons for action may appear twice in the process

[15] Raz *Ethics in the Public Domain* at 215.

of the compliance with law: first, at the stage of the translation of these reasons into legal rules by legal authorities and, secondly, at the stage of ascertaining the meaning of those legal rules by those to whom they are addressed.

This, however, is not as problematic as it may at first seem. It is not contradictory to claim, at the same time, that (1) to treat the law as a legitimate authority means to surrender the appeal to the original (non-legal) reasons in deciding about one's action, on the basis that the law effectively translates those reasons into its directives, and that (2) in order to identify the meaning of the legal directives we need, at times, to refer back to those original (non-legal) reasons. Acceptance of these two propositions, untidy though it may seem, has the advantage of saving the concept of law from patently counter-intuitive conclusions, according to which a number of legal standards would have to be denied the status of law precisely because in order to ascertain their meaning the subjects need to resort to the reasons that triggered the elevation of these standards to legal status in the first place.

This, indeed, is the meaning of 'standards' in those contexts when, in legal theory, they are contrasted to 'rules' (not to be confused with Dworkin's rules/principles distinction).[16] When the law denies enforceability to those contracts that 'unreasonably' restrain trade, or prohibits 'establishment' of a religion etc, then it calls upon its subjects to replicate in their minds the reasons for action that it now purports to 'pre-empt'. In order to fix the meaning of those standards (and therefore, of the authoritative directives of law) its subjects must go back to the original reasons for enacting them in the first place. To be sure, it is not merely a simple replication of the process of translation of the original reasons into directives because the very fact of already having those (and other) legal directives in force introduces some important constraints upon the meanings that can be given to them (and this is the point of Dworkin's theory of 'constructive interpretation' in law).[17] A subject, or an enforcer, of a legal standard does not have the same freedom of interpretation as the legislators and voters had when they argued for the introduction of the rule in the first place. If a legal standard prohibits, for example, the establishment of a religion, then there are limits as to which actions, under the interpretative conventions of a given legal order, may be viewed as the unconstitutional establishment of religion. However, within those constraints, in order to ascertain exactly what is and what is not prohibited (for instance, whether state financial aid to religious schools counts as 'establishment' or not), a subject and an enforcer of this legal directive will have to enquire

[16] See, in particular, Duncan Kennedy 'Form and Substance in Private Law Adjudication' Harvard Law Review (1976) 89: 1685–778; Kathleen Sullivan 'The Supreme Court, 1991 Term—Foreword: The Justices of Rules and Standards' Harvard Law Review (1992) 106: 22–123; Jeremy Waldron 'Legal and Political Philosophy' in Jules Coleman and Scott Shapiro (eds) *The Oxford Handbook of Jurisprudence and Philosophy of Law* (Oxford: Oxford University Press, 2002) 352–81 at 354–6.

[17] Ronald Dworkin *Law's Empire* (London: Fontana, 1986) 62–8.

into the underlying purposes, principles, and/or policies that it is supposed to implement. We know that the law mediates between the background policies and principles and specific authoritative decisions, and in order to identify the meaning of the mediating directives we sometimes need to look back to the original reasons that inspired them.

Indeed, law-makers may justifiably intend, in some circumstances, to force us to do just that, for instance in order to introduce some necessary flexibility into the law at the stage of its application (because flexibility at the point of law-making may often be politically unfeasible); or to avoid incidences of substantive injustice caused by the scrupulous application of a by-and-large justified rule; or to reduce the levels of over- and under-inclusiveness that necessarily occur when the background policies and principles are 'translated' into rough-and-ready rules, or for a whole host of other reasons—such as, to promote civic deliberation in the process of adjudication.[18] We (ie the subjects and enforcers of those directives) will then need to engage in the ascertainment of the meaning of those background principles and policies, and also in a rather complex balancing of the values at stake, thus largely replicating the moral balancing (although within the constraints of valid interpretative conventions) that initially led to the adoption of the directive. We may express this proposition in the language of Dworkin's 'constructive interpretation', or in the language of theorists of so-called 'inclusive positivism' who claim that law, at times, incorporates moral standards into the meaning of its authoritative rules. Either way, Raz's view that essential to the very notion of authority is the idea that the meaning of authoritative directives should be identifiable without recourse to the original reasons that the directives supposedly pre-empt cannot be squared with the pervasive presence of 'standards' (as opposed to 'rules') in legal directives. Nor can it be squared with the fact that the distinction between standards and rules is more a matter of degree than of a sharp divide: many directives, which at first blush look like straight rules, may be 'corrupted by exceptions'[19] to the point at which they more closely resemble standards.

3. 'Service Conception' and Democracy

While Raz's normal justification thesis is, as we have just seen, unhelpful in describing how such legal standards actually operate, its conception of legitimate authority is defensible if one remembers that it is not a *normative* thesis about how legitimacy should be generated but rather a *conceptual* analysis of what it means for authority to be legitimate. The source of misunderstanding

[18] See Sullivan 'The Supreme Court, 1991 Term—Foreword: The Justices of Rules and Standards' 67–9.

[19] ibid at 61.

about Raz's conception may be that Raz himself is not quite clear about this distinction between the possible aspirations of his project. One of his critics, Scott Hershovitz, claimed that the 'normal justification thesis' neglects the importance of the procedural mechanisms of democracy:

> If a government's electoral system favors some interests in society, or appears corruptly financed, or causes portions of the population to be marginalized and voiceless, we are quick to judge it illegitimate, or at least less legitimate than it might be otherwise. Where these deficiencies are present, it counts for little that a government may produce substantively good decisions, decisions that the normal justification thesis [of Raz] would hold authoritative.... This shows us one way in which the normal justification thesis is incomplete as a theory of legitimacy for political authorities: Governments that fulfill it may fail to be legitimate on procedural grounds.[20]

Hershovitz is, in my view, wrong, and the source of the confusion is that, in offering his conception, Raz is less interested in the problem of legitimacy than in that of authority; his avowed aim is to tell us what it means for one person or entity to have authority over another: 'It is an account of authority relations between a legitimate authority and those subject to it'.[21] To construct the concept of authority, Raz chooses to take, as a point of departure, the notion of *legitimate* authority. It is only once we learn what legitimate authority means (that is, that it applies only the dependent reasons, and so on) that we can discover what a less-than-legitimate authority is: by identifying what features it lacks in comparison with a legitimate one. And so we learn from Raz that 'the law either claims that it possesses legitimate authority, or is held to possess it or both', and that even if the law fails to possess legitimate authority, it is a conceptual truth that it must at least 'claim' to do so.[22] (As Dworkin has observed, this is in many respects a bizarre proposition, but we may leave this matter to one side here.)[23] So it is not the case that, according to Raz, we first develop a concept of authority and then add to it the conditions of its legitimacy; rather, the converse seems to be the case, as the very concept of authority is not intelligible without a prior notion of legitimate authority. (It is rather as if we defined 'postage stamps' by defining 'valid postage stamps' first, and only then explained that there are also stamps which lack some conditions of validity—but the very idea of a 'postage stamp' is unintelligible without knowing first what a valid stamp means.) This is confirmed when Raz says that '[a]uthority in general can be divided into legitimate and *de facto* authority. The latter either claims to be legitimate or is believed to be so....';[24]

[20] Scott Hershovitz 'Legitimacy, Democracy, and Razian Authority' Legal Theory (2003) 9: 201 at 216.

[21] Raz *The Morality of Freedom* at 64.

[22] Raz *Ethics in the Public Domain* at 215.

[23] Dworkin 'Thirty Years On (Book Review of *The Practice of Principle* by Jules Coleman)' 1666–7.

[24] Raz *Ethics in the Public Domain* at 211.

either way, any authority, whether legitimate or not, derives conceptually from the property of legitimacy.

Legitimacy, or the lack thereof, is in the eyes of the critical observer, a property of a de facto authority, which either commands 'legitimacy' by virtue of the beliefs of its subjects, or at the very least claims to be legitimate, even if it fails to engender this belief among its subjects. Under Raz's definitional proposal, an 'authority' that neither claims legitimacy nor is believed to be legitimate is a contradiction in terms. This seems acceptable; indeed, we have a different vocabulary for a political power that does not even try to create pretensions of legitimacy: tyranny, occupation force, naked power etc. The use of the language of 'authority' carries a modicum of an honorific acknowledgment of a (real or at least claimed) connection between the exercise of the authority and certain beliefs held by the subjects of the authority (namely, the reasons for action that they have independently of the existence of the authority itself). An 'authority' that did not even pretend to respect such a connection, and yet was successful in controlling the behaviour of its subjects, would not even be an 'illegitimate' authority; it would not be an 'authority' at all, and it would represent nothing but naked power. Whether the 'authority' is legitimate or not is a matter of its degree of success (in the eyes of a critical observer) in establishing a close connection between its directives and the background reasons that would otherwise guide the actions of the law's addressees—in Raz's terminology, 'reasons which apply to the subjects of those directives'.

Viewed in this way, Raz is immune to the criticism that he neglects the importance of procedural devices of democracy. His project is to suggest a concept of authority that necessarily relies upon a prior concept of legitimacy, rather than to propose a normative political theory about what are the necessary and sufficient conditions of legitimacy. But the concept of authority he outlines lends itself well to the democratic interpretation suggested by Hershovitz: it is only a matter of interpreting the meaning of 'the reasons which apply to the subjects' of authoritative directives. We may recall that Raz claimed in his 'dependence thesis' that the very concept of (legitimate) authority requires that directives be based 'on reasons which apply to the subjects of those directives'; the whole point of the 'service conception' is to place the (legitimate) authorities in the position of mediating between the subjects and 'the right reasons which apply to them'.[25] But what reasons can 'apply to the subjects' *other than those that they actually have*? To be sure, one can suggest perhaps that paternalistic non-democratic authorities (perhaps in the idealized version offered by John Rawls when he described decent and well-ordered, although illiberal, societies)[26] can better identify the reasons that 'apply to the subjects' than can the subjects themselves. This, however, is a

[25] ibid at 214.

[26] John Rawls *The Law of Peoples* (Cambridge, Mass: Harvard University Press, 1999) especially at 59–88.

matter of normative political philosophy: manifestly not what Raz engages in when describing his 'service conception'. So it is perfectly compatible with Raz's theory to claim that the *only* way for the authorities to ascertain 'the reasons that apply to the subjects' of authoritative directives is by asking those subjects themselves, through democratic elections, representative bodies, referenda etc. Combining such a (very plausible) normative political philosophy with Raz's 'service conception' brings about precisely what Hershovitz claims (although he presents his claim as a criticism of Raz's thesis), namely, that the only authority that can be legitimate under the service conception is one that is procedurally democratic.

The fact that Raz's conception *also* can be reconciled with a non-democratic, paternalistic theory (according to which the authorities are legitimate if they properly discern the reasons relevant to their subjects without asking the subjects themselves what they take those reasons to be) is not an argument against the service conception because Raz might simply retort that, as a matter of normative political philosophy, he considers the paternalistic conception deeply implausible. Therefore, while Raz's understanding of legitimate authority is broad enough to accommodate various democratic and non-democratic political theories alike, the use of this concept does not reveal indifference towards democratic procedures. This is quite simply a separate debate (about how to go about identifying the reasons relevant to the subjects of authority) and Raz is free to claim that it has only one plausible outcome.

4. Justification and Obligation

At the start of this chapter, I announced that I would deal with justification, legitimacy, and the obligation to obey the law but thus far I have focused exclusively on legitimacy; it is now time to consider the other two categories. Let us begin with the relationship between the legitimacy of law and the obligation to obey it. There is an understandable temptation, at a common sense level, to draw a tight conceptual connection between the two: while there is no reason to obey a law which is illegitimate, or the legitimacy of which is in doubt, what is the point (the argument may go) of ascertaining the legitimacy of a given law other than to identify our obligation to obey it? A finding that a law is legitimate may *appear* redundant unless it is necessarily connected to the validation of the duty to obey it. Indeed, it can be argued that we may at times have an obligation to obey laws that are perhaps less-than-legitimate, and so have an unquestionable obligation to obey the legitimate law. Consider John Finnis's proposition that 'if an unjust [legal] stipulation is, in fact, homogeneous with other laws in its formal source, in its reception by courts and officials, and in its common acceptance, the good citizen may (not always) be morally required to conform to that stipulation to the extent necessary to avoid weakening "the law", the legal system (of rules, institutions, and dispositions) as a whole'.[27] This is because, in the case of disobedience to a particular unjust law that is an aberration in an otherwise reasonably just system, we should be concerned about not undermining the effectiveness of the legal system as a whole in pursuing the common good. Hence, it may seem that in the case of a law that we consider to be legitimate (by our own criteria, whatever they may be) our moral obligation to comply must be all the stronger.

The connection, however, is not as close as it would seem at first sight, and it is significant that for a number of legal theorists the obligatory nature of laws does not necessarily follow from their legitimacy. Kent Greenawalt, for example, identifies a number of different correlates of the idea of a legitimate political authority, and the proposition that the governed should obey the directives of those with authority is only one among a number of others possible, such as that those with political authority are justified in issuing certain kinds of directives to those they govern, or that they are justified in using force to induce compliance, or that the governed should not interfere with such uses of force etc.[28] Similarly, Robert Ladenson has suggested that: 'The right to rule is . . . a justification right . . . [which] by itself implies nothing about either the subject's duty of allegiance to the state or of compliance with the law'.[29] Indeed, the view that the notion of legitimate authority merely connotes that the authority is *justified* in issuing directives to the subjects, but not that the subjects have a corresponding duty to comply with these directives, seems to be quite widespread in current legal theory.

To see clearly why this disconnection of legitimacy and obligation is eminently convincing, it suffices to consider again Raz's understanding of legitimate authority (the 'service conception'). According to this conception, as we have seen, those complying with the directives of the legitimate authority are more likely to attain the goals relevant to them. This means that these original reasons that people espouse identify important aspects of their well-being, broadly understood, and that they are more likely to attain this well-being if they comply with the authoritative directives rather than attempting to achieve it unilaterally (or, in other words, through acting on those reasons directly). The *only* implication of this conception is that it is rational, or wise, or prudent, for the subjects of an authority to follow authoritative directives (which ex hypothesi, under a legitimate authority, correctly incorporate the original reasons) rather than try to find their own way of attaining those aspects of their well-being. This can be accepted; no one, however, has a *duty* to be rational, or wise, or prudent! This is

[27] John Finnis *Natural Law and Natural Rights* (Oxford: Oxford University Press, 1980) 361–2.

[28] R Kent Greenawalt *Conflicts of Law and Morality* (New York: Oxford University Press, 1987) 50–1.

[29] Robert Ladenson 'In Defense of a Hobbesian Conception of Law' in Joseph Raz (ed) *Authority* (Oxford: Basil Blackwell, 1990) 36–7.

consistent with what Raz had claimed well before he formulated his 'service conception of authority', namely that there is no general moral obligation to obey the law. More specifically, he showed that such an obligation does not follow from our undeniable duty to support and uphold good institutions (and so, in the later language, the institutions that properly translate our original reasons into authoritative directives). The duty to support good institutions, Raz says, gives birth to an obligation to obey only those laws that guarantee the functioning of a democratic government, while '[i]t provides reasons to obey other laws only to the extent that by doing so one sets a good example or that by failing so to act one sets a bad example: that is, only to the extent that obedience to these other laws strengthens or prevents weakening the laws on which the democratic character of the government is founded'.[30]

To establish such duty to obey requires some *additional* normative argument, over and above the arguments certifying the law as justified. If I choose to ignore the directives issued by legitimate authorities (directives that, by definition, better reflect the reasons which apply to me than any unilateral action I could take), I may make my life more difficult, and fail to attain most efficiently the goals identified by my original reasons—but I have not breached any obligation on my part. I *would* have breached an obligation if, for instance, by disregarding the authoritative directives and acting on my own reasons directly I failed to discharge duties of fairness to my fellow citizens (who *do* follow the authoritative directives in a way that pre-empts their own, original reasons for action); or if I undermined the law's effort to provide the best coordination of individual actions in pursuit of public goods; or if I reneged on an implied promise to obey the law, which others might have legitimately read into my conduct and relied on in their actions, and so on. However, each of these grounds for alleging a breach of obligation requires an *additional* theory about the bases of my obligation: that, for example, the law parallels the schemes of cooperation that generate reciprocal duties of fairness; or that law is generally efficient in coordinating individual actions to deflect collective-action problems and that when it is certified as such, we all have a duty to contribute to such an efficient outcome; or that our continued presence in the society can be viewed as analogous to an implicit promise to be bound by a legitimate law etc. Each of these theories may or may not be persuasive—and, as we know, entire libraries can be filled with philosophical and legal literature arising from the disputes and disagreements over these, and other, proposed grounds for a political obligation. One thing, however, is clear: these are *additional* theories that are necessary to provide a moral basis for a duty to comply with a legitimate law, and that a concept of legitimate authority, such as that proposed by Raz, evidently does not ground, per se, such a duty.

[30] Joseph Raz *The Authority of Law* (Oxford: Oxford University Press, 1979) 241.

Of course, Raz's is not the *only* theory of legitimate authority. It is worth looking at those theorists who, in contrast to Raz, Greenawalt,[31] Ladenson and others, draw a strict connection between legitimacy and the duty to obey. Perhaps the most interesting version of such a conception was recently proposed by A John Simmons who describes (what he calls) a 'Lockean account' (which is also his, Simmons's, preferred one) of state legitimacy in the following way:

> A state's (or government's) legitimacy is the complex moral right it possesses to be the exclusive imposer of binding duties on its subjects, to have its subjects comply with these duties, and to use coercion to enforce the duties. Accordingly, state legitimacy is the logical correlate of various obligations, including subjects' political obligations. A state's 'legitimacy right' is in part a right held specifically against the subjects bound by any state-imposed duties, arising from morally significant relations – in Locke's case, consensual relations – between state and subject.[32]

Simmons goes on to elaborate the last point in this quotation, namely on the nature of the 'special moral relationship with any particular subject'[33] that gives the state a moral legitimacy, which in turn creates a duty to comply on the part of the subjects. For Locke, as for Simmons, the moral justification of a state is one thing, the validation of its legitimacy quite another. Moral justification is a matter of identifying, and applauding, the general quality of a state, such as its unique ability to solve various coordination problems, to institutionalize and enforce rights, to suppress violence etc. To justify states we need to show that they are beneficial, and of course not all states are beneficial; hence, not all states are justified. If a state *is* justified, we may, at best, have a duty not to undermine it and perhaps even positively to support it—but not necessarily to obey it. Obedience is another matter: it requires some special relationship between the state and a particular subject, because '[t]he fact that a state or a business has virtues that can be appealed to in order to justify its existence cannot by itself argue for its having special rights over particular individuals'.[34] Those 'special rights' constitute the state's legitimacy—and they have to be defended on some other grounds (which Simmons characterizes as a 'morally significant relationship' between the state and a particular individual) than merely the net benefits of having a state (or *that* state) in order to justify its existence.

Thus far I have been dealing with legitimacy without making any distinction between the legitimacy of particular rules and the legitimacy of a system of legal rules as a whole. Indeed, as I suggested earlier, legitimacy may be a matter of degree, and the legitimacy of a system may be seen as emerging from the recognition of the legitimacy of a great many specific legal directives that it contains.

[31] I should add that one of Greenawalt's seven possible 'correlates' of a state's legitimacy is a duty to obey it by its citizens. I have here taken into account only those 'correlates' where no such implication is proposed.

[32] A John Simmons 'Justification and Legitimacy' *Ethics* (1999) 109: 739–771 at 746.

[33] ibid at 748.

[34] ibid at 752.

From the citizens' point of view, however, which is the only perspective relevant to the obligation to obey, disobedience can normally be expressed only with regard to specific legal rules, not to the system as a whole. In such circumstances, as John Finnis noted, 'your allegiance to the whole system ("the law") is put on the line: either you obey the *particular* law, or you reveal yourself... as lacking or defective in allegiance to the *whole*, as well as to the particular'.[35] It would appear, therefore, that there is an important asymmetry between the problems of legitimacy and of the obligatory nature of the law: the former crystallizes only at the level of particular law, while the latter does so at both the particular and systemic level.

This distinction between the particular and the systemic needs not concern us here, however, as the asymmetry just noted does not affect the relationship between legitimacy and obligation in a way damaging to the argument here. After all, if legitimacy is based, as in Simmons's work, on special grounds that link the state with the individuals, then these grounds may equally concern specific laws or the system as a whole. And if legitimacy is based on the original (pre-legal) reasons being correctly encapsulated in legal directives, as Raz understands it, then legitimacy is even more readily identifiable at the level of particular rules. Similarly, repeated disobedience to a great number of particular laws amounts to a general habit of disobedience which may be based on a citizen's refusal to grant legitimacy to the legal system as a whole. However, there is no reason why we cannot say that someone may accord general legitimacy to the system as a whole while at the same time refusing to obey a particular law on the basis that he or she finds it illegitimate.[36]

Simmons's conception nicely demonstrates a general proposition that I want to make at this point, in bringing together the three concepts that I referred to at the start of this section: justification, legitimacy, and the obligation to obey the law. The general thesis is this: *either* justification and legitimacy are taken to be substantively the same thing (or, to be more precise, rely on substantively the same arguments) and then the obligation to obey requires separate moral arguments from those used to support the other two (as in Raz, Greenawalt, and Ladenson) *or* justification and legitimacy are two different things (each requiring different sorts of moral arguments) and then the obligation to obey follows necessarily from the validation of a state as legitimate (as in Simmons). To simplify, within the trichotomy of 'justification–legitimacy–obligation to obey', the notion of legitimacy is strategically central: either we align it with justification (and have a reasonably weak notion of legitimacy, equivalent to the state being justified in

[35] Finnis *Natural Law and Natural Rights* at 317 (emphases in the original).

[36] Consider Dworkin's proposition: 'A state is legitimate if its constitutional structure and practices are such that its citizens have a general obligation to obey political decisions that purport to impose duties on them. An argument for legitimacy need only provide reasons for that general situation. It need not show that a government, *legitimate in that sense*, therefore has moral authority to do anything it wants to its citizens, or that they are obligated to obey every decision it makes' Dworkin *Law's Empire* at 181 (emphasis added). The italicized words indicate the availability of yet another 'sense' of legitimacy, namely pertaining to *specific* legitimacy of particular laws.

issuing directives) or with an obligation to obey (and then we have a strong concept of legitimacy, equivalent to the duty of compliance).

What we *cannot* have is the simple alignment of all three concepts with each other because then we lose sight of the crucial fact that we do not have a duty to obey a state merely on the basis that it is doing what it is supposed to do. Whether we conceptualize the fact that the state is performing well its proper functions in the language of Raz's service conception of legitimate authority (and say that the state is correctly incorporating the dependent reasons into its authoritative directives, thus giving its subjects rational reasons to suppress their own independent reasons for action and to act on the state directives directly), or in the language of Simmons's moral justification of a state, is ultimately unimportant. What *is* important is the awareness that in the chain of reasoning: 'justification–legitimacy–duty to obey' we always have *two* separate argumentative steps, not just one; and that we should avoid the non-sequitur of moving directly from a moral justification of a state to the political obligations of citizens.

5. 'Democracy without Values'?

The preceding parts of this chapter had as their aim to clear the conceptual field, by reflecting upon what is at stake in attributing (or refusing) the property of legitimacy to a given legal rule, legal system, or a state. My argument was that the very concept is ambiguous, and it is important to be clear whether we use legitimacy as akin to justification (from which a duty to obey does not necessarily derive) or in a stronger sense as necessarily grounding the duty to obey, in which case legitimacy must be based on some other foundations than merely those necessary to justify a given legal rule, legal system, or a given state. I have suggested that legitimacy, at least in its first meaning, and as described by Joseph Raz, has a strong, although one may say contingent, connection with the requirements of procedural democracy. It is *contingent* because the connection between the legitimacy of legal directives (in Raz's understanding) and the democratic process is a matter of our empirical knowledge about how best to ensure that legal directives actually resonate with the preferences that people espouse. And it is not a matter of its definitional criteria: we can theoretically imagine a non-democratic technology for the government to track people's preferences. But while contingent, it is nevertheless very *strong* because the availability of such 'technologies' is extremely unlikely in the world as we know it and, in any event, even if we had them, the whole aspect of deliberation, persuasion, and change of preferences under the influence of other people's argument would be lost, thus eroding much of the weight of such a putative non-democracy based legitimacy.

The remaining parts of the chapter build on this conclusion, and go a step further in the overall argument, by inquiring into whether a procedural democracy is enough. I will raise the question, foreshadowed already in the introductory passages of this chapter, about whether procedural, or input-based, democracy is sufficient to ground legitimacy of the law, or whether we need in addition some substantive, output-based criteria, identifying some desirable contents of the law (at least, as a non-negotiable minimum) to satisfy the necessary conditions for legitimacy.

An example of an explicit and persuasive (to many) articulation of the output-based conception of democracy, which I will use as the starting point for my analysis of such conceptions, was made some time ago, by Pope John Paul II speaking before the Polish Parliament (Sejm). The Pope urged his audience—the parliamentarians of a newly democratized state—not to ignore the importance of the right moral values: 'Whilst the autonomy proper to the life of a political community must be respected, it should also be borne in mind that a political community cannot be seen as *independent of ethical principles*'.[37] He then went on to quote his own Encyclical, *Veritatis Splendor*, of 1993: 'As history demonstrates, a *democracy without values* easily turns into open or thinly disguised totalitarianism'.[38] As we can see, the Pontiff phrased the questions of the conditions of democratic legitimacy in a remarkably similar way to that in which I framed the issue at the start of this chapter: namely, that democracy must be enhanced with values—'output democracy', in my proposed vocabulary—in order to provide a strong basis for the legitimacy of democratically established legal directives.

'A political [democratic] community cannot be seen as independent of ethical principles'; 'a democracy without values easily turns into open or thinly disguised totalitarianism'... This is a call for democracy *with* values; for an output-based or values-enhanced democracy. What is the meaning of this call? The only way we can make sense of it is, I believe, by imagining what the opposite would be like: what a democratic community 'independent of ethical principles' or a 'democracy without values' might look like. Just as we can sometimes articulate intelligibly the shape of a positive precept (say, 'wealth with wisdom') only by realizing the shape and the consequences of its negative counterpart ('wealth without wisdom'), so we can give a proper meaning to the call for infusing democracy with values only by thinking about what 'democracy without values' would be like, and what would be wrong with it.

However, such a thought experiment is less easy than it may at first appear. Even at first glance, democracy as a system is based on particular, strong (and, by implication, controversial) moral values. The very choice of a democratic system, and a commitment to the maintenance and defence of democracy against the alternative institutional systems, is not in itself value-neutral. Perhaps the most obvious moral value that is necessarily presupposed by a democratic system is that

[37] John Paul II 'Address to the Polish Parliament' 11 June 1999, available at <http://www.vatican.va/holy_father/john_paul_ii/travels/documents/hf_jp-ii_spe_11061999_warsaw-parliament_en.html> part 5 (my emphasis).

[38] ibid part 5, quoting Pope John Paul II *Veritatis Splendor* 6 August 1993 (my emphasis).

of equal moral agency of every human being, expressed in their equal capacity to influence public decisions. What other reasons would we have to adopt a majority-rule based institutional design (which is, subject to all possible caveats and reservations, the irreducible hard core of any democracy) if we had not adopted, as an overarching political value, some precept about the equal moral agency (or dignity) of all?

At this point one might protest that there is a major and unforgivable simplification in this account: there is no single, canonical conception of democracy, and the implications for the equality of voters are different if we opt for a purely majoritarian-procedural theory of democracy, or a constitutional conception with strong substantive rights limiting the scope of the majority decision, or a deliberative democratic conception that attempts to overcome the procedural-constitutional distinction and identifies the main criterion of democracy in deliberation among the citizens with the aim of justifying their collective decisions to one another.[39] This is true, and in Chapter 2 I will further discuss various understandings of democracy and their connections with the principle of majority rule. At this point, however, all that matters is that, regardless of where, how, and to what extent the majority rule operates, it inevitably does rely on some prior egalitarian presuppositions (again, a point to be developed in more detail in the next chapter).

Under many plausible and empirically testable conceptions, the conferral of a (more-or-less) equal vote upon every adult citizen, in deciding about matters of common concern, is irrational and arbitrary. People vary widely in terms of their intelligence, knowledge, experience, moral integrity, honesty, contributions to public welfare, courage, and so on. Each of these attributes (and many others) could be shown to be relevant to the exercise of a right to affect public decisions; hence, each could constitute a ground for reducing or enhancing one's vote on public issues, for instance, in parliamentary or presidential elections. It would not seem implausible, for example, to believe that in a society 'where newspapers, periodicals, books, and other printed matter canvass and debate campaign issues, a State might conclude that only those who are literate should exercise the franchise'.[40] If, intuitively, we found such radical departures from a 'one person–one vote' principle objectionable (as, I take it, we usually do) then it must be because there are some powerful moral values that would be offended by such a departure. Of course, we may be hesitant to embark upon such a path also for non-moral reasons: we might think, for instance, that it will be increasingly costly to test and assign the vote based on any of such proposed criteria; or that it

[39] For this trichotomy of procedural, constitutional, and deliberative democracy, see Amy Gutmann and Dennis Thompson *Democracy and Disagreement* (Cambridge, Mass: Harvard University Press, 1996) 26–51.

[40] *Lassiter v Northampton County Bd. of Elections* 360 US 45, 52 (1959), cited by David R Ortiz 'The Democratic Paradox of Campaign Finance Reform' Stanford Law Review (1998) 50: 893–914 at 909 n 62.

might increase the potential for corruption and moral hazard; or we may reject it because any agreement to such a proposed reassignment of votes would itself have to be subject to a justifiable reweighing of votes, which runs us into an infinite regress etc. But while each of these objections is serious, taken together they would not be weighty enough if we thought that the principle of one person–one vote was fundamentally *morally* flawed; furthermore, we would be much more determined than we currently are to find a better system, and only then start worrying about the practical difficulties of putting the alternative into practice.

So it is like ascertaining the existence of a planet not by observing it directly but rather by drawing inferences from the puzzling behaviour of other, visible planets. The fact that we intuitively reject, on moral grounds, suggestions for apportioning the vote on the grounds of, for example, intelligence implies the assumption of a powerful value (or set of values) that trump these, otherwise prima facie plausible, grounds for differential assignment of the right to vote. What might this other powerful value be? Not surprisingly, democratic theorists disagree among themselves about its specific articulation, and the different versions of our conception of democracy reflect different understandings of this value. Any attempt to identify a single value or a set of values accepted by all those who espouse democracy is ultimately futile: democracy is, to use Ronald Dworkin's characterization applied to political ideals in general, both an 'interpretive' and an 'integrated' ideal.[41] It is, first, 'interpretive' in the sense that people not only disagree about the value of democracy but also disagree about what democracy really is, and no 'Archimedean' standpoint is available in order to establish, in a descriptive manner, the meaning of democracy before we get on with the debates about its worth. And, secondly, it is an 'integrated' ideal in the sense that the meaning and value of democracy are only revealed through their place in a larger constellation of values, which mutually reinforce and confer worth upon each other.[42] This combined interpretive and integrated nature of the ideal of democracy is nicely revealed in this elegant reflection by the historian of ideas, John Dunn, on the changing meanings given to the word 'democracy' after the American revolutionaries have embraced it with such enthusiasm:

> From then on it is relatively easy to follow this word as it moves onwards with the stream of history, sometimes hurtling through rapids, sometimes drifting out in great slow eddies, or disappearing for lengthy intervals into stagnant pools. It is also easy to see why it attracts or repels so many different users, summoning up allegiances or fomenting enmities. It is even easier to see why it constantly loses definition along the way,

[41] See Ronald Dworkin 'Hart's Postscript and the Character of Political Philosophy' OJLS (2004) 24: 1–37 at 7–9 and 14–16.

[42] The 'integrated' character of the concept of democracy should not be confused with another claim that Dworkin makes about the concept, namely its 'dependent' character; see the discussion in Chapter 2.6 of this book.

stretched in one direction then another, and largely at the mercy of anyone who chooses to take it up.[43]

One might perhaps think that the characterization of democracy as both interpretive and integrated (in the Dworkinian sense) detracts from the argument that there is a foundational value behind democracy, such as that of equal moral agency. In fact, it only *strengthens* the view that democracy is value-based in a sense that renders the concept of 'democracy without values' largely meaningless. For we may disagree over what specific account to give the values that justify democracy in the first place: some will discern irreducibly theological grounds for such values,[44] while others will insist that they are based upon equal rationality free from any transcendental presuppositions.[45] These different articulations of democracy-justifying values will yield somewhat different conceptions of democracy itself, and there is nothing puzzling or embarrassing about this. As Dunn remarked, immediately following the just-quoted account of the changing fortunes of the word 'democracy' throughout history: 'what still remains harder to see is just how it aids or impedes those who do choose to use it, augmenting their political strength, exposing their deceit or blurring their comprehension of their own goals'.[46]

'Democracy' may become associated with a whole range of values, ideals, and ideologies—this much we know. What matters is that there must be *some* values that have to be adopted and defended, and whose general contours are by and large egalitarian, in order to counter and outweigh the prima facie rational arguments for elitist, aristocratic, or technocratic models of collective decision-making. These by-and-large egalitarian values must be powerful enough to defuse the arguments about the wisdom of apportioning the power of the vote as a function of a person's competences as measured by a person's intelligence, education etc. They must be able to convince us that when it comes to fundamental decision-making about, for example, which major political party should govern for the next four or five years, or what should be the nation's choice on joining a major international alliance, or whether abortion should be punished by law or not, each adult citizen's qualification to make an informed choice (or, more precisely, the qualifications of each person who cares to vote) is as good as that of any others. I will have much more to say about this egalitarian rationale of majority rule in Chapter 2; here it will suffice to assert that our intuitive acceptance of the one person–one vote system shows, through something like a reflective

[43] John Dunn *Setting the People Free: The Story of Democracy* (London: Atlantic Books, 2005) 161.

[44] See eg Jeremy Waldron *God, Locke, and Equality: Christian Foundations in Locke's Political Thought* (Cambridge: Cambridge University Press, 2002) 44–82; Larry Siedentop *Democracy in Europe* (London: Allen Lane, 2000) 192–8.

[45] See Ronald Dworkin *Sovereign Virtue: The Theory and Practice of Equality* (2000).

[46] Dunn *Setting the People Free: The Story of Democracy* at 161.

equilibrium analysis, that we do accept an egalitarian background ideal as a relatively 'fixed point' in our commonly accepted constellation of values.

It may perhaps be objected that the above remarks apply only to a '*politique politisante*' rather than a '*politique politisée*'; that even though at the level of the general design of a democratic system, its legitimacy is assured by a strong value-based justification, nevertheless, at the level of the actual application of the design in everyday political life, the connection between democracy and values cannot be taken for granted. The urge to infuse democracy with values—an output democracy conception—can therefore be located at the level of the everyday workings and implementation of the design, rather than the design itself. It is *there* (so the argument may go) that the danger that democracy will become disconnected from substantive moral value is real, and it is there that the warnings against 'a political community independent of ethical principles' maintain their force and validity. To think otherwise would be a sign of naive faith in the self-perpetuating force of the moral values that underlie the choice of a democratic system in the first place: the hope that the values that justify the adoption of democracy would reveal themselves at each 'use' of the system.

Democracy, under such a naive faith, would be akin to what John Rawls dubbed 'perfect procedural justice': an institutional system that guarantees that any specific distributive decision is always and necessarily just, *in terms of standards of justice independent of the procedure itself.*[47] With regard to democracy, it would reflect a hope that once we put a democratic system in place (justified, as it is, by certain values), each outcome of the democratic game will express those very values. However (the argument might continue), just as in real life, we do not have the luxury of 'perfect procedural justice' (other than some hypothetical examples invented to illustrate the concept itself, such as—in an example provided by Rawls—a system in which the person who divides a cake will be the last to pick up his or her slice),[48] so that we cannot hope for democratic procedures that will always and necessarily give effect to the values that justify the system as a whole. The best that we can hope for in the area of distributive justice is to set up systems of 'imperfect procedural justice' (which maximize the likelihood of achieving procedurally just outcomes); similarly, in the case of the democratic legitimacy of political systems we can hope, at best, for institutional designs that will maximize, but never guarantee in each instance, the achievement of outcomes that are legitimate by virtue of their congruence with the values that justified the choice of system in the first place.

There is an immediate temptation to give a quick answer to the objection described in the preceding paragraph, which should, however, be resisted. The temptation is to appeal to the concept of '*pure* procedural justice', which is different from the perfect and imperfect types of procedural justice in Rawls's

[47] See John Rawls *A Theory of Justice* (Oxford: Oxford University Press 1971) 83–7.
[48] ibid at 85.

taxonomy in that it dispenses altogether with outcome-based criteria of justice: pure procedural justice obtains whenever the correct procedure is strictly adhered to (as in sports or gambling, in which we do not have any outcome-based criteria to judge whether the result is just). In contrast, perfect and imperfect forms of justice use outcome-based criteria, and the only difference between imperfect and perfect justice is that the latter guarantees, whereas the former merely maximizes, the congruence of the outcome with our standards of justice. The initial response that I have in mind would be to suggest that the problems raised by democracy are more akin to the *problématique* of pure procedural justice than to that of (im)perfect procedural justice, in that the only democratic game in town is procedural and we should not concern ourselves with the 'fit' between the outcome of a democratic game with the outcome-based standards of democracy, but only with the compliance of political (including legislative) procedures with purely procedural rules.

As I have already noted, this temptation should be resisted: the 'answer' provided here is decidedly too rash. Even in Rawls's initial introduction of the three-way division between forms of procedural justice, serious doubts can be raised about its 'pure' manifestation: do we really refer to the outcomes of sports competitions or gambling as 'just' merely because they comply with the rules of procedure? To my ear, such a characterization is out of place in such situations; the conferral of the status of 'justice' in these cases is contrary to the semantic intuition many of us have. This would suggest that the language of procedural justice is always and necessarily a reflection of the 'justness' of the outcome.[49] This impression is only strengthened upon consideration of the problems of democratic legitimacy. To say that once a democratic system is in place any outcome will be, by definition, democratic because we do not have an independent outcome-based notion of democratic legitimacy seems contrary to our intuitions. Rather, the opposite is true: we feel that if the democratic majority, in accordance with a democratic procedure, were (for example) to deprive members of an ethnic minority of their fundamental rights, then the outcome would be illegitimate as contrary to the foundational values of democracy itself. So we *do* have criteria of a democratically legitimate outcome after all; and, if we support democracy it is not because we believe that *by definition* anything that such a system produces is legitimate but rather because we believe that democracy, more than any other system, maximizes the attainment of values that we endorse. It is not by virtue of a definitional identification of legitimacy with the scrupulous observance of procedural rules, but rather through our real-life experiences of how different systems connect with values, that we may endorse democracy; to do so merely by definitional fiat would be weak and unconvincing.

[49] For more on this, see Wojciech Sadurski 'Social Justice and Legal Justice' Law and Philosophy (1984) 3: 329–54 at 346–53.

Thus, the easy way out by invoking pure procedural justice is not available to us, and the best we can do is to uphold democracy as a device similar to imperfect procedural justice: a system that maximizes the achievement of democracy's foundational values, although it falls short of guaranteeing that each and every instance of a democratic procedure will perfectly reflect those values. The distinction between '*politique politisante*' and '*politique politisée*' therefore stands, and the fear that a political community will render itself 'independent of ethical principles' cannot be easily dispelled, it appears, by a general appeal to the ethical principles foundational of democracy itself.

So we need to think a little harder about what the opposite of a value-enhanced democracy would look like, and what dangers may accompany a 'political community independent of ethical principles'. There are two main ways in which a disconnection of democracy from moral values can possibly be imagined to occur, and reflection upon these two *negative* scenarios may bring us closer to a *positive* idea of what democracy-plus might be. The first way in which such a disconnection could take place may be understood at the level of the motivations of political actors in a democracy (both voters and their representatives in the parliamentary assemblies): if their decisions are motivated not by value-based considerations but by some other grounds deemed antithetical to an infusion of democracy with values. Let us call this aspect 'motivational'. The second manner in which such a disconnection may be imagined is when political decisions acquire validity solely by virtue of being adopted in a procedurally proper way, regardless of the degree of congruency between these decisions and the foundational values of a democracy. This, as we have seen, would be a sign of adopting a 'pure procedural justice'-like approach to democracy, and seems unsatisfactory because it ignores the fact that we construct democratic legitimacy in a way more akin to imperfect procedural justice. The gap between perfect and imperfect justice raises the spectre of decisions that are procedurally correct and based on a system that, by and large, maximizes the attainment of democracy's foundational values, but that may, in particular instances, be inconsistent with those values. Let us call this dimension 'constitutional' (for reasons that will become obvious later). These two examples of apparent disconnection of democracy from values should be kept apart because they generate different problems for the issue of democratic legitimacy in the face of society's value pluralism.

6. 'Democracy without Values' in the Motivational Sense

The first level at which we may (theoretically) perceive and deplore 'value-free democracy' is that of the motivations of voters and their representatives. Here a short aside is in order: for the purposes of democratic theory as discussed here, the distinction between individual citizens and political actors, such as the members of legislative bodies, is irrelevant: we assume a full continuity between the motivations, intentions, preferences, and so forth of the individual voters and their representatives in parliament (a point to which I will refer below as the 'continuity thesis'). Of course, we know that this assumption is naive and not very realistic but as a matter of normative democratic theory it does not make any difference whether we consider the motivations of the institutional actors or of individual citizens. Or, to put it differently, a citizen qua voter is also a political institution (as Rawls put it, 'ideally citizens are to think of themselves *as if* they were legislators'),[50] and only as such is considered relevant for the purposes of democratic theory.[51]

At this motivational level, the separation of democracy from values can be discerned in the reliance of voters and their representatives upon their *interests* rather than values and ideals. Democracy is eroded of values, it can perhaps be said, when public decisions are motivated by the calculus of interests rather than of ideals, and when the 'input' to political decision-making consists of our own perceptions of our interests rather than ideas about the public good. To take an example, if my motivation in voting for a particular taxation scheme (or voting for a party on the basis of its taxation programme) is guided only by the question: 'Which of the alternative tax schemes will be the best for me?', then this results in a deplorably value-free democratic process; the right question should have been: 'Which of the alternative tax schemes best corresponds to a defensible idea of justice in taxation?'

This particular example shows, incidentally, that a 'motivational' understanding of the output democracy conception is immune to the possible charge that it adopts an illiberal stance in the controversy between perfectionism and anti-perfectionism concerning the debate over the proper limits of state action in enforcing moral values. 'Democracy-plus', in this version, may be but need not be illiberally perfectionist. If perfectionism is understood in a broad, and not necessarily illiberal way, as the proposition that the role of the state includes the strong commitment to personal autonomy (which requires a high degree of respect for individual choices of ways of life and which is well captured by the 'harm principle'),[52] then the democracy-plus call for acting on values rather than on interests *is* perfectionist but in a non-objectionable manner—from a liberal standpoint at least. It may simply mean nothing more than that a polity should aim at the implementation of some notions of the social good, and that the accommodation of particular interests should be informed by some public

[50] John Rawls 'The Idea of Public Reason Revisited' in Rawls *The Law of Peoples* at 135 (emphasis in the original).

[51] On this last point, see Christopher L Eisgruber *Constitutional Self-Government* (Cambridge, Mass: Harvard University Press, 2001) 50; Bruce Ackerman *We the People: Foundations* (Cambridge Mass: Harvard University Press, 1991) 232–43 and 297–314.

[52] For such a 'perfectionistic' understanding of autonomy and of the harm principle, see Joseph Raz *The Morality of Freedom* (Oxford: Oxford University Press, 1986) 412–20; see also, generally, Vinit Haksar *Liberty, Equality, and Perfectionism* (New York: Oxford University Press, 1979).

ideals of justice. If, however, perfectionism is taken to mean that the state should enforce some ideals of private morality that express some controversial notions of individual virtue (that the state should identify and coercively promote superior ideals of human excellence),[53] there is nothing in the call to act on values rather than on interests (whatever it may mean, as will be discussed shortly) that creates a necessary bias in this direction within democracy-plus. The demand, for example, that in the debate on redistribution through taxation we should be guided by our ideals of public good rather than by our particular interests is not illiberally perfectionist: it takes no stand in the dispute about the role of the law in shaping private morality (the notion of 'the good', as contrasted to 'the right', in Rawls's parlance) of the citizens.

But the continuity thesis, suggested in the first paragraph of this part of the chapter, can be challenged in a way that resonates with the debates concerning 'perfectionism', that is, by appeal to the notion of neutrality of legislation towards competing moral conceptions. It can be claimed that, even if we adopt the ideal of 'moral neutrality' of the state, and attempt to discern the indicia of this neutrality in the motivations of the legislators, it cannot go all the way down; we must not expect individual voters to be neutral on issues of private morality.[54] It is one thing, it may be argued, for the state to attempt to be as neutral as possible on the controversial issues of private morality; it is quite another to expect citizens to reflect such neutrality in their decisions and conduct. While the former ideal may be a useful way of articulating the liberal political ideal, the latter demand (addressed to individuals) can be seen as absurd.[55] This 'absurdity', however, can only arise if we confuse the perspective of an individual as a private person and an individual as a citizen-voter. Being neutral in our private capacity on moral issues is just a fancy and somewhat confused manner of saying that we are uncertain, or agnostic, about some controversial moral matters. But being neutral when we act in our public capacity as voters (or, more generally, as citizens) has no air of absurdity or confusion: it simply means that we act on a distinction between our notions of private morality and our notions of the public good. Naturally, the distinction itself is controversial and open to challenge but *if* we accept that the distinction can be made, or at least attempted, then it can be drawn equally

[53] For this understanding of 'perfectionism' see, inter alia, Carlos Santiago Nino *The Ethics of Human Rights* (Oxford: Oxford University Press, 1991) 132–6, 142–3; see also Tim Gray *Freedom* (London: Macmillan, 1991) 167. The *locus classicus* of a liberal rejection of perfectionism is, of course, in Rawls *A Theory of Justice* at 325–32, restated in John Rawls, *Political Liberalism* (New York: Columbia University Press, 1993) at 194–5, 292–5.

[54] While a discussion of that point is beyond the scope of this chapter, it should be acknowledged that for some liberals, including William Galston and Joseph Raz, even the notion of political neutrality as addressed only to law-makers is incoherent; see William Galston *Liberal Purposes* (New York: Cambridge University Press, 1991) 79–97; Raz *Morality of Freedom* at 108–122. For my critique of Raz's criticism of the principle of neutrality see Wojciech Sadurski *Moral Pluralism and Legal Neutrality* (Dordrecht: Kluwer Academic Publishers, 1990) 99–111.

[55] See Jeremy Waldron *Liberal Rights* (New York: Cambridge University Press, 1993) 154.

well in the mind of an individual voter as in the minds of the legislators, and in consequence relied upon by the collective legislator in its law-making. After all, in a democracy it is the citizens, and not just the legislators as their representatives, who 'exercise final and coercive power over one another in enacting laws and in amending their constitution'.[56] Therefore, the continuity thesis seems immune to the criticism.

The distinction between these two types of motivations, interests and values, corresponds to a classical debate between adherents of a 'pluralistic' conception of democracy and those preferring a Rousseauian one. The former—taking their inspiration from Jeremy Bentham—find it both empirically plausible and normatively acceptable that people vote on the basis of their interests, and the aggregate public decision that tries to accommodate those various and divergent preferences is the only matrix of a 'public good' that we can have. The latter, following Jean Jacques Rousseau, reject interests-based decisions as inappropriate in a democracy; whoever (whether a voter or a representative of the voter) tries to gauge his or her interests as the basis for their decisions, answers the wrong question—the one that should not be asked in the public forum. The only relevant question to ask is: 'which of the alternative proposals is most congruent with my view about the public good?' Even though we know, *contra* Rousseau, that we will encounter fundamental disagreements among members of society in answering this type of question, it will be a *different* disagreement from that generated by conflicts of interests.

A call for output democracy, or 'democracy-plus', under this interpretation amounts, therefore, to a rejection of a Benthamite vision and endorsement of a Rousseauian democracy in which people vote on the basis of ideals rather than interests.[57] Why would such a choice provide us with a step towards morally legitimate democracy, in the sense of its infusion with moral values? The best answer I can think of is by linking the interests/values distinction to the liberal principle of legitimacy: the principle that the use of coercive powers against a person can be legitimate only if that person can accept the reasons that stand behind the law or policy that authorizes this coercive use. There is an important strand in liberal thinking that links legitimacy with the consent of the governed. Not the *actual* consent, of course, because such a requirement would undercut the whole search for the principles of political legitimacy; we would end up with the anarchistic idea that each individual is bound only by those laws to which he or she has agreed. But consent, hypothetical at least, is needed in order to confer some degree of legitimacy upon the laws which, after all, can never enjoy the unanimous support of

[56] Rawls *Political Liberalism* at 214.

[57] On this contrast, see the excellent discussion in Jeremy Waldron, *Liberal Rights*, 392–421; see also Rawls, *Political Liberalism*, 219–20 (endorsing Rousseau's view of voting as 'ideally expressing our opinion as to which of the alternatives best advances the common good', and contrasting it with the view that 'people may properly vote their preferences and interests').

all citizens. In a weak but plausible version, the liberal principle of legitimacy postulates that only laws that are based upon arguments and reasons to which no members of society have a rational reason to object can boast political legitimacy, and as such be applied coercively even to those who actually disagree with them. A contemporary *locus classicus* of the liberal principle of legitimacy is Rawls's *Political Liberalism*: 'Our exercise of political power is fully proper only when it is exercised in accordance with the constitution the essentials of which all citizens as free and equal may reasonably be expected to endorse in the light of principles and ideals acceptable to their common human reason'.[58] Rawls further elaborates upon this conception in his discussion of the concept of 'public reason', that is, publicly recognizable standards of right and wrong. He also suggests that, as a test, we might inquire as to whether a particular argument for a new law belongs to the category of 'public reason' by considering whether it could be used in a written opinion of a supreme court.[59] Another way of expressing the same thought is the 'endorseability by all' thesis, which can be found in Habermas's suggestion about how individual interests may appear in public deliberations: 'In practical discourses, only those interests "count" for the outcome that are presented as inter-subjectively recognized values and hence are *candidates* for inclusion in the semantic content of valid norms'. Habermas concludes: 'Only *generalizable* value-orientations, which all participants (and all those affected) can accept with good reasons as appropriate for regulating the subject matter at hand...pass this threshold'.[60] The implication is clear: some arguments, even if actually present in the minds of legislators or policy-makers, are not qualified to figure in the public defence of a law; the law must be defensible in terms that belong to a forum of principle rather than an arena of political bargains and plays of naked interest.

This last point suggests that the liberal principle of legitimacy operates, more often than not, in a negative (or weak) fashion, namely, to discard *illegitimate* laws rather than to certify the law as a legitimate one. A law cannot claim any legitimacy towards me if it is based upon arguments and reasons that I have no reason to accept. For instance, if the best (or the most plausible) justification that can be given for a law is in terms of a religious sectarian creed and I happen not to espouse that creed then I have no good reason to recognize the law as legitimate. Or if the law is based upon an argument that casts me out from the political community (for example, an argument that considers my racial group as inherently inferior to other groups), then there is no moral reason why I should recognize this law as

[58] Rawls *Political Liberalism* at 137. A broader wording of 'the ideal expressed by the principle of legitimacy' is: 'to live politically with others in the light of reasons all might reasonably be expected to endorse', ibid at 243. For yet another statement of the liberal principle of legitimacy see Rawls *Political Liberalism* at 217.

[59] ibid at 254.

[60] Jürgen Habermas *The Inclusion of the Other: Studies in Political Theory* (Cambridge, Mass: MIT Press, 1998) 81 (both emphases in original).

legitimate: I cannot identify with the reasons that triggered the adoption of this law in the first place. The denial of legitimacy to such a law is based on the view that there must be some connection between the law and myself qua subject of the law—a connection that establishes some rational reasons to identify the good for myself in the law. The connection must be between the substance of the law and the preferences, desires, convictions, or interests of each individual subjected to it. If, under rational examination, no such connection can be detected, then I have no reasons to accept the law as legitimate. If, however, I disagree with the wisdom of a given law but would agree that it is based upon arguments that I can recognize as valid, then a *necessary* condition for its legitimacy has been met. This point has been expressed well by Jeremy Waldron: 'If there is some individual to whom a justification cannot be given, then so far as *he* is concerned the social order had better be replaced by other arrangements, for the status quo has made out no claim to *his* allegiance'.[61]

As it stands, the formula is fraught with ambiguity: from the fact that a justification *can be given*, it does not follow that it *will be accepted* as framed in terms of public reason just as, to return to Rawls's formula, it does not follow from the diagnosis that citizens 'may be expected to endorse' the constitution that they actually endorse it. The actual acceptance requirement would turn the *hypothetical* consent test into a *real* consent (a clearly unreasonable requirement) but, on the other hand, the hypothetical acceptance standard makes the test both easy to manipulate and difficult to apply. There is a space between what citizens can reasonably be expected to accept and what they actually accept, and the liberal principle of legitimacy reflects the tension between these two poles of the continuum of consent: an insufficient pole of hypothetical, rational consent and an unrealistic pole of an actual (even if only tacit) consent.

The liberal principle of legitimacy is intimately connected with the idea of public reason. However, the very idea of 'public reason', as expounded by Rawls, is rather troublesome. Rawls operates with two understandings of public reason which are not necessarily equivalent. The first one is revealed in the 'equal endorseability by all' criterion; the second, in his extended distinction between political and comprehensive conceptions, with the proviso that public reason must safely place itself within the former. As to the first understanding, Ronald Dworkin has expressed doubts as to whether public reason, so understood (in Dworkin's interpretation it is characterized as the 'doctrine of reciprocity'), *excludes* anything at all. As Dworkin argues: 'If I believe that a particular controversial moral position is plainly right... then how can I not believe that other people in my community can reasonably accept the same view, whether or not it is likely that they will accept it?'[62] But the effectiveness of this objection is not obvious. In fact, I may well believe that my moral position is plainly right but *under an impartial observer's perspective*

[61] Waldron *Liberal Rights* at 44 (emphases in the original).

[62] Ronald Dworkin *Justice in Robes* (Cambridge, Mass: Harvard University Press, 2005) 252.

(which is crucial here, when making a judgment about the public reason status of a given position) my moral position may be incapable of being acceptable to all. For instance, my moral position (which I still believe plainly right) is based on the religious views not shared by all, or if it assumes an unequal moral standing to all. In fact, Dworkin further concedes that moral positions based on religious convictions are such that not everybody has a reason to embrace them, and yet he maintains that 'Rawls offers no reason to think that the test of reciprocity excludes any reasonable convictions *beyond religious convictions*'.[63] Now *this* would, in itself, be a significant use of public reason (and a significant demonstration that public reason requirement does exclude many moral positions) but there is surely more to it, namely those positions which under an impartial observer's test deny some groups and categories equal moral standing at the outset.

The second formulation of public reason in Rawls is, however, more problematic. This is the requirement of locating public reason within the arguments that can properly be considered 'political' (hence, positioned within an overlapping consensus) as opposed to comprehensive ones. I do not wish to rehearse a very rich literature containing the arguments objecting to the exclusion of comprehensive moral conceptions from the public discourse, and deploring the inevitable impoverishment of the public discourse resulting from such exclusion, as well as the blatant lack of realism revealed by such a directive. What I do want to observe, however, is that there is no necessary equivalence between the first and the second formulations of public reason: it is not the case that only narrow, non-comprehensive moral conceptions can be reasonably acceptable to all. Public reason in its first formulation seems to be broader and more ecumenical than in the second, and the test of 'reasonable endorseability' by all (the first formulation) need not go so far as to disqualify all arguments appealing to comprehensive moral views from the discourse about the legitimate law. To be sure, this broader or more ecumenical (and at the same time, more realistic) character of public reason is conditional upon our understanding that what matters is a hypothetical endorsement rather than the actual one, and the adoption of an impartial observer perspective. So, in the end, there is an inevitable tension, in the public reason conception, between the hypothetical and real endorsement by all citizens.

This *tension*, luckily, is not a *contradiction* and does not render the liberal principle of legitimacy chimerical for two reasons. First, and perhaps obviously, the subject matter of the consent is not the wisdom or justness of the law but only a certification that the reasons that may be rationally supplied for its defence belong to 'public reason': that is, that they are not 'sectarian' (in the sense that they cannot be endorsed by all)[64] but belong to the category of reasons that may properly be cited in defence of a law. Arguably, it is easier to elicit consent that the reasons

[63] ibid at 253 (emphasis added).

[64] For the same usage of 'sectarianism' see Joshua Cohen 'Deliberation and Democratic Legitimacy' in David Estlund (ed) *Democracy* (Oxford: Blackwell, 2002) 87–106 at 98.

provided for adopting a law fall into this category than to seek universal agreement with the specific justification of a particular law: the former is a more lenient test than the latter. Secondly, and more importantly, it does not particularly matter that the criterion of acceptance is discerned in a hypothetical rather than a real manner because (consistent with my earlier argument about disconnection of legitimacy as justification from a duty to obey the law) what we are concerned with is the legitimacy of the law rather than citizens' duty to obey. For this reason we may well identify the locus of legitimacy in the eyes of an impartial observer rather than in the eyes of citizens themselves. This distinction, between an impartial-observer perspective and that of an actual citizen corresponds to a distinction drawn by Simmons between generic and transactional evaluations in political philosophy: the former correspond to the general moral virtues of political arrangements, the latter to the specific, actual interactions between individual persons and their polities.[65] Here we can content ourselves with the former (generic) because our aim is to ground the system's legitimacy (understood as its justification) rather than the obligation of citizens to comply with its directives. Hypothetical consent becomes, then, merely an 'expository device' of a critical observer's reasoning (just as in Rawls, the original position is an expository device of our individual reasoning about justice),[66] leading to the conclusion that the law indeed is legitimate (that, in Raz's language, it properly incorporates in its directives the reasons which apply to its subjects).

This is perhaps most clearly viewed in the case of Dworkin's conception of legitimacy, based as it is upon 'the model of principle': our institutions are legitimate if they operate within a community that genuinely takes 'integrity' as central to politics, and which therefore 'expresses a concern by each for all that is sufficiently special, personal, pervasive, and egalitarian to ground communal obligations'.[67] At first blush, there is very little room in this version of the liberal principle of legitimacy for any consent by citizens, hypothetical or otherwise, and the certification of the institutions as legitimate (and of the community as principle- or integrity-based) results from a judgment as to how well they fare under the standards of the group that generated the proper associative obligations. In these cases, 'the members of a group must by and large hold certain attitudes about the responsibilities they owe one another',[68] including that they 'must suppose that the group's practices show not only concern but an *equal* concern for all members'.[69] This latter judgment (that the group treats all with an equal concern) need not necessarily be actually shared by those who are on the receiving end of coercive action; however, on the other hand, if even the *other* members

[65] Simmons 'Justification and Legitimacy' at 764. But note that Simmons uses different notions of 'justification' and 'legitimacy' from the ones adopted here.

[66] Rawls *Theories of Justice* at 21.

[67] Dworkin *Law's Empire* at 216.

[68] ibid at 199.

[69] ibid at 200 (emphasis in the original).

of the group cannot reasonably attest to the institutions' attitude of treating all with an equal concern then those institutions clearly lack a threshold condition of legitimacy.

Returning to the values/interests distinction with which we began, it can now be seen that this distinction is a very imperfect and crude proxy for the distinction between those justifications of laws that *are* properly part of public reason, and hence that can be accepted as valid by all those to whom they apply (even if, in practice, some will not agree with the substance of the laws) and, on the other hand, those justifications that *cannot* be offered to all citizens because they violate the liberal test of legitimacy. The first distinction (values *versus* interests) is not well correlated with the second (proper justifications of law in terms of public reasons *versus* justifications that not everyone can be expected to accept, and therefore that are beyond the limits of public reason), and it is the *latter* distinction that is crucial to the issue of legitimacy, the main question that has occupied us here. The first distinction is secondary, and to the degree that it does not track the latter distinction, it is of no special relevance for us.

Why would anyone have thought that the interests/values distinction was important for the legitimacy of law and policy under something like a liberal principle of legitimacy? The reason might be this: it *could* be claimed that if the best justification for a particular law is that it meets the interests of a group X, then if I am not a member of a group X, I have no reason to accept this law. But it is enough to articulate this argument in this way to see how implausible it is. For one thing, not every interest-based argument must be 'sectarian' in this way: there may be laws that implement the interests of everyone or nearly everyone, by providing solutions to coordination problems. They will still be justified in terms of interests but nevertheless they may figure as 'public reason' in that they are justifiable to (almost) everyone. This is because self-interest is not necessarily antithetic to fairness. One example of cases when self-interest may be the basis of a claim which is justifiable in terms of fairness is when any of the actors involved in a particular joint practice can contribute the requisite level of a public good and yet it seems unfair to require just one actor to shoulder all the costs of such contributions from which everyone else benefits. In such cases, there is a ground for spreading the burdens of contributions to a production of public good, and the self-interest based claims of such an actor provide then, as Jack Knight and James Johnson nicely put it, 'a significant part of the normative scaffolding in terms of which fairness can be defined'.[70] For another thing, even if a legal rule's main justification is that it implements the interests of group X, as a non-X member I may still recognize the importance of meeting this group's interests, on the basis of my notions of fairness, compensation for past deprivation etc. It may be argued,

[70] Jack Knight and James Johnson 'What Sort of Equality Does Deliberative Democracy Require? in James Bohman and William Rehg (eds) *Deliberative Democracy: Essays on Reason and Politics* (Cambridge: MIT Press, 1997), 279–319 at 290.

of course, that then the best justification for this law is in terms of justice rather than in terms of X's interests, but this only serves to illustrate how uncertain and unreliable the very distinction between interests and values is in the first place.

This is confirmed by common sense. When a particular person votes, for example, for a particular tax scheme which in fact will make her richer, does she vote on the basis of her interests, or of her sense of justice (she genuinely believes that she deserves it), or on the basis of her view about the public good (she believes that it is the most efficient scheme, which will, incidentally, also make her richer)? It is difficult to separate these different justifications from each other, and the most sensible observation would be that, usually, we make our public decisions on the basis of a complex mix of such, and other, justifications. And it seems to be a category mistake to oppose values to interests because interests, when properly generalized and certified as legitimate, acquire a status of values. In the words of Habermas: 'Once [an interest] is translated into an inter-subjectively shared evaluative vocabulary, it is no longer tied to contingent desires and preferences and can achieve, as a candidate for value-generalization in moral justification, the epistemic status of an argument. What enters discourse as a desire or preference survives the generalization test only under the description of a value that appears to be generally acceptable to all participants . . . .'[71]

Matters become even more complicated if the example does not refer to a law that has clear material benefits and costs to the voters (such as a tax scheme) but rather concerns complex moral judgments about the rightness or otherwise of a particular practice, and the law's proper reaction to it. What would it take to vote on the basis of one's 'interests' on issues such as abortion, euthanasia, or capital punishment? A 'Benthamite' picture would probably be that a vote based on interests would mean that someone who feels that she is likely to terminate her pregnancy, or terminate her life, or be punished for murder, will vote, respectively, for a liberal regime of abortion and euthanasia, and against the death penalty. But such a preposterous supposition would be an obvious travesty, ignoring what we know about why people support or oppose such laws. The subject matter of these laws simply does not lend itself to an interest-based motivation although, arguably, we *could* think of arguments in favour of them that would not pass the public-reason test. In these areas, calls for value-based motivations (and, more broadly, for a value-enhanced democracy) simply sound redundant. Another way of expressing the same thought would be by using the language of a mix of 'personal' and 'external' preferences, the latter being indistinguishable from personal affirmations of the common good. This was well expressed in the classic polemic by HLA Hart regarding Ronald Dworkin's theory based upon the personal/external preferences distinction. Hart invited Dworkin to focus on those 'cases where the external preference is *favourable* to, and so supports, some personal preference or want for some good or advantage or liberty . . .'. Hart further

[71] Habermas *The Inclusion of the Other: Studies in Political Theory* at 81–2.

gives the following example: 'Suppose . . . the issue is freedom for homosexual relationships, and suppose that . . . it was the disinterested external preferences of liberal heterosexuals that homosexuals should have this freedom that tipped the balance against the external preferences of other heterosexuals who would deny this freedom'.[72] Here the language of 'external preferences' is just a manner of speaking about one's values concerning justice.

We may generalize this point. A society does not have normativity-free zones; it is, so to speak, normatively saturated. Some subject matters—*most* subject matters belonging to the public area—yield individual choices based on values. In this sense, a call for a value-based democracy (understood in the first, motivational, sense discussed here) is empty: it is not the case that democracy *should not* be value-free but rather that it *cannot* be so. That the motivations of citizens and their representatives in taking public decisions will not be free of values is not a *real* problem: what *is*, however, is that they will differ, often fundamentally, as to the choice of values. This is therefore a 'problem' of moral pluralism and not of value-free democracy. The warnings of the adherents of democracy-plus against 'a political community . . . *independent of ethical principles*'[73] are therefore either very weak, or they are a proxy for a warning against a community 'independent of *the right* ethical principles'. The very weak interpretation amounts to a warning against moral indifference or apathy: against citizens and their representatives ignoring all moral values when voting on public issues. But such a fear is largely unfounded, as we have seen, and the warning is for this reason practically meaningless. However, if the warning is understood in the latter sense, then it is incompatible with the liberal-democratic order that attempts to create legitimate law for people who differ greatly over the moral values they believe to be right. The strong interpretation amounts to a plea for a polity that enforces morality in the strongly 'perfectionist' manner identified earlier in the chapter: it is a political community that coercively imposes ideals of individual good and virtue upon those who do not necessarily share them.

7. 'Democracy without Values' in the Constitutional Sense

The second level at which the legitimacy of democratic laws might be seen to be contingent upon their incorporation of the right values is at the 'constitutional' level which is of a different nature from the 'motivational' one. It does not concern the motivations of the decision-makers (voters and legislators alike) but the value-laden limits upon the substance of democratically adopted decisions: it

[72] HLA Hart 'Between Utility and Rights' Columbia Law Review (1979) 79: 828 at 842 (emphasis in the original).

[73] John Paul II 'Address to the Polish Parliament' 11 June 1999, available at <http://www.vatican.va/holy_father/john_paul_ii/travels/documents/hf_jp-ii_spe_11061999_warsaw-parliament_en.html> part 5 (my emphasis).

therefore concerns the 'output' rather than the 'input', so to speak. The general idea here is that democratic decisions, in order to be legitimate, must comply with certain substance-related requirements, or that they cannot transcend certain substance-related constraints. I will call this dimension 'constitutional' for the obvious reason that the identification of the substantive limits that a legislator is not permitted to overstep is widely seen to be one of the main functions of constitutions, and in particular of constitutional charters of rights.

I will be brief in discussing this aspect of democratic legitimacy—not because it is unimportant but because it has been dealt with so expansively in the literature on constitutional theory.[74] For my present purposes, it is important only to indicate that this second dimension, of the output democracy, or values-enhanced democracy, raises different problems in the face of moral pluralism from the first, 'motivational' dimension. The issue here is not so much that a fear of moral indifference or apathy is generally unfounded (as was the case with the motivational dimension) but rather that, in the process of the articulation of the meaning of vague constitutional pronouncements, actual moral disagreement over moral values is merely *replicated* rather than deflated. We may well accept, as a starting point, that the legitimate exercise of authority in a democratic state requires us to assume that there are *some* limits to what the authorities can decide. Indeed, the acceptance of the principle of respect for human rights itself necessarily also means that there are substantive limits to what authorities can do to individuals. (There may also be other implications of the human rights principle: for example, that there are some opportunities that must be provided to citizens, and the language of opportunity does not translate easily into the language of limits, except trivially. However, human rights include also, amongst other things the idea of limits.) The 'problem' is that, faced with moral disagreement in society, even if the constitution is accepted consensually (which is a presupposition adopted only for the sake of argument), the actual articulation of the general constitutional rights translates the general moral disagreement into a disagreement as to whether a particular authoritative directive transcends the limits imposed by the constitution.

This is not the weak observation that, at the margins, people will disagree about the specific 'penumbra' of a particular vague concept implicated in various constitutional rights. Rather, it is that the disagreement will often be fundamental and central to the meaning of a right-as-limit. For example: whether freedom of speech mandates or prohibits limitations on paid political advertisements, or whether the right against discrimination prohibits, permits, or mandates affirmative action in university admissions, or whether the right to life requires or prohibits assistance in terminating the life of a terminally-ill patient on demand.

[74] For two excellent expositions of this idea, see Michael J Perry 'What Is "Constitution"? and Other Fundamental Questions' in Larry Alexander (ed) *Constitutionalism: Philosophical Foundations* (Cambridge: Cambridge University Press, 1998) 99–151; Richard S Kay 'American Constitutionalism' in Larry Alexander (ed) *Constitutionalism: Philosophical Foundations* 16–63.

These and a myriad other controversies can easily be understood in terms of constitutional rights but our disagreements on the interpretation of these constitutional rights will simply replicate the prior disagreement over the moral issues that these rights were supposed to resolve. We will not only disagree over whether a proposed law transcends a substantive limit imposed by a constitutional right but, even more fundamentally, over what interpretation of a right constitutes a *limit* on the exercise of state authority in the first place. Is a ban on euthanasia a limit on what can be done to a person (with the subsequent discussion about where exactly this limit lies), or rather is a legal opportunity of terminating one's life with the help of a doctor a limit on what can be prohibited and enforced against a person? The answers, of course, will be a direct reflection of prior and more fundamental moral disagreement. Thus, while we may well all agree that there should be *some* limits to what the state can do to individuals, once we start debating what constitutes a limit, not to mention where the limits should properly lie, the constitutional pronouncements of rights will turn out to be singularly unhelpful.[75]

This is not to say that rights provisions are irrelevant, or without significance. On the contrary, we know that they play a very significant role politically in providing, in various legal systems, judicial or non-judicial bodies with the grounds for decisions that may invalidate, or reinterpret, the laws adopted by legislatures. There is, however, no reason to adopt a position of institutional fetishism and to assume that a constitutionally identified institution that has the power to displace the choices of other bodies with its own is, *eo ipso*, 'right' in the articulation of the meaning of a controversial constitutional provision. Indeed, a disagreement between two bodies, for example between a parliament and a constitutional (or a supreme) court (or to be more precise, between the majorities of these collective bodies), will more often than not merely reflect a moral disagreement existing in the society as a whole about what, in terms of a vague constitutional provision, constitutes a limit on state action, and where that limit should properly lie. The power of such an extra-parliamentary body to pronounce on the decisions of the parliament simply adds one step to the constitutionally prescribed procedure that has to be followed in order for the decision to be final and legitimate; however, it still remains a procedure-based legitimacy, not a values-based one. The law as corrected in a process of judicial review is not necessarily more *within the limits* defined by constitutional rights than a law without such a correction, but the review does make a difference in terms of what counts as a legitimate procedure for the issuing of legal directives. As a judge of the US Supreme Court once famously said: 'We are not final because we are infallible, but we are infallible only because we are final'.[76]

[75] For further discussion, see Wojciech Sadurski 'Judicial Review and the Protection of Constitutional Rights' OJLS (2002) 22: 275 at 294–6.

[76] *Brown v Allen* 344 US 443, 540 (1953) (Jackson J concurring).

The conferral on a particular institution of the power to strike down laws on the basis of their (alleged) inconsistency with constitutional rights is a matter of institutional fiat which adds (rightly or wrongly—this is beyond the scope of this book) one step in the correct procedure to be followed.[77] The decisions that emerge from such a procedure acquire democratic legitimacy, just as those that issue from a procedure where no such possibility of review exists acquire democratic legitimacy. There may be good political arguments related to the institutional competence of various organs for creating or removing such a power. One is the simple argument about the fragmentation of legislative powers: the more 'veto points' are built into the law-making system (not only constitutional courts, but also a bicameral legislature, executive veto, complex systems of screening proposed bills by parliamentary or extra-parliamentary committees etc) the lower the likelihood of arbitrary, impulsive, unreflective law-making. Another popular argument concerns the (alleged) higher capacity of constitutional courts (or similar bodies) to conduct their deliberation in a dispassionate and impartial way, without pressure from interest groups or political parties. Yet another argument is that various institutional incentives built into constitutional courts, but absent from parliamentary bodies, such as a very long (or life) tenure, guarantees of high and non-reviewable income, incompatibility of judicial tenure with other professional or political positions etc, ensure that judges care more about their reputations than immediate interests and thus try harder to get to the heart of the matters before them. Now these, and myriad other, arguments about constitutional judicial review are controversial and subject to rebuttal. But, again, this is not the place for that discussion. My point is that the argument about enhancing the legitimacy of law-making by injecting the right values into the decision is *not* affected by any particular view we may hold about the best institutional design of the law-making.

It *would* be affected if we could plausibly believe that constitutional judges (or any other institution which would enforce the substantive limits upon the parliamentary law-making) had a better insight into the true meaning of constitutional rights. But such a belief would be unfounded. An articulation of a constitutional right—whether by a legislature or by a court—is not so much an act of making a vague concept simply more precise but rather, when fundamentally divergent interpretations are available, under the accepted canons of interpretation,[78] it is an act of endowing a concept with moral value, which is the only reason we endorse this concept in the first place. For the rights are meaningful to us—morally significant—only insofar as they represent a moral value, but if a given proposed

[77] For my views about merits and demerits of judicial constitutional review, see Wojciech Sadurski *Rights Before Courts: A Study of Constitutional Courts in Postcommunist States of Central and Eastern Europe* (Dordrecht: Springer, 2005).

[78] It resonates with Waldron's recognition that 'disagreements about rights are often about central applications, not just marginal applications', Jeremy Waldron 'The Core of the Case Against Judicial Review' Yale Law Journal (2006) 115: 1346–406 at 1367.

'right' cannot be understood in a way which is morally valuable to us, we have no reason to endorse that right in the first place. I think that it is a different way of saying what Joseph Raz meant when he suggested that 'rights' are 'intermediary steps' or 'intermediary conclusions in arguments from ultimate values to duties'; they are, Raz added 'points in the argument where many considerations intersect and where the results of their conflicts are summarized....'[79]

It is much more than merely making a more general concept more specific—a job which can properly be seen as capable of being entrusted to judges, that is officials without strong democratic legitimacy etc. It is, rather, an act of actually making a fundamental choice for the society which (when a given constitutional right is capable of widely different interpretation) had *not* been prefigured by a constitutional choice. Now it may well be that not every constitutional right—not every right written into any constitutional document in the world—is of such a nature; in some cases future decisions by political actors as to the articulation of a given right *have* been largely pre-empted by the act of constitution-making (such as with regard to a constitutional right against extradition from one's own state, for instance, even though some leeway of choice as to the meaning of 'extradition' is still left to the future rights-articulators). But at least some of the most important constitutional rights are of such a nature that it is only in the process of articulating them that we can endow them with the value which supports our endorsement of that right in the first place—and it is around these rights that the whole debate about judicial review centres. And if what I have just suggested is correct—if we have no reason to believe that one institution as compared to others have a better insight into the true meaning of constitutional rights—then output democracy cannot really build upon the notion of substantive, value-based constitutional limits on democratic procedures.

Conclusions

The upshot of this chapter may seem disappointing to those who believe (as almost all of us do) that the value of democracy lies not in the process itself but rather that it leads to morally and politically admirable outcomes: that it protects rights, respects equality, implements self-determination etc better than any other system. The conclusions of this chapter seem to go against the current popular disenchantment with purely 'procedural' democracy which, as the experience of the 20th century shows, is not a panacea for all social ills, and often lacks sufficient self-defence mechanisms against those who would use democratic procedures to pursue inhuman, oppressive, and discriminatory goals—and demolish democratic institutions in the process. But such a reading of my conclusions would be unwarranted: I do not call for indifference as to 'values' and for exclusive concern with the proper 'procedures'. If anything, my conclusion is the opposite: I am

[79] Raz *The Morality of Freedom* at 181.

suggesting that our values are normally and routinely engaged with democratic procedures, and any criticism of 'merely' procedural democracy can be properly read as a disappointment that a particular democratic system gives effect to some values other than those espoused by the critic. This sense of disappointment is hard to reconcile with the acceptance of moral pluralism and disagreement as a pervasive, persistent, and significant feature of contemporary societies.

Disappointment of this sort, in particular, should not lead one to deny legitimacy to laws that have been adopted in accordance with proper democratic procedures. This, however, is not a recipe for blind obedience to democratically adopted laws; as I argued in Part 4 of this chapter, it is not the case that each individual is necessarily (morally) obliged to comply with every *legitimate* law. The disconnection of legitimacy from the duty to obey—a disconnection advanced for reasons discussed earlier—has the consequence of deflating the apparent drama of what to do about laws adopted in a procedurally correct manner in a democracy and yet which strike us as morally wrong. A democratic and liberal legal system can and should provide room for disobedience to legitimate law, but this question is beyond the scope of this book; what is important is that a finding that a given law is legitimate does not necessarily lead to the conclusion that it must always be complied with by those who disagree with it. However, we need a language in which to express the combination of recognition of legitimacy and refusal to obey on moral grounds; and if we were to incorporate the 'right' values into our test for the legitimacy of law, then this possibility would no longer exist.

But isn't it too cavalier to claim that values are indeed involved in a democratic procedure? What are these values, and are they significant enough to confer legitimacy upon the laws resulting from these procedures? More importantly, how do these values resonate with the fundamental ideal of equality, for instance if we know that democratic legislatures occasionally adopt, through the use of democratic procedures, laws which treat individuals and groups unequally? These questions will be addressed in the next chapter.

suggesting that our values are normally and routinely engaged with democratic procedures, and any criticism of 'merely procedural' democracy can be properly read as a disappointment that the particular democratic system gives effect to some values other than those espoused by the critic. This sense of disappointment is hard to reconcile with the acceptance of moral pluralism and disagreement as a pervasive, persistent, and significant feature of contemporary societies.

Disappointment of this sort, in particular, should not lead one to deny legitimacy to laws that have been adopted in accordance with proper democratic procedures. This, however, is not to argue for blind obedience to democratically enacted laws, as I suggest in Part 3 of this chapter, [illegible]

2

Political Equality and Majority Rule

In Chapter 1, I claimed that the very choice of a democratic system—even understood in a purely procedural manner—reveals an endorsement of some substantive values, insofar as the majority rule (which, I asserted, is an irreducible core of democracy) is underwritten by some egalitarian values: majority rule, I asserted, makes sense only if we believe in the fundamental political equality of citizens. But at that point it was just that: an assertion, and here I propose to defend it. In doing so, I will rely on certain widespread intuitions about the legitimacy-conferring power of majority rule. The structure and the aspiration of the argument developed in this chapter, needs some explanation at the outset.

As a starting point, I assume that the legitimating force of majority rule (hereinafter MR) is so pervasive that we rarely question or even realize it: we usually just take it for granted. All sorts of collective decisions are taken by majority, even if not always by a *simple* majority: the election of a new pope by the conclave of cardinals, the laws passed by parliaments, the verdicts laid down by courts, the regulations adopted by clubs and associations, as well as the decisions between friends about where to eat out together. There are, of course, some important exceptions to this pervasive authority of the principle of majority. There are contexts in which unanimity is required (as in many jury systems or in some voluntary organizations using blackballing for the admission of new members) and, conversely, there are contexts in which only one person, or a few persons, are in a privileged position to make the decisions for the group: consider for instance some of the decisions in a family, in the army, or in a church structure. It is, however, precisely because these are *exceptions* that we take the majority decision as a *norm* in the legitimacy-conferring decision rule.

This is not to deny the force of a popular counter-argument against the uses of MR: 'The majority is not necessarily right'. We all know this, and in those circumstances in which the rightness of the decision relies significantly on the ascertainment of some empirical *facts*, this challenge may be effective. Consider, for example, the issue of establishing the criminal guilt of a particular celebrity: holding a national poll on his guilt or innocence, with a verdict by majority, seems like a particularly bad decision procedure in this case. This does not mean, however, that the rule of majority has no place in this example at all, but rather that the constituency of the decision-makers has been identified in an inappropriate way. Once we have decided, in a more reasonable manner, the proper range of decision-makers, be it a jury or a panel of professional judges, we may well establish that, in the situation incurred by the inevitable uncertainty about the truth of the facts, we do need to settle for a decision by majority. (Or we may not: we may require unanimity or a qualified majority. But a majority decision is not to be regarded as absurd in such cases.) Similarly, when the 'rightness' of a decision does not rely on the decision being based on the ascertainment of certain verifiable facts but on the justice of the outcome, there is no guarantee that a decision taken by majority will be right in that sense: '[a]lthough in given circumstances it is justified that the majority (suitably defined and circumscribed) has the constitutional right to make law, this does not imply that the laws enacted are just'.[1]

But my point is not that MR applies or should apply to *all* collective decisions, but rather that it is intuitively taken as a norm about the sources of *legitimacy* of many types of collective decisions in a wide range of contexts. I do not necessarily want to defend MR as the best collective decision rule, all things considered; instead I am interested only in its legitimacy-conferring power, via its egalitarian character (which I intend to demonstrate in this chapter). But I wish to emphasize that my aspiration is even more modest than that: I do not wish to claim that MR always respects the equality of participants (or stakeholders), and does it better than any other collective decision rule, but only that it respects equality better than any other decision rule once the alternative is presented as a choice between only two options based on the ranking of the latter. First, we may have other plausible procedures of collective decision-taking: we may for instance, decide to reach decisions not on the basis of the aggregation of preferences, but by applying certain rules about fair division.[2] Suppose a decision needs to be made about the allocation of certain resources among a number of people, and the aggregate claims exceed the stock of available resources: we may then resort to division rules which do not rely on aggregating preferences at all (eg the best offices in a given office building to be allocated on the basis of seniority). It may be said that some rules of fair division will respect the equality of the stakeholders better than any aggregative procedure. But, secondly, even within the category of aggregative procedures, we may establish rules differing from MR, which may be claimed to be more egalitarian, for example the rules of proportionate consideration. Suppose the three of us always go together to the cinema: two of us prefer comedies, while one favours thrillers. To apply a majority rule here would give the two-thirds a 100 per cent dominance in the choice and one-third 0 per cent. So there may be a better way: we may determine that out of each three movies seen together, we will see comedies twice and a thriller once. This is a so-called 'positional' decision procedure. And there may be others: we may use a so-called Borda count,[3] which

[1] John Rawls *A Theory of Justice* at 356.

[2] The point made in this paragraph is inspired by Mathias Risse 'Arguing for Majority Rule' *Journal of Political Philosophy* (2004) 12: 41–64.

[3] Risse 'Arguing for Majority Rule' at 43.

gives each voter a possibility of assigning a number of points (starting with the lowest, going up to the highest, according to each individual ranking) to each option or candidate, and the result will be based on the summing up of all the votes and selecting those at the top. This last method is particularly well suited for the selection of a multi-member body. Indeed, to use simple MR would violate the principle of equality in this case. This is because MR, used without deep qualifications, would be satisfied by a system whereby a majority elects *all* members of the elective body, an outcome clearly violating the principle of equal weight of every vote.[4] But also in a larger range of cases such 'positional' methods may be more sensitive to the principle of equality of voters (and/or of stakeholders) than MR. The supremacy of MR (in terms of its egalitarian character) is demonstrated in this chapter only vis-à-vis other decision rules within the pair-wise votes; when the choice is to be made for one option within a simple alternative. So a theory of MR must be accompanied by a meta-theory about when the collective choice should be reduced to a simple alternative. Providing such a meta-theory is beyond my ambitions here; but it would have something to do with (among other things) the need to reduce complexity and the desirability of presenting plain choices to voters.

Subject to these qualifications, it can probably be accepted that in our conventional thinking, we accept intuitively MR as a legitimacy-conferring procedure in a great number of contexts, groups, and types of decisions. But why should we do so? MR is not self-justifying, and we should find out what can possibly account for this legitimating force of MR in numerous and diverse circumstances. Such an exploration *may* be motivated by a critical aspiration: one may try to show that MR, considered *in abstracto*, has no sufficient justifying force to endow it with a universally legitimating power. This will not be my approach here: the pervasive force of intuitive support for MR is much too powerful to make it vulnerable to a philosophical challenge, and in any event I have no stake in launching or supporting such a challenge. Rather, I wish to discern some good justifying rationales behind MR which can be seen as endowing MR with a legitimating power.

One possible line of argument may appeal to output-legitimacy; that is the legitimacy of decisions based on their consequences. If one of the indicators of output-legitimate decisions is that their results will maximize satisfaction of those to whom they apply, then obviously if more people prefer decision D-1 to D-2, the choice of D-1 over D-2 is likely to produce more satisfaction. It is also likely to ensure higher compliance with the decision, because it better resonates with the preferences of those who will be required to comply with it. This is a utilitarian argument for MR (another consequentialist argument will be discussed in more detail in Part 1 of this chapter), and I will *not* make any use of it in this chapter: not because it is insignificant, but because it tells us nothing directly about the

[4] See further Jonathan Still 'Political Equality and Election Systems' *Ethics* (1981) 91: 375–94 at 384–5.

egalitarian potential of MR (my real interest here) and, in any event, because the outcome-oriented conception of legitimacy is a very partial, incomplete, and controversial view of legitimacy.

My argument will be that MR is thoroughly egalitarian in its rationale, and that it is this aspect of equality which is intrinsic to MR that can account for the legitimating power of MR. What sort of equality we are referring to will need to be clarified at a later stage; for the time being what is important to emphasize is that the burden of this chapter will be to show and defend the relationship between MR and the equality of citizens.

If this link can be properly established, then the implication will be that, given the intuitive legitimating force of MR (treated here as an axiom), the real legitimating work is done via the principle of equality of people as citizens. This implication resonates quite well with a conventional, liberal-egalitarian conviction according to which 'equal concern is a precondition of political legitimacy'.[5] On the face of it, this conviction may seem to apply only to the social *outcomes* of the decisions, rather than the involvement in the process. However, the principle of equal concern for the interests of all is usually (and plausibly) combined with the anti-paternalistic understanding that 'everyone is assumed to be the best judge of his or her own good or interests';[6] hence the requirement of the equal right to participate in the political process, if the aim of equal consideration of the interests of all is to be attained. As the authors of an excellent essay on deliberative democracy have noted, the question of equality 'is an especially pressing problem insofar as we are concerned with the legitimacy or otherwise of democratic institutional arrangements'; in a democracy, they observe, legitimate decisions are those which arise from the deliberation of all, and 'most defences of democratic deliberation insist that this criterion of legitimacy requires a strong form of equality'.[7]

This insight applies, in my view, to a broader range of institutions and circumstances than just the relationship between the state and its citizens. In any event, I will not try to justify *why* the principle of equality has, and should have, a legitimating force. Thus the project of this chapter can be schematically defined as follows: the belief in a legitimating power of the MR will be *taken for granted* as an empirical fact of our widespread moral convictions; the *core* of the argument will be the relationship between MR and the principle of equality; and the *implication* will be that it is this equalitarian ingredient that truly accounts for the legitimating force of MR. This is how I will proceed. First, to clear the way for further argument, I will answer the question of whether the intuitive connection between MR and legitimacy cannot be better established by non-egalitarian

[5] Ronald Dworkin *Sovereign Virtue: The Theory and Practice of Equality* at 2.

[6] Robert A Dahl 'Procedural Democracy' in Peter Laslett and James Fishkin (eds) *Philosophy, Politics and Society* (Fifth Series, Oxford: Basil Blackwell, 1979) 97–133 at 126.

[7] Jack Knight and James Johnson 'What Sort of Equality Does Deliberative Democracy Require?' in James Bohman and William Rehg (eds) *Deliberative Democracy: Essays on Reason and Politics* (Cambridge, Mass: MIT Press, 1997) 279–319 at 280.

explanations, such as what I will call a 'shortcut link' which refers to the stabilization of the commitments of people to the system as a whole, even if they happen to be outvoted in a given instance (Part 1). I will then consider two interesting 'puzzles' about MR, frequently discussed in democratic theory: about the alleged insensitivity of MR to varying intensity of individual political preferences (Part 2) and the customary ban on vote trading (Part 3). In both of these cases, my single concern will be about how dominant practices in these two fields affect the equality-legitimacy link. I will then move to the central part of the argument, and review the claim that the principle of unanimity, or at least of a qualified majority, better expresses egalitarian values than that of a 'bare' MR (Part 4). Having established the good egalitarian credentials of MR, I will then consider and rebut an important argument against them, formulated by Hans Kelsen, namely that the equality-MR link is based on an erroneous view about the 'aggregation of wills' (Part 5). This argument will lead to the most important last three Parts, in which I will consider and rebut the general claim that MR, or purely procedural democracy, cannot be a good expression of political equality, insofar as it allows for the adopting of decisions which are fundamentally inegalitarian in their outcomes. I will first consider the status of a distinction between outcome-oriented and process-oriented conceptions of political equality, and will resist the calls for an outcome-oriented conception (Part 6). Next, I will argue that some of the dilemmas which have been drawn, notably by Ronald Dworkin, with regard to the idea of equal political influence or equal political impact, can be addressed by a proper understanding of the concept of equal opportunity in the field of politics (Part 7). On this basis, I will argue that there is a strong connection between this ideal of equal opportunity and the principle of MR (Part 8). This conclusion, if successful, fulfils the aspiration of showing the fundamentally egalitarian character of 'procedural' democracy, with MR as its main ingredient.

1. Majority Rule and Legitimacy: a Shortcut Link?

Before addressing the merits of the main argument of this chapter, a preliminary remark is in order. The general gist of the argument developed here is not only that majority rule is based on substantive equality principles (which serves to support a more general observation that even merely 'procedural' democracy has substantive moral moorings) but also that there is a normative connection between majority rule and the legitimacy of law, and that the work of mediating between majority rule and legitimacy is done largely through egalitarian values (whose specific nature still remains to be ascertained). But one may observe that there are other, perhaps simpler, ways of discerning a link between MR and the legitimacy of the law without any need for reconstructing the egalitarianism underlying MR and then showing that this egalitarianism goes some of the way towards legitimating the law.

One such way is by focusing on a function that MR typically serves: it stabilizes the commitment of people to the system as a whole, by making it feasible for those who are in an outvoted minority on a given law to remove this law in the future. The closer the law-making system comes to a simple majority rule, the easier such a possibility becomes; by contrast, any departures from a single majority rule (qualified majority requirements) favour more entrenched preferences of the current majority, and consequently lead to the unlikelihood of today's minority accepting the legitimacy of the system and abstaining from undoing the majority's rulings through violent means. This is a feature of MR which Ian Shapiro describes as the 'institutionaliz[ation of] the perpetual possibility of upsetting the status quo',[8] and which he then identifies as one of those findings in the public choice literature which are 'less threatening to democracy's legitimacy than is often assumed'.[9]

There is no doubt that this incentive for people to remain loyal to the system is an important merit of majority rule; it makes the task of undoing the results of today's decisions less overwhelming tomorrow than many other decision-making rules. And there is no doubt that the revocability of individuals holding governing positions is an extremely important democratic achievement; perhaps the most important feature of democracy, under realistic and hence rather minimalist expectations of what are the main advantages of a democracy. As John Dunn noted, 'The predicament of being governed by those whom a clear majority can eventually dismiss is far less dire than the corresponding predicament of being governed indefinitely by those of whom you can hope to rid yourself only by rising up and overthrowing them by force of arms'.[10] No one can reasonably dispute this judgment. But is the revocability of individuals and of laws really a satisfactory argument to support the *legitimacy* of the law-making system as a whole? I have some doubts about it. For one thing, the link between this feature of MR and the legitimacy of law-making rests on a number of additional conditions which may or may not be fulfilled, and therefore the link is very contingent. Without entering into too much detail (which would require providing an empirical political science analysis), the link exists when the majority/minority division is fluid, when various minorities of today have a reasonable chance of entering into majority-constituting coalitions, and when the cleavages between preferences cut across various social classes. If these conditions are not met (ie when there are groups constituting 'permanent minorities'), and when there is a single dominant cleavage within society, majority rule is of no use for today's 'losers' and the incentive for them to accept the legitimacy of the system does not arise, or must be found in features of the system other than in the MR.

[8] Ian Shapiro *The State of Democratic Theory* (Princeton: Princeton University Press, 2003) 14.
[9] ibid at 16.
[10] John Dunn *Setting the People Free: The Story of Democracy* at 164.

Secondly, there is something bizarre, perhaps even perverse, about a proposition that the legitimacy-generating feature of a given law is that it can easily be undone. It is equivalent to saying that a particular official is legitimate on the basis that she can be easily removed from office. Let us pursue this analogy for a moment. The easy removal of an official *may* be an indirect indication of her legitimacy in the sense that it signals that she was appointed (or elected) into the office through legitimacy-endowing processes, such as the election or appointment by a body authorized to make such decisions. But it just shows that it is not the fact of easy removal per se which endows the official with legitimacy, bur rather the fact that she has been *democratically elected* in the first place. Similarly, it cannot be the fact of an easy change of the laws which may endow the law with legitimacy. We need some *positive* features of the law in question, or of the law-making process which led to its enactment, rather than the consolation for those who dislike the law that it can be easily overturned, if we want to identify the sources of its legitimacy.

But one must not quibble too much: there *is* an element of legitimacy-building in the feature of MR depicted by Ian Shapiro, and by other political theorists, and described as the institutionalization of the possibility of upsetting the status quo. The link between this feature of MR and legitimacy is, however, not to be found in the political stability which it apparently enhances nor in the loyalty of the opposition it produces (even though it certainly does that, under some empirical conditions mentioned above), but rather in the fact that it creates a certain type of *equality* between those who have won (the majority) and those who were outvoted (the minority) on a given proposal. What sort of equality is it? An analogy will help explain this. Consider two athletes: one has just won the competition, whereas the other, on the face of his recent record and his capacities, is well within the reach of winning in the next game. This likelihood of winning in the future renders them both 'equal' to each other in the meaningful sense of the word, and in the sense in which two athletes of highly *different* capacities are not 'equal'. It is not just a trivial proposition about varying degrees of difference; it is rather that the differences, kept within certain limits, do not amount to inequality. All members of a given class are 'equal' by virtue of the likelihood of victory, and the marginal distinctions of capacities do not count for the purpose of recognizing the fact of equality. (We can claim, without any absurdity, that Juventus, Inter, and AC Milan are 'equally good' football teams even though at any time when we make this statement they will almost certainly occupy different positions in the current ranking.) This is what John Rawls dubbed the relationship of equality by virtue of having a 'range property' which he described (in the context of a discussion where he based equality on the natural capacities of individuals) in the following example:

[T]he property of being in the interior of the unit circle is a range property of points in the plane. All points inside this circle have this property although their coordinates vary within a certain range. And they *equally* have this property, since no point interior to a circle is more or less interior to it than any other interior point.[11]

There are many contexts in which equality is a matter of all persons meeting a particular threshold, such as when meeting a particular legal requirement (say, of age for voting eligibility) is all that matters for equal qualifications for a particular benefit, and the marginal differences in the degree of satisfying a particular condition are irrelevant. But this type of equality may also apply to some moral and political arguments, which do not have a rough-and-ready threshold condition (as in legal classifications) and where the moral or political condition, theoretically at least, lends itself to judgments of degrees, but where we refuse to grant any relevance to such degrees. Precisely that type of equality occurs also, I believe, when there is a reasonable likelihood of becoming a winner in the political voting game next time round, and this likelihood is higher in the MR-based process than when a more qualified majority is required. Admittedly, this is a vague and rather unsatisfactory description—but the only reason why I include it here is in order to show that what may seem to be a legitimacy-enhancing factor of MR in fact boils down to its egalitarian characteristics.

2. Majority Rule and Intensity of Preferences

One of the central puzzles raised in democratic theory about MR is that it seems to presuppose the equal intensity of perceived interests and of espoused preferences, which is (as the argument goes) deeply implausible: 'A man who is passionately opposed to a given measure and a man who is slightly favorable but does not care greatly about it are given equal weight in the [majoritarian] process of making final decisions'.[12] This is often seen to be a perversion of equality, and therefore either a basis for proposals departing from MR or at least as a proof that the MR procedure is not really equality-based. It is only this last argument that is of interest to the present discussion.

To begin with, one needs to observe that a point at which MR is actually employed does not exhaust the entire political decision-making process in a democracy, and that the adoption of MR may actually presuppose (rather than being a departure from) the existence of elements of the process which *are* sensitive to differing intensities of political preferences. As Henry B Mayo observed in his classic book: 'Intensity of feeling—often an acute political phenomenon—has abundant opportunity to make itself felt in the many political processes which

[11] John Rawls *A Theory of Justice* at 508 (emphasis added). Rawls's concept of 'range property' has been taken up by Waldron in his interpretation of the Lockean idea of the equal rationality of human beings; see Jeremy Waldron *God, Locke, and Equality* (Cambridge: Cambridge University Press, 2002) at 76–81.

[12] James M Buchanan and Gordon Tullock *The Calculus of Consent* (Ann Arbor: University of Michigan Press, 1965) 132.

are open' and which, one may add, are connected in various ways with the process of voting.[13] MR applies only to the final stage of the decision-making process which follows, and is responsive to an earlier stage consisting of the deliberation of various proposals. Undoubtedly, differing intensities of views affect the way in which a deliberation takes place since those who feel stronger about a matter will probably participate in the debate more actively and more forcefully than those who are indifferent or apathetic about the issue who will not care to take part or will make only very meek expositions of their views. If the voting stage is affected (as it should be in the ideal model of democracy) by what was going on in the deliberation stage, then the final vote will be sensitive, although indirectly, to intensities of preferences.

The second way in which MR coexists with intensity-sensitive mechanisms is as follows. To say that when 'we vote' each vote counts equally, without regard to the motives for voting and thus to the intensity of preferences underlying the vote, is correct but only as a shorthand of something much more complex, which in fact *does* recognize the unequal intensities of preferences. We rarely 'vote' for and against a specific proposal: as citizens, we do so only in these rare moments when there is a referendum on a single issue. In such circumstances, for a number of reasons (such as ignorance as to how others will vote, high transaction costs involved in the collaboration to make strategic alliances, secrecy of the ballot making it impossible to verify the performance of the commitments undertaken previously) we are unable to engage in processes where unequal intensities can be recognized. (It is only at the margins that these unequal intensities can be registered: those who do not care at all about a given issue, or whose preference is of extremely weak intensity, can, and do, abstain from participating in the referendum thereby reducing the perverse effect of unequally counting intense preferences equally.) But more often than not, we as citizens 'vote' for our representatives on the basis of the broad package represented by a party (or individual) platform, and the actual voting on the specific proposals is done by the representatives. The mechanisms of representative democracy of course allow, (and indeed, in an ideal model, encourage) the processes of negotiation and bargaining in which preferences of unequal intensity will be compared, and the resultant 'exchanges of votes' will occur. As James Buchanan and Gordon Tullock observe in their classic study, '[S]uch exchanges significantly affect the results of political process. It seems probable that this fact provides one of the major reasons for the widespread use of representative democracy'.[14]

One does not have to represent this process in a cynical way as 'horse-trading' or 'logrolling'—compared with market exchange in which the goods gravitate to those who can extract better value from them, measured by the willingness and

[13] Henry B Mayo *An Introduction to Democratic Theory* (New York: Oxford University Press, 1960) 178.

[14] Buchanan and Tullock *The Calculus of Consent* at 134.

capacity to pay. One can view the process as a virtuous mechanism of finding the optimal solutions through mutual compromises in the environment of trust, for which representative mechanisms (again, in their optimal embodiment) are uniquely tailored. It is clear that these mechanisms (which derive their existence from MR because representation is based on the majority vote in the elections) are intensity-sensitive, and so MR is not totally blind to unequal intensities of preferences. In fact, this dimension of intensity can also be present at the stage of the popular vote in the elections, albeit in an indirect way, by being reflected in the voters' preferences where some aspects of the 'packages' presented to them by the parties (or the individual candidates) will overshadow other aspects. Buchanan and Tullock have dubbed this effect an 'implicit logrolling' which may be orchestrated by political entrepreneurs who 'keep firmly in mind the fact that the single voter may be so interested in the outcome of a particular issue that he will vote for the one party that supports this issue, although he may be opposed to the party stand on all other issues'.[15]

Thus unequal intensities of preferences are not fully invisible in the MR-based process. It is, however, true that when it comes to the most paradigmatic use of the MR procedure: a single vote on a particular proposal taken in isolation from other votes and processes, it does not register the inequality of intensities. This may not be so bad from the point of view of egalitarian values served (as it is argued here) by MR. One problem about trying to factor different intensities of preferences into a design of the political process would be that it would be necessarily reflective of intensities of *expressions* of preferences which may be a function of many factors which are irrelevant for the intensity of preferences themselves, but have to do with purely subjective characteristics such as differences in temperament, emotionalism etc. As Peter Jones has observed:

> Some people seem to feel more strongly than others about almost everything. Some become excited without good reason; others fail to become excited when they have good reason. Taking account of intensity of preference may therefore favour over-sensitive busybodies to the disadvantage of long-suffering stoics.[16]

One could respond perhaps that this is a notorious fact about all attempts to register in politics the features corresponding to a state of mind. In politics, all that we see are the external expressions of those states of mind, and this cannot be an argument against trying to make politics responsive to the avowed preferences: we must hope that there is a degree of correlation between the expressions of preferences and the preferences themselves. But in the special instance of trying to reflect the intensity in the aggregation of preferences, the problem noted by Jones is of a different character. When A expresses a preference P-1 and B a preference P-2, the danger of a false inference from the expressions of preferences

[15] ibid at 135 (footnote omitted).

[16] Peter Jones 'Political Equality and Majority Rule', in David Miller and Larry Siedentop (eds) *The Nature of Political Theory* (Oxford: Oxford University Press, 1983) 155–82 at 162.

as opposed to the preferences themselves is minimal: we may doubt whether the preferences have been formed in a rational way, but it is hard to doubt that these *are* really the preferences of A and B at a given moment, unless we consider the facts which render these expressions insincere. But when A expresses a preference P-1 in an enthusiastic and emphatic way, and B's preference P-2 strikes us as bland and weak, these differences may very well (and very plausibly) be due to the differences in the excitability and temperament between A and B. And if it is the case (which our common sense suggests often *is* the case) then any attempt to factor in this difference of intensities into the social outcome would in fact violate, rather than respect, the equality of A and B.

This serves to focus the argument on intensity on the only issue which is of interest here. Remember, we are not concerned with whether, in general, it is a regrettable fact that MR tends to disregard the differing intensities of preferences of voters, but more specifically, whether this feature of MR shows that our intuitive endorsement of MR cannot claim support from any *egalitarian* values. Whatever the defects of MR can be as far as the intensity of preferences is concerned, the question for us is only if these defects deprive MR of its egalitarian credentials. So far my argument has been that they do not: either because MR presupposes (or at least coexists with) processes which are sensitive to differing intensities, or because redesigning MR in a way which would make it alert to different intensities would be harmful rather than beneficial for the very equality which we claim to discover as underlying MR. Without denying the force of these contentions, they cannot be *decisive* for the claim according to which intensity-insensitive MR gives effect to the political equality of persons. The decisive argument must neither be extraneous to MR (as the former proposition is) nor negative (as the latter is): it must be both intrinsic to, and positively about, MR and its relationship to the equality of persons. Such an argument must be based on a recognition that there may be a difference in the intensity-of-preferences problem when we look at the process of political decision-making at its *input* as well as at its *output* ends. When we look at the decision-making from the point of view of *outputs*, disregarding unequal intensities indeed upsets the equality between persons. For, when we consider citizens as fundamentally stakeholders in the decisions, an equal recognition of preferences of those who have high stakes and low stakes in the decision violates the principle of equal treatment. Consider the strong feelings about the construction of a new factory by those who will have to live next to it and weak feelings of those who will be unaffected by the negative externalities of the new production: to place one and the other on an equal level and merely to count the votes is not egalitarian.

But viewed from the point of view of the *input*, the relationship between intensity-insensitive MR and equality is different. Or at least, it is different if we recognize (as we should) that people's political opinions express not merely their interests but also their judgments about values. While interests have the dimension of intensity which should be counted in the calculus of social decision, the judgments about values do not.[17] The force with which we hold a particular value is not indicative of its worth. The intensity of judgment is not a symptom of its quality: '[e]ven among rational and impartial persons those with greater confidence in their opinion are not, it seems, right'.[18] Consequently, all that counts for the political process which attempts to reflect individual judgments of members of the group is the fact that each of us espouses a particular judgment and not how strongly we espouse our respective values. The fact that I believe in the need to permit doctor-assisted suicide and you are against it is fundamentally the only relevant fact for the political process leading to a collective decision on this issue: how strongly we hold on to our beliefs is not relevant, at least if the process purports to respect our politically equal status. By contrast, if the political process were to attach more importance to one of us only, because one of us has stronger feelings about the issue, it would treat us in an objectionably unequal way, because it would penalize another person for factors which are irrelevant to the exercise of a citizen's role of influencing the collective decision. Now there *may* be an equality-respecting reason for differentiating the importance of your and my opinion about the subject on the basis that your stakes are higher than mine in the social outcome (I am a suffering patient wanting to die; you are a young and healthy person) but this is precisely where the input and output perspectives on the issue diverge. In so far as the input perspective matters, and as long as the point of the political process is not merely to take into account expressed interests, but also expressed judgments, the insensitivity of MR to differing strengths of preferences is a requirement rather than a negation of the political equality of citizens.

In the end, and somewhat ironically, this argument supports a certain argument expressed by Buchanan and Tullock on this subject. I am saying it is 'ironic' because these two scholars have, of course, harshly criticized an intensity-insensitive design of the political decision-making system. But at the outset of their discussion of the subject, they offered (almost *en passant*) the following analysis, which I will quote at length because it captures well the nature of the argument that I have in mind:

> As with certain other aspects of political theory, there seems to have been a failure here [ie in the literature on voting rules] to distinguish between positive analysis and normative theory. Implicit in much of the discussion of majority rule has been the idea that individual votes *should* be treated as reflecting equal intensities of preference, quite independently of whether or not the norms agree with the facts in the case. This idea, in turn, probably stems from the more fundamental norm of democratic organization—that of political equality. Political equality may be fully accepted as essential to any form of democratic process, but this does not imply that individual votes on particular issues should be considered *as if* they reflect equal intensities of preferences over all participants.[19]

[17] For this reason, Rawls rejected the idea that 'the intensity of desire is a relevant consideration in enacting legislation', *Theory of Justice* at 230; see also ibid at 361.

[18] Rawls *Theory of Justice* at 261.

[19] Buchanan and Tullock *The Calculus of Consent* at 126 (emphases in original).

I think that Buchanan and Tullock have it exactly right here, although they would probably not approve of the use I am making of their statement. Indeed, exactly as they insist, the insensitivity of the process towards varying intensities of preferences is mandated by political equality. It is based on an 'as if' proposition: if we want to respect political equality of citizens-voters, we must treat their preferences *as if* they were of equal intensity. But of course, they are not, and Buchanan and Tullock are at pains to debunk this myth, in their (as they claim) 'positive analysis' as opposed to a 'normative theory'. What we are interested in here, however, is a 'normative theory': the theory about how the voters *should* be treated, if we wish to respect their political equality. And if the nexus between the intensiveness-insensitivity of the conventional account of MR and the principle of political equality is established so firmly by the *detractors* of the former, then we can be satisfied that this insensitivity is a meaningful symptom of the egalitarian credentials of MR, as we intuitively endorse it.

3. Vote Trading and Equality

The line of thought proposed here to explain the intensity-insensitivity built into MR can also account, mutatis mutandis, for our intuitive and widespread hostility towards the commodification of votes, ie vote selling. This is a pervasive feature of our democratic practice everywhere: while abstention from the exercise of a right to vote is almost everywhere[20] considered as a right correlated with the right to vote under an MR regime (and does not raise any difficult problems from the point of view of an egalitarian defence of MR), the trading of votes for money or for other goods or favours is generally considered to be contrary to good democratic practices. The intuitive rationale for this hostility is worth exploring here. No doubt, much of our hostility is based on practical considerations: we understand that, in the world as we know it, the temptation of the poorer people to trade whatever minimal value their vote may have for them (even if we understand the value of the vote for them in expressive terms, and not merely in terms of the marginal impact that an individual vote may have)[21] in exchange for much needed money or food may be so strong that, if such practice is permitted, it would, when generalized, significantly distort the picture of societal preferences as revealed by the voting. But if we put aside, for the sake of

[20] I put aside those few cases where an exercise of a right to vote is considered to be a matter of legal obligation, as in Australia, which can be considered to be an aberration rather than the norm. These cases may raise interesting theoretical issues from the point of view of the equality-rationale for MR, but I will not be pursuing this question here.

[21] For an exposition of the expressive theory of voting, see Geoffrey Brennan and Loren E Lomasky 'Large Numbers, Small Costs: The Uneasy Foundation of Democratic Rule' in Geoffrey Brennan and Loren E Lomasky (eds) *Politics and Process: New Essays in Democratic Thought* (Cambridge: Cambridge University Press, 1989) 42–59.

argument, this practical consideration, we may consider the more theoretical reasons underlying our widespread hostility to votes' buying and selling. After all, one may claim that according to the equality rationale supporting MR, votes can be considered just the same type of commodity as any other scarce goods: people derive value from these goods, and since they are allowed to trade with others in order to achieve the most optimal distribution (satisfying the Pareto optimality test) for a great number of any other goods, why not add the value derived from exercising a right to vote to the list of these goods, and allow free trading of votes to the highest satisfaction of everyone?

This way of putting the question immediately suggests some lines of response. One strategy of responding to the objection would be along the lines of the argument focusing on the general limits of the commodification of many other goods:[22] after all, votes are not the *only* valuable goods which we remove from the range of tradable goods. In Walzer's words, 'we can buy and sell universally only if we disregard real values; while if we attend to values, there are things that cannot be bought or sold'.[23] The boundaries of commodification are of course historically and culturally contingent but at least in some places, and at any given time, a great many goods are not subject to trading: exemption from military service or from jury duty, human life, honours or aristocratic titles, children, marriage, offices, official decisions (the buying of which is normally called bribery), bodily organs, salvation.[24] These cases of today's quasi-universal non-commodification do not usually raise important objections in terms of equality. Just the contrary: it is in terms of equality that we often object to proposals aiming at the commodification of certain goods (think about purchasing the exemption from military service in a time of war) even if one may be tempted to think that equality (or social justice) might be improved if we allowed the worse-off to sell some goods usually perceived as non-commodifiable.[25] Perhaps, at a general level, all we can say is that equality cannot be an argument against or in favour of market exchanges, and that, at this general level of argument, we must resort to other, non-equality-related arguments about the dangers resulting from the commodification of the goods generally considered non-commodifiable, such as the degradation and erosion of the worth of values associated ideally with these goods, the depletion of opportunities for altruism, and slippery-slope arguments claiming that, once admitted into the market sphere, some goods will gravitate from the non-market sphere and leave the space of non-market empty even for

[22] See, generally, Margaret Jane Radin 'Market-Inalienability' Harvard Law Review (1987) 100: 1849–937.

[23] Michael Walzer *Spheres of Justice* (Oxford: Basil Blackwell, 1983) 97.

[24] As this non-exhaustive list indicates, in some places and at given times at least some forms of these 'blocked exchanges' were unblocked, and the goods listed were turned into commodities which could be purchased. For a nice discussion of 'what money cannot buy', see ibid at 97–9.

[25] For a discussion of this temptation, see Margaret Jane Radin 'Justice and the Market Domain', in John W Chapman and J Roland Pennock (eds) *Markets and Justice: Nomos* XXXI (New York: New York University Press, 1989) 165–197 at 187–8.

those who do not choose the market regime.[26] Presumably, some of the reasons against the commodification in general are applicable to a prohibition on vote trading.

But before I consider these reasons, it is important to realize that the prohibition on vote trading is not absolute: we normally oppose trading votes for material goods but not votes for *votes*. 'Vote exchange' happens routinely at the political level, and is considered to be a legitimate part of the political process: my representatives in the parliament agree today to support a proposition A (even though I do not like it all that much) in exchange for a support of your proposition B tomorrow which is of much higher importance to me than opposing proposition A.[27] As I have suggested earlier, this is an indirect form of factoring the intensity differences into the MR regime, which is characteristic of a representative system and, far from being deplorable, it adds (in a generally non-objectionable way) an intensity dimension to MR in that it promotes deliberation in the process, because it requires the representatives of different constituencies to talk to each other and to weigh and balance competing arguments.

But if we allow the (indirect) trading of votes for votes, why not take it a step further and allow the trading of votes for other goods, eg money? (Remember that the only perspective on this question which we are interested in here is from the point of view of the *equality*-rationale of MR; all other reasons for the rejection of vote trading are outside of our interest here.) There is one *bad* answer which should be discarded at the outset: the answer which relies on the special value of the vote in expressive terms. According to this answer, it would be acceptable, under an equality rationale, to trade votes for money if the value of votes to the voters corresponded to the marginal impact that a vote had on promoting the collective decisions favoured by a voter. But since (the argument goes) this theory is deeply implausible, and we must find a different interpretation of the value of the vote, for instance in terms of its expressive significance, under these alternative interpretations the expressive value of the vote is so incommensurable with the value of money that we cannot imagine any promotion of equality as a result of the permissible trading of votes for money.

This, I believe, is not a good argument, and not merely just because the critique of the utilitarian theory of voting from the standpoint of an expressive theory is not necessarily convincing,[28] but also because the incommensurability argument goes only so far. If we *can* legitimately measure a great number of emotional, aesthetic, and sentimental gratifications in monetary terms (as we do), then what is special about the expressive value of the act of voting (as compared with many other tradable expressive values) which renders it inappropriate to alienate it for

[26] See ibid at 168.

[27] See Buchanan and Tullock *The Calculus of Consent* at 131–5.

[28] For a mild critique of the expressive theory of voting, see Dennis C Mueller 'Democracy: the Public Choice Approach' in Brennan and Lomasky *Politics and Process: New Essays in Democratic Thought* 78–96 at 82–7.

monetary values, which in turn can bring us other expressive or emotional gratifications which we may happen to value more? This way of putting the question shows that the answer relying on the expressive value of voting does not in itself provide us with a satisfactory rationale for the non-commodification of votes, but merely refers back to a more fundamental answer about the special nature of voting which in turn cannot be given in terms of the expressive value that the voting has for the voters.

The right answer can be given, I believe, in terms similar to those I have employed earlier (in Part 2) for the argument about disregarding the differences in intensity of preferences in the MR procedure of collective decision-making. If voting is seen as promoting the utility of the voters (in serving their interests) then vote-trading would be acceptable under the equality rationale (subject only to an additional proviso, developed below). But if, and insofar as, voting is about the judgments about a good society then the selling of votes is inconsistent with the principle of the equality of voters. This is because the sort of equality which is furthered by MR is the equality of impact on the collective decisions about a society: it is not about equality in the specific satisfaction of desires or meeting of the preferences. This sort of equality, the equality of voters as equal autonomous persons who can equally affect the shape of their society, cannot be improved by the trading of votes for money because the equal impact of the voters, after vote trading, will be eroded, even if other aspects of equality will be promoted. If A trades his vote with B for money then A and B will reach a more optimal distribution of votes/money in terms of satisfaction of their interests (A makes a better use of extra money than of a vote, B prefers an extra vote than the money he paid for it) but they are no longer equally influential judges about the ideas of justice that are to prevail in their society. *This* equality, if it had existed before, has been lost for the duration of the surrender of a vote by A.

But there is another equality-based argument against the alienability of votes, an argument which would hold even insofar as we consider votes as devices for furthering the voters' individual interests. Even if, as a result of vote-trading between A and B, a sort of equality is established between them, the inequality between A and C (who does not trade *her* vote for money with anyone) arises: 'it is wrong for A to sell her vote to B not because of any injury to A or B, but because their trade dilutes the value of C's vote'.[29] The inalienability of votes serves not only to prevent the situation in which some people's views do not count at all, but also the situation in which some people's votes count for *more* than others (with no role by those others in this new and unequal dispensation). This cannot be

[29] David R Ortiz 'The Democratic Paradox of Campaign Finance Reform' Stanford Law Review 50 (1998) 893–914 at 912. As Ortiz aptly puts it, 'A and B's trade creates negative externalities because the value of everyone else's vote is partly defined according to the independence of A and B's voting', ibid at 912. See, similarly, Harry Brighouse 'Egalitarianism and Equal Availability of Political Influence' *Journal of Political Philosophy* (1996) 2: 118–41 at 122.

tolerated under the egalitarian rationale for MR, and so this egalitarian rationale accounts well for our intuitive hostility to votes-for-money trading.

4. Majority Rule, Unanimity, and Equal Respect

The precise nature of the background values which underlie democracy as institutionalized through the procedures of MR is, of course, a matter that notoriously divides various theorists of democracy. We may well adopt, as a starting point, a stipulation by Rawls that 'the main variation in the extent of equal political liberty lies in the degree to which the constitution is majoritarian', and that, consequently, '[w]henever the constitution limits the scope and authority of majorities, either by requiring a greater plurality for certain types of measures, or by a bill of rights restricting the powers of the legislature, and the like, equal political liberty is less extensive'.[30] But it is just a starting point. To say that MR represents a form of equality may be seen as not particularly illuminating because the 'one person one vote' rule is (one may claim) egalitarian[31] only in a formal and admittedly objectionable sense: it ignores the unequal resources that various voters have at their disposal to persuade others to vote in a particular way. Consequently, the rigorous application of the 'one person one vote' rule may lead to drastically unequal results that counter the principle of equal concern, substantively understood: the result of a majority decision (with a one person one vote principle respected) may, for example, lead to the unequal treatment of members of a minority.[32]

This last argument has been made forcefully by Charles Beitz (author of arguably the most important work on political equality in recent years) in the context of a broader argument according to which MR cannot be properly defended on the basis of the more fundamental principle of the equal moral status of persons. This is not to say, Beitz claims, that MR is indefensible: on the contrary, it is, under normal circumstances, the best decision-making procedure, but its rationale must be found elsewhere. For instance, as Beitz believes, in the claim that it is 'the social decision procedure most likely to produce outcomes to which no one

[30] Rawls *Theory of Justice* at 224.

[31] At this point I wish to reiterate a general caveat, made already in the introductory paragraphs of this chapter, at pp 42–3, that the link between political equality and voting by majority, applies only to the situations when voters are faced with a simple alternative (two options only), and, in particular, when the subject of their vote is not an election of a multimember body, but either a policy decision formulated as a simple alternative or the election of a single-person body.

[32] For this argument, see Charles Beitz *Political Equality* (Princeton: Princeton University Press, 1989) 64. The distinction between equality as expressed in an equal vote and equality revealed in the substance of the decision corresponds to Dworkin's distinction between 'detached' and 'dependent' interpretations of democracy (focused, respectively, on the input and the output of political decisions); see Dworkin *Sovereign Virtue* at 185–90.

will have good reasons to object', which is another way of saying that 'it is more likely than any other to produce substantively correct decisions'.[33]

Beitz bases his argument against the equalitarian credentials of MR on the opposition between two theoretical points of reference: the May/Ackerman notion of neutrality in collective decision-making, on the one hand, and the Rousseauian view about majority and unanimous voting, on the other hand. The former founds the idea of neutrality (leading to the majority decision) on the notion of equal respect for people, and is (according to Beitz) mistaken. The latter is considered correct by Beitz because it is said to derive normal majoritarian decision-making from sources other than equality, while the locus of equal respect is found in unanimity voting which, in Rousseau, is reserved only for the most extraordinary, constitutive choices. The first theoretical point of reference is a theorem formulated in a classical article by Kenneth May, who showed that only the procedure of simple majority can satisfy four, reasonably thin, conditions: those of decisiveness, equality, neutrality, and positive responsiveness.[34] In his *Social Justice in the Liberal State,* Bruce Ackerman used May's theorem (with a slightly changed vocabulary) in the service of his own theory, integrating a defence of MR into his conception of social justice, consistently with the overall constraint of neutrality.[35] The details of Ackerman's argument (as well as May's) are beyond the scope of this chapter. What matters for our current argument is that, according to Beitz, the May/Ackerman account relies on conditions which 'reflect an implausibly narrow understanding of the more basic principle [of the equal respect for persons], from which substantive concerns regarding the content of political outcomes and the context of public deliberation have been excluded....'.[36]

Suppose it is the case; indeed, in Ackerman's conception of neutral discussion the criteria of neutrality are outcome-independent. But the problem is that, as Jeremy Waldron has remarked, in case of disagreement we are simply unable to identify the criteria of the content of political outcomes which support the ideal of equal respect for persons.[37] What counts as treating people with equal respect is often at the very heart of the controversy about a particular law or policy. If the outcome were to be determinant of whether the political process respects the equality or not between people then we would be unable to come up with any workable criteria for political equality: they would simply be at the mercy of substantive conceptions of the good espoused by different contestants.

[33] Beitz *Political Equality* at 66.

[34] Kenneth O May 'A Set of Independent Necessary and Sufficient Conditions for Simple Majority Decision' *Econometrica* (1952) 20: 680–4.

[35] Bruce A Ackerman *Social Justice in the Liberal State* (New Haven: Yale University Press, 1980) 274–93.

[36] Beitz *Political Equality* at 64.

[37] Waldron *Dignity* at 161–2.

Does the Rousseauian conception, invoked in this context by Beitz, indeed provide us with the right basis for the majoritarian procedure in a way which abstracts it from the ideal of equal respect? Can Rousseau, in other words, be used as the support for the disconnection between MR and the principle of equal respect for persons? I do not think so. Beitz's account of Rousseau relies on a radical disconnection between the majoritarian and the unanimous procedures, allegedly to be found in Rousseau; while the latter (ie unanimity) could be identified with equal respect for people, it cannot underline the decision procedure applied in routine situations. '[O]n Rousseau's view equal respect for persons is modeled by the unanimity requirement of the initial contract situation and is reflected in the standard for assessing political outcomes accepted there...' says Beitz.[38] For my part, I do not read Rousseau as containing such a radical distinction between unanimity-decision circumstances (where the principle of equal respect seems to be properly observed) and circumstances allowing for the operation of majority rule (where, Beitz claims, the principle of equal respect cannot be found). I find in Rousseau a fundamental *continuity* between the unanimity and majority rule: both are oriented towards the detection of the general will, although in different contexts. Unanimity is reserved for constitutive decisions because the stakes are too high to allow any objectors to stay in the polity: when setting up a polity, we must all agree to its constitutive principles, and those who do not agree, simply stay outside:

> There is one law only which by its nature requires unanimous consent. That is the social pact.... If, then, at the time of the social pact, there are some who oppose it, their opposition does not invalidate the contract, it only keeps them from being included in it; they are foreigners among the Citizens.[39]

But the routine law-making decisions cannot stick to the unanimity rule because under such a requirement *no* decisions would be taken most of the time: it is a regrettable fact, for Rousseau, which he accepts only grudgingly and with a sense of loss, as an unavoidable second-best.[40] Nevertheless, the constitutive-stage unanimity rule still importantly prefigures the majority rule on the less important occasions: majority rule is for Rousseau, so to speak, the closest we can get to unanimity in non-ideal situations. The governing principle is the same: that the whole point of collective decisions is to identify the 'general will', or the

[38] Beitz *Political Equality* at 63; similarly at 54.

[39] Rousseau 'Of the Social Contract' in *The Social Contract and Other Later Political Writings* edited and translated Victor Gourevitch (Cambridge: Cambridge University Press, 1997) 123.

[40] In *Considerations on the Government of Poland* Rousseau distinguishes between the unanimity which is required for 'the formation of the body politic and for the fundamental laws that bear on its existence', on the one hand, and on the other hand, those less important issues for which either a simple majority rule or a qualified majority set at 'any number of proportions... depending on the importance of the matters [under consideration]', *Considerations on the Government of Poland and on Its Projected Reformation* in *The Social Contract and Other Later Political Writings* 217–18.

common good. Now how well the majority mimics the unanimity-modelled general will is for Rousseau an empirical question and it may well be the case that both epistemic defects and moral vices will contaminate the majority in a way preventing it from detecting the general will. Rousseau is explicit about it: having described the right motives for an individual voter (which consists in assessing the consistency of the proposal with the general will) he adds a crucial proviso: 'This presupposes... that *all the characteristics of the general will are still in the majority*: once they no longer are, then regardless of which side one takes there no longer is any freedom.'[41]

Consequently, if the constitutive-stage unanimity decisions do give effect (as Beitz believes) to the principle of equal respect to all persons, so do the majority decisions, albeit in a less perfect way. It is important to emphasize that I offer this interpretation of Rousseau not as an exercise in the exegesis of the great classical thinker but as a contribution to the debate on the relationship between majority rule and the equality principle. Rousseau is instructive in this context precisely because Beitz's established link between the pursuit of the general will and the egalitarian principle of respect for all *is* compelling. Still, one need not accept the Rousseauian theory of majority rule as a pale shadow of the unanimity principle (which is the way I read Rousseau)[42] to see the former as expressing a significant egalitarian stance. Indeed, at this point, we may perhaps challenge the underlying insight in Beitz's use of Rousseau, namely, the idea that the unanimity requirement expresses equal respect for persons. Perhaps it does, but only in a rather limited and questionable way: the unanimity requirement creates a guarantee that no one will be coerced to comply with the requirements based on views that she does not share. There is, admittedly, an important equality ingredient revealed in the words 'no one' in the preceding sentence: everyone is *equally* protected against a duty to comply with unwanted directives. This may be seen as a good prudential rule, that everyone is equally protected against the costs of having to comply with unwanted rules.

It may certainly be prudential (a point to which I will return shortly), but is it egalitarian? It is quite obvious that a unanimity regime creates a very important *inequality*: those who support a particular directive count for much less than those who oppose it if unanimity is required for the adoption of the directive. In fact, any decision-making procedure, other than a simple majority rule, creates an immediate inequality between proponents and opponents of a proposed decision, and the further we go in departing from a simple majority rule, the more unequal their positions become. To this extent, unanimity is a power of veto

[41] Rousseau 'Of the Social Contract' at 124 (emphasis added).

[42] I do not claim my reading of Rousseau to be the only correct one, all I claim is that it is *a* plausible one. One should take heed of Henry Mayo's observation, made precisely with regard to the relationship between the majority principle and the general will in Rousseau: 'Of Rousseau it is possible to prove quite contradictory propositions by selected quotations; one sees it done all the time', Mayo *An Introduction to Democratic Theory* at 181.

given to a single opponent whose opinion becomes, in this manner, weightier than the opinions of all proponents of a directive put together. This is an obvious defect, from the point of view of equality, of any special majority rule, and all the more so, of the unanimity rule.

The prudential defence of the unanimity rule is also questionable. Both decisions and *non*-decisions have costs for an individual, so to say that unanimity is a good prudential policy presupposes that the costs of bad collective decisions (from the person's point of view) prevail over the costs of not having good collective decisions. But such a calculus is question-begging: there is nothing prudentially rational in preventing me and the other individuals who form a majority, from enacting good common rules simply on the basis that if the rules happen to be bad, I will not need to work towards forming a majority against these rules. Favouring the unanimity rule (or a special majority rule) involves a bias towards the status quo: departures from the status quo require stronger support than maintaining it. But this is irrational, and if there is one great lesson to be drawn from both the public choice theory and the economic analysis of law, it is that omissions are also costly, and not just commissions, which means that in assessing the costs of action, we also need to compare them against the costs of inaction. Unanimity rules violate this precept because they seem to be based on the unstated presumption that the costs of inaction are nil (or at least, are necessarily lower than the costs of positive action). As Ian Shapiro rightly observes, 'we may feel in certain circumstances that failures to act collectively, rather than collective action itself, should shoulder the burden of proof'.[43] If we consider (as we should) a non-decision as a choice or a course of action which has it costs and benefits, just as it has its opponents and proponents, then we increase our protection for the individual by modifying the threshold for a vote above a simple majority: by moving from a simple majority towards unanimity, we reduce the weight of every single proponent of a new decision and increase accordingly the weight of every individual opponent.

The force of the principle of unanimity (and of the hostility against the use of majority rule qua an egalitarian rule) is exploited in a claim based on a hypothesis such as this:

> [I]magine you, me, and a third person in the same room. Two of us decide that you should give your life to serve us. Is our decision legitimate, do you have an obligation to obey simply because we were a majority within the room?...On the face if it, you can claim that our decision 'enslaves' you and denies you 'equal status' with us.[44]

[43] Shapiro *The State of Democratic Theory* at 19 (footnote omitted). See, similarly, James S Fishkin 'In quest of the social contract' in Brennan and Lomasky *Politics and Process: New Essays in Democratic Thought* 183–93 at 185 and James S Fishkin *The Dialogue of Justice* (New Haven: Yale University Press, 1992) 56–7.

[44] Robert A Burt *The Constitution in Conflict* (Cambridge Mass: Harvard University Press, 1992) 27–8.

But this example, provided by Robert A Burt, shows that the decisions taken by the majority may lead to drastically inegalitarian results. This is clear and banal since the majority can exploit, oppress, and even enslave a minority. But this does not show that the majority rule itself does not presuppose *some* egalitarian moral principles, related to the decision-making process itself. And, *a contrario*, it does not show that unanimity does support a notion of equality superior, or more refined, to that of the one presupposed by the majority rule. Burt's example is instructive, though, because he explicitly uses the language of 'legitimacy' and of the 'obligation to obey'. Note that the (intuitively persuasive) lack of such legitimacy (and of obligation to obey) of the exploitative decision taken by Burt's characters is not (or at least, not necessarily) the result of a violation of some fundamentally egalitarian norm about the political process but rather of the moral heinousness of the outcome. We can explain our revulsion against the outcome imagined by Burt without resorting to the language of (in)equality but rather ruminate, from a Kantian-like perspective, about the moral vice of an instrumental treatment of some persons to the benefit of others—and this shows that equality is an unreliable asset in defending unanimity against majority rule.

So why would anyone think, as Beitz clearly does, that the unanimity rule (in contrast to MR) expresses the principle of equal respect? One possible defence of the unanimity-equality nexus is based on a radical distinction between the foundational and the post-foundational stages of politics with unanimity defended strongly at the foundational, or constitutional, stage. This is the line of argument favoured by Buchanan and Tullock in *Calculus of Consent*, and of course it has since then been the dominant approach of the public choice movement which relies on a clear and radical dichotomy between the constitutional and non-constitutional level, or the levels of setting and applying the rules of the game. Indeed, this dichotomy is seen by many as central to the very idea of constitutionalism.[45] This is fair enough, and for analytical purposes, we can adopt a 'foundational' conception of constitutionalism, and the correlated fiction that there are moments in the life of the society where everything is being designed from scratch—much as this fiction is unrealistic. But why would this distinction lead to the privileging of unanimity at the level of *foundations* of the legal system? In *Calculus of Consent*, this is never made properly explicit but rather is taken for granted: the advantages of the unanimity rule are presented in a way which does not rely on the centrality of the foundational versus non-foundational politics. The crucial virtue of the unanimity rule in Buchanan and Tullock's book is that it 'will insure that all external effects will be eliminated by collectivization',[46] ie that it is the only rule which guarantees that an individual will not suffer any negative externalities from a collective action—because he will be able to veto it

[45] For an emphatic assertion of this dichotomy from a public-choice perspective, see Geoffrey Brennan and Alan Hamlin 'Constitutional Political Economy: The Political Philosophy of *Homo Economicus*?', *Journal of Political Philosophy* (1995) 3: 280–303 at 287–8.

[46] Buchanan and Tullock *The Calculus of Consent* at 89.

ex ante. However, this is not an equality-based rationale (because it establishes a single dissenter in a much more powerful role than each of the remaining actors), and as a prudential guarantee it is subject to the objection just made, ie that it unreasonably distinguishes between risks of action and of inaction. (Not to mention that it puts aside the increasing transaction costs of reaching any decision as we move from the simple majority towards the unanimity regime.[47]) But the case launched by Buchanan and Tullock for unanimity rule stands or falls with equal weight whether it is applied to the foundational (constitutional) or to day-to-day politics. This is implicit in the explanation provided by them for the (grudging) approval of majority rule 'as one among many practical expedients made necessary by the costs of securing widespread agreement on political issues when individual and group interests diverge':[48] majority rule is adopted for purely contingent, practical reasons related to transaction costs rather than its inherent virtues. Whatever advantages it may have, therefore, occur as pale derivatives of the unanimity rule; hence, it is difficult to see any crucial role for the dichotomy of the constitutional and non-constitutional activities in this picture.

About a quarter of a century after co-authoring the book with Tullock, James Buchanan made this distinction more explicit while yet again praising the unanimity rule and criticizing the popularity of the majority rule. He drew a distinction between three spheres of politics: enforcement of the actual law, collective action within the realm of existing law, and changing of the law. Buchanan further argued that within the first and the third spheres, majority rule should have no application. In particular, in the third (foundational) sphere, the only rule permitted according to his contractarian premises is that of unanimity.[49] To be sure, he later makes a concession to the real world in which the 'abstract contractarian logic need not be pushed to its extreme, which would require that constitutional changes be reached only through unanimous agreement'.[50] Nevertheless the theoretical rationale for unanimity rule at the constitutive level remains a puzzle. Buchanan's contractarianism is not of a Rawlsian variety, ie the individuals are not behind the veil of ignorance while negotiating the terms of the constitutional dispensation; hence, the contract cannot be viewed as a modelling device of our own moral argument about the impartiality-constrained ideal conception of justice.[51] In this more recent article of Buchanan, the unanimity rule at the constitutional stage is defended on the basis of an analogy with exchanges on a market where an exchange of apples and oranges will take place only if it is seen

[47] The transaction costs are further brought into the picture by Buchanan and Tullock *The Calculus of Consent* at 90–1.

[48] ibid at 96.

[49] James M Buchanan 'Contractarian presuppositions and democratic governance' in Brennan and Lomasky *Politics and Process: New Essays in Democratic Thought* 174–82 at 179.

[50] ibid at 181.

[51] For his self-characterization by comparison to the Rawlsian theory, and in particular for the rejection of the 'veil of ignorance' in the original contract, see James M Buchanan *The Limits of Liberty* (Chicago: The University of Chicago Press, 1975) 174–5.

as 'value enhancing for both parties', and we are told that 'a change in the constitution (in the rules) is not different in this fundamental respect [ie in the mutual value-enhancing condition] from a simple exchange between two traders'.[52] But if that is so (as opposed to, as one would expect, the constitutional change being compared with the negotiation between the traders about the rules to govern their trade), the specificity of the foundational stage is all but lost, and the above-mentioned equality-based and prudential objections to the rule of unanimity remain valid.

So if possible defences of the connection between the unanimity principle (or at least, a qualified majority requirement) and the principle of equal respect for all participants in the decision-making are unsuccessful, what can account for the persistence of various, widely accepted, departures from the principle of simple majority towards unanimity? In particular, one may consider it puzzling that whenever the significance of decisions to be taken is particularly high, departures from simple majority are viewed with general approval—various voting rules on constitutional amendments around the world are a good example. It is not only with respect to constitutional changes but also to particularly significant political decisions that the calls for heightened majority requirements are often made. A good example is provided by an old article by Jürgen Habermas about civil disobedience as a litmus test for a democratic order. In that article, Habermas discussed a controversy in West Germany in the early 1980s about the stationing of new US missiles there; Habermas used it as an occasion to develop the theory of civil disobedience as supplementing normal democratic procedures in cases of decisions of particularly high significance and with irreversible consequences. Against this background, he asked whether 'fundamental decisions concerning security policy, with which extreme risks are associated... may be supported by the threadbare legitimating cover of a simple parliamentary majority'.[53] The answer was negative, and this was because the conditions which allow for majority rule to have a legitimizing effect on the decisions were deemed to be rarely met in reality: one such condition was that '[t]here should be no minorities by birth',[54] another, that such decisions should not 'diverge from the ideal results of a discursively achieved agreement or a presumptively just compromise',[55] and the third, that 'the majority cannot be permitted to make irreversible decisions'.[56] At this point, only the third condition is of interest to us because the first and second defects of majoritarian decisions taint also supra-majoritarian decisions, or (to look at the matter from the opposite side) taint the procedure which allows for a veto against a simple majority. But the third condition is of a different nature, and

[52] Buchanan 'Contractarian presuppositions and democratic governance' at 179.

[53] Jürgen Habermas 'Civil Disobedience: Litmus Test for the Democratic Constitutional State' *Berkeley Journal of Sociology* (1985) 30: 95–116 at 109.

[54] ibid at 111.

[55] ibid.

[56] ibid.

it connects with the point about our intuitive support for reinforcing the decision rules for particularly important decisions (irreversibility being only one, but a significant, indicator of importance). After all, just as the opponents of an 'irreversible' decision may complain that the decision is too momentous to be decided by a simple majority, so would proponents of a proposed decision complain that the *failure* to take that decision will cause such irreversible consequences that the power of non-decision must not be left to a simple majority. And so the puzzle is this: if my argument about the lack of connection between a heightened majority (and unanimity) and the principle of equal respect is correct then one would expect the opposite argument: the more important the subject matter of a decision is, the more we would expect the insistence on a simple majority because the more we then have reason to respect equally all the participants and stakeholders in the decision.

Or do we? An argument can be plausibly made that the requirement of strengthened majority protects other values than equal respect for decision-takers, and that these other values served by those decisional requirements can help resolve the puzzle just mentioned. Two such values come to one's mind, the first being intrinsically and the second only contingently connected to the heightened majority requirements. The first is the principle of conservatism, understood here in its literal rather than judgmental sense: that there are usually good prima facie reasons to stick to the currently established ways, and any change must be supported by particularly stringent rationale—more stringent, any way, than the rationales for maintaining the status quo. Strengthened majority rules serve in a trivial manner the principle of conservatism because they make it more difficult, and therefore less likely, to change the law in force. But while the connection between the super-majority rules and the principle of conservatism is obvious, the strength of that principle is limited. It can, roughly, rely on three types of rationale. First, the law that has been in force for a significant time is likely to be better known than the law about to be enacted—and the knowledge of the law is a significant factor for compliance, and hence of its effectiveness. The second rationale is about the importance of settled expectations: people draw a set of expectations based on the existing law, and organize their life and their plans around it. Even if the law is sub-optimal, it enters as a datum in people's minds, and people develop, with time, strategies of 'making the best of it'. This is particularly true of constitutions, which are perceived as being of a long duration, and therefore people factor into their strategies the existing constitutional frameworks. The third rationale is about the unexpected consequences of changes; even if we can justify a change by reference to its predicted advantages, we cannot properly anticipate all its consequences, including the negative ones. And since we cannot anticipate those negative side-effects, our calculus of the costs and benefits of change is usually distorted towards the optimistic calculation. Now it is clear that none of these rationales establishes a conclusive, or even particularly strong, objection against change: the existing law may be so obsolete or unjust that the advantages of change will easily overcome the objections arising from the principle of conservatism. Indeed, the very fact of change may be advantageous in itself, regardless of its specific content, by infusing the people with a sense of hope, enthusiasm, and energy. So, discussed *in abstracto*, it is implausible to elevate the principle of conservatism to a rank of a powerful argument for delaying constitutional changes.[57] What matters, however, is that such a principle is often widely endorsed, even if only implicitly, and in particular when it comes to constitutional changes it seems to be a powerful factor contributing to a requirement for a heightened majority.

The second reason why heightened majority rules *may* seem to be attractive may have to do with the understandable call for deliberation in the process leading to the adoption of decisions on particularly important matters. It is quite plausible that the higher the majority the proponents of a new decision (say, of constitutional amendments) have to muster, the more they will have to go down the path of a deep societal deliberation about their proposal; they will have to use various channels and devices of sensitizing the community to the problems which their proposal addresses, and attempt to popularize their proposed solutions. A heightened majority requirement may therefore be seen as an incentive for deliberation, and the similarity between this proposition and Bruce Ackerman's dualist theory of ordinary politics/constitutional politics is quite obvious. In Ackerman's scheme, the main reason for directing certain issues into a constitutional track ('higher lawmaking', as he calls it) is precisely in order to compel the proponents to mobilize public deliberation: 'Throughout the period of mobilized deliberation, the movement [aiming at a constitutional amendment] will have to gain support for its initiative time and again in lawmaking assemblies. Such repeated successes will be unlikely if a majority of citizens does not support it decisively against all plausible alternatives'.[58]

While this latter connection (between the higher majority requirements and the deliberative character of the decision-taking process) may in some circumstances be plausible, it is nevertheless quite contingent; there may well be cases of genuinely deliberative processes leading eventually to a decision taken under a simple majority rule (as in various genuinely deliberative parliamentary debates) and, on the other hand, there may be cases of very impoverished deliberations notwithstanding a high majority threshold (when a decision is adopted under a qualified majority rule, but the debate has been largely technical and confined to a small elite). Further, there is a normative and not merely an empirical problem here. If it is true, as I have argued before, that the departures from a simple majority requirement counter the principle of equal respect, then how can the *unequal* positions of participants in the debate co-exist with the deliberative

[57] See, similarly, Joseph Raz 'On the Authority and Interpretation of Constitutions: Some Preliminaries' in Larry Alexander (ed) *Constitutionalism: Philosophical Foundations* (Cambridge: Cambridge University Press, 1998) 152–93 at 174–6.

[58] Bruce Ackerman *We the People*: *Foundations* at 286 (footnote omitted).

nature of the process? They can, but only within certain limits. It is true that severe departures from the equality of the political impact may have a negative effect on the deliberative character of the process. On the other hand, a strong insistence on the equality of the impact is not necessarily optimal from the point of view of the cognitive quality of the decisions, which in turn favours the quality of the deliberations. As David Estlund has argued, there may be genuine trade-offs between equality of political impact on the one hand and the quantity of the impact as well as the resultant epistemic quality of political deliberation, on the other.[59] This is because, Estlund argues, there may be some epistemic advantages derived from having more input overall, and sometimes the extra input will be provided only if there is an inequality of input: '[t]he gains may not be produced but for the incentives provided by the unequal distribution [of political input]'.[60] In such cases, equalizing overall political input downwards will bear epistemic costs, that is, it may simply result in producing worse decisions. Estlund concedes that, everything else being equal, more equality of political influence is (cognitively) superior to inequality, but when we factor in the question of the quantity of input, it may turn out that we can buy more quantity by tolerating a degree of inequality, and then we need to decide about trade-offs between these two factors, and therefore the advantages of having a wider discussion may outweigh the disadvantages of a degree of unequal influence. For our purposes the significance of Estlund's conclusions is that the unequal impact of participants does not necessarily damage the deliberative quality of the process, and so the incentive for deliberation may be, at times, a plausible rationale for departures from a simple majority rule.

There is finally one tempting, but ultimately unsuccessful, way of reconciling the attraction of qualified majority with the egalitarianism of a simple majority rule: it is by deriving the legitimacy of the qualified majority principle from the legitimacy of a simple majority's decision at the time of the constitutional entrenchment of such a method of decision-making. It can be claimed that if the majority decides to adopt a qualified majority procedure (or even a requirement for unanimity) at a foundational moment, then we can have the best of both worlds: the benefits of qualified majority (such as the presumption against changes or an incentive for deliberation) and, on the other hand, the legitimacy of the equality-respectful simple majoritarianism. But this will not do. First, there is something presumptively illegitimate about a simple majority deciding to entrench a qualified-majority procedure for certain subject matters. Suppose that 50 per cent plus one member of the constitutive assembly decide at the point in time T-1 that all decisions on future changes in the constitution will require a 66 per cent majority. Next suppose that, at T-2, there is a 55 per cent majority

[59] David Estlund 'Political Quality' in David Estlund (ed) *Democracy* (Oxford: Basil Blackwell, 2002) 175–212.

[60] Estlund 'Political Quality' at 196.

support for a constitutional change. Surely each member of that 55 per cent majority at T-2 can now complain that her vote has a less equal weight than each vote of the 45 per cent minority (something which we have shown above), and in addition each majority member can plausibly refuse to see the nucleus of equal respect in the decision of the former 50 per cent plus one constituent majority at T-1 to entrench such an inequality for the future? They (that is, the complaining 55 per cent majority at T-2) may still find *some* good reasons in the entrenchment of the qualified majority rule, but the principle of equal respect is not one of these good reasons. This goes to the very heart of the discussions about the theory of constitutional entrenchment in terms of a collective pre-commitment: even if we found some justification in the entrenchment of certain areas against a simple majority, and further compare this to a pre-commitment of a collective agent to observe certain rules, a conception which in itself is controversial,[61] we still are unable to say that the pre-committing decision taken under a simple majority rule endows all future decisions taken under a qualified majority with the value of equal respect for decision-takers. (Such an ex post facto laundering of decisions taken under a regime departing from simple majority would be equivalent to saying that if the original decision about removing certain issues from the field of public debate was taken under the unrestrained freedom of deliberation then all the future proceedings operating under such a gag rule would enjoy the qualities of unrestrained deliberation, which is absurd.) So if we believe seriously that the constituent, or founding, power prefigures in a meaningful sense the future operations of the polity, then the original simple majority rule should be replicated rather than abandoned in the subsequent operations of the system.

5. Majority Rule and the 'Aggregation of Wills'

A legal theorist who insisted strongly on *not* trying to rest MR upon the principle of equality was Hans Kelsen. For Kelsen, in his 1929 essay 'On the Essence and Value of Democracy', the problem was how to reconcile MR with the principle of the political autonomy of individuals; a project strikingly similar to that of Rousseau whose solution to the problem relied, as we saw, on political freedom understood as the congruence of collective decisions with the general will, and with MR considered as a second-best device tailored to detect the general will. But Kelsen's solution was entirely different; the strength of political freedom (in the state which must take collective decisions binding on all, including on those who disagree with them) is judged by Kelsen by the ease with which the outvoted minority can alter the laws they do not like. This, Kelsen says, applies equally to

[61] See Jeremy Waldron 'Precommitment and Disagreement' in Larry Alexander (ed) *Constitutionalism: Philosophical Foundations* (Cambridge: Cambridge University Press, 1998) 271–99.

the members of the majority who have changed their minds since the decision was taken: 'The legal irrelevance of such a change of will reveals only too clearly the *alien will*, or—speaking non-metaphorically the *objective validity of the social order* to which [the voter] is subject. He must find a majority for his change of will if he, the individual, is once again to be free'.[62] This is best done under the simple majority rule: the higher the majority necessary to change the law, the more difficult such a change is, and the higher the political *unfreedom* of Kelsen's individual. Here, Kelsen says, we are faced with a paradox: 'That which earlier, at the founding of the state order, served to protect individual freedom, in accordance with the idea of freedom, becomes its shackle if it is no longer possible to escape the order'.[63] 'That' refers, of course, to the unanimity requirement. It was a freedom-protective guarantee at the 'founding', stage but becomes a hindrance for political freedom at the stage of the operation of the system.

Kelsen's solution shares its weakness with the political conception of the legitimacy of majority rule, discussed earlier, in Part 1 of this chapter. No doubt, it is an important virtue of a democratic law-making system that it should leave open the avenues for the revisions of enacted laws, just as it is an important advantage of a democratic political system over its rivals that 'a steady and substantial majority can be confident that it holds the power to dismiss rulers it has come to loathe'.[64] And yet, it would be ironic to connect political autonomy with the ease with which disliked law can be repealed. I find it an unattractive conception of political freedom to be told that, while the laws which govern my behaviour are objectionable (ex hypothesi), I can nevertheless work towards repealing them, and the repeal is easier than in any other alternative system of law-making. This sounds to me like an excessively thin, negative, and defensive account of what political autonomy is grounded upon. But, for our present purposes, what is important is the use Kelsen makes of this idea, in negating the link between MR and the principle of equality. Having established the conception of political autonomy as founded on the (comparative) ease of repeal of unwanted legislation, he goes on:

> From this idea the *majority principle* is to be derived. Not, however—as it tends to happen—from the idea of equality. That everyone's human will is equal is indeed a precondition of the majority principle. But this being equal is only figurative; it cannot mean that human will or personalities can actually be measured or added together. It would be impossible to justify the majority principle by saying that more votes have a greater total weight than fewer votes.[65]

[62] Hans Kelsen 'On the Essence and Value of Democracy' in Arthur J Jacobson and Bernhard Schlink (eds), Belinda Cooper (trans) *Weimar: A Jurisprudence of Crisis* (Berkeley: University of California Press, 2000) 84–109 at 87 (emphasis in original).

[63] ibid at 87.

[64] Dunn *Setting the People Free: The Story of Democracy* at 164.

[65] Kelsen 'On the Essence and Value of Democracy' at 87 (emphasis in original).

Note that Kelsen links together two separate ideas: a contention that MR is equality-based and a proposition that we can somehow aggregate different individual wills, and that the total aggregate of a greater number of wills has a higher 'weight' than the aggregate of a smaller number. It is on the basis of the implausibility (in Kelsen's eyes) of the latter that the former is rejected. He makes this link explicit as he continues: 'If one attempts to derive the majority principle only from the idea of equality, it does indeed have that purely mechanical, even senseless, character with which the autocratic side reproaches it. It would only be the roughly formalized expression of the experience that the many are stronger than the few....'[66]

I think that Kelsen is right in rejecting the 'mechanical' idea of a larger number of expressed wills representing a 'greater total weight' but that he is wrong in believing such a view to be intrinsic to the egalitarian justification of MR. His rejection of the 'mechanical' view is made easier by the fact that he operates with vague metaphors which may stand for different things. If we consider a 'greater weight' of the aggregate of a larger number of wills as similar, in a purely mathematical way, to the putting together of a number of boxes of equal size, each of which represents one person's 'will', then such an image is indeed implausible and 'senseless'. Revealed preferences are not like physical objects which can be weighed. But we do not need to espouse such a mechanical image in order to rest MR on the prima facie equal moral competence of each individual whose life is affected by collective decisions. (It is prima facie only because it may be weakened by specific disqualifying facts—as in the cases of criminals denied a right to vote, or enhanced by special circumstances, such as when an individual has a special stake in the decision, disproportionately higher than other members of the group. But what we are interested in here is why we should adopt equality as a default position; or as a normal state of affairs, the departures from which would call for special justifications.) We can disconnect the egalitarian defence of MR from a 'mechanical' account of aggregation of votes ridiculed by Kelsen, by agreeing with Waldron that majority rule is egalitarian in an undisputed sense, in that, when employed in the process of decision-making it 'attempts to give each individual's view the greatest weight possible...compatible with an equal weight for the views of each of the others'.[67] There is no 'mechanical' image of adding wills in order to achieve the highest possible 'weight' behind Waldron's formula. It does not presuppose to abandon the mechanical imagery, that is, that a view aggregating a larger number is somehow superior to the view aggregating a smaller number of opinions. There is no aggregation of views or opinions at all

[66] ibid at 87.

[67] Jeremy Waldron *The Dignity of Legislation* (Cambridge: Cambridge University Press, 1999) 148; for a general argument linking the principle of equal consideration of interests with an equal vote, see Thomas Christiano *The Rule of the Many: Fundamental Issues in Democratic Theory* (Boulder: Westview Press, 1996) 53–71 and, more recently, Thomas Christiano 'The Authority of Democracy' *Journal of Political Philosophy* (2004) 12: 266–90.

necessary to render the egalitarian perception of MR meaningful. Rather, it relies on an argument which is distributive as opposed to aggregative, or individualized as opposed to collective: it says that *if* we are to use each person's preference in a prima facie equal way to that of all others, then we cannot use any other procedure for collective decisions than MR.

This can be represented in the form of a principle of 'minimal decisiveness'. If there is an evenly split vote, then, under a majority rule, a single person's vote is decisive. If you know (or suspect) that your group is split in half regarding a particular outcome, then your vote determines the social outcome, as does, individually and taken one by one, every other person's vote who voted like you. Thus, according to Ackerman: 'If, say, there are 99 people in the Assembly, then majority rule gives me a decisive voice when the rest of you are split 49–49; and the same is true of your decision as well'.[68] Now the force of this argument is limited because the perfect split, which is necessary to make a single vote count, is hardly imaginable in political circumstances but it indicates a way of reasoning about how MR can have a distributive, as opposed to aggregative, legitimating effect. In Ackerman's account, the force of this argument seems to rely on a hypothetical contention: we may persuade the citizens of the benefits of the simple majority rule by telling them that this is the only rule which, in the situation of a perfect split, *would* make a single vote of any citizen decisive for the collective outcome; in the words of Ackerman, majority rule positively responds 'to the considered judgments of any citizen when this will serve to break a tie'.[69] But then, *any other* publicly announced rule for collective decision-making may make a single citizen's vote decisive for the outcome:[70] under a unanimity rule, if I know (for the sake of argument) that everyone else is in favour of a proposal, my single dissent will be decisive, as will be the case in any qualified majority rule, as long as I know that only one vote is needed for the satisfaction of the particular majority requirement. So this 'minimal decisiveness' is not an argument for MR as such but rather it points to *a pattern of arguing* about different voting rules, which do not rely on crude aggregative imagery of wills assembled into a larger whole.

Such a pattern, I would suggest, is not too superficial or convoluted to serve as a model to reflect on the individual motivations of the voter in a large polity. The well-known puzzle about an apparent irrationality of the individual voter going to the polls, even though the impact that she can make on a result that would be favourable to her is incomparably smaller than the costs of voting, has led various public choice theorists to develop a theory which *would* reconcile this cost-benefit assessment with the belief in the basic rationality of a great number of voters in any elections in democracies. Their real motivations are, we are told, not to contribute to the result which they favour but rather because they derive satisfaction

[68] Ackerman *We the People*: *Foundations* 282–3.

[69] ibid at 283.

[70] As is, incidentally, acknowledged by Ackerman himself, ibid at 283.

from the act of expressing support for certain candidates or causes. Advocates of the expressive conception tell us that, if someone votes for X, it is not because one prefers X to other alternatives, but rather because one prefers *to vote* for X.[71] But quite apart from whether this solution really restores our belief in the rationality of voters (is it rational to 'like to vote' for X without necessarily liking X?), the point is that there is little resemblance between this theory and widespread intuitive knowledge about the psychology of voters (based also on introspection) which suggests that we do believe that we make a difference by voting in a particular way because we accept, rightly or wrongly, an argument of the 'What if everyone…' form. Now the way in which a critique of this expressive theory of voting connects with our non-aggregative approach to the image of majority rule is this: every voter, taken separately, in effect models herself as a person whose vote does make, individually, a difference, not unlike in the minimal decisiveness conception. Consider the following scenario imagined by Denis Mueller: '[O]ne might imagine a process in which each year one citizen is selected at random and allowed to make the decisions for the community (perhaps to save decision-making costs)'.[72] This highly stylized example serves Mueller to argue that the motives that such a single decision-maker has could be ethical (about the good of the community) rather than selfish 'because he knows that next year someone else will be making the community's decisions and he wants that person to feel compelled by the same moral imperative as he is to make decisions on everyone's behalf'.[73]

But my purpose in using this example is different from Mueller's: I claim that it is realistic, psychologically speaking, to model our voting behaviour on the motives of this single decision-maker, and that in the voting booths we can identify ourselves with the conduct of this person, not just in terms of the motives underlying a decision but also in our perception of our impact. And such a modelling is not based on aggregative terms where a single voter is viewed as a replaceable parcel of a larger whole, but rather that we perceive ourselves as individuals who behave as if our choices can make an equal difference. Any other decision procedure—unanimity requirement, or special majority rule—gives some individuals a much higher influence on the collective decisions compared with others. This is not to say that there cannot be other, non-egalitarian arguments for MR (as we have seen before, there are some very plausible arguments). And this is not to say that MR cannot be employed for non-egalitarian ends: this indeed is the whole point of the present discussion, that a species of equality which is behind the MR may conflict with other types of equality which may be negated by the individual cases of resorting to MR. But all that is being argued here is that

[71] This is a paraphrase of Brennan and Lomasky *Politics and Process: New Essays in Democratic Thought* at 51.

[72] Mueller 'Democracy: the Public Choice Approach' at 85.

[73] ibid at 86.

MR is based, among other arguments, on a meaningful form of political equality, and thus Kelsen's critique of egalitarian arguments for MR as allegedly linked to the 'mechanical' image of aggregating individual wills is unpersuasive.

Kelsen's representation of an aggregation of wills, in a 'mechanical' way, can be compared with a 'physical' interpretation of Locke's defence of majority rule: 'it is necessary the Body should move that way whither the greater force carries it, *which is the consent of the majority*: or else it is impossible it should act or continue one Body, *one Community*, which the consent of every individual that united into it, agreed that it should....'[74] There is a temptation to understand this argument for majority rule in a purely physicalist way, corresponding to Kelsen's depiction of the 'mechanical' aggregation of human wills. But this temptation should be resisted, as Waldron has persuasively shown in his discussion of this passage from Locke. The society that accepts the choice made by the majority is not viewed by Locke (or by Waldron for that matter) as 'the body [which] as a whole moves either north or south in accordance with the tendency of the greater number of its elements, as a result of their cumulative motion'.[75] It is not the 'force' or the 'weight' that makes the majority prevail, but rather the normative significance of individual consent which endows the preference expressed by the majority with authority, argues Waldron, relying on John Dunn's suggestion that one possible interpretation of Locke's proposition is 'to see the concept of force as moralized by the notion of consent....'[76] As Waldron puts it, 'consent does not carry physical weight or even pure political force; rather, it carries moral force with regard to the purposes for which consent is required'.[77] It is a normative theory with no physicalist (or mechanical) connotation; it can be stated as the idea that consent is ultimately the irreducible, fundamental element which can endow collective decisions with authority. Since the fact of consent is not subject to degree, the only way to 'aggregate' individual consent into a collective preference is by counting each person as one, as a result of which majority rule is the only procedure consistent with both (1) the equal value of each individual consent, and (2) the maximum strength given to each consent. Respecting only the first condition does not necessarily lead to majority rule, because equal value may be respected while not taking into account anyone's views (or by tossing a coin to take a decision when people disagree) but the combined respect for both of these conditions may be put into effect only through the MR procedure. When, therefore, we accept without objection the operation of the majority rule, we accept, at least implicitly, the rule of an equal respect for everyone's view about the matter subjected to a collective decision.

[74] John Locke *Two Treatises of Government*, Book II, quoted in Jeremy Waldron *God, Locke and Equality* at 129 (emphases in original).

[75] Waldron *God, Locke and Equality* at 129.

[76] John Dunn *Political Thought of John Locke* (Cambridge: Cambridge University Press, 1969) at 129.

[77] Waldron *God, Locke and Equality* at 130.

6. Outcomes and Procedures: 'Detached' and 'Dependent' Conceptions of Democracy

Can the egalitarian credentials of majority rule be challenged by referring to the (possibly) unequal outcomes produced by the uses made of majority rule? The question is somewhat misleading because it collapses various types of possible 'outcomes' into one category even though different types of outcome may have a different status from the point of view of their significance in relation to political equality itself. Ronald Dworkin's distinction between what he calls a 'detached' and a 'dependent' conception of democracy, understood as the system of political equality, is useful here. For Dworkin, a detached conception is the one where we can certify that a system is democratic on the basis of the characteristics of the process alone. In contrast, a dependent conception 'supposes that the best form of democracy is whatever form is most likely to produce the substantive decisions and results that treat all members of the community with equal concern'.[78] In this latter version one may observe that democracy is in fact a derivative of justice, or substantive equality: our controversies regarding which system treats people with equal concern, in whatever fields of distribution, may be decisive for our views about whether the system is democratic. But on such an undifferentiated view of democracy, the specificity of political power (and therefore political equality) disappears, and our attention to politics as one particular arena of equality turns out unwarranted. A 'dependent conception', without any further qualifications, clashes with our linguistic usages: we frequently do indeed draw the line between justice (or equality) in the political arena and justice in the field of distribution of material resources.

We may, of course, become convinced that economic justice is more important than political democracy: that democracy in the field of equal political impact is worthless in the face of drastic economic injustice. This is, for example, the position espoused by Philippe van Parijs, for whom democracy is not 'an independently important ideal' but merely an 'institutional instrument, from which it is legitimate to deviate *if* the pursuit of the ideal [of justice] requires it'.[79] However, it is a *normative* position which is certainly respectable but which needs a properly normative defence: for van Parijs, for example, one of the arguments leading to such a conclusion is the observation that adherence to democratic rules leads to closed-borders regimes, anti-immigration rules, and in consequence, growing economic and other inequalities on the world scale.[80] This normative argument obviously cannot be adopted on the basis of a mere definitional fiat according to

[78] Dworkin *Sovereign Virtue* at 186.

[79] Philippe van Parijs 'Justice and Democracy: Are they Incompatible?' *Journal of Political Philosophy* (1996) 4: 101–17 at 110 (emphasis in the original, footnote omitted).

[80] ibid at 108–9.

which we would agree to call political justice only a system, which leads to a just economic distribution. In fact, such a fiat would make it impossible to claim that political democracy may coexist with economic injustice, something that seems to be not only proper but a rather commonplace observation. In our everyday language we distinguish between the calls for greater democratization in the political field (in terms of more equal and fuller empowerment of people in collectively deciding about their destiny) and the calls for greater social justice. Even though both these calls (and others) must eventually be included in a broader, more comprehensive social ideal, they are clearly distinguishable from each other, and our moral language should preserve rather than blur this distinctiveness.[81]

Further, we may, of course, claim that political democracy in a context of sharp economic injustice cannot be a *real* democracy, because those suffering economic deprivation and exploitation are rendered so vulnerable and dependent that they are simply unable to exercise free political choice and that, on the other hand, those who are very rich will find ways of converting their economic clout into a political influence. This is quite obvious, and for these reasons the distribution of economic resources cannot be insulated in any realistic analysis from political procedures, which assign influence in collective decision-making. We know that those who exercise a disproportionately high control over economic resources can affect political outcomes in all sorts of ways, including by influencing the process of public deliberation (through media, advertising etc) or by threatening to withhold their investments, unless their preferences in terms of outcomes are satisfied. But this very plausible observation relies upon a set of empirical propositions and, again, cannot be adopted simply by virtue of opting for a 'dependent' conception of democracy as a conceptual choice.

We need to be clear about what is at stake in arguing for a 'detachment' of political equality from the various laudable ideals of social justice. This is not just a matter of respect for our linguistic usages, which leads us frequently to distinguish between calls for a higher political democracy and calls for a fairer distribution of other goods than political influence. After all, our linguistic usage may not be accepted by all, and may rest on a confusion which blurs rather than clarifies a proper articulation of the normative issues at stake. The choice between a detached and a dependent conception is of a *normative* character, rather than relying on a conceptual analysis of the word 'democracy'. The choice of a detached conception rests upon a contention that equality in political power is a valuable, attractive ideal, which is not parasitic on a more encompassing ideal of equality in a society, and that we should in effect be concerned about how power is distributed (that is, about *how* collective decisions are made), irrespective of, or in addition

[81] See similarly David Miller *Principles of Social Justice* (Cambridge Mass: Harvard University Press, 1999) 15; Robert E Goodin 'Democracy, Justice and Impartiality' in Keith Dowding, Robert E Goodin and Carol Pateman (eds) *Justice and Democracy: Essays for Brian Barry* (Cambridge University Press: Cambridge 2004) 97–111 at 97–8.

to, our concern about *what* is the substance of these decisions and how they shape the distribution of other (other than political power) resources. This is, of course, a normative position; it rests upon a judgment that we have legitimate interests in participating in political life, which is an important (although not the only, and not necessarily paramount) human good, separable from the good of having our other interests protected by the outcomes of political decisions. Hence, there is nothing neutral about a choice between a 'detached' and a 'dependent' conception, whatever the further contours of the conception may be.

This suggests that opting for a detached concept of political equality incurs benefits (which will be explained below) but also a *price*. The costs of disconnecting the spheres of political and material equality are fittingly illustrated in a somewhat melancholic account provided by John Dunn to describe the historic journey of the idea of democracy from Athenian times to our days:

> Democracy became in effect the regime name of the route towards equality, gracing whatever institution volunteered to shoulder its responsibility of pressing on towards that elusive goal. It was not until the change in expectations had run its course, and the defenders of equality had formally surrendered, that the claim to a special tie to democracy was surrendered along with it.... Democracy has altered its meaning so sharply since Babeuf because it has passed definitely from the hands of the Equals to those of the political leaders of the order of egoism.[82]

This is not a particularly uplifting picture, and it identifies the losses stemming from identifying democracy with political equality, and political equality with equal impact (or influence) of all adult citizens upon collective decisions, regardless of how it affects the patterns of distribution of wealth and status in a society in which these decisions are taken.

So, perhaps, one should attempt a normative defence of a *dependent* conception by developing a purely instrumentalist defence of democracy (democracy as valuable only insofar as it leads to other valuable goods) and of individual interests, claiming that it would be mistaken to consider the good of equal political influence (or the good of influence in politics, as such) to be of value independently of the values which can be promoted through exercising the political influence? I, for one, would consider such an argument morally and politically problematic, for reasons I will develop later. But at this point, it is important to identify what is at stake in the choice between a detached and a dependent conception of democracy. And one way of thinking about it is by considering trade-offs between political equality and other spheres of equality. If we opted for a fully dependent conception, we would have to accept that any reduction of political equality can be compensated by an increase of another type (for instance, material) of equality. But if we insist upon political equality as a specific domain of equality, separable from others, we do not need to accept such trade-offs as necessarily justified, and

[82] Dunn *Setting the People Free: The Story of Democracy* at 152–3 and 160.

we may wish to protect democracy (understood, under a detached conception, as a distinctive ideal) from the sacrifices justified by increases of material equality.[83]

We might wish to defend this stance by claiming, for example, that political equality and other types of equality are incommensurable for the reason that political equality is about the distribution of second-order resources: of resources which enable the adoption of decisions about the distribution of resources, and which therefore should not be mutually tradable. (Politics need not be *only* a second-order resource: it may also be a first-order resource as a means leading directly to individual satisfaction and fulfilment regardless of the effects of one's political influence for the pursuit of other resources.[84] But the degree to which politics *is* about second-order resources leads it to become incommensurable with these other first-order resources.) Of course, we need not go so far as to insist that no reduction of democracy is ever justifiable in the face of demands for social justice, but the very fact that we are prepared, at least partly, to entrench democracy against marginally higher improvements in social justice, reveals an implicit normatively-based choice of a detached conception.

7. Equality of Influence, of Impact, and of Political Opportunity

It is one thing to say that, on normative grounds, we may wish to preserve the sense of specificity of political equality by opting for a detached conception of democracy, and another to show that we can articulate the terms of political equality in such a way that they do not collapse into non-political goods, and also do not render political equality seriously unappealing. At the same time, the terms of political equality should be such that they are sufficiently 'thick' to make them morally attractive, for we can always define political equality in such a thin way that it will escape the danger of collapsing into non-political justice, but will not seem attractive enough to be worth pursuing. When, for instance, John Rawls defines 'the principle of (equal) participation' as the principle requiring 'that all citizens are to have an equal right to take part in, and to determine the outcome of, the constitutional process that establishes the laws with which they are to comply',[85] then this ideal is not vulnerable to collapsing into non-political goods but, under one (pedantic) interpretation at least, it is not ambitious enough to be attractive. For we can all have an 'equal right' to take part in the political process

[83] See, similarly, Christiano *The Rule of the Many: Fundamental Issues in Democratic Theory* 56–7.

[84] 'The time and thought that [a citizen] devotes to forming his [political] views is not governed by the likely material return of his political influence. Rather it is an activity enjoyable in itself that leads to a larger conception of society and to the development of his intellectual and moral faculties', Rawls *Theory of Justice* at 234.

[85] Rawls *Theory of Justice* at 221.

and to determine the outcome but it does not follow that, once we participate and determine the outcome, the actual level of determination of the outcome will be roughly similar for the different participants.

It is now worth returning to Dworkin, since he explicitly deals with the question of collapsing political justice into other goods. Soon after drawing the distinction between a detached and a dependent conception, he highlights an important caveat: 'We must be careful not to confuse that distinction with a different one, between two types of outcomes or consequences of a political process': a distributive and a participatory one.[86] The former refers to the consequences of political decisions regarding various resources: about acquisition and transfer of wealth etc, and therefore corresponds, by and large, to economic justice. The latter (participatory outcomes) are about symbols, agency, and community. Symbolic consequences are about affirming an equal membership in the community of all those who have a right to vote. Agency consequences build connections between an individual moral experience and politics: they rely not simply on a vote, but also on expressing our commitments in the public deliberation. Communal consequences are defined by Dworkin as those which permit individuals to 'share[] fully in the pride or shame of collective decisions' and in 'nourishing a cohesive and fraternal political community'.[87]

But these three types of 'participatory' consequences sound to me suspiciously like the attributes of the *process* rather than of the outcome: they are about what meaning we can attach to the fact of voting, and also how it connects with the pre-voting stage, that is, the stage of the public deliberation which precedes the vote. This process-related character of these consequences is perhaps most evident at the symbolic level which emphasizes that particular procedural forms have clear expressive consequences that are related to the message sent by a particular procedure about its participants; in Beitz's words, this is related to the 'idea that fair institutions should express public recognition of the equal worth of persons, conceived as autonomous centres of deliberation and action'.[88] Anything other than a one-person-one-equally-weighted-vote is demeaning to those who will get a lesser vote, regardless of the substantive outcomes of the voting. But surely the question is not the characterization of these (or the other) aspects of democratic decision-making as belonging to the *process* itself as opposed to its *outcome*, and the significance of Dworkin's distinction between a detached and a dependent conception of political equality must, for us, be deeper than whether we can ascertain that a procedure is egalitarian on the basis of the process only (as the detached conception would seem to dictate) or on the basis of consequences (as the dependent conception seems to warrant). A temptation to settle for such a simplistic distinction (where the detached/dependent distinction relies simply

[86] Dworkin *Sovereign Virtue* at 186.
[87] Dworkin *Sovereign Virtue* at 187.
[88] Beitz *Political Equality* at 92.

on the process/outcome distinction) should be resisted as uninteresting, if only because of the inevitable arbitrariness in characterizing particular phenomena as belonging to the category of processes or of outcomes.

This arbitrariness is illustrated by Dworkin's own examples about the three 'participatory consequences' cited above. However, there is more to it than that. A truly central role in Dworkin's argument about political equality is played by yet another distinction: between equality of impact and that of influence. The difference is that, while the impact a person makes is defined as 'the difference he can make, just on his own, by voting for or choosing one decision rather than another', the person's influence is defined as 'the difference he can make not just on his own but also by leading or inducing others to believe or vote or choose as he does'.[89] I will not attempt to summarize in full the use that Dworkin makes of this distinction (which, in the frame of his reasoning is quite complex), but will limit myself to identifying the broad framework relevant here. When applied to the considerations of political equality, 'impact' is not a useful category, Dworkin claims: in vertical relations (as between citizens and officials) equality of impact is just unthinkable, while in the horizontal dimension (as between different citizens) it is not ambitious enough because it cannot account, for instance, for the importance of freedom of speech, of political associations etc in contributing to political equality. This would seem to leave 'equality of influence' as the only attractive interpretation of political equality. Not so, warns Dworkin: trying to propel equality of influence (in the sense just defined) to the forefront would counter a great number of important features of a liberal-democratic society because we would need to equalize not only those sources of influence which many of us consider to be illegitimate (such as unequal financial means), but also those which are perfectly legitimate sources of unequal influence, and which are based on the fact that 'some people are more politically motivated or trained or charismatic than others'.[90] If we tried to equalize some of the sources of *these* inequalities (which in turn lead to unequal influence) it 'would conflict with other egalitarian goals'[91] and more generally, it would be 'incompatible, even in principle, with other attractive aspects of an egalitarian society'.[92] We would, for example, either be compelled to reduce the influence in politics overall, or try to convince people not to attempt to influence others in ways which can be traced to their specific experience or commitment or reputation etc. In the broader strategy of Dworkin's argument, this conclusion serves not as an argument for returning to equality of impact but rather as a demonstration that a 'detached' conception of democracy cannot provide a sufficient basis for any convincing notion of political equality. The alternative is to opt for a 'dependent' conception which would rely on distributive values (ie related to the distributive consequences of

89 Dworkin *Sovereign Virtue* at 191.
90 ibid at 196.
91 ibid at 196.
92 ibid at 198.

the decisions) as being relevant for political equality, and which would preserve the ideal of 'equality of impact', but only with respect to those collectively decided issues which are 'choice sensitive', ie where the adequacy of a solution 'depends essentially on the character and distribution of preferences within the political community'.[93]

But such a 'dependent' conception raises the spectre of diluting the specificity of political equality as compared to other aspects of equality and social justice. The remedy, namely the insistence on the equality of impact in choice-sensitive areas, is illusory for two reasons. First, it brings us back to an unsatisfactory search for 'equality of impact' if it is understood in a way that distinguishes it from 'equality of influence' because it does not account for various aspects of equality in the deliberation phase. Indeed, equality of impact is met when all have one vote even in circumstances where there are stark inequalities as regards access to the means of political communication, etc. Secondly, it is confined to the 'choice-sensitive' area, while the demarcation of this area from choice-insensitive matters is fundamentally contingent and arbitrary, and as such, as a second-order determination, is choice-insensitive, as Dworkin himself concedes.[94] According to a certain expansive approach of the field of choice-insensitive issues (and the approach *is* likely to be expansive, whenever rights figure prominently in our constitutional landscape because, as Dworkin suggests, choice insensitive issues correlate with the issues of 'principle' as contrasted to the issues of 'policy' in Dworkin's own old distinction)[95] the sphere of relevance of 'equality of impact' may be quite narrow and all we end up with to guide our judgment about political equality are the outcome-dependent distributive consequences. The consequence of dropping the ideal of equality of political influence is therefore that, in order to make a judgment on political equality, we need to rely directly on judgments relating to distributive justice more generally.

In the end, if we accept Dworkin's reasoning, we are faced with a dilemma: either to adopt the ideal of equality of influence (with the perverse consequences attributed by Dworkin to such an ideal, as noted above) or to collapse the judgment of political equality into an undifferentiated judgment on social justice, insensitive to the specificity of claims for *political* equality. (We can extend the list of options by adding a purely formal 'equality of impact', fully satisfied whenever each person has one vote, period.) But are we really compelled to face such an unpalatable choice? I do not think so, and I believe that the way out can be offered by a reflection about the ideal of equality of political *opportunity*—an ideal which Dworkin fails to consider, and yet which seems to be particularly well suited to address the specific concerns raised by him. Let us recall the main reason why he urges us to reject the ideal of equality of influence: it is because it is unable to discriminate among different sources of political inequality, some of

[93] ibid at 204. [94] ibid at 204–5.
[95] ibid at 205.

which may be legitimate and others not. If we were to equalize political influence across the board, we might wish to reduce the impact on a political discourse exercised by those who are more influential because of their higher motivation, intelligence, experience, reputation earned through record of service for public causes etc, and such an attempt would have perverse effects. If, however, we wish to equalize only those sources of political inequality which are illegitimate, then we might as well drop the ideal of equality of influence and talk directly about the aspects of inequality which we consider illegitimate. This is how we can paraphrase Dworkin's argument.

But such a gambit has an obvious cost (in the loss of the specificity of *political* equality, as compared to other fields of equality and distributive justice), so why not try to rescue the notion of equality of political influence while discarding its undesired and perverse consequences? The danger depicted by Dworkin is precisely the risk that in various other areas equality is normally addressed by the notion of (genuine) equality of opportunity.[96] In the conventional language, equality of opportunity can be presented, in a somewhat stylized manner, as occupying a space halfway between a *purely formal* equality of opportunity and the equality of *outcome*, where the distinguishing criterion relates to the grounds of access to the means of satisfying the conditions regulating the distribution of a particular good. When only very few of such grounds matter for our judgment of equality of opportunity (EO) to be satisfied, and they are thin and easily met (for instance, a citizenship in a given state) then we will call, often disparagingly, such an ideal a 'purely formal' equality of opportunity, because it is blind towards the many grounds of unequal access which, we know, are significant. If, on the other hand, all possible grounds of unequal access count for a judgment of equality of opportunity, then such an ideal effectively collapses into an equality of outcome because any unequal outcome is taken to be a sufficient symptom showing there was an inequality of access. A meaningful ideal of genuine equality of opportunity must be thicker than a formal EO (because it must be sensitive to a number of factors, which render more difficult the access for some of us to the conditions required in the distribution of desired goods) but at the same time stop short of collapsing into equality of outcome, because it must acknowledge that some causes of unequal outcomes are (or at least, may be) legitimate. Hence, the way of finding a right position between a formal EO and an equality of outcome is, for genuine EO, to discriminate between the legitimate and illegitimate sources of unequal access to the satisfaction of the conditions which figure as criteria for the distribution of scarce and desired resources.

This is precisely the concern that Dworkin raised as a reason for rejecting the principle of equality of political influence, arguing that it was impossible to distinguish between the legitimate and the illegitimate causes of unequal influence.

[96] See Andrei Marmor 'Authority, Equality and Democracy' *Ratio Juris* (2005) 18: 315–45 at 331–3.

To better reflect on how the language of genuine EO can provide a solution for this problem, let us consider a standard example of an application of the language of EO in the admission to a university. A 'formal' principle of EO is satisfied when there are no conditions of entry such that they cannot ever be fulfilled by some groups of candidates, for instance of race or place of birth, and therefore which would a priori exclude some applicants. But that is not sufficient for satisfying ourselves that genuine EO has been met because the other conditions which determine access to the university may be such that they are much more difficult to satisfy for some candidates than for others. If some candidates attended much better secondary schools which better equipped them with the required qualifications at the point of entry to the university, whereas the others, through no fault of their own, had no access to the better secondary schools, then we cannot recognize university access as satisfying the principle of EO. In contrast, if some of the prospective applicants have not achieved the necessary qualifications merely because they had chosen to devote more time to sport, then they cannot complain about inequality of opportunity. So EO crucially depends on a distinction between those causes of unequal access to qualifications required at the point of selection which can be deemed legitimate and those which we consider illegitimate.

The matter is, however, more complicated than that. Suppose we have a theory about the causes of unequal access that are illegitimate and those that are not; for example, that the causes which can be traced back to a person's own, freely taken choices are legitimate, and those which can be traced back to the circumstances over which a person has no control are illegitimate. But 'tracing back' is a long and tedious process in the cases of EO analysis because any access at a particular point in time is conditioned by factors which have affected the access to goods at an earlier stage, and which are relevant to the acquisition of qualifications required for today's selection, and this earlier access had already been conditioned by an even earlier one... etc. EO requires 'not merely that there should be no exclusion from access on grounds other than those appropriate or rational for the good in question, but that the grounds considered appropriate for the good should themselves be such that people from all sections of society have an equal chance of satisfying them',[97] and each 'access' in one's life is affected by an *earlier* crucial access in one's life. In our university access example, even if we are satisfied that the opportunities for secondary school access have been equalized, if, nevertheless, the access to equally good primary schools had not been equalized, the access to qualifications supplied by the secondary school will (partly) reproduce the inequalities of this earlier stage, which in turn will have reproduced inequalities of access at an even earlier stage etc.[98]

[97] Bernard AO Williams 'The Idea of Equality' in Hugo A Bedau (ed) *Justice and Equality* (New Jersey: Prentice-Hall, 1971) 116–37 at 132.

[98] Wojciech Sadurski *Giving Desert Its Due* (Dordrecht: D Reidel, 1985) 198–204.

Now this multi-tiered structure of EO may *seem* to disqualify this ideal altogether: either we stop the chain of argument at a certain stage (in which case our myopia about the earlier unequal access is condemnable as arbitrary) or we trace it to the earliest causes, some of which may be based on unequal genetic endowment (which, after all, is also outside a person's control) in which case not only do we reduce the ideal *ad absurdum* but also conflate EO fully with equality of outcome. This is because the very notion of an 'opportunity' to something (to X) means that the only thing that stands between me and X is my own choice, will, effort etc. But this already presupposes a certain theory about my own choice, will, effort, and so on, being fully under my control, and not being predetermined in a way which is outside my control. Not only does this argument raise a spectre of infinite regress but, more damagingly for the equal-opportunity argument, it rests the determination of equality of opportunity upon some fundamental metaphysical problems related to free will and determinism, on which philosophers deeply disagree and 'ordinary people' usually do not have a clue.

But this does not shatter the ideal of EO because there is a certain ambiguity in the notion of a source of unequal qualifications being 'illegitimate', and our everyday language of EO relies upon this ambiguity in a way which rescues the ideal of EO from the charge of absurdity. At times, we use the notion of illegitimate sources in a thick moral way whereby a source of inequality is 'legitimate' only if it can be fully and exclusively accounted for in terms of a free individual choice (as in our example of a free choice to devote more time to sport rather than to academic study, as a result of which a person has lower qualifications than those required at the point of entry to the university). But often such purely choice-dependent factors are not easily available, and in any event this argument often raises the complicated issues of the relationship between a free choice and choice-independent factors (perhaps the free choice to devote more time to sport was genetically conditioned?). When the point of such perplexity is reached, we usually do *not* abandon the language of EO altogether but rather use a second meaning of 'illegitimate' sources: they are factors which (even though they do condition a person in a choice-independent way) we do not *want* to be equalized because it would lead to deplorable and sometimes even perverse consequences. This is a 'consequentialist' rather than thick moral sense of the illegitimacy of sources of unequal qualifications which enters into the reasoning, in order to prevent the EO discourse from collapsing into absurdity. Consider our earlier argument: even if, along the lines of some arguments on free will and determinism, we reached the conclusion that our willingness to undertake efforts (say, to study rather than to play) is genetically predetermined, we do not want to equalize the genetic potentials. Thus our equal-opportunity argument considers this particular factor as legitimate for the differentiation of outcomes, the operation of which does not negate the existence of equal opportunities. One can obviously protest at this point that in using the consequentialist argument we are putting a cart before a horse: we are assessing whether the opportunities were equally distributed from the predicted consequences of the steps aimed at equalizing them. Indeed, this is precisely what we are doing, but this should not be seen as a defect, but as a regular and proper feature of our moral discourse, and our language of EO should be sensitive to *both* of these understandings of the illegitimacy of factors of inequality.

Consider this example from Bernard Williams's classical article on equality:

> [o]ne is not really offering equality of opportunity to Smith and Jones if one contents oneself with applying the same criteria to Smith and Jones at, say, the age of 11; what one is doing there is to apply the same criteria to Smith as affected by favourable conditions and to Jones as affected by unfavourable but *curable* conditions. Here there is a necessary pressure to equal up the conditions....[99]

The emphasis should be on the word 'curable', which should play an operative role here, and 'curability' is a matter not only of the theoretical feasibility of remedies, but also of a practical cost-benefit calculus. Some unequal conditions may be 'curable', but only with such a great cost in terms of damages to other important values that, for all practical purposes, we consider them to be beyond the reach of any remedies.

What is important for us here is that, if EO is viewed in this way, then it resonates with the argument of Dworkin, which led him to the rejection of the ideal of equality of influence (in the Dworkinian strict sense of 'influence' as contrasted to 'impact'). Indeed, one of the main reasons for rejecting this ideal was that the imaginable ways of equalizing the political influence would lead to highly unattractive results, and the way Dworkin depicts the ways in which these results would be unattractive evokes the perversity of some ways of equalizing the factors of qualifications, under the EO analysis. For instance, one way of rendering influence more equally distributed would be by limiting the resources that people can freely spend on the means of politically influencing others; as Dworkin says, it would 'prevent some people from tailoring their resources to fit the lives they wanted though leaving others, who had less interest in politics, free to do so'.[100] To translate this scenario into the language of EO, such a result would counter EO in a plain and obvious way because it would equalize the outcomes conditioned by inequalities which can be traced fully to choice-sensitive factors. Another strategy of equalizing 'influence', Dworkin claims, would be by 'educat[ing] people not to attempt to influence others, with respect to political decisions, *except in ways that do not rely on special advantages they might have, in experience or commitment or reputation*, and also to attempt to resist being influenced by other people whose arguments might have special force traceable to such advantages'.[101] To translate this into the language of EO: we would be restoring political equality but in a way which would bring about some obviously appalling

[99] Williams 'The Idea of Equality' at 133 (emphasis added).
[100] Dworkin *Sovereign Virtue* at 197 (footnote omitted).
[101] ibid at 197 (emphasis added).

consequences. It would be perverse to try to bring about equality of opportunity by making it impossible for the better arguments to influence public opinion more strongly than the worse ones, even if the strength of the argument could be traceable to individual factors which cannot themselves be 'deserved' in a morally meaningful way. For consequentialist reasons we therefore consider the differences in political persuasiveness as 'legitimate' factors of different opportunities, even if these factors cannot be traced back to purely choice-sensitive causes.

These two main hypothetical strategies of equalizing influence under Dworkin's conceptual framework,[102] which play the role of the 'parade of horribles' and thus lead him to the rejection of the ideal of 'equality of influence', can therefore be accommodated into the language of EO, and the perverse implications of adopting the ideal of equality of influence can be well handled by the discourse of equality of political opportunity. This would mean that, if we can speak meaningfully of equality of political opportunity (and if this allows us to come to grips with the problems that the parallel ideal, that of equality of political influence, would generate) then perhaps we need not collapse the language of political equality into that of undifferentiated equality or social justice, as the 'dependent conception' of Dworkin's analysis would inevitably demand. The ideal of equal political opportunity would seem, therefore, to preserve those aspects which Dworkin found missing from the ideal of equal political influence (such as the distinction between legitimate and illegitimate sources of unequal influence) and at the same time preserve the specificity of political equality, which was the aspiration articulated earlier, in Part 6.

8. Equality of Political Opportunity and Majority Rule

How is the principle of equal political opportunity related to MR? The relationship is only indirect. Equal political opportunity applies quite obviously to the deliberation stage of the political process. It is with respect to *this* stage that the concept of equal *influence* was developed in the first place (and indeed, it was *defined* in terms which have relevance to the deliberation stage only), and the ideal of equal political opportunity enters the stage as a remedy to the defects that the ideal of equal influence had. But it is worth asking: an opportunity *to what* should be equalized, under the principle of EO?

From an individual's point of view, the purpose of deliberation is twofold: first, it is to acquire the best ideas and information for oneself; second, to affect the views of other people. Equal political opportunity is, obviously, mainly concerned

[102] There is also a third strategy in Dworkin's reasoning, namely that of reducing the role of influence of politics overall, see ibid at 197, but Dworkin quickly discards it as so self-evidently unacceptable, that it cannot be seriously entertained in a democratic society. He is of course right, and its short appearance in Dworkin's argument does not affect the discussion here in any way.

with the second function of deliberation, because it is the second function that relates to political *influence*. What can equal opportunities, with regard to this second function, be opportunities *for*? I suggest that the object of the opportunities (that is, the benefit which the opportunities lead to) is located somewhere halfway on the spectrum between being able to *communicate* one's views and being able to actually *convince* the audience of one's views. The former interest is too weak: a mere ability to communicate is too thin a good for people to want to attain it, without more. Any Hyde Park speaker has already attained this good, and the thinnest regime of freedom of speech (understood merely as the absence of censorship and physical restraint) easily satisfies this ideal. The latter good, an ability to convince one's audience of one's own views, is too strong to lend itself to equalization. The likelihood of convincing the audience is largely dependent on the listeners' *prior* views, which belong to the category of factors that are outside of the speaker's control, and that are not the subject of the 'equalization' in the equal-opportunity discourse. This is due to various causes of disagreement between people, which can be explained neither by a lesser rationality of some people as compared to others nor by the fact that those different views are merely rationalizations of people's narrow interests, which themselves are different. John Rawls labelled these reasons 'the burdens of judgment'.[103] In Rawls's view, those burdens include the fact that the evidence relating to a case is often conflicting and complex; there may be disagreement about the weight of different kinds of considerations that are relevant; concepts are often vague, indeterminate, and subject to hard cases; our experiences are different and these differences affect the way we assess evidence, etc. Even assuming that listeners are fully receptive to the speakers' arguments, a number of decisive factors for the effectiveness of persuasion are, and should remain, outside of the power of speakers.

So if the ability to communicate one's views is too weak, and the ability to convince one's audience is too strong, and neither can, therefore, be considered as the objects of a political opportunity, what could be a plausible good between these two extremes? It can probably be characterized as the ability to effectively get one's own political message across to the audience one wants to reach. Anything less is an insignificant good; anything more is implausible because it engages the factors which are, and should remain, outside the control of a person making this communication. But it is quite plausible to claim that equal political opportunity in the deliberation stage of collective decision-making should mean an equality of opportunity to reach one's desired audience, to get one's message across, to be heard. This is more than an opportunity to speak, and less than an opportunity to convince; it is an opportunity to convey one's message to the audience which the speaker wants to reach. Because deliberation is largely carried on through speech, the ideal of equal opportunity with respect to speech can properly be applied here. Elsewhere, I have argued at some length about the attractiveness

[103] John Rawls *Political Liberalism* (New York: Columbia University Press, 1993) 54–8.

of an ideal of an 'equal opportunity to be heard' as a plausible and meaningful interpretation of equalizing expressive opportunities.[104] I will not be summarizing my conclusions here, beyond stating that the ideal of equality of opportunity seems to capture well the various policies aimed at equalizing access to media of political communication because '(1) being heard by one's audience is an important social good which many people seek, and (2) we may legitimately and meaningfully aim to reduce the impact of those factors which are outside the speaker's control and affect his or her access to the means of effective speech'.[105]

What sort of institutions and procedures are needed to maximize such an equality of opportunity to influence a given audience? It is hard to make any specific recommendations at that level of abstraction. What is clear is that the equalization of these opportunities at the stage of political deliberation implies at least the following dimensions of deliberation: (1) impact upon the agenda-setting, including the capacity to initiate public deliberation about a chosen subject; (2) access to the information relevant to public decision-making; (3) access to the forums of deliberation, and in particular mass media, in the sense that the existing inequality of power and resources do not affect the chances of contributing to a public deliberation; (4) guarantees that the penalties for being converted to one's opponents' views are not prohibitive, hence, that it is politically and socially plausible that we may persuade others to our views; (5) ensuring that the procedures of the deliberation are neutral in relation to the different substantive viewpoints, in the sense that a procedure itself does not privilege any particular discussant.

None of these requirements is straightforward or uncontroversial. *Regarding (1)*, the capacity to set the agenda is dependent upon the pre-existing deliberation and the outcomes of earlier discourses; those who have been 'winners' in the deliberation so far will naturally be privileged in setting the agenda for the future. There is never a 'fresh start' in which the agenda is set for the next public deliberation, but rather there is a continuity in the sequence of deliberations; hence, an inevitable tendency towards the petrifaction and entrenchment of the pre-existing hierarchies of deliberative powers.

With respect to (2): unequal access to the information relevant to the deliberation will inevitably have a differentiated effect on the participants' capacity to influence others. This does not apply only, or mainly, to the 'technology' of deliberation, so to speak, but primarily to the substantive issues at stake, and those who do not know what policies will advance or damage their interests or their conceptions of justice will be highly disadvantaged vis-à-vis those who know. Hence, as Thomas Christiano suggests, '[e]galitarian institutions are charged with the task of disseminating understanding widely so that individuals have the means of informing themselves of how to advance their interests and convictions.... Hence, democratic institutions ought to be structured in such a way as

[104] Wojciech Sadurski *Freedom of Speech and Its Limits* (Dordrecht: Kluwer, 1999) 73–98.
[105] ibid at 85.

to provide wide and roughly equal access to information relevant to democratic decision-making'.[106] But this is a very tall order, and the main thrust of this task is fulfilled not by the institutions of deliberation themselves but by educational institutions: the success of achieving equality of opportunity with respect to political deliberation is therefore largely parasitic upon the equality of educational opportunity. In addition, some viewpoints may rely upon a much more technical, and thus difficult to acquire and disseminate, knowledge than others: an appeal to 'common sense' or widespread prejudices may make an argumentative task easier than an appeal to a scientific knowledge which would debunk popular conventional wisdoms.

With respect to (3): what would, even in ideal circumstances, equal access of proponents of different viewpoints to forums of deliberation, look like, considering that those whose views are socially less popular are inevitably less privileged in their access to the media than others? Would it mean, literally, an equality of access (so that fringe groups and major parties would have more or less equal time in public broadcasting, which would lead to perverse results because the need to give equal time to all the eccentric fringes would devalue the deliberation time across the board) or would it mean access in proportion to the influence already enjoyed as reflected in, say, the recent election results of particular parties (which would be clearly discriminatory against the emerging, new viewpoints and would merely perpetuate the status quo of existing political influence)? More importantly, with respect to (3), how do we disconnect the actual political deliberations from vastly unequal financial resources that people are able and willing to put into public spheres such as mass media? We may think of ways of immunizing some media (such as public broadcasters) from financially powerful interests but, as long as there are 'powerful players, who make it their business to shape the terms of the public debate through financial contributions they make available to politicians and political campaigns',[107] deliberative opportunities will remain drastically unequal. Deliberations aim at affecting the existing structures of power and resources, but at the same time they are carried on within those structures, and inevitably reproduce existing inequalities.

With respect to (4): if the penalties that a participant to a debate suffers in case he accepts the opponent's arguments are extreme and dramatic (such as excommunication or a *fatwah*) then the likelihood of persuasion (which is the aim of deliberation from the participants' perspectives) is extremely low, and hence the opportunities for achieving one's deliberative aim is lower for those whose opponents face such dramatic consequences. On the other hand, equality of penalties (or rewards) for conversion is impossible to establish because it would imply (among other things) equal stakes that all participants would have in the results of a given deliberation, which is impossible. So perhaps all that can be aimed at

[106] Christiano *The Rule of the Many: Fundamental Ideas in Democratic Theory* at 85–6.
[107] Shapiro *The State of Democratic Theory* at 30.

is the establishment of certain threshold conditions under which no one faces particularly dramatic consequences of conversion.

With respect to (5): the goal of having a procedure which is outcome-neutral is chimerical. Deliberation always takes place within institutions, and the latter frame the deliberation in a way which is never outcome-neutral. Studies show that factors internal to the deliberation itself, such as the sequence in which particular actors speak, or the point at which the deliberation is terminated, affect the outcome: different designs of the deliberation itself, will generate different outcomes within the same initial range of viewpoints.[108] So even if a design in these respects is purely arbitrary and not tailored to privilege any particular viewpoints, some viewpoints *will* be privileged and others disadvantaged, thus reducing equality of opportunity. Perhaps all we can do is ensure that the reduction is minimal, and that the design is established under the 'veil of ignorance' as to who in particular will be affected and how by any such design.

So much for equal political opportunity at the stage of political deliberation. When it comes to the stage of actual decision-making we obviously do not need to find an interpretation of the good of political *influence*: by voting (either in the elections or in a referendum or in the parliament) we do not try to *influence* anyone but we actually take the decision. It is too late to talk about influence at this point, and thus also about political opportunities to affect the decisions. MR is therefore an institutional embodiment of what Dworkin called 'equal *impact*': a weight that a person's vote has (taken on its own) in the collective decision-making. But there is an indirect connection between equal impact and equal political opportunity, which parallels the connection between voting and deliberation. If there was *no* vote at the end of the road (for instance, if the decision was to be taken by a reasonably benevolent dictator who would tolerate all sorts of deliberations but did not care about them one bit when taking the decisions, or if the decisions were taken by lottery) the deliberation would be meaningless. It could still go on but people would have no intelligible motivations to participate in the first-order deliberation (about the actual decisions to take), although obviously they would have good reasons to participate in the second-order deliberation (about how to change the decision-making process). Therefore, it would not matter whether the deliberation stage respected the condition of equal political opportunity, or of equal influence, or of equal whatever. In contrast, when the decision-making procedure does respect the principle of equal impact, then an equal opportunity to affect the views of those who will be taking the decision acquires an urgent value. Equality at the output of the system radiates upon the importance of equality at the input, so to speak. For if our adoption of the system of MR is motivated by strong egalitarian reasons (as has been the main theme of this chapter) and gives an expression to the principle of equal impact, then we do

108 Knight and Johnson 'What Sort of Political Equality Does Deliberative Democracy Require?' at 291.

not want to upset this political equality by a lack of equality at an earlier stage, which in turn significantly informs the final stage. There should be a degree of continuity in the egalitarian credentials at all stages of the process, if equality is our true reason for opting for MR.

It is important to be clear about this connection. It is not the case that if we violate the principle of equality of political opportunity at the deliberation stage, then the equality of impact at the stage of decision-taking (in the institutional form of MR) is in some way damaged. The point is rather that the adoption of MR at the final stage reveals our intention to give effect to the principle of equality in the political process, and therefore the *integrity* of this intention demands that we try to respect it at the earlier stages of the process as well, especially since these earlier, deliberative stages, inform the substance of the decision itself.

Conclusions

Political equality, which underlies and supports majority rule, is an important though limited ideal. It can coexist with, and is not necessarily discredited by, unequal political outcomes which result from the recourse to majoritarian procedures. Equality of political opportunity and of political impact have a powerful legitimating significance for democratic decisions, and need to be assessed in a way which is at least partly detached from controversies about what constitutes equality in the outcomes of these processes. We adopt a democratic rule for reasons that are egalitarian through and through, but it is at this point that our egalitarian consensus ends. It is not the case that political equality is more or less egalitarian than a substantive principle of equal concern but rather that, in a pluralistic community, we would not agree on the common criteria determining which outcomes are substantively equal (that is, which express, in their substance, the principle of equal concern for all citizens), while we may more likely agree on standards of equality within the process. The detachment of political equality from substantively equal concern as displayed in laws and political decisions renders it possible for us to establish that the very adoption of a democratic procedure reveals a prior acceptance of a strongly egalitarian premise; a premise weighty enough to prevail over the arguments (whatever they may be) for a non-democratic system of government.

There is one issue which has been placed, deliberately, outside the bounds of my argument in this chapter. I have not discussed the question of who constitutes the demos within which the majority counts for the purposes of MR: an implied presupposition has been that the demos corresponds more or less to the range of people to whom the collective decisions apply, and who are expected to comply with them. But it is, of course, a risky presupposition, and the 'more or less' clause may hide the real problems. Some exclusions from the demos are taken almost universally for granted: of children, of the mentally incompetent, or of those criminally punished. Others are less obvious and are (justifiably) under increasing scrutiny: the exclusion of long-term residents, nationals of other countries, for example. A determination of the bounds of the demos is crucial for any fully-fledged conception of democracy, because, even if my argument about the link between MR and equality is correct, a fundamental inequality may be caused by a disenfranchisement of some groups of people for the purposes of ascertaining majority. As Robert Dahl had persuasively argued while criticising Schumpeter's democratic theory, it is one thing to say 'System X is democratic in relation to its own demos' and another to say 'System Y is democratic in relation to everyone subject to its rules'.[109] Naturally, it is only the latter which is meaningful. This is because ultimately what we are interested in (in this chapter, in any case) is the relationship between equality (as displayed by MR) and the *legitimacy* of a democratic system, and by placing some people outside the bounds of the demos, the system fails to make out the claim of the legitimacy of its laws as applied to them.

This is, at least, a prima facie proposition which can be rebutted in some specific circumstances, which may redeem the legitimacy of the system's directives addressed to those who have not made it to its demos, such as children or foreigners. Why these groups *may* have reasons to consider the system as legitimate is unrelated to the principle of equality: clearly, they have not been given an equal status in the law-making process. But this just goes to show that there may be other bases of legal legitimacy that do not relate to equality; there was nothing in my argument which required an assertion that equality (as displayed through MR) is the only possible source of law's legitimacy. But it is an *important* source, and a source which in a democratic system is a norm, while other grounds of legitimacy (eg towards children or foreigners) are exceptions.

[109] Dahl 'Procedural Democracy' at 112.

3

Legal Equality

Legal equality is a particularly troublesome ideal, and in this chapter I will attempt to make sense of it. I will begin by locating it at two different conceptual levels: the level of application of the law and that of the content of the law, and by emphasizing the need to distinguish between the two (Part 1). After a short restatement of this rather banal point, I will spend the remainder of the chapter discussing equality at the latter, substantive level. I will suggest that it is at the same time a non-negotiable (occupying a position lexically prior to other legal ideals shared by its proponents) and a fundamentally ambiguous ideal (Part 2), and that it must not be understood as a requirement that a legal system should minimize, and ideally avoid altogether, classifying individuals by means of legal rules (Part 3). I will then discuss, and reject, what I take to be probably the most popular approach to legal equality, namely a view that certain characteristics of individuals, when used as a basis for classifications, necessarily render a classification discriminatory (what I will call a 'per se theory' of discrimination (Part 4).

Based on the critique of 'per se' theories, I develop a more positive argument, starting from the insight that the key to the test for equality lies in the relationship between classification and purpose, which is a promising track but which may yield a danger of circularity that can be avoided by heightening the level of scrutiny applied to the fit between the classification and the purpose (Part 5). Nevertheless, we need some good reasons for heightening the level of scrutiny of the legislation, and these reasons must be embedded in a general theory of what renders a classification discriminatory. Through a use of the method of 'reflective equilibrium', I will propose some indicia which help us identify the circumstances when we should be suspicious that the classification is tainted as discriminatory by certain wrongful motives for legislation (Part 6). This, I hope, coheres into a substantive conception of legal equality which is a *working* conception, in that it does not fully collapse into a statement of an overall approbation for a given legal rule.

Perhaps one methodological point is worth making right at the outset. Since this chapter is devoted to a *legal* category, much of the material is legal in nature and focuses upon the language and arguments used in legal texts, in particular judicial opinions. This is natural; arguments developed by judges in upholding or invalidating various legislative distinctions give us a good insight into what those legal officials consider constitutes improper 'discrimination', and by implication, what they consider legal equality to mean. The uses of these legal arguments are, however, on a par with the arguments developed by legal academics: the aspiration of this chapter is not doctrinal (in the sense of identifying what is a valid legal rule in a particular legal system) but theoretical, and so judges' opinions do not carry for me, for the purposes of this chapter, any particular authority, other than a theoretical one. Readers will easily recognize that there is a clear preponderance of US-based material and in particular judgments of the Supreme Court of the United States (although, occasionally, other countries will provide illustrations for the points made here). This is because, in my view, the reasoning by the judges of the highest US judicial body provides us with the richest intellectual material for contemplating various aspects of discrimination (which is not to say that it is usually convincing). But I will be using this material in a way which, I hope, makes it perfectly capable of applying in a more universal manner, in a way which is perhaps too stylized (which is another way of saying: simplistic) to a good US constitutional lawyer. My intention is to identify the general patterns of argument which are often hidden behind the technical-legal formulae, and which, when abstracted from a particular legal context, are translatable into an argument capable of being used in a different legal system. For example, the language of different 'standards of scrutiny', so characteristic of the United States 14th Amendment jurisprudence, is not *that* different from the language of 'proportionality' which is favoured by European constitutional courts. The general pattern of reasoning is very similar: it is to test the structure of relationship between the means used by a legislation (which draws various distinctions among citizens) and the aims it seeks to achieve. When studying legal categories, we often consider particular technical concepts, but if the aim is theoretical rather than doctrinal, we should treat those technical concepts merely as indicators of general patterns of argument which are similar, if not identical, in different countries.

1. Equality *before* and *in* the Law

It has become commonplace to point out, and complain, that even extreme forms of discrimination may coexist with the observance of a 'formal' principle of equality before the law. As an Australian judge once said: 'Formal equality before the law is an engine of oppression destructive of human dignity if the law entrenches inequalities "in the political, economic, social, cultural or any other field of public life"'.[1] Jack Balkin encapsulated this observation well: '[T]he discourse of equality [under the Equal Protection Clause of the US Constitution] has been

[1] *Gerhardy v Brown* 59 ALJR 311, 337 (1985) (Austl) (Brennan J) (quoting s 9(1) of the Racial Discrimination Act (Austl 1975).

used not only to further egalitarian norms but to perpetuate and preserve racial hierarchy'.[2] This is because the standard of equality, as applied to legal rules, is sometimes understood as a principle governing the enforcement of legal rules, *whatever they are*, and it is in other times understood as a principle governing the substance of these rules. Another way of articulating the same distinction is by saying that the principle of equality before the law can apply either to the bodies that only apply the law or to the lawmakers themselves.[3] One way of appreciating that the generic notion of 'equality before the law' captures two different normative phenomena is by a simple textual analysis of some important constitutional texts. Consider, as a representative example, equality provisions of the Canadian Charter of Rights and Freedoms of 1982. Article 15(1) of the Charter reads, in part: 'Every individual is equal *before and under the law* and has the right *of equal protection* and equal benefit of the law *without discrimination*....'[4] Unless the draftsmen deliberately chose to be repetitive in one sentence, a strong implication is that they believed that there was a difference between equality 'before' and equality 'under' the law, and also that they believed that the precept of 'equal protection of the law' is not identical with the injunction against discrimination.

The fact that the principle of equality, as applied to law, can be located at two different levels, the level of the enforcement of a rule and the level of the substance of a rule, is parallel to the analogous bifurcation of the notion of justice. Justice, as Chaim Perelman and many other writers have pointed out, can be seen as consisting of two parts: a formal component which requires that like cases be treated alike, and a substantive component which supplies the standards of what the relevant equalities among individuals are from the point of view of the treatment in question (in other words, from the point of view of that particular benefit, or that particular burden, the distribution of which is under consideration).[5] The adoption of a maxim of distribution related to the 'substantive' component is conceptually independent from the first component, namely the principle of treating equal cases equally. Indeed, it has been pointed out that the principle of equal treatment of equal cases is not an 'egalitarian' principle at all but rather that it necessarily follows from a general principle of rational behaviour which, inter alia, requires similar conduct in similar circumstances. The application of the principle of 'equal treatment of equal cases' is merely a manner of speaking about treatment of people according to general and abstract rules, as opposed to an ad hoc treatment, case-by-case treatment, or treatment triggered by arbitrary impulses and whims. As soon as there are general rules in operation

[2] JM Balkin 'Agreements with Hell and Other Objects of Our Faith' (1997) 65 Fordham L Rev 1703 at 1712 (footnote omitted).

[3] Robert Alexy *A Theory of Constitutional Rights* (trans, Julian Rivers) (New York: Oxford University Press, 2002) 260.

[4] The Canadian Charter of Rights and Freedoms (Constitution Act 1982, Part I) Article 15(1) (emphasis added).

[5] See Chaim Perelman *Justice, Law, and Argument: Essays on Moral and Legal Reasoning* (Dordrecht: D Reidel, 1980) 10–11.

which prescribe the way individuals should be treated, the individuals will be treated 'equally' (at the level of enforcement) if they are treated according to a rule because a rule prescribes the proper treatment of individuals defined in terms of their relevant characteristics rather than as separately enumerated individuals. As long as these characteristics are taken into account in decisions about the class of individuals who are to be afforded a given treatment prescribed by the rule, they are treated equally. Whether treatment is *just* in a more substantive sense (characterized by Perelman as 'concrete')[6] is a matter of judgment determined by the reasoning at a second level, that is, the level of 'substantive' justice, which in itself is not informed by the considerations of equality.

This bifurcated nature of the concept of *justice* applies also to the concept of equality before the law. Equal treatment of individuals from the point of view of a given legal rule is nothing other than the treatment of those individuals in accordance with this rule, regardless of its content. It is, therefore, a *proper* treatment understood as consistency between the rule and its enforcement. As Robert Alexy puts it, 'It simply requires that every legal norm be applied to every case falling within its ambit and to no case not falling within its ambit, which is tantamount to saying that legal norms must be followed'.[7] The word 'equality' in the notion of 'equality before the law' (at the level of enforcement) does not do any independent work. It is indeed redundant since exactly the same meaning is conveyed by the term 'proper enforcement of a rule', which is enforcement of a rule in accordance with its substance. The word 'equality' in this first sense of legal equality may as well be discarded, but semantic innovation is not my aspiration here. The persistence of the word 'equality' in this particular context may be explained by rhetorical functions of the notion, and should be respected. However, it is important to realize that 'equality *before* the law' (as I will call it henceforth), in the sense of equality in the enforcement of rules, whatever they are, is a proxy for something else; namely, for the proposition that the valid rules should be enforced as fully as possible in accordance with the stated contents. It demands that if there is a rule R which prescribes a treatment T to all individuals who posses a characteristic C, then a good legal system should maximize the likelihood of a state of affairs in which all who possess C would be given T, and no one who does not have C should be given T.

This is, of course, a greatly simplified inference from the notion of 'equality before the law'. For instance, T may also be afforded to some people who do not have C but who have a characteristic D, which under a separate rule is triggering a treatment T which happens to be identical with treatment T triggered by C. (For instance, a person A and a person B who are situated differently under a rule R-1 may have to be treated differently under that rule but, since B is also treated under a rule R-2, it may well happen that under that rule he will turn out to be treated

[6] ibid at 11, 20–22.

[7] Alexy *A Theory of Constitutional Rights* at 261 (footnote omitted).

identically to A: A is a thief and B is not but B is a bribe-taker and the penalty for bribes may turn out to be the same as for theft. This of course is not a violation of the principle 'treat different cases differently' for the simple reason that we are all within a constant field of operation of a high number of different rules and the range of modes of treatment that they provide—for instance, penalties—is reasonably narrow). However, all that is important here is that 'equality before the law', in the sense of equal enforcement of a rule, is not based on any equality-related rationale. It is equivalent to the principle of uniform enforcement of the same rule to, and exclusively to, all the cases that are defined as relevant by that very rule. It does not follow that this principle is self-evident, and/or that it is a requirement of pure rationality without any normative component. Indeed, the vision of a good law which maximizes the state of affairs in which all who have C would be given T, and no one who does not have C should be given T, requires justification, as any other normative vision of a good law, and may be contested. But, and this is the point of the present argument, the justification for this vision, and alternatively challenges to this vision, cannot be articulated in egalitarian terms without running into circularity.

Nevertheless, it is one thing to say that the principle of treatment of people in accordance with a rule is not self-evident, and it would be another thing to say that it is widely contested and that in practical moral and political disagreements its proponents carry a burden of argument equal to those who argue *against* the treatment of people according to general rules. While as a matter of abstract moral theorizing it may be useful and interesting to require a good moral justification of any normative principle, however widely shared, in practical moral reasoning it is widely accepted that the legal treatment of people in accordance with publicly stated rules is presumptively good. The exceptions from treatment according to the rules should be precisely that—the exceptions. One need not share Fuller's view that there is a strong connection between the formal principle of treatment according to a rule and a substantive set of right moral principles, in other words, that there is a connection between the 'inner' and 'external' morality of law.[8] Furthermore, it is unnecessary to argue against the point that sometimes, in the case of particularly oppressive rules, the only good thing that one can say about a legal system is that it does *not* always practise what it preaches. Consequently, one can perhaps argue that in an oppressive legal system it is actually a good thing that not *all* people identified by a rule as having a characteristic relevant to a particular treatment, are actually treated in such a way. This is not the point. The point is that in routine legal situations, which do not reach the level of extreme oppressiveness, there is a general presumption in favour of treatment of people in accordance with general rules. The rules apply to a larger class of people rather than on an ad hoc, case-by-case basis. This presumption is rebuttable but it is

[8] See Lon L Fuller *The Morality of Law* (New Haven: Yale University Press, 1977) 132–3, 157–9 (1969, revised edn).

nevertheless quite strong. That is why the principle of 'equality before the law', understood as an enforcement of legal rules in accordance with their own content, is relatively unproblematic.

This is not to say that in practice there will be no disagreements about what is required by this principle. But these disagreements and controversy will flow either from (1) uncertainties about which valid rule applies to a given situation, or from (2) uncertainties about how to define the relevant individual characteristics that are conditions of a given treatment, and (3) whether some specific individuals do indeed possess those characteristics. These three types of disagreement are the stuff of daily operations of any legal system, and they are very often difficult to answer in a compelling way. These difficulties, however, do not hinge upon the theoretical complexities of the concept of equality before the law.

2. Equality in Law: a Non-Negotiable, Fundamentally Ambiguous Ideal

Probably no other legal postulate has provoked so many debates, discussions, and disagreement as that of equality *in* law. We should not find this surprising. While many other concepts advanced as the essential values to be implemented by a just legal system (such as liberty, welfare, security, certainty, and community) are also vague, lending themselves to differing conceptions of their 'true' scope and boundaries, the problem with the ideal of equality is different. Its specificity hinges on two features: non-negotiability and fundamental ambiguity.

The non-negotiability of the principle of legal equality means that those who are postulating this ideal are usually unwilling to accept any trade-offs between equality and other values, even those which they themselves would recognize as attractive. While the attitude of 'non-negotiability' with respect to any other social ideal protected by law may in principle seem unduly rigid, with regard to equality it does not usually strike us as unreasonable. On the contrary, many of us would consider it bizarre if a law-maker (or a legal commentator) were to argue along the following lines about a proposed legal rule: 'While this rule admittedly introduces a degree of inequality before the law, this is more than compensated by the other benefits produced by the rule.' The intuitive response to this sentence is that its first part conclusively disqualifies the rule in question, and that no alleged benefit, whatever its extent, could ever redeem it. In this sense, 'equality before the law' is 'lexically prior' to other values.[9] This is in clear contrast to most other ideals typically associated with a just legal system. Proponents of liberty, utility, wealth maximization, and legal certainty are usually prepared to accept some limits upon the implementation of these ideals if the surplus in the

[9] On the concept of 'lexical priority' see John Rawls *Theory of Justice* at 42–3. Rawls assigns lexical priority to the principle of equal liberty within his set of principles of justice, ibid at 43.

implementation of other, competing ideals, makes up for the losses. Hence trade-offs are usually seen as acceptable—except with regard to legal equality.

The second distinguishing feature of legal equality is its fundamental ambiguity. By this, I mean not just the vagueness of a concept which lends itself to different interpretations, conceptions, and criteria for implementation; rather and more fundamentally and disconcertingly, what is referred to is that one and the same ideal can be understood as implying two, mutually antithetical, but equally prima facie reasonable, sets of specific prescriptions. This goes beyond 'mere' conceptual ambiguity. Compare, for example, the ideal of equality before the law with that of liberty protected by the law. Consider a specific controversy related to the latter principle: the dilemma as to whether laws committed to the protection of individual liberty can impose coercive restraints upon individuals to protect them against self-inflicted harms. In general, one could, prima facie, adopt a principle that coercing people for their own good is inconsistent with the principle of liberty. Of course, the matter cannot end there. It is not necessary to rehearse the arguments made in an extensive literature on 'paternalism'[10] in order to conclude that a certain degree of coercion-backed protection against self-inflicted harm can be permitted (some would even say, mandated) by the principle of legally-protected liberty. A number of reasons may be given to justify this: (1) certain harms are so great and irreversible that they will annul the future liberty of an individual to act in a particular way; the process of forming preferences for a particular action may be distorted by many extraneous factors which can then be countered by paternalistic coercive interference; (2) the process of transforming preferences into individual choices is affected by ignorance on the part of an agent who is unaware of vital facts which render the choice incongruent with a preference; (3) the consent of an agent who enters into a transactional agreement with another, which is harmful to the first party, is not genuine; (4) the only way of giving effect to an individual's true preferences, in a situation of collective action and the resulting Prisoner's Dilemma, is to impose coercive norms which ensure that the process of implementing individual preferences is not eroded by a perverse incentive structure which rewards non-cooperative action by individuals etc. Each of these cases, seeming to justify a rebuttal of our prima facie distaste for paternalistic interferences, requires a judgment of degree, for example, about how 'genuine' a party's consent was. But the ambiguity that results from the possibility of disagreement about this judgment of degree is a 'mere' ambiguity, rather than a fundamental one. Such ambiguity stems from the notorious fact that values allow for degrees. It is *not* that the value is itself inherently ambiguous. Such an inherent ambiguity would occur, in our example, if, *regardless of judgments of degree*, two individuals could still in good faith disagree over whether

[10] See, generally, Rolf Sartorius (ed) *Paternalism* (Minneapolis: University of Minnesota Press, 1983); Joel Feinberg *Harm to Self: The Moral Limits of the Criminal Law* (vol 3, New York: Oxford University Press, 1986).

the principle of liberty, properly understood, allows for paternalistic interferences with individual action or not.

The ambiguity of the ideal of equality is precisely of that sort, and it differs from the 'mere' ambiguity sketched above because individuals can, and frequently do, disagree in good faith about its application, and may propose mutually antithetical specific prescriptions, without this being affected by any judgments of degree related to the values used in the process of argument. The controversy about affirmative action is perhaps the most obvious example. Apart from any other arguments used by parties to the controversy, both proponents and opponents of the principle of affirmative action believe that their positions are *mandated* by the principle of equality before the law. In contrast to my other example above—about liberty and paternalism—the disagreement here is not about the degree to which equality can be reasonably *restricted* by some affirmative action without losing its bona fide egalitarian character but rather about whether the essence of the concept of equality is such that, under some empirically verifiable circumstances, it will mandate or prohibit affirmative action. This is, therefore, not a contest between different approaches to implementing the same ideal but rather about the content of the ideal of equality itself: the question is which concept of equality best expresses, and accounts for, the moral and political importance equality holds in the eyes of the contestants. To use Dworkin's terms, it is a typically 'interpretive' concept of value, ie one which lends itself to controversies not merely about 'how important [equality] is or when it should be sacrificed to other values, but what it is'.[11] In other words, the concept of legal equality is not just a neutral baseline upon which substantive controversies arise; disagreement about the very concept of equality, its meaning and parameters, is itself an element of these controversies.

There is a temptation, in this context, to dub legal equality an 'essentially contested concept' with an obvious reference to WB Gallie's classic formulation.[12] This I will resist: Gallie's formula has become, I suspect, more often quoted than seriously studied and, as a result, is sometimes misused by those who would apply it to all vague, controversial, or contested notions.[13] What Gallie had in mind was not only that such concepts are (to use his vocabulary) 'appraisive', but also that they refer to internally complex practices, address multiple parts and features of the practice, are open to modification in light of changing circumstances, and are also capable of being used both aggressively and defensively. These criteria, taken together, still do not mark a distinction between essentially contested

[11] Ronald Dworkin 'Hart's Postscript and the Character of Political Philosophy' at 8. I have substituted the word 'equality' for 'justice' in Dworkin's sentence. Dworkin earlier had undertaken a more elaborate discussion of interpretive concepts in *Law's Empire* at 46–9 and 65–8.

[12] WB Gallie 'Essentially Contested Concepts' *Proceedings of Aristotelian Society* 56 (1956) 167–98.

[13] As is also noted by Waldron: see Jeremy Waldron 'Is the Rule of Law an Essentially Contested Concept (in Florida)?' Law and Philosophy (2002) 21: 137–64 at 148–53.

concepts and those 'which can be shown... to be radically confused'.[14] Gallie added two conditions which any paradigmatically 'essentially contested concepts' must meet: they must be 'derivations... from an original exemplar whose authority is acknowledged by all contestant users of the concept';[15] additionally, continuous competition amongst various usages of the concepts is 'likely to lead to an optimum development of the vague aims and confused achievements' they capture.[16]

To make what is perhaps at this point a premature assertion (because it anticipates this chapter's later argument) I do not believe that the controversies around the understanding of legal equality fulfil the first of these two final conditions. In this sense, equality differs from the examples given by Gallie himself: 'Christian life', Art and Democracy, in that they (in his interpretation) do, indeed, all relate back to a certain original point of reference. But what 'original exemplar' holds together various contestants in the controversies about equality? Perhaps it *could* be said that those controversies all have a certain common *concern* which they try to address in different ways, so that their answers are different solutions to a single question which would play the role of Gallie's 'original exemplar'. But, to put it somewhat flippantly, if equality is an answer, what was the question? It is unlikely that behind those various contested answers in terms of equality there is just one single concern.

Moving along these lines would lead to a considerable watering down of Gallie's notion of 'essential contestation'. Perhaps we should heed Gallie's own warnings against over-extending this category. It is interesting—and not often acknowledged by those using Gallie's category—that Gallie refrained from characterizing the concept of 'social justice' as essentially contested. As Gallie said, such a notion 'suggests a bridge between those appraisive concepts which are variously describable and essentially contested and those whose everyday use appears to be uniquely describable and universally acknowledged'.[17] Equality can be seen as such a bridging concept as well. It occurs as a limited number of variants, and it does not derive in any obvious way from 'an original exemplar', as Gallie's original examples of essentially contested concepts did.

Gallie makes one interesting observation at the end of his essay when he reflects upon some of the consequences of recognizing a concept as 'essentially contested'. An 'optimistic' view would be that, once people realize that a concept about which they disagree is essentially contested, they may in turn recognize that the uses of such concepts by their rivals may be of some 'permanent potential critical value' to their own uses of the concepts, which may later lead to raising the quality of argument. But next Gallie introduces a more pessimistic scenario. If we continue to believe (however mistakenly) that our own use of a concept is the one

14 Gallie 'Essentially Contested Concepts' at 180.
15 ibid at180.
16 ibid at 186.
17 ibid at 187.

that is capable of 'honest and informed approval' by all (hence, is not essentially contestable) we may persist in the hope of persuading opponents of our viewpoint. However, once the essentially contested nature of a concept becomes clear, we may just abandon any effort at persuasion, instead applying non-persuasive means against our opponents.[18] Although often disregarded by enthusiastic supporters of Gallie's category, this sheds an interesting light on what Gallie meant by 'essentially contested concepts', and explains why it would not be helpful to incorporate legal equality, as understood here, into this category. The argument which follows, especially in parts 4 and 5 of this chapter, is offered as one that can be accepted through an 'honest and informed approval' by all who use it. One must not hold on to a naive illusion that this will actually happen; but lack of agreement about the meaning of a concept such as legal equality does not prove that it is *essentially* contestable: it only shows that it is in fact widely contested. The fact of a broad contestation is very unlikely to lead the protagonists of the controversy to abandon all efforts at persuasion and, in Gallie's words, 'to cut the cackle, to damn the heretics and to exterminate the unwanted'.[19]

3. The 'No Differential Treatment' Standard

Before we inquire into whether we can design a standard which will work as a test for equality *in* the law, as opposed to equality *before* the law, that is, one which will help us scrutinize the *substance* of legal rules from the point of view of their congruency with the ideal of equality, we need to consider the temptation of opting for a 'no classifications at all' standard. Some believe that a good legal system that respects the equality of its citizens should not draw any legally relevant distinctions between citizens whatsoever. In his *Social Contract,* Jean-Jacques Rousseau claimed that the laws which truly represent 'the general will' must be such that every legal act 'either obligates or favours all Citizens equally, so that the Sovereign knows only the body of the nation and does not single out any one of those who make it up.... [I]t is never right for the Sovereign to burden one subject more than another. ...'[20] For different reasons,[21] the United States Supreme Court's Justice Jackson expounded a similar instruction to legislators in *Railway Express Agency v New York*: '[T]here is no more effective practical guarantee against arbitrary and unreasonable government than to require that the principles of law which officials would impose upon a minority must be imposed

[18] ibid at 194–5.
[19] ibid at 194.
[20] Jean-Jacques Rousseau 'Of the Social Contract' at 63.
[21] Rousseau's maxim was based on his understanding of the 'general will' as the true expression of popular sovereignty, and on his strong dislike of 'factions' and other intermediary political forms (ie located between an individual and the state). Jackson's maxim is based on purely prudential grounds.

generally'.[22] But this is both an impossible and unattractive ideal. It is impossible because you cannot treat everyone in the same way; 'the same' means the same treatment of the same individuals, and since no individuals are exactly the same in every possible respect (otherwise they would be one and the same individual), the principle of 'the same treatment' means the same treatment of individuals who possess the relevant characteristics to the same degree. The flip side of this is that individuals who do not have the relevant characteristics to the same degree must be treated differently. The 'no-classifications at all' principle is also patently unappealing. Intuitively, we can think of circumstances in which it would be prima facie unfair (and, in an important sense, non-egalitarian) to accord the same treatment to two individuals, regardless of (what we consider to be) relevant differences between them.

The significance of this last point needs to be considered in some detail. The argument against the 'no classifications' precept applies both to the 'holistic' (so to speak) dimension and to the individual rules. In the first dimension, our argument (referred to as Type 1) is opposed to an ideal of *a legal system as a whole* which would, in the name of legal equality, postulate as few classifications as possible. On the level of individual rule (referred to as Type 2), the argument rejects a belief that there is something wrong, even if only prima facie wrong, with differential treatment of the addressees of that particular rule, if legal equality is of value. The latter dimension is more interesting than the former. We usually make our judgments with regard to particular individual rules rather than to the system as a whole. And even if we make holistic judgments about a legal system as a whole for offending the values of legal equality, this is usually because we have a limited number of particular rules in mind that we believe offend against this value, and we do so in the belief that the discrimination resulting from these individual values is of such magnitude that their inegalitarian character contaminates the entire legal system. Moreover, the legal system as a whole can be tainted by discrimination only through the discriminatory character of its individual rules. So it is only if the latter, the individually oriented argument of Type 2 about no prima facie stricture against differential treatment, is correct that a holistic argument of Type 1 against the ideal of 'no classifications' can be justified, and not the other way round. We should therefore focus on the argument of Type 2 and keep in mind that whenever the 'no classifications in the legal system as a whole' ideal is discussed, it is meaningful only as a shorthand for the 'prima facie wrongness of differentiations' of the ideal as applied to individual rules, and only as such should be accepted or (as is the case of the present argument) criticized.

What arguments are there for such an ideal? No doubt, our common intuitions strongly argue for it; in our everyday language we often associate differentiated treatment with unequal treatment, and equality in legal rules is habitually seen as a simple matter of treating everyone by a legal rule in the same way. In the

[22] *Railway Express Agency v New York* 336 US 106 (1949) at 112 (Jackson J concurring).

next part of this chapter I cite some examples of an almost seamless transition, in various legal arguments, from 'classification' to 'discrimination', and as much as we may object to the theoretical coherence of this connection it no doubt enjoys a strong support from widespread moral intuitions and linguistic usages. But (and this may be seen as one major lesson of the argument of this chapter) these intuitions should be resisted and such usages countered: this is one of these cases when moral intuitions are an unreliable source of normative argument and when widespread linguistic usages express rather thoughtless convictions. Or so I wish to argue. If one puts to one side these intuitive convictions (that are, admittedly, in the best of times rather unreliable as a source of a normative argument), one can reconstruct two strategies of building a case for the argument of Type 2 about a prima facie wrongness (from the point of view of the ideal of legal equality) of the differentiation of the treatment of the rule's addressees. A good illustration of both these strategies is the treatment of the legal right to equality by Robert Alexy in his major book on a theory of constitutional rights.

The first strategy is of lesser importance and I will only briefly comment on it, concentrating instead on the second. The strategy relies upon a presumption for an undifferentiated treatment, resulting in the placement of a burden of argument upon the defenders of the differentiation of treatment. In Alexy's book, this emerges in the inter-relations between two precepts which are like two sides of the same coin: (a) 'If there is no adequate reason for permitting an instance of differential treatment, then similar treatment is required', and (b) 'If there is no adequate reason for permitting an instance of similar treatment, then differential treatment is required'.[23] As Alexy observes, if we adopted the second precept we would be understanding the most general equality rule 'treat the same similarly and differences differently' as consisting of two symmetrical prescriptions, but this is (according to Alexy) not so. Such 'symmetry' would avoid placing a burden of the argument on the defenders of either parts of the general rule—which is what Alexy rejects. In tracking the jurisprudence of the German Constitutional Court which had established that an arbitrary differentiation occurs whenever 'a persuasive and reasonable ground...cannot be given for the legal differentiation'[24] Alexy insists upon the burden of the argument being placed on the proponents of a differentiation but not on the advocates of the same treatment. Asymmetry (supported by Alexy) of the two parts of the general precept 'Treat the same similarly and different cases differently' privileges the first part vis-à-vis the second part in the allocation of the burden of argument. To give effect to this asymmetry, Alexy reformulates the precept (b) into (c): 'If there is an adequate reason for requiring differential treatment, then differential treatment is required'. It is clear that this precept has a different structure from the precept (a) in that the precept (a) applying, as it does, to the cases warranting a similar treatment

[23] Alexy *A Theory of Constitutional Rights* at 271.
[24] Quoted ibid at 270 n 34.

does not require its advocates to discharge the burden of the argument that there are indeed reasons for such a similar treatment. Whereas precept (c), applying to differential treatment, accepts differential treatment only when the reason for requiring such a treatment is satisfactorily shown, hence the asymmetry which 'maintains the burden of argumentation in favour of similar treatment'.[25]

But why exactly would we accept this asymmetry, and the resulting privileging for the *same* treatment which then becomes a default position for the observance of the principle of legal equality? The arguments provided by Alexy are strikingly question-begging and even tautological: they are question-begging where the presumption in favour of similar treatment is based on the value of equality (because what precisely is at stake is the meaning of equality when the lawmaker faces a choice between a differentiated and a similar treatment), and they are tautological when equality is defined *in terms* of a privileged position of a similar-treatment option. Arguments in favour of asymmetry hold that, with full symmetry, the principle of equality 'would lose any tendency towards equality',[26] and, whereas the more extended explanation of the rationale of asymmetry holds: 'The asymmetry between similar and differential treatment norms has the consequence that the general principle of equality is indeed a principle of *equality*, which prima facie requires similar treatment and only permits differential treatment if this can be justified by competing reasons'.[27] This passage illustrates the question-begging and tautological nature of the arguments for asymmetry. To say that to preserve the overall equality we need to privilege similar treatment and place the onus on those who demand dissimilar treatment (on the basis that the persons to whom the rules are applied are dissimilarly situated) is to pre-empt *by definition* what is at stake in the normative discussion. Why would, in abstract terms, similar treatment be 'closer' to the ideal of equality prior to knowing how similar or different the persons are with respect to the aims of the rule? There is an undisclosed presumption here that, deep down, equality *is* similarity of treatment and that any departures of similarity of treatment are to be treated with suspicion. This presumption performs an important function and therefore needs to be carefully articulated and defended. It seems to me that such a general articulation is remarkably implausible, and therefore this move from 'classification' to 'discrimination' (or, in Alexy's language, from similarity of treatment to equality) simply will not do.

The second strategy is more challenging. It relies upon a distinction between 'legal equality' which is equated with same treatment, and equality of conditions as a result of the use of legal rules which only comes about through differentiated

[25] ibid at 273.

[26] ibid at 272. The passage from which these words are taken is summarizing the views of another German legal scholar, A Podlech, with whom Alexy partly disagrees, but not in a manner that weakens his view of asymmetry being a condition for maintaining the 'tendency towards equality'.

[27] ibid at 273 (emphasis in original).

treatment with the privileging of the former over the latter. This strategy is also deployed by Alexy in a sophisticated and interesting fashion in his treatment of constitutional rights to equality. He introduces a distinction between similar/differential treatment as applied to acts and as applied to consequences; he assimilates similar treatment as applied to acts ('in common with a widespread usage') with 'legal equal treatment', or legal equality, and differential legal treatment leading to equalisation in circumstances, with 'factual equality'.[28] To put it simply, equality in acts equals legal equality whereas equality in consequences equates to factual equality. Thus defined, legal equality must take some precedence over factual equality, at least as far as the adjudication by a constitutional court (the matter which is the main background for Alexy's considerations) is concerned, although the character of this precedence does not collapse into a simple priority rule. Where there is a conflict of principles of legal equality (that is, similar treatment through legal rules) on the one hand and of promoting factual equality through differentiated legal treatment on the other, Alexy assures us that we do not need to abdicate from legal recognition of any force of the latter; we do not need, for instance, to recognize that the latter is merely 'an unenforceable norm' which may bind the legislature but has no place in judicial scrutiny.[29] Rather, Alexy says, a solution should be 'based on the theory of norms'[30] along the following lines: 'the principle of factual equality plays the role of a reason for a right to a certain instance of legal difference, in particular a legal difference that serves the promotion of factual equality. It gives rise to a subjective right to the promotion of an element of factual equality'.[31]

So far so good: up to this point the characterization of similar legal treatment as the proper site of 'legal equality' seems reasonably innocent because the dissimilar legal treatment, although denied the status of legal equality even if leading to egalitarian consequences, is also elevated to the rank of a 'subjective right', so what is the problem, one might ask? Here is the catch: what the just-mentioned 'subjective right' is a right *to*, is only 'the promotion of an element of factual equality', factual equality is a 'subject matter of a principle' and it is just too bad that, as any principle, it is not a 'definitive but [a] prima facie reason[]'.[32] As such, it 'can be trumped by competing principles', and judging by Alexy's view of the competition between the relevant principles, factual equality is not likely to do all that well in this contest.

This is mainly for two reasons, which are worth considering in some detail here as they are crucial to the whole argument. The first reason is that factual equality (produced, it is recalled, by a differentiated treatment which is the cause of the problem) will necessarily compete with legal equality '*because each legal difference of treatment in pursuit of factual equality is by definition a limitation*

[28] ibid at 276.
[29] ibid at 278.
[30] ibid at 279.
[31] ibid at 280.
[32] ibid at 280.

of the realization of the principle of the principle of legal equality'.[33] The significance of this phrase for the entire argument justifies italicizing it in full: an initially innocent sounding definitional fiat of equating similar treatment (equality in acts) with legal equality now discloses its fundamental normative effect so powerful as to compete with, and most likely prevail over, the differentiated laws aimed at equality. The most fundamental issue in the theory of legal equality (the issue which shows its main force in the case of affirmative action, but not only, of course) is 'resolved' here by definition. That this is precisely what Alexy has in mind is confirmed by a quotation from a German Constitutional Court's judgment which he cites with approval and which he attaches as a footnote to the just-quoted sentence: 'The Federal Constitutional Court has this conflict [of legal equality and factual equality] in mind when it states that "even the social state principle does not authorize every form of social engineering, which would destroy the requirement of equality" '.[34] We now see the price we have to pay for the definitional fiat: if equal legal treatment *is* a similar treatment of persons, then any differentiation is necessarily ('by definition') an infraction of legal equality, and has to be seen as at least prima facie regrettable (if we do indeed respect legal equality, and who doesn't?) But why would we adopt such a significant theory 'by definition'? In fact, this is precisely what we object to when we note (also in this chapter) an objectionable sleight of hand in those arguments which seamlessly move from legal 'classification' to legal 'discrimination'. If legal equality indeed demands a similar treatment (equality 'in acts') then legal classification equals discrimination (even if aimed at 'factual equality'). But if *this* is the true outcome of equating legal equality with similar treatment (equality in acts) then it should be argued about openly rather than imported into the argument through the guise of a definitional convention. And our earlier illustrations of affirmative-action controversies show that such an equation is precisely the central normative proposition which many would reject.

There is also a second argument given by Alexy for the privileging of so-understood legal equality over the principle of 'factual equality': an institutional argument about the respective fields of legitimate authority of a constitutional court and that of the legislature. The entire argument that Alexy develops is informed (as already mentioned) by his analysis of the judgments of the German Constitutional Court in adjudication under the German Constitution's equality clause (Article 3(1) of the Basic Law which provides that 'everyone is equal before the law'), so no wonder that the concern about how far the constitutional judges can go in replacing the legislative choices with their own under this general equality clause is an important factor in the argument. The problem is, to what extent should this institutional concern inform our understanding of the contours of 'legal equality', especially when contrasted in a questionable (as I have just tried

[33] ibid at 281 (emphasis added, footnote omitted).
[34] ibid at 281 n 78.

to show) way to so-called 'factual equality'?[35] According to Alexy, the 'formal principle of the discretion of the democratically legitimated legislature in structuring society is... the second main counter-principle to the principle of factual equality';[36] the second, that is, in addition to the principle of legal equality. Now we see the true and momentous political consequence of a seemingly innocuous 'definitional' convention of identifying the equality of 'acts' with 'legal equality' and equality of 'consequences' with the 'factual' one. The attempt to promote 'factual' equality is now articulated as being oriented towards the 'structuring [of] society', and once characterized in such a way, it is obviously not the domain of a constitutional court, especially if the legislature has different ideas about it. This is accompanied by some quite plausible gestures of judicial restraint vis-à-vis the legislature: in the words of the German Federal Constitutional Court, which Alexy cites with approval, in the domain of equal treatment the legislature has 'a very wide discretion',[37] and in the words of Alexy himself, the subjection of the legislature to the constitutional principle of equality does not 'lead[] to an uncontrolled jurisdiction on the part of the Federal Constitutional Court to impose its values without limit on the legislature'.[38] One such limitation is precisely the privileged status of 'legal equality' over the 'factual equality' in the court's reasoning, with a relatively free range for the legislature to promote 'factual equality' when it so wishes.

But such an institutional gambit, without more, will not do because the members of the legislature themselves also want to know what understanding of equality should guide their actions, and want to know how far they can go in advancing the 'factual equality' to the detriment of 'legal equality'. The question of the degree to which a constitutional court may upset the choices of legislature is secondary as compared to the earlier, conceptual question about where the genuine equality resides when more equal outcome needs to be achieved through a differentiated treatment of unequally situated groups of persons. Once we have characterized such an action as violating 'legal equality' for the sake of the 'factual' one, we have strongly biased our conceptual and normative argument against differentiated treatment. Such a conceptual and normative analysis must operate *across the board*, ie, apply to the legislature, the executive, and the constitutional judiciary alike, and at which point of the making of authoritative decisions each of these branches can enter the stage, and with what force it can replace the choices of a different branch with its own, is a matter which is secondary and external to that conceptualization of legal equality. So the institutional

[35] Note that from now on in my discussion of Alexy I will be consistently considering the term 'factual equality' in inverted commas, not only to signify that it is a quotation from Alexy but also to mark my distance from his use of this concept, distinguished as it is in Alexy's theory from 'legal' equality.

[36] ibid at 281.

[37] ibid at 269, quoting a judgment of the Constitutional Court, BVerfGE 17, 319 (330).

[38] ibid at 274.

argument for privileging legal equality over 'factual equality' cannot be treated as a 'counter-principle' to factual equality, a counter-principle that would operate on the same plane as the counter-principle of legal equality. It is, at best, a veiled form of a political recommendation for a qualified judicial restraint in overturning legislative choices, a recommendation which should come *after* we have already sorted out the relevant competing principles at stake.

To be sure, Alexy does not suggest that in a competition of legal and 'factual' equality, the former principle should always prevail even in the constitutional court's reasoning (much less in the reasoning by a legal theorist). He uses at some length an example of the German Constitutional Court's decision on legal aid which illustrates a triumph of 'factual equality' over the 'legal' one. As Alexy reports, an early case in the line of the court's decisions on legal aid considered whether a refusal to provide legal aid for some procedures, despite a legal requirement for legal representation, breached the constitutional principle of equality before the law.[39] In Alexy's characterization, the regular non-provision of legal aid to all is consistent with equality as applied to 'acts' (hence, legal equality) but inconsistent with equality as applied to 'consequences' (hence, 'factual equality') because the non-provision of legal aid to all would prevent the poor but not the rich from pursuing legal remedies.[40] Alexy approves of this outcome, and justifies it under his conceptual scheme as proof that there may be certain justified instances when 'the principle of factual equality takes priority over competing principles'.[41] So, in the end, the *practical* consequences of contrasting legal equality with 'factual equality' *à la* Alexy may be minimal. But then they may not be; at the same time as depicting the legal aid case as demonstrating the possibility of giving effect to 'factual equality', Alexy cites the opinions which hold that the case was not particularly typical: the application of the constitutional guarantee of access to courts greatly facilitated the identification of the ways in which to achieve 'factual equality' in this case, rendering the case 'relatively straightforward'.[42] On a theoretical level, however, once we distinguish 'legal' and 'factual' equality in the way Alexy does, we stack the cards against the use of differentiated treatment as a perfectly legitimate way of giving effect to legal equality, and we employ a presumption against it in a way which finds no satisfactory rationale in the principle of equality itself.

So much for the 'no classifications' standard of legal equality. Once we have rejected it, we see that the principal task that legal theory faces, as far as equality in the law is concerned, is to identify criteria for legal classifications of individuals which render those classifications discriminatory and thus offensive to the ideal of legal equality. Since *some* classifications of individuals are inescapable (and morally required), it is important to determine the test for non-discriminatory

[39] BVerfGE 2, 336, discussed in Alexy, ibid at 276 and ff.
[40] Alexy, ibid at 276.
[41] ibid at 283.
[42] ibid at 283.

classifications. As a preliminary matter, it is important to realize that the test itself should meet certain conditions.

First, the test should have a 'working' character, that is, it should be capable of being accepted by people regardless of their fundamental substantive views about the overall justness of a given legal regulation. This is for the following reason: if we thought that the requirement of equality in the law collapsed fully into an overall judgment of the 'justness' of a regulation then all our considerations of equality in the law, as the specific normative ideal of law, would be redundant; we might as well talk directly about the requirement that the law be substantively just. However, our conventional discourse suggests that the ideal of equality in the law is narrower and more specific than an ideal of overall justness. It is an 'intermediate' ideal, which is more specific than the substantive ideal of justice, while being more general than the set of particular judgments about particular legal regulations.[43] A 'working' test of nondiscriminatory discrimination should be capable of being accepted by people who are on different sides in disagreements about justice. It does not follow that the test is morally neutral; what does follow is that it is at least possible for two people to agree about the discriminatory character of a given legal classification, while disagreeing, all things considered, about whether the classification is just.

The second condition of a test for non-discriminatory classifications is that it should be relatively independent of the actual views of people to whom it is purported to apply; hence, it should not be fully 'subjective'. Consider a test for equality in the law proposed by Friedrich Hayek which, for brevity, I will call the 'double majority' test.[44] Hayek recognizes that '[t]he requirement that the rules of true law be general does not mean that sometimes special rules may not apply to different classes of people if they refer to properties that only some people possess'.[45] However, '[s]uch distinctions will not be arbitrary, will not subject one group to the will of others, if they are equally recognized as justified by those inside and those outside the group'.[46] Hayek further explains:

> So long as, for instance, the distinction is favored by the majority both inside and outside the group, there is a strong presumption that it serves the ends of both. When, however, only those inside the group favor the distinction, it is clearly privilege; while if only those

[43] I borrow the notion of an 'intermediate ideal' from Joseph Raz, who applies it to assertions of rights; see Joseph Raz *The Morality of Freedom* (Oxford: Oxford University Press 1986) 181.

[44] Friedrich A Hayek *The Constitution of Liberty* (Chicago: Henry Regnery, 1960) 153–4, 209–10. The label 'double majority' is my characterization of Hayek's principle and not his own. It should be also noted that, strictly speaking, Hayek is concerned with a test for the 'generality' of law, rather than for equality. But the context and argument suggest that what Hayek calls 'generality' corresponds to what I call 'equality in the law' in this chapter. At one point, Hayek describes the 'double majority' condition as 'one important requirement' of 'equality before the law' (ibid at 209), the other requirement being the unforeseeability of 'how a law will affect particular people' (ibid at 210).

[45] ibid 154.

[46] ibid 154.

outside favor it, it is discrimination. What constitutes privilege to some is, of course, always discrimination to the rest.[47]

But this will not do. One should realize than under the 'double majority' test, even a perfectly unimpeachable distinction will likely be defeated so long as a group that is defined by a regulation as carrying a particular burden objects to it. Likewise, it will be defeated by the objection of non-beneficiaries. Such views are very likely to be voiced and yet, in our everyday moral habits, they are usually not taken to be *sufficient* evidence that the rule in question is discriminatory. Can we really say that, since the majority of a group picked out by a rule would rather not carry this particular burden, the rule is *for that very reason* discriminatory? What is wrong about Hayek's 'double majority' test is that it makes a finding of discrimination wholly dependent upon whether or not those to whom the rule applies consider it justified. But we must be able to distinguish between a judgment that a rule is discriminatory, and a finding that the majority considers it discriminatory. This is the difference between 'positive' and 'critical' morality, to use an old-fashioned distinction;[48] between, on the one hand, a description of prevailing standards within the community, and a normative judgment, on the other. If we, as citizens, are to draw guidance from a normative theory in shaping our preferences, then the normative theory cannot depend on our prior views about the matter under consideration. If a single citizen is to respond to a question about whether she considers a proposed regulation discriminatory, then her answer must not depend upon how others answer and whether, at the end of the polling, there it receives double majority approval. In this sense, a test for non-discriminatory classifications must be independent of the subjective views of persons to which those classifications apply.

4. 'Per Se' Theories and Immutable Characteristics

The first test that I will consider relies upon a proposition that there are certain criteria of classifications that inevitably and necessarily render the classification discriminatory. In other words, the use of some properties of individuals by legal rules is per se discriminatory when such rules deploy these properties to divide individuals into beneficiaries of the relevant legal benefits (or, conversely, bearers of legal burdens) and those who are not. This is this test's main feature, and for this reason I will be calling it the 'per se test'. One striking fact about the 'per se test' is that it is as widely accepted in legal thinking as it is theoretically implausible. This combination of pervasiveness and philosophical unsoundness is truly puzzling. By far the most popular practical version of a 'per se test' is the concept

[47] ibid 154.
[48] See HLA Hart *Law, Liberty, and Morality* (Oxford: Oxford University Press, 1963) 20.

of 'colour-blindness', a theory suggesting that any classification based on the race of citizens is either presumptively or (in a stronger version) conclusively discriminatory. In United States jurisprudence, the notion of 'colour blindness' was first articulated as a vehicle of protesting invidious discrimination against African-Americans in a famous dissent by Justice Harlan: 'Our Constitution is color-blind, and neither knows nor tolerates classes among citizens.... The law regards man as man, and takes no account of his surroundings or of his color....'.[49] The slogan of 'colour-blindness' persisted, despite the change of context, and was adapted to judicial and jurisprudential objections to affirmative action.[50]

Very similar thoughts can be found in the recent decisions of the US Supreme Court and in particular in two decisions on affirmative action in public university admissions of 2003.[51] In his dissenting opinion in *Grutter*, one of these two cases, Justice Thomas declared that '[t]he Constitution abhors classifications based on race',[52] that the Equal Protection Clause 'prohibit[s]... classifications made on the basis of race',[53] and that 'racial classifications are *per se* harmful'.[54] Even more tellingly, throughout his dissenting opinion Thomas uses the words 'racial classification' interchangeably with 'racial discrimination';[55] a race-based 'classification' also becomes, in his language, 'racial discrimination' which, as he puts it,

[49] *Plessy v Ferguson* 163 US 537 (1896) at 559 (Harlan J dissenting).

[50] For some examples of judicial uses of 'colour blindness', see eg *DeFunis v Odegaard* 416 US 312, 331–4 (1974) (Douglas J dissenting); *Fullilove v Klutznick* 448 US 448, 523 (1980) (Stewart J dissenting). For examples of the uses of colour-blindness in legal scholarship, see eg Alexander M Bickel *The Morality of Consent* (New Haven: Yale University Press, 1975) 132–3; Richard A Epstein 'Affirmative Action for the Next Millenium' Loyola L.Rev. (1998) 43: 503, 504–7.

[51] *Grutter v Bollinger* 539 US 306 (2003) and *Gratz v Bollinger* 539 US 244 (2003). Both originated with the University of Michigan admission programmes, which, if taken together, present a truly Solomonic package: in *Grutter v Bollinger*, the Court narrowly (by five justices to four) upheld the Law School's admission programme; in *Gratz v Bollinger* the Court, on the same day, and with multiple cross-references to its companion case, struck down as unconstitutional (by six to three) a somewhat different affirmative-action system for undergraduate selection. The criteria by which the cases were distinguished, and which were crucial to the two admission systems' upholding or invalidation concerned, first, the degree to which each selection programme, respectively, was 'individualized'; secondly, the role of an applicant's status as a member of a given racial group in the decision to admit (in particular, whether such membership was only one among many *indicia* of diversity, and whether or not it could have been a 'decisive' factor in the student's admission); and lastly, and perhaps most importantly, about how 'narrowly tailored' a given system was to attaining a compelling purpose of diversity of a student body.

[52] *Grutter* at 353 (Thomas J dissenting).

[53] ibid at 368.

[54] ibid at 371.

[55] See eg the following passage, in which Thomas J contrasts two types of departures from 'meritocracy' in university admissions: so-called 'legacy preferences', under which the children of alumni may be given preferences, and race-conscious preferences for members of under-represented minorities: 'What the Equal Protection Clause does prohibit are *classifications* made on the basis of race. So while legacy preferences can stand under the Constitution, racial *discrimination* cannot. I will not twist the Constitution to invalidate legacy preferences.... The majority should similarly stay its impulse to validate faddish racial *discrimination* the Constitution clearly forbids', *Grutter*, at 368 (Thomas J dissenting) (footnote omitted, emphases added). What is merely a 'classification' in the first sentence, becomes 'discrimination' in the second and third.

'the Constitution clearly forbids'.[56] This restatement of 'colour blindness' appearing in Thomas's dissent culminates with the approving citation, by Thomas, of Harlan's 'colour blindness' dictum in the latter's *Plessy* dissent.[57] However, these two statements are separated by 97 years, during which all formal legal racial discrimination in the United States was abolished. Harlan's dissent attached to a judgment upholding racial segregation in public transport;[58] Thomas's dissent to a decision to uphold a public university's admissions programme that aimed at enrolling as students a 'critical mass' of members of under-represented minority groups, including African-Americans, Hispanics, and Native Americans. Yet the maxim *seems* to be exactly the same, in the implication that it is the very use of race (or colour) which is per se discriminatory, not the purpose for which this characteristic of individuals is invoked by a legal rule or, alternatively, the relationship between the property of race and the evil that the law purports to address.

Of course, the colour-blindness version of a 'per se theory' of non-discriminatory classifications is not confined to American jurisprudence nor is it unopposed within American judicial thinking on equality and discrimination.[59] In an important decision of the Australian High Court concerning the legality of a particular provision of a state law which restricted access of non-Aboriginal people to Aboriginal land, the then Chief Justice Gibbs stated bluntly: 'Speaking broadly, that subsection [of the Racial Discrimination Act] deals with acts of racial discrimination, i.e. with acts which make a distinction on racial grounds'.[60] It is the 'i.e.' which is truly problematic here: racial *discrimination* is simply equated with a *distinction* on racial grounds. To emphasize this point, Gibbs provided a hypothetical reversal of a situation created by the above rule: 'I see no distinction between the effects of [the provisions of the state act under challenge, which allowed exclusion of non-Aborigines], and that of a law which provided as

[56] ibid.

[57] ibid at 378 (Thomas J dissenting).

[58] In *Plessy v Ferguson* the Supreme Court upheld a 1890 Louisiana statute requiring railroads to provide 'equal but separate accommodations for the white and coloured races', and barred persons from occupying rail cars other than those assigned to their race, 163 US 537–8.

[59] '[R]acial classifications are not *per se* invalid under the Fourteenth Amendment', *University of California v Bakke* 438 US 265 (1978) at 356 (Brennan, White, Marshall, Blackmun JJ, concurring in part and dissenting in part); see also ibid at 407 (Blackmun J concurring in part and dissenting in part) ('In order to get beyond racism, we must first take account of race'). Actually, the 'colour blindness' theory has never become the law in the United States; see *Fullilove* (n 62 below) at 482 ('we reject the contention that in the remedial context the Congress must act in a wholly "color-blind" fashion').

[60] *Gerhardy v Brown*, 59 ALJR 311, 315 (1985) (Austl). The 'subsection' to which Chief Justice Gibbs refers in this sentence is s9(1) of the Racial Discrimination Act 1975 (Austl) which reads: 'It is unlawful for a person to do any act involving a distinction, exclusion, restriction or preference based on race, colour, descent or national or ethnic origin which has the purpose of nullifying or impairing the recognition, enjoyment or exercise, on an equal footing, of any human right or fundamental freedom in the political, economic, social, cultural or any other field of public life'. For a detailed analysis and critique of this decision, see Wojciech Sadurski 'Gerhardy v Brown v the Concept of Discrimination: Reflections on the Landmark Case that Wasn't' Sydney L. Rev. (1986) 11: 5–43.

follows: white men and women who are traditional owners of land in a particular town have unrestricted rights of access to that town; no-one else may enter it without their permission'.[61] The reversal of black/white roles serves as a rhetorical amplification of the point that it is the very use of race (*whatever* race) which is the *indicium* of the discriminatory character of the law in question, and that it is the racial distinction per se that taints the law as discriminatory.

To see more clearly what is wrong with the colour-blindness maxim, it is useful to invoke one further statement of it, this time, in a dissent by Justice Stewart in *Fullilove v Klutznick*,[62] a US Supreme Court decision upholding certain state government preferences for minority business enterprises. Stewart (joined by Justice Rehnquist) restated the maxim by saying: 'under our Constitution, any official action that treats a person differently on account of his race or ethnic origin is inherently suspect and presumptively invalid'.[63] Stewart goes on to formulate 'one clear lesson' to be drawn from the 'history' of the Supreme Court's treatment of racial classifications, 'under our Constitution, the government may never act to the detriment of a person solely because of that person's race'.[64] This is followed by an important sentence which brings us as close as we get in Stewart's dissent—and in the whole American equal-protection jurisprudence—to the rationale offered for colour-blindness: 'The color of a person's skin and the country of his origin are immutable facts that bear no relation to ability, disadvantage, moral culpability, or any other characteristics of constitutionally permissible interest to government'.[65]

At first blush, there is something puzzling about this sentence: it consists of two parts, one of which is true but banal and the other, interesting but patently untrue. True and banal is the characterization of colour (alongside country of origin) as immutable characteristics. The second part of the sentence lists a number of factors potentially 'of... interest to government', hence, which *can be* grounds for the conferral of benefits or imposition of burdens upon individuals but none of which, in Stewart's view, is related to one's skin colour or country of origin. This is patently untrue, at least as concerns one of the factors enumerated, namely 'disadvantage'. In many places and times in history, both skin colour and country of origin have influenced, if not determined, social advantage and disadvantage. Much of the majority's argument in *Fullilove* hinges upon the fact that Congress could reasonably adopt a special set-aside for minority business enterprises because 'minority businesses have been denied effective participation in public contracting opportunities by procurement practices that perpetuated the effects of prior discrimination'.[66] The majority's argument relies on a view that, when prior discrimination was based

[61] 59 ALJR at 317.
[62] *Fullilove v Klutznick* 448 US 448 (1980).
[63] ibid at 523 (Stewart J dissenting) (citations omitted).
[64] ibid at 525 (footnote omitted).
[65] ibid at 525.
[66] ibid at 477–8 (Burger CJ delivering the opinion of the court).

on racial grounds, 'disadvantage' *was* determined by one's race; hence, 'a person's skin' bears a clear relation to that person's 'disadvantage', contrary to Stewart's explicit statement. For his part, Stewart could of course take issue with the majority's premise in various ways, for example, by pointing out (what he could consider to be) the regulation's over- or under-inclusiveness, or the weakness of empirical findings concerning past disadvantage. But instead he chooses to advance a general principle: not that, *in this particular case,* beneficiaries' skin colour bears no proper relation to the disadvantage targeted by the proposed law, but rather, that 'the color of a person's skin' is *in general* unrelated to disadvantage.

Why should Stewart choose to pronounce, with such confidence, a proposition that so obviously flies in the face of social experience? We need to recognize that most of the work in Stewart's argument is done by the word 'immutable': 'The color of a person's skin and the country of his origin are *immutable* facts that bear no relation to ... any ... characteristics of constitutionally permissible interest to government'.[67] Putting proper emphasis on 'immutable', Stewart's proposition ceases to be an obviously false statement concerning empirical correlations of individual characteristics with disadvantage, and can be read, instead, as a purely *normative* thesis about which characteristics must never be relied on by governmental regulations. That is why 'colour', for Stewart, is accompanied by mention of 'the country of origin', preparing the ground for a citation from *Hirabayashi*[68] which follows immediately after the sentence I have so far been interpreting: 'Distinctions between citizens solely because of their ancestry are by their very nature odious to a free people whose institutions are founded upon the doctrine of equality'.[69] Note that the *Hirabayashi* court does *not* mention 'immutability' in this context. Stewart, however, establishes the link between race and country of origin by claiming, for the former, the same presumptive illegality already established in *Hirabayashi* for the latter—the relevant similarity being that both these factors are equally 'immutable'. In this context, Stewart's must be seen as a purely normative principle. The citation from *Hirabayashi* does not attempt to establish any empirical relation between a property of an individual (ancestry) and factors of permissible interest to government, such as disadvantage, but rather states a rule that classifications based on ancestry are discriminatory per se. This is the principle that Stewart extends to the other immutable characteristic, namely, skin colour. Canadian legal theorist JC Smith expressed the same principle in more abstract terms: 'No rule may differentiate between people in terms of properties the possession of which is immediately knowable and determinate at birth for every person, and which are never after subject to change for the persons possessing them'.[70]

[67] ibid at 525 (Stewart J dissenting) (emphasis added).

[68] *Hirabayashi v United States* 320 US 81 (1943).

[69] ibid at 100, quoted in *Fullilove* (n 62 above) at 525 (Stewart J dissenting).

[70] JC Smith *Legal Obligation* (London: The Athlone Press, 1976) 124. Smith further makes clear that what really matters is a person's capacity to change his or her group membership, and

The salient question at this point is, what is it about 'immutability' per se that makes a characteristic an impermissible basis for legal classification? We have moved from a very specific level (enumeration of some particular 'impermissible' characteristics, such as colour and ancestry) to a more general level (identification of their common trait, namely immutability) so now we need a theory that would explain the wrongness of classifications based on *any* immutable properties of individuals. For, obviously, there are many other characteristics which are immutable, and yet which do not strike us as rendering a classification necessarily discriminatory: eg the characteristics of physical health in recruitment to the army, intelligence in admission to university, beauty in the selection of catwalk models etc. Vice versa, we can also identify a great number of classifications based on characteristics which are perfectly 'mutable' (such as wealth) and yet which figure as classifying criteria in clearly discriminatory laws (for example, property qualifications for voting eligibility in general elections). The general proposition that the very fact of immutability, as such, renders a classification discriminatory is so incongruent with our intuitive judgments about which laws are discriminatory and which are not, that it requires a particularly convincing moral theory to support it.

However, it is very difficult to find an explicit moral justification for hostility to classifications based on immutable characteristics; antipathy to them usually arises without argument. One has therefore to reconstruct this theory, in trying to find the best possible backing for the thesis that it is presumptively wrong for the law to classify people along the lines of immutable characteristics. The most obvious justification that springs to mind is connected to an intuitive feeling that there is something particularly unfair in categorizing and selecting people on the basis of characteristics beyond their own control. The general intuition can be made more specific in two ways. In the first instance, we can say that immutable characteristics are, by their very nature, much more tightly linked to individual *identity* than are the alterable characteristics which are more defining of a person's changeable *roles* in society. Under this argument, 'immutability' is just a proxy for identity-defining characteristics. Yet, unless this equivalence is a matter of definition, which would make the argument circular, it is a very imperfect proxy for identity. There are some characteristics which are immutable but which do not define anything particularly significant about individual identity (for example, freckles on one's skin); there are also characteristics which *may* be highly defining, but which are alterable (for example, membership of a political party). But even if immutability did properly capture identity-constituting characteristics, it would still be question-begging to say that legal classifications

thus to become (or cease to be) an addressee of a norm: 'It is only a law limited solely in terms of a property determined at or by birth, such that a person can neither choose nor change it, which offends the principle of equality before the law by excluding a determined class from the domain of the rule... Differentiations between persons must take place in terms of actions and events rather than the properties of personal and group identification.' ibid at 124–5.

based on identity-defining characteristics are necessarily more suspect than those based on more contingent properties. Presumably, this argument would have something to do with the perceived dangers of 'identity politics' where rights and burdens granted on the basis of group identity may be seen, for instance, as leading to balkanisation and division in society.[71] Notwithstanding, as stated, this argument is much too vague and contingent to amount to a solid case against such classifications.

A second (and better) reason why one might consider 'immutability' as a suspicious criterion of legal classification is the unfairness of imposing legal burdens upon individuals when defined by criteria which do not allow them, as bearers of those burdens, any opportunity to get rid of those burdens (by escaping the burdened group). This was one of the reasons why Brennan J, in his concurring opinion in *Bakke,* would have applied 'intermediate' rather than simple, rational-basis scrutiny, to classifications based on race, gender, and illegitimacy.[72] Each of these properties, Brennan J explained, 'is an immutable characteristic which its possessors are powerless to escape or set aside'[73] adding that 'such divisions are contrary to our deep belief that "legal burdens should bear some relationship to individual responsibility or wrongdoing" '.[74] The key feature disqualifying immutable characteristics as a basis for legal classifications, therefore, is that individuals so classified cannot, through acts of their own volition, *escape* burdensome classifications. Yet, just articulating this reason is sufficient to discredit it. It is analogous to an argument that hate speech addressed against a racial minority would be less harmful if members of that minority could easily change their skin colour. Heightened protection against discrimination (and likewise against insult) should not be contingent upon the inescapability of a protected category. Consider the case of discrimination (or, in a parallel argument, offensive speech) against gay men and lesbians. Would it make any difference to the wrongness of the discrimination (or the offence) if we found a strong empirical confirmation that sexual orientation is an inborn characteristic, rather than a freely chosen 'lifestyle'? Corollary to the view that 'alterability' of sexual orientation should lessen protection against homophobic discrimination is the argument that gay men and lesbians may easily avoid discrimination by changing their sexual orientation to

[71] For a depiction of the dangers of granting rights based on group identity, see Claus Offe ' "Homogeneity" and Constitutional Democracy: Coping with Identity Conflicts through Group Rights' *Journal of Political Philosophy* (1998) 6: 113–41 at 124–39.

[72] *Bakke* (n 59 above) at 360–2 (1978) (Brennan, White, Marshall, and Blackmun JJ concurring in part and dissenting in part). It is important to emphasize that Brennan J is not a proponent of the per se illegality of race-based classifications; indeed, the burden of his argument is to support race-conscious remedial regulations, such as the one under challenge in *Bakke.* However, the context of the argument from which the citations in the main text are taken is the justification of a stricter than usual scrutiny of race-conscious classifications (ie intermediate scrutiny); this argument is preceded by another which shows why remedial racial classifications should not trigger strict scrutiny, which would be likely to invalidate the classification under challenge; see ibid at 356–8.

[73] ibid at 360.

[74] ibid at 360–1, quoting *Weber v Aetna Casualty & Surety Co*, 406 US 164, 175 (1972).

a heterosexual one, and so no heightened protection—reserved for 'truly immutable' characteristics—is warranted. But this argument collapses, because the central question is whether it is *fair* for a society to impose a penalty (in the form of lower protection against discrimination) upon members of a group who do not renounce the relevant conduct, values, or set of beliefs.

The immutability criterion's weakness is equally obvious in considering religious groups. Religion is usually listed, along with race, as one of those characteristics which should be banned from serving as a basis for legal classifications of citizens.[75] Superficially, it could be a counter-argument to the 'immutability' theory because, while religion is certainly viewed as constitutive of personal identity, and to a very high degree, there is nothing 'immutable' about it. Perhaps, however, the immutability argument should be split into one of 'entry' and 'exit' points: it *might* be claimed that, while we all have the opportunity to abandon a particular religion ('exit'), we do not 'enter' religions voluntarily, rather being born into them. But this is obviously untrue in a great number of cases: for non-believers who at a certain stage of their life discover a religious truth for themselves, or for those who convert from one faith to another. Why should those people whose religious affiliation was *not* a matter of conscious choice enjoy a higher level of protection against discrimination? Such a suggestion could only be justified by identifying the involuntariness of a given characteristic (lifestyle, beliefs, preferences, etc) with depth of commitment. This is patently implausible. On the contrary, it would seem that we are often *more* committed to those values, relationships, and lifestyles which we have chosen voluntarily or, at least, to those which we *can* abandon but prefer to retain, notwithstanding a feasible exit option. So, the immutability argument seems at odds with the 'constitution of identity' argument, if depth, or strength, of commitment is seen (as it should be) as indicative of those characteristics defining a person's identity to a very high degree.

The example of religion also suggests that the very act of drawing a line between immutable and mutable characteristics, and then characterizing a given property as falling on one or the other side of the line, is not neutral towards members of a group defined by this property. Whether you believe religion to be an immutable or mutable characteristic depends to a large extent on whether you are religious or not: secular liberals tend to describe religion as an 'alterable' characteristic which

[75] See eg *Edwards v California* 314 US 160, 185 (1941) (Jackson J concurring) (describing 'race, creed or color' as constitutionally irrelevant). Title VII of the US Civil Rights Act of 1964 prohibits discrimination based on 'race, color, religion, sex, or national origin' in employment 42 USC § 2000e–2(a) (1982). The Canadian Charter of Rights and Freedoms prohibits discrimination based, in particular, on 'race, national or ethnic origin, colour, religion, sex, age or mental or physical disability', s 15(1). See also Universal Declaration of Human Rights art 2 (1984) (no distinction of any kind based on, inter alia, religion; American Declaration of the Rights and Duties of Man art 11 (1948) (no distinction as to, inter alia, creed); Council of Europe 1950 Convention for the Protection of Human Rights and Fundamental Freedoms art 14 (no discrimination based on, inter alia, religion).

can be affected by a person's choice, while those with a religious outlook complain that such an approach trivializes and distorts the nature of religious commitments. According to Michael Sandel, a liberal approach 'depreciates the claims of those for whom religion is not an expression of autonomy but a matter of conviction unrelated to choice' and fails 'to respect persons bound by duties derived from sources other than themselves'.[76] Perhaps there is a tendency (although by no means universal) for adherents of a given set of beliefs, values, and commitments, to perceive them as not having been freely chosen, not being 'mere preferences', and not capable of being discarded through an act of free will. Indeed, in the passage just quoted, Sandel further complains that a liberal approach to religion (linking religion with the exercise of free choice) 'may miss the role that religion plays in the lives of those for whom the observance of religious duties is a constitutive end, essential to their good and indispensable to their identity'.[77] If any group's self-awareness is positively built upon a sense of originating from something other than free choice then any attempt by the law to classify some characteristics as 'immutable' and others as 'alterable' is non-neutral between groups characterized by immutable characteristics and those who are not. If, as the case of religion shows, there is a link in people's minds between recognition of the strength of a commitment and characterization of a commitment as unrelated to choice, then a legal characterization of some properties as immutable is parasitic upon a judgment about the depth, strength, sincerity, and significance of the given belief or commitment. As a result, not much remains of 'immutability' as such—it merely becomes a vehicle for disguised distinction between beliefs which the government respects to a greater extent, and those which it respects less, and to which it thus accords lower legal protection against discrimination.

The upshot is that the 'immutability' of a characteristic is, in itself, neither a sufficient nor a necessary condition of the discriminatory nature of a classification based on that characteristic. There are classifications based on 'alterable' characteristics that are manifestly discriminatory, and classifications based on 'immutable' characteristics that are perfectly unobjectionable. But the lessons to be drawn from the above discussion are not limited to 'immutable' characteristics. It is impossible to identify *any* characteristic which inevitably implies that a classification based upon it violates the principle of legal equality. In this sense, the argument against 'immutability' as a test for discrimination is meant to serve as an argument against the whole 'per se' family of tests of non-discriminatory classifications. And yet, so far, I have proceeded as if the only prima facie plausible rationale for a 'per se theory', in particular in its colour-blindness version, was the immutability of grounds of prohibited classifications. But is it the only, or the only plausible, rationale for any 'per se' theory? Naturally, the answer here

[76] Michael J Sandel 'Freedom of Conscience or Freedom of Choice?' in JD Hunter and O Guinness (eds) *Articles of Faith, Articles of Peace: The Religion Liberty Clauses and the American Public Philosophy* (Washington: Brookings Institution, 1990) 74–92 at 89.

[77] ibid at 89.

is no and, insofar as there may be other rationales for such theories, the argument thus far against a per se approach may be seen as inconclusive. As a result, in concluding this section of the chapter, we need to contemplate the other candidates for such a rationale.

A good place to start looking for such a rationale is the two 2003 affirmative action cases which I have already mentioned, *Grutter* and *Gratz*,[78] because it was precisely in these decisions that a strong connection between race-based classifications (an indicium of a 'per se theory') and strict scrutiny (which brings us close to outright prohibition) was made. Indeed, majority judgments (O'Connor J in *Grutter*; Rehnquist J in *Gratz*) in both these cases begin with, and use as an organizing principle for the argument that follows, a restatement of the current doctrine of the US Supreme Court that all racial classifications must be reviewed under strict scrutiny.[79] And yet, there is precious little in either opinion by way of defence and justification of this link, despite its central importance in each case. Certainly, the justices now endorsing this link can be partly excused for omitting a justificatory theory on grounds that the principle can be plausibly depicted as an established, authoritative doctrine of the court, going back at least to Powell J's opinion in *Bakke*, and reinforced by equal-protection decisions ever since. From our perspective, however, this misses the point because our aim is to reconstruct such a justificatory theory from the ('per se' theory's) judicial endorsements.

The majority decision in *Grutter* lacks any such justificatory theory, directly or indirectly expressed the view that all racial classifications should trigger strict scrutiny is asserted, not argued for. So too Chief Justice Rehnquist's majority opinion in *Gratz*—although perhaps he nears a hint at justification, in quickly supplementing his assertion of strict scrutiny of racial classifications with an emphasis (attributed, with approval, to Powell J in *Bakke*) on 'considering each particular applicant as an individual, assessing all the qualities that individual possesses . . .'.[80] Implicit, here, would be the theory that a race-based classification is inherently anti-individualistic and that it considers persons only as members of larger classes rather than in their own right. But this will not do, because classifications based on properties such as *race* are still not distinguishable in any meaningful way from any other classification, based on different types of individual properties, which also create classes of individuals from the point of view of that rule. In other words, Rehnquist J's approach does not identify what it is that makes race qualitatively different, so that race-based classifications must be treated with greater suspicion than any other legal categories. And, if the reason is that race (and few other characteristics) is more 'group-defining', in that it is less apt to

[78] *Grutter v Bollinger* 539 US 306 (2003); *Gratz v Bollinger* 539 US 244 (2003).

[79] *Grutter* at 326; *Gratz* at 270.

[80] *Gratz* at 271.

be changed by individual action, then we have arrived back at the immutability theory.

Perhaps better attempts at justification are to be found in the dissenting opinions. In *Grutter*, Thomas and Kennedy JJ each devote considerable attention to the question of the standard of review. In a rare attempt explicitly to justify his antipathy for all racial classifications, Thomas J states: 'The Constitution abhors classifications based on race, not only because those classifications can harm favored races or are based on illegitimate motives, but also because every time the government places citizens on racial registers and makes race relevant to the provision of burdens or benefits, it demeans us all'.[81] This sentence holds the nuclei of three distinct arguments: that racial classifications may be detrimental to their purported beneficiaries; that they are (note, 'are', rather than 'may be') based on illegitimate motives; and that they 'demean us all'. The third is a purely rhetorical claim unsupported by further argument;[82] the second is neither explained nor accompanied by further argument elsewhere in the dissent; the first, however, is developed at greater length. Later, Thomas J makes the general announcement that 'racial classifications are *per se* harmful',[83] and attempts to show that race-conscious preferences for minority applicants are harmful to minorities themselves—because those admitted as a result of racial preference are relatively unprepared and, therefore, will necessarily 'under-perform' (requiring continued racial preference, throughout the years of study and at the hiring stage), and also because it generates doubt vis-à-vis minority students who would have been admitted without racial preference.[84] Hence, racial preference creates the 'problem of stigma', and a 'badge of inferiority' that tars all members of a preferred group.[85]

I do not need here to go into the merits of these arguments; for present purposes, all that matters is that they are purely contingent, hinging on empirical findings and, as such, cannot serve to justify universal hostility towards racial classifications per se. A system of preferential admissions *may* produce a phenomenon of stigma; equally, however, a very low number of minority students (in the absence of a system of preferences) may stigmatize minority members even further by reinforcing the stereotype that members of these minorities are not qualified to study at elite professional schools. It may well be that any phenomenon of stigma will be more than offset by real advantages derived by minority students from an opportunity to access such studies, and, on balance, will be seen as

[81] *Grutter* at 353 (Thomas J dissenting).

[82] The sentence quoted is followed immediately by a quotation from Thomas J's concurrence in *Adarand Constructors Inc v Pena* 515 US 200 (1995) which announces, without more, that racial classifications 'have a destructive impact on the individual and our society', *Grutter*, at 353 (Thomas, J dissenting, quoting *Adarand* at 240, Thomas J concurring in part and concurring in judgment).

[83] *Grutter* at 371 (Thomas J dissenting).

[84] ibid 372–73.

[85] ibid 373.

worth suffering, for the sake of the overall benefits the system brings. Girardeau Spann has put it nicely: 'One is better off having resources than being thought well of while continuing to languish in a perpetual underclass.'[86] After all, if minorities experienced preferential admissions as bringing *disadvantage*, rather than benefits, one would expect minority groups, organizations, and leaders to protest strongly against such preferences and, notwithstanding some individual African-American scholars' and writers' opposition to affirmative action,[87] it is not the case that minority groups *en masse* are rejecting such programmes: if anything, the reverse seems to be true. In such circumstances, it is hard to see why the Supreme Court (even by the mouth of its only African-American member) should be announcing to minorities what is truly in their best interest. Thomas J's arguments fail to explain why it would be the case that any legal classification drawn in terms of race will necessarily or always disadvantage those individuals whom the policy behind such a classification attempts to benefit and, crucially, what especially distinguishes race from all other criteria of legal classification so as to produce such perverse consequences.

One other dissenting opinion in *Grutter* offers an explicit explanation as to why any racial classification, regardless of its aim, should be strictly scrutinized by the courts. After deploring the majority's failure, in his view, properly to apply strict scrutiny, Kennedy J recounts the history, post-*Bakke*, of judicial affirmations of 'the absolute necessity of strict scrutiny when the state uses race as an operative category',[88] offering this explanation: 'Preferment by race, when resorted to by the State, can be the most divisive of all policies, containing within it the potential to destroy confidence in the Constitution and in the idea of equality.'[89] But 'confidence in the Constitution' and in 'the idea of equality' will be undermined only if it turns out that race-based classifications are necessarily and inherently unconstitutional and contrary to the principle of equal protection of the laws—precisely the issue in debate. If, *arguendo*, race-based classifications can be, under some circumstances, warranted by the Constitution then confidence in the Constitution will be undermined by *rejection* rather than acceptance of race-conscious affirmative action by the State. Inconsistency with the Constitution cannot at the same time figure as the premise and conclusion of the argument—as it does in the passage just quoted. 'Divisiveness', to which Kennedy J refers, will be a morally weighty argument only if the reasons for the disapproval of race-conscious affirmative action are based on good constitutional arguments. Otherwise, any state action which benefits or burdens a particular group (racial or otherwise) may be 'divisive', in the sense that its non-beneficiaries may resent

[86] Girardeau A Spann 'The Dark Side of Grutter' *Constitutional Commentary* (2004) 21: 221–50 at 238.

[87] eg Thomas Sowell *Affirmative Action Around the World: A Comparative Study* (New Haven: Yale University Press, 2004).

[88] *Grutter* at 388 (Kennedy J dissenting).

[89] ibid 388.

it; just as school desegregation could be seen as 'divisive', for raising the ire of segregationists. 'Divisiveness', without more, carries no moral or constitutional weight. Indeed, that legislators are not entitled to track the patterns of unreasonable prejudices and social animus, even if the interest in public peace and harmony would, superficially, argue for the policy of placating racists, is a principle long established by the US Supreme Court[90]—and it is precisely this principle that withdraws all moral and constitutional significance from Kennedy J's 'divisiveness' argument: either 'preferment by race' is constitutional, and whether it is divisive or not is immaterial, or racial preference is unconstitutional, and the policy has to be struck down, divisive or not.

For the sake of completeness, one last attempt to justify strict scrutiny should be mentioned, as potentially helping to clarify the status of race and other 'immutable characteristics', under a plausible theory of judicial review of equality-related regulations. In the same year that *Grutter* and *Gratz* were decided, the US Supreme Court also handed down the momentous decision, *Lawrence v Texas*,[91] in which it struck down a Texas penal provision prohibiting private homosexual conduct even between consenting adults. In her separate opinion, O'Connor J described in the following way the determinants of the level of scrutiny under the Equal Protection Clause:

> Laws such as economic or tax legislation that are scrutinized under rational basis review normally pass constitutional muster, since 'the Constitution presumes that even improvident decisions will eventually be rectified by the democratic processes'. We have consistently held, however, that some objectives, such as 'a bare... desire to harm a politically unpopular group', are not legitimate state interests. When a law exhibits such *a desire to harm a politically unpopular group*, we have applied a more searching form of rational basis review to strike down such laws under the Equal Protection Clause.[92]

Here is a theory behind stricter scrutiny completely different to, and much more attractive than, a 'per se theory'. Even if the first part of the proposition by O'Connor J (that deferential scrutiny is justified by the ease of legislative revision of a challenged law) is implausible, as Robert Post has rightly noted,[93] the second part is sensible: a legislative desire to harm an unpopular group calls for a more exacting scrutiny. This stricter scrutiny may, but does not have to, be justified, *á la* John Hart Ely,[94] by the difficulties faced by unpopular minorities in trying to amend statute through normal democratic processes (as 'unpopular', they will find it difficult to co-opt other groups to form majority alliances capable of

[90] See eg *Palmore v Sidoti* 466 US 429 (1984).

[91] 539 US 558 (2003).

[92] ibid at 579–80 (citations omitted) (O'Connor J concurring in the judgment) quoting *Cleburne v Cleburne Living Ctr* 473 US 432, 440 (1985) and *US Dept of Agriculture v Moreno* 413 US 677, 686 (1973) (emphasis added).

[93] Richard C Post 'The Supreme Court, 2002 Term: Foreword: Fashioning the Legal Constitution: Culture, Courts, and the Law', Harv. L. Rev. (2003) 117: 4 at 51.

[94] John Hart Ely *Democracy and Distrust* (Cambridge, Mass: Harvard University Press, 1980).

democratic reversals). The ease of legislative reversal is a speculative and *ex ante* unverifiable criterion, and in any event, why should courts tolerate a blatantly discriminatory provision even if there is some hope that, some time in future, the provision will be struck down? What about the victims who suffer discrimination in the meantime? However, a case for stricter scrutiny *can* be made here, directly and straightforwardly, by reference to a particularly important right at risk, namely 'the right not to be harmed merely because one belongs to an unpopular group'.[95] One may claim that, notwithstanding the perspective of legislative reversal, such laws, once passed, must be seen with suspicion and hostility, and deference to law-makers in these cases is unfounded. But of course, the very exposition of the theory behind this argument for strict judicial review immediately reveals it as being very far from any 'per se theory', such as colour blindness, or gender blindness, or any other immutable-characteristic-blindness. The operative words in the conception encapsulated in the last quoted passage from O'Connor J are 'desire to harm'. It is the 'desire to harm a politically unpopular group' which calls for a suspicion; not the desire to benefit, nor the desire to classify in any other way which cannot be captured by the word 'harm'. The purpose of a classification is, under this theory, as important as the nature of the group picked out by the law. It is, therefore, the inverse of any 'per se theory'.

5. Relevance, Circularity, and Levels of Scrutiny

A critique of 'per se' theories leads to a positive alternative candidate for a test of non-discriminatory classifications. What was wrong with 'per se theory' was that, as a matter of principle, it disregarded any link between a classification and its purpose. In contrast, the relevance-oriented theory identifies this link as the main benchmark for judging whether a given classification is discriminatory or not: non-discriminatory classifications are those that differentiate among individuals in terms germane to the acceptable purposes of legislation. Yet the test's apparent simplicity is deceptive. Given inevitable uncertainties about legislation's specific purpose, there is a temptation to infer its objectives from the terms of legislation itself, hence from the classification, in which case the whole exercise becomes circular. Suppose a critic of legislation claims that the classification, C-1, is not rationally related to the purpose of the legislation, P-1. A supporter of the legislation might respond that it is not the case that P-1 was the only purpose of the legislation, or even *a* purpose of legislation. After all, legal acts do not always parade their purposes on the face of their texts and, in any event, legal acts usually target a number of purposes, attempting to attain them to varying degree. The very fact that the legislator has used classification C-1, the defender of the

[95] Post 'The Supreme Court, 2002 Term: Foreword: Fashioning the Legal Constitution: Culture, Courts, and the Law' at 51.

statute might say, suggests the desire to achieve an aggregate of purposes P-1, P-2, and P-3, with P-2 and P-3 being in a more satisfactory relationship to C-1 than P-1 was. If those purposes are inferred from the classification used by the legislator, there can, however, be *no* circumstances in which any legislation can ever be criticized as violating the relevance test. As noted by Terrance Sandalow, in his classic article:

> The potential multiplicity of legislative objectives means that it will always be possible to draw from the terms of a statute legislative purposes to which the statutory classification is rationally related. The burdens or benefits created by a statute suggest at the very least a purpose to burden or benefit all those who share the classifying characteristic. The statutory classification must be rationally related to that purpose because the purpose has been derived from the classification.[96]

Schlesinger v Ballard,[97] a 1974 US Supreme Court decision, usefully illustrates the danger of such circularity, as well as the route to overcoming it. Under challenge was a differential promotion system for men and for women in the United States Navy. More stringent criteria applied to men (a male officer who twice failed to be selected for promotion was subject to mandatory discharge) resulting in different periods of tenure for male and female officers. One male officer challenged this classification as discriminatory. Stewart J, writing the majority opinion, disagreed with the petitioner's argument, finding instead the different situations of male and female officers relevant to the purpose of the statute under challenge. Male and female line officers in the Navy were 'not similarly situated with respect to opportunities for professional service'[98] because of restrictions on female participation in combat duty. It was, therefore, rational for Congress to believe that 'women line officers had less opportunity for promotion than did their male counterparts',[99] and that more lenient rules of discharge for women were consistent with the goal of creating more fair and equitable programmes of career advancement.[100] Brennan J (in a dissent joined by Douglas and Marshall JJ) disagreed. As he complained: '[T]he Court goes far to conjure up a legislative purposes which *may* have underlain the gender-based distinction here attacked'.[101] This was unjustified, according to Brennan J, as there was 'nothing in the statutory scheme or the legislative history to support the supposition that Congress intended... to compensate women for other forms of disadvantage visited upon

[96] Terrance Sandalow 'Racial Preferences in Higher Education: Political Responsibility and the Judicial Role' U. Chi. L. Rev. (1975) 42: 653–703 at 659–60. See also, generally, Note, 'Legislative Purpose, Rationality, and Equal Protection', Yale L.J. (1972) 81: 123 at 128: 'It is always possible to define the legislative purpose of a statute in such a way that the statutory classification is rationally related to it'.

[97] 419 US 498 (1974).

[98] ibid at 508.

[99] ibid at 508.

[100] ibid at 508.

[101] ibid at 511 (Brennan, Douglas, and Marshall JJ dissenting).

them by the Navy'.[102] This neatly illustrates the circularity problem described above: unless the purpose is ascertained independently of the terms of classification, any analysis of the relevance of the classification to its purpose will be circular, and therefore meaningless.

While this is one aspect of disagreement between the majority and the dissent in *Ballard*, there is another, related, dimension which concerns the standard of scrutiny by which gender-based classifications should be tested. For our purposes, this is an important point because it indicates a way of overcoming the circularity problem identified above. Stewart J's majority opinion in *Ballard* is framed within a simple rationality requirement: it does not explicitly discuss the level of scrutiny but rather implicitly assumes that all that is required, in order to redeem the classification, is to see whether it is rationally related to a permissible purpose. The dissenters, in contrast, require more. They claim that 'a legislative classification that is premised solely upon gender must be subjected to close judicial scrutiny' defined as follows: 'Such suspect classifications can be sustained only if the Government demonstrates that the classification serves compelling interests that cannot be otherwise achieved'.[103] Heightening the level of scrutiny (in contrast to the simple requirement of a classification's relevance to the goal pursued) consists of two steps: a requirement that a purpose pursued by the legislation must be 'compelling', rather than merely 'permissible'; and a requirement that the classification be a 'necessary' way of achieving this purpose (so that the purpose 'cannot be otherwise achieved').

This last point embodies a certain over-simplification, however. Identifying a means as 'necessary' to attain a particular goal is a shorthand formulation which cannot be taken literally: the class of 'necessary' means is dependent upon the identification of alternatives, and yet some alternatives (which do not carry the defect of a measure under scrutiny) may be so outlandish that to cite them as an argument that our measure under scrutiny is *not* a necessary one (and does not pass the test) would be disingenuous. This is, I believe, what triggered O'Connor J's clarification, in *Grutter,* that '[n]arrow tailoring does not require exhaustion of every possible race-neutral alternative' but rather 'require[s] serious, good faith consideration of *workable* race-neutral alternatives that will achieve the diversity [of student body] the [U]niversity [of Michigan] seeks'.[104] This perfectly reasonable and commonsensical concession undermines the architectural elegance of the necessity requirement, and brings a degree of indeterminacy into the characterization of a given level of scrutiny as strict or otherwise; it was precisely this aspect that provoked the dissenters' claim in *Grutter* that, '[a]lthough the Court

[102] ibid at 511 (footnote omitted). According to one interpretation of *Ballard*, the majority simply legitimized the underlying inequality of the combat restrictions; hence, it allowed one inequality (in tenure provisions) to be justified by another (in combat restrictions); see Note, 'Toward a Redefinition of Sexual Equality' Harv. L.Rev. (1981) 95: 487, 496–7.

[103] ibid at 511 (Brennan, Douglas, and Marshall JJ dissenting).

[104] *Grutter* at 339 (emphasis added).

recites the language of our strict scrutiny analysis', it was in fact deploying a more deferential, and much less stringent, standard.[105]

It is worth pausing for a moment over this point because there is a deceptive straightforwardness to the 'necessity' scrutiny, whether in the US idiom of strict scrutiny or in the more European-sounding 'proportionality' test. In the United States Supreme Court jurisprudence (whose impact has of course radiated out to academic legal theory) both the appeal and the ambiguity of 'strict scrutiny' depend on the malleability of the notion of 'necessity' of means to ends. Many years ago, in a now largely forgotten case on affirmative action, *United States v Paradise*, O'Connor J protested against what she called 'a standardless view of "narrowly tailored" far less stringent than that required by strict scrutiny'.[106] *Paradise* was a case about a court-ordered plan for preferential promotions for African-Americans in the Alabama Department of Public Safety. The district court had decided that, due to past systematic exclusion of minorities from employment in the department, one half of all promotions should go to African-Americans if qualified applicants were available; the Supreme Court upheld the plan by six to three, largely on the basis that it served a compelling state interest in remedying past and present discrimination by a specific state actor. Dissenting, O'Connor J complained that the district court had used a quota without considering any alternatives, making it impossible to suggest that this was 'necessary'. On this basis alone, she concluded that the quota could not survive strict scrutiny (which she sometimes describes with reference to 'necessity', and at other points, and somewhat more vaguely, as 'narrow tailoring'[107]). Driving home her point, however, she reiterated that, 'to survive strict scrutiny, the District Court order must fit with greater precision than any alternative remedy'.[108]

Although allegedly 'strict', this test is significantly more lenient than the traditional 'necessity'. It is one thing to say that a classification, in order to survive scrutiny, must be 'necessary' to achieve a compelling aim; it is another to say that it must fit the attainment of this aim better than any alternative remedy. The former test allows for trumping of racial classifications even by less precise alternatives, wherever the costs of this diminished 'precision' are outweighed by the benefits of not using a racial classification, with all its usual drawbacks. The latter test (of 'fitting the aim with greater precision than any alternatives') does not allow for such a calculus: a racial classification will survive strict scrutiny if all the alternatives fit the aim less precisely. Such a prediction is relatively easy to make if, for instance, 'less precisely' means postponement in time, or higher side-effects in terms of under- and over-inclusiveness, or higher costs. Hence, the test

[105] *Grutter* at 380 (Rehnquist J dissenting); similarly, ibid at 387–8 (Kennedy J dissenting); ibid at 362 (Thomas J dissenting).

[106] *United States v Paradise* 480 US 149, 197 (1987) (O'Connor J dissenting).

[107] ibid at 201.

[108] ibid at 199.

of 'greater precision', described by O'Connor J herself as 'strict scrutiny', is in fact substantially different (and much more lenient) than her own test of necessity.

The European tradition of 'proportionality' analysis is even better evidence of the malleability and inconclusiveness of the 'necessity' criterion. The idiom of proportionality (as preferred jargon for arguing about the balancing of various rights and other goods when some rights have to be restricted) is here entangled with the notion of 'necessity' more intimately than in the American taxonomy of different levels of scrutiny (which may be seen as separating the notion of necessity from a more lenient notion of relevance). For example, in the case law of the European Court of Human Rights (ECtHR), the requirement of 'necessity' contained explicitly in Articles 8–11 of the European Convention on Human Rights (which demands that restrictions on the rights of privacy, of freedom of religion, freedom of expression, and freedom of association must be, among other things, 'necessary in a democratic society') has actually acquired a meaning synonymous with 'proportionality'; or, to put it more precisely, the test of 'proportionality' has been found to be an important factor in establishing whether the 'necessity' requirement has been met. The ECtHR has advanced, in a number of decisions, the same authoritative interpretation of the Convention's formula 'necessary in a democratic society': interference with a right must correspond to a 'pressing social need' and be 'proportionate to the legitimate aim pursued'.[109] As one commentator has noted, 'from "necessity" to proportionality is but a small step'[110]—and one that has been repeatedly taken. Indeed, the notion of 'pressing social need' has been authoritatively established as a test for 'necessity'. Under this interpretation, 'necessity' qua proportionality is a rather flexible notion that allows for a relatively broad range of measures to be found 'necessary'—even if they are not 'necessary' in the sense of being 'indispensable', or being *sine quae non*. Significantly, at times, the ECtHR jurisprudence has also held 'necessity' to be analogous to the requirement that reasons for a restriction be 'relevant and sufficient'.[111]

On the face of it, this last proposition rests on a confusion: a measure may be relevant (ie related to achievement of its aim) and sufficient (that is, once the measure is applied, the aim will be achieved without requirement for further action) and yet not 'necessary' because that same aim can be achieved by using some other means. For instance, if we wish to make sure that there are no car-related traffic accidents in our suburb, we may prohibit (and make physically impossible) the entry of cars into the suburb. The measure will be 'relevant' (there is a connection between the means and the aim) and 'sufficient' (applying, and strictly

[109] See eg *Goodwin v United Kingdom* (1996) 22 ECHR 123, 143–4; for discussion see Alastair Mowbray *Cases and Materials on the European Convention of Human Rights* (London: Butterworths, 2001) 411–12, 448.

[110] Marc-Andre Eissen, quoted by Mowbray, ibid at 413.

[111] See P van Dijk and GJH van Hoof *Theory and Practice of the European Convention on Human Rights* (3rd edn, The Hague: Kluwer Law International, 1998) 81.

enforcing it will be enough to achieve the goal) and yet hardly 'necessary', in the sense of being *sine qua non*. In turn, if we find that a given measure *is* necessary (under a 'but for' test) then it is ipso facto proportionate: if a legislator is required to pursue a particular goal, and a measure is 'necessary' to achieve that goal, then this measure cannot be found to be disproportionate. Holding any genuinely 'necessary' measure disproportionate would amount to disabling legislators from pursuing a goal that they are obliged or entitled to pursue.

Taken on its own, the notion of 'relevance' is an extremely rudimentary threshold test which, in itself, hardly does any work at all. As Robert Alexy puts it, the test of relevance (which he translates into English as 'suitability'), used by the German Constitutional Court in its three-tiered principle of proportionality,[112] can be conceptualized as a maxim that 'excludes the adoption of means obstructing the realisation of at least one principle without promoting any principle or goal for which they were adopted'.[113] However, if the measure in question does not promote 'any principle or goal' for which it was adopted, then this can be seen as so irrational as to defeat the legislative restriction, even without further investigation into how it 'obstructs' realization of any other principles. At the other extremity of the spectrum, the test of 'necessity' is very difficult to meet because it involves a counterfactual: namely, an inquiry into whether there are any other measures imaginable which are less intrusive (or otherwise problematic) than the proposed one, and which would also lead to the constitutionally mandated goal. Theoretically, postulating 'necessity' as a criterion for a measure's constitutionality must result in its invalidation, as long as we can plausibly think of some other measures that do not have the defects that triggered our scrutiny in the first place, while *also* attaining the goal pursued by the measure under challenge.

If that were the end of the story, the distinction between 'necessity' and 'relevance' (or 'suitability', 'rational basis' etc) scrutiny would be sharp, and any blurring of the lines between these types would be a sign of conceptual confusion. But it is not, and the distinction sketched in the previous paragraph is highly pedantic, and ultimately useless. It does not take into account the 'efficiency' of the attainment of the goal—understood as the degree of achievement of that goal, relative to the extent of any negative side effects (defined in terms *other* than the failure to achieve fully the goal). Suppose that a measure under challenge, M-1, which has a defect (for instance, in restricting a constitutional right R-1), is adopted by the legislator in order to achieve goal G. Under a pedantic reading of the necessity test, M-1 is unconstitutional if we can plausibly think of another measure, M-2, that is also capable of achieving G but that does not restrict (or restricts to a lesser extent) R-1. But what if M-2 achieves G to a lesser extent than M-1 does, and/or produces higher negative side effects (in terms other than the

[112] The three tiers are: the principles of suitability (relevance), necessity, and proportionality *stricto sensu*.

[113] Robert Alexy 'Constitutional Rights, Balancing, and Rationality' Ratio Juris (2003) 16: 131–40 at 135.

restriction of R-1) that are also constitutionally relevant? It is this situation which seems to be well captured by O'Connor J's 'greater precision than any alternative remedy' requirement.

The two possible scenarios just depicted—relative under-attainment of the pursued goal, and relative excess of negative side-effects—may be considered as two *different* situations, raising somewhat different problems from the point of view of means-ends efficiency.[114] For our purposes, however, they can be collapsed into a single net inefficiency variable. Our question is this: is it enough, to dub a measure 'necessary', that a measure is the most efficient (ie compared with other imaginable measures leading to the same goal)? If the answer is yes, then the test of necessity is really the one of relative efficiency, and the use of the word 'necessity' is misleading and redundant; necessity is watered down, and the architectural elegance of the taxonomy of different levels of scrutiny (with a sharp line separating necessity from relevance) is eroded. If the answer is no, the price to pay for the integrity of the taxonomy of levels of scrutiny is high: the test is rendered pedantic, divorced from reality, and virtually unattainable (because we can almost always identify another measure leading to this goal if the relative under-attainment or side effects do not disqualify a new measure from defeating the one under challenge).

The lesson which can be drawn from this analysis is not that the use of the 'necessity' requirement in the scrutiny of law is meaningless. Rather, the 'necessity' test must be seen for what it really is: a shorthand for something that is less than necessity, in the literal sense of the word, and which is located somewhere on a spectrum ranging from mild efficiency, at one end, to strict necessity at the other. Under mild efficiency, a challenged measure will be redeemed if it is even marginally superior over alternative measures, in terms of degree of attainment of the goal and lower negative side effects; whereas under strict necessity, the availability of any feasible alternative measure, no matter what its costs in terms of under-attainment or side effects, amounts to a disqualification. The foregoing analysis also demonstrates the malleability of the 'necessity' requirement, hence also of the taxonomy of levels of scrutiny. But malleability is not the same as meaninglessness, and from now on in this chapter I will proceed as if the different levels of scrutiny can be meaningfully distinguished from each other (ie as if 'necessity' *was* meaningfully different from mere relevance), subject to the caveats just made.

Consequently, in what follows, I will employ a highly stylized, simplified distinction between 'strict' and 'lenient' scrutiny. In doing so, I take my cues from the tiers-of-scrutiny analysis of the US Supreme Court, and cut across the increasingly complex—at times confusing—scholarly and judicial controversies surrounding two questions: first, of the precise meaning of any of the three

[114] For an analysis considering these two situations separately, see Wojciech Sadurski *Rights before Courts* (Dordrecht: Springer, 2005) 269–70.

tests—rational-basis, intermediate, and strict;[115] and, secondly, of the assignment of particular types of classification to any of these tests. While these issues go beyond the subject matter of this chapter, a key point is that the very heightening of the level of scrutiny (whether to an 'intermediate' or to the 'highest' level) can be seen as a way of overcoming the circularity problem discerned above, at the beginning of this section of the chapter. To explain why, it is useful to simplify the taxonomy of levels of scrutiny, reducing it to two extreme instances: lenient scrutiny (also called rational-basis scrutiny) and strict scrutiny. The argument about strictness also applies to an 'intermediate' level, but with correspondingly less force, depending on the distance separating 'intermediate' from 'strict' scrutiny.

Beforehand, however, it is important to canvass briefly the *ramifications* of both ideal types of scrutiny of legal classifications. They may be roughly described in the following way. First, lenient scrutiny expresses a low degree of suspicion by the scrutinizer (a constitutional judge, a citizen-critic, a legal scholar etc) that the classification gives effect to invidious discrimination; strict scrutiny, in contrast, is triggered by heightened suspicion that the classification in question is discriminatory. This is a fundamental point, discussed in greater detail in Part 6 of this chapter. Secondly, whereas lenient scrutiny is likely to uphold legislation containing a classification under challenge, strict scrutiny is likely to invalidate legislation as discriminatory. Thirdly, rational-basis scrutiny displays a high tolerance for inevitable under- and over-inclusiveness of legislation. In other words, a relatively broad range of cases which are not captured by legislation and yet which should be captured by it because of its purpose, and, conversely, a relatively broad range of cases which fall under a classificatory scheme even though they should be left out, do not necessarily defeat the scheme as discriminatory. In contrast, strict scrutiny, in its extreme version, permits no under- or over-inclusion whatsoever: all, and only those, who are similarly situated with respect to the purpose of the law should be included in the category identified. Fourthly and lastly, under lenient scrutiny, the burden of argument rests on the critic, who must provide compelling arguments that a classification is discriminatory; under strict scrutiny, the onus shifts onto the legislator, who needs to prove the classification non-discriminatory.

As I forewarned, this presentation simplifies and schematizes the contrast between 'lenient' (or rational-basis) and 'strict' scrutiny—the concepts which I am using, not as terms of art with specific technical meanings in the 14th Amendment jurisprudence but rather as broad descriptions of two opposite ideal

[115] A rational-basis scrutiny examines whether a classification is *rationally* related to a *legitimate* state purpose; it is usually applicable to ordinary economic and social classifications. The 'intermediate test' is usually characterized as requiring that a classification must serve *important* governmental objectives, and must also be *substantially* related to the achievement of these objectives. 'Strict test' usually means that the classification must be shown to be a *necessary* means to a *compelling* or *overriding* state interest.

types of scrutiny of legal classification applicable within any legal system that entrenches a principle of equality in the law. The task now is to show how the move from 'lenient' to 'strict' scrutiny, with all the ramifications described above, helps overcome the circularity problem immanent in relevance theory. Under lenient scrutiny, all that is required is a *permissible* purpose; strictness of scrutiny consists of restricting the range of purposes which may figure in the justification of a classification by adding the requirement that they should be of compelling importance. To recall an earlier argument, the problem of circularity arose in the first place from the fact that the classification will always be relevant to the purpose, if the purpose has been inferred from the terms of the classification itself. Manufacturing a purpose, ex post facto, becomes possible where the criteria for acceptability of purposes are lax. To be sure, *some* purposes will still be disqualified under the 'permissibility' criterion. But it is unlikely that the legislator will frequently pursue an impermissible purpose, ie one forbidden by explicit constitutional rules. Only rarely has the US Supreme Court struck down legislation on grounds of impermissible purpose, for example a purpose informed by hostility to a particular racial group.[116] It has been observed that 'the requirement of permissibility seems little more than a caveat intended to make the formula [of the equal protection] logically secure against the assertion that "this classification is valid because it is rationally related to the purpose of promoting inequality" '.[117] But avoiding such an eccentric 'defence' of discrimination is, arguably, a marginal and atypical task in the scrutiny of legal classification. Much more usual is its use in resisting the manufacture of purposes which *are* permissible (in the sense of not violating any specific constitutional prohibition against the governmental purposes being pursued) and which have been inferred from the terms of the classification rather than from external sources. This is precisely the nature of Brennan J's objection in *Schlesinger v Ballard*, described earlier.[118] In these circumstances, the requirement of 'permissibility' is incapable of avoiding the danger of circularity; however, the problem can be remedied by tightening up the criteria for 'purpose' which may figure in the scrutiny of relevance. If not just *any* permissible purpose will do, the possibilities for the scrutinizer to manufacture purpose are accordingly reduced. At the limits, the range of particularly 'important' or 'compelling' purposes is very narrow; so are the opportunities for a defender of the legislation to redeem it, by inferring those purposes from the terms of a classification itself. If classification C-1 does not lead rationally to the purpose P-1 but is defended, instead, on grounds of the purpose P-2 which is more germane to the terms of classification, the latter defence becomes more

[116] See eg *Yic Wo v Hopkins* 118 US 356 (1886) (refusing laundry licences to Chinese people because of racial hostility deemed impermissible and therefore in violation of the equal protection clause).

[117] Note, 'Development in the Law: Equal Protection' Harvard L. Rev. (1969) 82: 1065–92.

[118] ibid 125–6.

difficult if we insist, in addition to relevance, that the purpose P-2 should be important and not just 'permissible'.

As this indicates, and as stated earlier, one useful way of looking at levels of scrutiny is through the lens of the degree of tolerance for over- and under-inclusion. Suppose a legislator draws a classification C related to the purpose P; as a result of the classification, all members of the group X are subject to conferral of a particular burden or benefit. Inevitably, there will be some members of X who, while suffering the burden or enjoying the benefit, will not contribute to attainment of purpose P. This is a case of over-inclusion. Conversely, there will be some non-members of X who will escape the burden or miss out on the benefit in question, even though their being so advantaged or disadvantaged would be instrumental to P. This is a case of under-inclusion. Over-inclusion and under-inclusion are inevitable consequences of regulating social affairs by rules rather than on a case-by-case basis because rules' criteria never fully correlate with the justifying bases for the classifications they make.[119] The discrepancy between a classification's justifying basis and its criterion, leads to the twin phenomena of under- and over-inclusion.

Suppose you are a legislator who is to determine criteria for eligibility for drivers' licences, and one of your key purposes is to maximize road safety. You decide that one criterion (one of necessary conditions) will be age: people under 18 (for the sake of argument) are not eligible. There is an obvious discrepancy between the justifying basis (picking out all and only those who promise to be good and responsible drivers) and the basis of classification. But there is only so much that we can do to individualize criteria of classification without incurring enormous administrative costs, on one side, and enhancing the discretionary powers of those responsible for deciding about whom to award licences, on the other. For this reason, in many cases we are prepared to live with the inevitable over- and under-inclusiveness of rules, considering this as a cost that is outweighed by the benefits of a lower administrative burden, and a lesser risk of arbitrariness stemming from inflated administrative discretion.

In different spheres of legal regulation we are prepared to accept varying degrees of over- and under-inclusion: the higher the level of scrutiny of the relationship between a classification and its purpose, the lower is our tolerance for over- and under-inclusion. It is also important to emphasize that, in particular circumstances, over- and under-inclusion may pose qualitatively different problems, warranting different levels of toleration. This largely depends on whether a given regulation imposes a burden or confers a benefit on a group. Offhand, it would seem that, in the case of burdens, over-inclusion is less tolerable, while in the case of the benefits, under-inclusion seems more objectionable. But this is a simplification because the conferral of a benefit on a group can be seen as a relative burden to those outside the group, so that over-inclusion may be seen to be grossly

[119] See Frederick Schauer *Playing by the Rules* (New York: Oxford University Press, 1991) 31–4.

unfair to those others. Consider again *Fullilove v Klutznick.* Special preferences in public contracts accorded to minority business enterprises (MBEs) were justified on the basis of compensating for past barriers to competitive access.[120] But of course, not all MBEs had suffered such discrimination, and not only MBEs suffered it. The lack of a complete correlation between the justifying basis and the classification criterion (MBEs) triggers under- and over-inclusion. In his plurality opinion, Chief Justice Burger anticipated, and refuted, both objections of under- and over-inclusion. As to the under-inclusion, his response was to invoke a 'one thing at a time' theory: 'a legislator may take one step at a time to remedy only part of a broader problem . . . .'.[121] This sounds convincing: a legislator should not be disabled from addressing a particularly important *part* of a broader problem because not the *whole* problem is thereby addressed. It has been stated that 'the legislature is free to remedy parts of a mischief or to recognize degrees of evil and to strike at the harm where it thinks it most acute'.[122] As to over-inclusion (which he characterizes as the objection that the classification 'bestows a benefit on businesses identified by racial or ethnic criteria which cannot be justified on the basis of competitive criteria or as a remedy for the present effects of identified prior discrimination'[123]) Burger CJ responds by describing the provisions for waiver and exemptions in the administrative scheme for MBEs.[124] He notes that that the statute envisages administrative scrutiny, to identify and eliminate from participation in the scheme those MBEs 'who are not "*bona fide*" within the regulations and guidelines; for example, spurious minority-front entities can be exposed'.[125] This would leave the problem of those MBEs which are not 'spurious', and yet which had not suffered past discrimination. In response to this aspect, Burger CJ notes that 'waiver is available to avoid dealing with an MBE who is attempting to exploit the remedial aspects of the program by charging an unreasonable price, a price not attributable to the present effects of past discrimination'.[126]

Burger CJ's answer indicates that, even in the context of benefits, over-inclusion may be treated as equally troublesome as under-inclusion. Indeed, in *Fullilove,* the answer to the problem of over-inclusion is more consistent with the call for a higher 'fit' of classification to purpose than is the answer to the under-inclusion problem. Under-inclusion is dealt with by an appeal to a 'one thing at a time' theory, an admittedly unsatisfactory answer under any scrutiny requirement stricter than the most lenient one. How do we know that the legislator, in some undefined future, will address the cases presently left out? As over-inclusion seems successfully remedied

[120] *Fullilove v Klutznick* 448 US 448 (1980) at 477–8.
[121] ibid at 485.
[122] Note, 'Developments in the Law: Equal Protection' at 1084 (footnote omitted).
[123] *Fullilove* at 486.
[124] ibid at 486–9.
[125] ibid at 487–8.
[126] ibid at 488 (references omitted).

by the combined devices of exemption and waiver, as described by Burger, there is a certain asymmetry between the two.

The final task before us now is to see how heightening of scrutiny addresses the initial problem of possible circularity in the relevance tests. It may be recalled that under the simple relevance model, circularity occurred because purpose was inferred from the classification itself, and such purpose reflected could not fail to be attainable by that classification. But a 'perfect fit' requirement (no over- and under-inclusion) reduces the possibility of ex post facto rationalizations of the classification. The reasons why are best explained by John Hart Ely and so important that he deserves to be quoted at length:

> The goal the classification in issue is likely to fit most closely, obviously, is the goal the legislators actually had in mind. . . . [W]here the requirement is simply the Court's standard call for a 'rational' relation between classification and the goal, [the fact that the goal that fits the classification best is unconstitutional] will seldom matter: even if the goal the classification fits best is disabled from invocation, there will likely be other permissible goals whose relation to the classification is sufficiently close to be called rational. The 'special scrutiny' . . . , however, insists that the classification in issue fit the goal invoked in its defense more closely that any alternative classification would. There is only one goal the classification is likely to fit *that* closely, however, and that is the goal the legislatures actually had in mind.[127]

We now see why, as scrutiny of fit between classification and purpose becomes stricter, the more difficult is the 'manufacturing' of purposes and the attempt to establish a classification's relevance to those purposes. As Ely shows, the application of stringent scrutiny can be seen as a way of discerning *actual* legislative motives. If those real purposes are improper, they taint the legislation as discriminatory. But if the classification can be seen as related to some proper purposes, and we insist upon a perfect fit, we will likely avoid the dangers of ex post facto reconstruction of purposes that renders the whole exercise circular.

6. Suspectness and Discrimination

As should be clear by now, a decisive step in the argument about discrimination is the determination of a proper level of scrutiny of the relationship between a classification and its purpose, and of the importance of the purpose itself. One and the same classification is likely to be validated as non-discriminatory under a lenient scrutiny and condemned as discriminatory under a more demanding test. To use an example already enlisted above, the age threshold for eligibility for a driver's licence will probably pass (in the eyes of most people) lenient scrutiny in which a relatively large incidence of over- and under-inclusion does not

[127] Ely *Democracy and Distrust* at 145–6 (endnotes omitted).

matter, but will fail a test intolerant of substantial under- and over-inclusiveness. An apparently preliminary decision about the character of the test is therefore largely decisive of the final result.

What considerations should inform decisions about the 'strictness' of scrutiny? American 14th Amendment jurisprudence employs, amongst other terms of art, a concept of 'suspect classifications', ie classifications which can be upheld only if shown to be necessary to accomplish a compelling state interest.[128] I propose to use this notion in a conventional, rather than a technical sense. 'Suspicion' is the right word in this context. We normally 'suspect' when we have doubts about something, while not being absolutely sure. For this reason, suspicion is an attitude well suited to the use of strict scrutiny: if we had *no doubts* about legislation, we would settle for a simple, lenient scrutiny; on the other hand, if we *knew* legislation to be discriminatory, no scrutiny would be needed and we might as well reach directly for our conclusion. However, it is somewhat glib to say that suspicion suffices to warrant strict scrutiny because we know that the decision to employ strict scrutiny is, more often than not, fatal to the classification in question. So we need more than mere 'suspicion'; we need at least some rough contours of what makes the suspicion justified. In turn, this can be spelled out only if we have some general theory about what constitutes 'discrimination'; we cannot describe our grounds of 'suspicion' unless we have at least some preliminary ideas about what constitutes discrimination in the first place.

One could perhaps protest, at this stage, that the whole framework of the relevance test turns out to be redundant. For the relevance test operates using varying levels of scrutiny; the decision about scrutiny is triggered by a degree of suspicion, and now it is claimed that the suspicion is justified in so far as it is informed by our theory about the nature of discrimination. But if we offer such a theory, what is the point of the whole framework of scrutiny of the relationship of the classification and its goal? We might just as well, this argument would go, directly test a given classification by the lights of our criteria of discrimination. But this objection fails to recognize that the 'theory' of discrimination required as a ground for ascertaining the level of 'suspicion' would amount to no more than a pre-theoretical judgment of what comprises the nature of discrimination. This is much too vague to serve as a standard of discriminatory classifications, being merely a belief about what renders a given treatment discriminatory, about what taints our treatment of others as unequal, and about what is the true evil targeted by the anti-discrimination principle. In order to be applied as a standard

[128] On racial classifications as suspect, see inter alia *Korematsu v United States* 323 US 214 (1944); *McLaughlin v Florida* 379 US 184 (1964); *Fullilove* at 508 (Powell J concurring). Race is not the only suspect basis of classification in the United States; alienage and national origin would be suspect (see, respectively, *Graham v Richardson* 403 US 365, 372 (1971) and *Hirabayashi v United States* 320 US 81, 100 (1943)) and, under certain interpretations, sex, although the Supreme Court itself has adopted an intermediary standard for sex-based classifications; see *Craig v Boren* 429 US 190 (1976).

for detecting discriminatory classifications this intuitive judgment must be translated into something more precise and capable of application.

Earlier in this chapter, I rejected two possible pre-theoretical judgments about the nature of discrimination: that it consists of *any* classification of citizens by legal means, and that it consists of the classification of citizens by legal means along lines determined by certain 'impermissible' characteristics, in particular, by 'immutable characteristics', such as race. An alternative approach discerns the nature of discrimination in the impermissible *motives* for imposing burdens (or conferring benefits) upon a particular class. There are classifications that may be irrational but which are not triggered by any wrongful motive; these can be seen as errors of judgment on the part of the legislator, and can be detected even by a rational-basis scrutiny, without any need for suspicion-based strict scrutiny. To set the level of eligibility for a driver's licence at the age of 30 would most probably be considered irrational, producing excessive under-inclusion intolerable even under a very lenient scrutiny. Hence, any further move towards strict scrutiny and the associated suspicion-triggered test, would be unnecessary. But when we reflect upon paradigmatically invidious discriminations in the past and at the present time, we do not usually come up with examples such as *this*. Rather, we think immediately about racist, sexist, homophobic, or religious discriminations that cannot simply be characterized as 'error in legislative judgment': they are evils, not mistakes. We consider them to be wrong because they stem from bad motives, not from merely mistaken judgments about a classification's rationality; and we believe that they are triggered by prejudice, hostility, dislike, self-imposed ignorance, unfair stereotyping etc. Tom Campbell has captured this well in asserting: 'discrimination is the perpetration of unjustifiable inequality in consequence of bigotry'.[129]

A motive-based view of the nature of discrimination resonates with a broader approach in constitutional theory which deems laws unconstitutional in so far as they are based on wrongful motives; the benchmark of unconstitutionality is within the area of motives rather than external effects.[130] This approach has been propounded in many areas of constitutional jurisprudence other than constitutional equality, especially in the fields of freedom of speech[131] and freedom of religion.[132] But we need not be concerned here with the broader theory of unconstitutionality. All that is relevant is whether the motive-based view properly captures strong intuitive convictions about the sources of the wrongness of

[129] Tom Campbell 'Unlawful Discrimination' in Wojciech Sadurski (ed) *Ethical Dimensions of Legal Theory* (Amsterdam: Rodopi, 1991) 153–70 at 163. See also Ronald Dworkin *A Matter of Principle* (Cambridge, Mass: Harvard University Press, 1985) 302, 314, 330; Dworkin *Law's Empire* 384, 396.

[130] On unconstitutionality based on impermissible legislative purposes, see Richard H Fallon Jr 'The Supreme Court, 1996 Term – Foreword: Implementing the Constitution' Harv and L.Rev. (1997) 111: 54–152 at 90–102.

[131] See eg *Texas v Johnson* 491 US 397, 414 (1989) ('the government may not prohibit the expression of an idea simply because society finds the idea itself offensive or disagreeable').

[132] For example, one of the three prongs of the test for the establishment of religion is whether a statute had a secular legislative purpose, *Lemon v Kurtzman* 403 US 602, 612 (1971).

discrimination. And, on the basis of my perception of what is usually seen as being *really* wrong about some unquestionably invidious discriminations, I believe that the response given by a motive-based view is a persuasive one. Consider, for example, the following argument in favour of a deferential scrutiny of legislation: '[T]he distinctive legislative response ... to the plight of those who are mentally retarded demonstrates that ... the lawmakers have been addressing their difficulties in a manner that *belies a continuing antipathy or prejudice* and corresponding need for more intrusive oversight by the judiciary'.[133] By clear implication, suspicion of 'antipathy or prejudice' would trigger more 'intrusive' scrutiny of legislation.

Like any motive-related theory of statutory unconstitutionality, however, this faces a fundamental problem: how to ascertain the legislator's *true* motives? Second-guessing reasons for action, including that of law-making, is an extremely risky enterprise, and arguments that the very attempt to discover true legislative motives is either theoretically incoherent, or practically impossible, are legion.[134] But these arguments have also been exposed to important rebuttals.[135] As far as our particular topic is concerned, it would fly in the face of common sense to say, for example, that in the case of racial segregation on public transport, we are fundamentally incapable of deciding whether a regulation was triggered by racist animus, hostility, and prejudice, or by some more benign motive, such as the aesthetic value of having people of different races sit together in different sections of a train.[136] As Richard Fallon has observed, 'In light of history and familiar psychology ... some types of actions—as identified either by their contents or their effects—can be seen in the aggregate as likely to reflect forbidden purposes'.[137] However, not all cases are so clear cut. Truly hard cases (for example, race-conscious preferential university admission or protective labour legislation for women etc) will call for the employment, in our decisions about the level of scrutiny of the classification, of a *working* theory of discrimination. To say, simply, that strict scrutiny is justified whenever any such classification appears to be based on prejudice, hostility, or other invidious motives would leave us with a standard almost impossible to apply in concrete cases. We need more objective *indicia* of wrongful motives in order to avoid the need to second-guess the true motives moving legislators to enact a particular regulation. In any event,

[133] *Cleburne v Cleburne Living Center* 473 US 432, 443 (1985) (emphasis added).

[134] See eg Dworkin *Law's Empire* at 313–24. See also *Edwards v Aguillard* 482 US 578, 636–9 (1986) (Scalia J dissenting).

[135] See eg Jeffrey Goldsworthy 'Originalism in Constitutional Interpretation' Federal L. Rev. (1997) 25: 1.

[136] This paraphrases a hypothetical example of Paul Brest's, about a school principal 'who seats the blacks on one side of the stage at the graduation ceremony and the whites on the other, and defends it in aesthetic terms' Ely *Democracy and Distrust* at 148, summarizing the argument in Paul Brest *Processes of Constitutional Decision-Making* (Boston: Little, Brown & Co 1975) 489.

[137] Richard F Fallon Jr 'The Supreme Court, 1996 Term – Foreword: Implementing the Constitution' Harv. Law Rev. (1997) 111: 54–152 at 95 (footnote omitted).

it should be emphasized that a motive-based theory of discrimination is not really concerned with the actual, subjective, psychological states of mind of legislators voting for this or that law but rather with the motives in an objective sense, that is to say, the intention that can be most reasonably or plausibly attributed to a person proposing or endorsing a particular legislative proposal. Such an approach to legislative intent is not puzzling; indeed, it is commonplace in constitutional interpretation. It was well captured by Justice Antonin Scalia who described it as 'a sort of "objectified" intent—the intent that a reasonable person would gather from the text of the law, placed alongside the remainder of the *corpus juris.* 'As Bishop's old treatise nicely put it, elaborating upon the usual formulation: "[T]he primary object of all rules for interpreting statutes is to ascertain the legislative intent; *or, exactly, the meaning which the subject is authorized to understand the legislature intended*" '.[138]

Before I offer my proposed indicia of suspicion that invidious discrimination is at work, it is useful to explain the methodology for identifying such indicia. The method is the same as in the case of identifying the motive-based view of discrimination as plausible. It can now be described more abstractly: it is akin to the method of 'reflective equilibrium' or any other coherence-based theory of moral argument. 'Reflective equilibrium', in Rawls's explanation, consists of achieving rough coherence between our 'considered convictions of justice' (understood as specific and intuitive moral responses to situations lending themselves to evaluations in terms of justice) and our 'principles of justice' (understood as general and abstract moral maxims).[139] The general underlying view is that we all hold certain moral beliefs of different levels of generality, and we hold them with different strengths of conviction. Rawls's methodology consists of using those judgments which we hold with the greatest force of conviction as our 'provisional fixed points', and then building on this basis a coherent set of both general, and specific, moral beliefs and judgments, if necessary, by altering the initial 'provisional' starting points. This method seems to be particularly well-suited to our purposes. Remember, we need to identify cases in which our initial 'suspicion' of discrimination is appropriate and in which a stricter than usual scrutiny of relevance needs to be undertaken. This means that, by the very nature of the exercise, we deal with 'hard cases' when we are of two minds about whether the classification is indeed discriminatory: otherwise we would not be talking about 'suspicion' but about certainty. Reflective equilibrium is designed precisely to test those 'hard cases' (as Rawls says: 'where our present judgments are in doubt and given with hesitation')[140] by an appeal to our fixed moral points (in Rawls's words, those 'judgments...which we now make intuitively and in which we have the greatest

[138] Antonin Scalia *A Matter of Interpretation* (Princeton: Princeton University Press, 1997) at 17, citation omitted (quoting Joel Prentiss Bishop *Commentaries on the Written Laws and Their Interpretation* (Boston: Little, Brown & Co. 1882), 57–8) (emphasis added by A Scalia).

[139] John Rawls *A Theory of Justice* (Oxford: Oxford University Press, 1971) 19–20.

[140] ibid at 19.

confidence').[141] In the area of anti-discrimination law, many of us are relatively uncertain about whether remedial racial preferences, or protective bans upon the employment of women in some positions, or the exclusion of women from active combat duty, are discriminatory or not. Furthermore, even if some of us have strong views about these matters, we face disagreement between rational people arguing in good faith about the acceptability of relevant regulations. But we do not have similar doubts, and we do not face similar disagreements, concerning, for example, whether racial segregation in public transport, refusal to grant voting rights to women, or religious tests for public office, are wrong. The point is thus to elaborate the test of prejudice, hostility, and other wrongful motives, using the latter (unquestionable) cases of discrimination as a starting point, so as then to be able to apply them to those moral disagreements and dilemmas actually faced by our societies.

Here I wish to offer three indicia of wrongful motivations, identified in such a fashion, through a 'reflective equilibrium' process. First, it is intuitively plausible to say that, historically, invidious discrimination has usually been a product of action by a politically powerful group against those unrepresented (or inadequately represented) in the political and legislative process. Hence, the burdens imposed by a majority (in a democratic system) or by a political elite, upon a minority or upon an unrepresented group, raise immediate suspicion of activation by invidious motives. In contrast, this suspicion is not warranted when a legislator grants *benefits* to a group that is beyond, or at the margin of, the political process, while burdens of the new regulation are to be borne by the majority whom the legislator represents. As said famously by Judge J Skelly Wright, 'when a decision maker chooses to disadvantage members *of his own* racial or ethnic group, it may hardly be supposed that he is acting out of prejudice, ignorance, or hostility.... When the majority group acts to disadvantage itself for the benefit of the minority, there should be a strong presumption of legality'.[142] And as stated earlier, in similar vein, by John Hart Ely: 'When the group that controls the decision making process classifies so as to advantage a minority and disadvantage itself, the reasons for being unusually suspicious, and, consequently, employing a stringent brand of review, are lacking'.[143]

The second ground for suspicion that a classification is motivated by hostility or prejudice is that it has the effect of perpetrating, strengthening, or freezing an existing pattern of disadvantage. One feature of discriminatory regulations has usually been that they, so to speak, add insult to injury, in petrifying the

[141] ibid at 19.

[142] J Skelly Wright 'Color-Blind Theories and Color Conscious Remedies' U. Chi. L. Rev. (1980) 47: 213, 234–5 (footnotes omitted).

[143] John Hart Ely 'The Constitutionality of Reverse Racial Discrimination' U. Chi. L. Rev. (1974) 41: 723, 735.

existing structure of social burdens and disadvantages.[144] In the American equal-protection doctrine, this test is reflected in the concept of 'discrete and insular minorities':[145] if the group that bears the burden of a regulation can be so characterized, there is a justified fear that the burden will exacerbate existing disadvantages. That fear is greatly allayed, on the other hand, if a group burdened by a regulation matches the description in *San Antonio Independent School Dist v Rodriguez*: 'the class is *not* saddled with such disabilities, or subjected to such a history of purposeful unequal treatment, or relegated to such a position of political powerlessness as to command extraordinary protection from the majoritarian political process'.[146] A broadly similar insight is expressed in Ginsburg J's dissent, in *Gratz,* where she mentions '[a]ctions designed to burden groups *long denied full citizenship stature*'[147] as requiring especially careful judicial scrutiny. We may conclude that in cases where the burden of a particular regulation falls *unevenly* on different groups, burdens borne by a group that is generally disadvantaged and traditionally worse off, raise much higher suspicions of prejudice or hostility than burdens suffered by the traditionally privileged.

The third indicium of suspicion is linked to the stigmatizing effect of the discrimination. One of the most powerful effects of unquestionably invidious discrimination is that, in addition to imposing disadvantage upon an already disadvantaged group, it also fosters a sense of the group's inferiority vis-à-vis the rest of the community.[148] Stigmatization may (and usually does) work in both ways: reinforcing a sense of inferiority on the part of victims, and confirming grounds for contempt towards victims in the eyes of perpetrators. Discrimination is, after all, the end result of a process whereby external differences (in race, class, religion) are transformed into differences of value, or worth, of particular groups.

[144] Frank Michelman suggests that one of the characteristics of 'invidious' discrimination is 'a high degree of adaptation to uses which are oppressive in the sense of *systematic* and unfair devaluation, through majority rule, of the claims of certain persons to nondiscriminatory sharing in the benefits and burdens of social existence', Frank I Michelman, 'The Supreme Court, 1968 Term – Foreword: On Protecting the Poor Through the Fourteenth Amendment' Harv. L. Rev. (1969) 83: 7, 20 (emphasis added).

[145] See *United States v Carolene Products Co* 304 US 144, 152 n 4 (1938): 'prejudice against discrete and insular minorities may be a special condition, which tends seriously to curtail the operation of those political processes ordinarily to be relied upon to protect minorities, and which may call for a correspondingly more searching judicial inquiry'. The concept of 'discrete and insular minorities' has been invoked with the aim of applying an intermediate, rather than strict, judicial scrutiny of benign racial classification; see *Bakke* at 361–2 (Brennan, White, Marshall, Blackmun JJ concurring in part and dissenting in part). It should, however, be noted that this is not a unanimously accepted view; see ibid at 290 (Powell J delivering the judgment of the court). See, generally, Wojciech Sadurski 'Judicial Protection of Minorities: The Lessons of Footnote Four' Anglo-Amer. L.Rev. (1988) 17: 163–81.

[146] 411 US 1, 28 (1973) (emphasis added).

[147] *Gratz* at 301 (Ginsburg J dissenting) (emphasis added).

[148] 'The distinction between discrimination against blacks and discrimination against whites is that the former is part of a system that stigmatizes the group and treats its members as inferiors, and the latter is not', Judith A Baer *Equality Under the Constitution* (Ithaca: Cornell University Press, 1983) 139.

Perhaps discrimination's most invidious effect is reflecting and strengthening stereotypes and prejudices against a group as a whole, so that it becomes a legal weapon in the service of an irrational hatred. The International Convention on the Elimination of All Forms of Racial Discrimination, in its preamble, links racial discrimination to 'doctrine[s] of superiority based on racial differentiation', which it describes as 'scientifically false, morally condemnable, socially unjust and dangerous'.[149] As the social scientist who has given the most illuminating account of the 'stigma' phenomenon has put it:

> By definition... we believe the person with a stigma is not quite human. On this assumption we exercise varieties of discrimination, through which we effectively, if often unthinkingly, reduce his life chances. We construct a stigma theory, an ideology to explain his inferiority and account for the danger he represents, sometimes rationalizing an animosity based on other differences, such as those of social class.[150]

Clearly, the stigmatizing effect is one of the major objects of attack by anti-discrimination law. The landmark decision in the United States, *Brown v Board of Education,* invalidated school segregation on the ground that it 'generates a feeling of inferiority as to [African-Americans'] status in the community that may affect their hearts and minds in a way unlikely ever to be undone'.[151] Racial stigma was characterized movingly by Brennan J in his concurrence in *Bakke,* by contrasting it to an effect of remedial affirmative action upon a non-member of a preferred minority:

> [Bakke was not] stamped as inferior by the Medical School's rejection of him.... [T]here is absolutely no basis for concluding that Bakke's rejection as a result of [the University's] use of racial preference will affect him throughout his life in the same way as the segregation of the Negro schoolchildren in Brown I would have affected them. Unlike discrimination against racial minorities, the use of racial preferences for remedial purposes does not inflict a pervasive injury upon individual whites in the sense that wherever they go or whatever they do there is a significant likelihood that they will be treated as second-class citizens because of their color.[152]

We now have three indicia of reasonable suspicion that a classification is motivated by wrongful reasons, such as hostility or prejudice: the fact that the regulation burdens a politically powerless group (or at least, a group under-represented in the law-making process); the fact that a regulation contributes to, or freezes, the existing pattern of social disadvantage; and that the burdens inflicted upon

[149] International Convention on the Elimination of All Forms of Racial Discrimination (1965), preamble.

[150] Erving Goffman *Stigma* (New York: Simon & Schuster, 1963) 15 (footnote omitted). Goffman develops his account around stigmas related to physical disabilities, but it applies equally well to racial, religious, and other stigmas as well.

[151] 347 US 483 (1954) at 494.

[152] *Bakke* at 375 (Brennan, White, Marshall, Blackmun JJ concurring in part and dissenting in part).

a target-group by a regulation in question have a stigmatizing effect. Arguably, these do not amount to a fully 'objective' test, and people may still disagree whether a given regulation matches any of these three conditions. Nonetheless, these indicia are certainly much less subjective, vague and indeterminate than a mere criterion of prejudice or hostility. Therefore, they lend themselves better to a *working* theory of discrimination which can be adopted by people who otherwise disagree about their fundamental values, such as justice.

Precisely because each of these three indicia allows for judgments of degree (which is why reasonable disagreements may occur, concerning whether a particular regulation matches any one of them), it is unnecessary to decide, in abstract terms, whether they should all be present or whether one is enough, to subject a given regulation to a heightened scrutiny. If there is a very high correlation between a given regulation and only one indicium, this would probably be sufficient to warrant stricter than usual scrutiny. But the presence of two, or all three, in a given regulation, certainly strengthens the case for strict scrutiny. The set of three together should be considered, not as a strict algorithm to detect discrimination, but rather as a translation of a broad and vague motive-based view into something more determinate and usable. In any event, it is rather clear that the three indicia are interrelated. It is also important to remember that, even if all are present, it will not be the end of the story; this only comprises a sufficient reason to subject a regulation displaying these characteristics to strict scrutiny. Ultimately, a discriminatory classification may pass this test;[153] this will be, however, a rare and unusual outcome. A telling fact is that the recent *Grutter* decision was only the second case in the history of the United States Supreme Court's equal protection jurisprudence in which a racial classification scheme was found to pass the test of strict scrutiny.[154]

Just as it is possible (although not very likely) that a legal classification will *pass* a strict test, so it is possible (although perhaps equally unlikely) that a legal classification will *fail* a lenient, rational-basis test. It is not impossible to think of examples of classifications which do not raise any suspicions that they were motivated by prejudice, hatred, or stereotyping, and where none of the three indicia of 'suspectness' can be detected, and yet which are so 'off the mark', as far as the relationship between the classification and its purpose is concerned, that

[153] In *Fullilove v Klutznik*, the plurality opinion written by Chief Justice Burger mentions, obiter, that the classification under challenge (ie special set aside contracts for minority business enterprises) 'would survive judicial review under either "test" articulated in the several Bakke opinions' (n 56 above) at 492, that is, also a strict test, compare *Bakke* at 291 ('Racial and ethnic distinctions of any sort are inherently suspect and thus call for the most exacting judicial examination') and ibid at 299 (racial and ethnic classification must be 'precisely tailored to serve a compelling governmental interest').

[154] The first was the now discredited *Korematsu v United States* 323 US 214 (1944), in which the Court for the first time established such a test for racial classifications, upholding the exclusion of Americans of Japanese extraction living on the West Coast from their homes in the time of perceived danger of Japanese invasion.

they have to be disqualified as discriminatory. There can be discrimination which does not match the paradigm cases of invidious discrimination which we know from history, but which, rather, results from fundamental errors of legislative judgment about the relevance of the means to the ends. Classifications based on such mistaken judgments are discriminatory but we do not need to engage any special moral insight in making this statement; those cases of discrimination can be routinely picked up with the use of simple (lenient) scrutiny which calls for the rational relationship of classification to its purpose.

Conclusions

In this chapter, my main concern was with articulating a substantive and plausible conception of the ideal of legal equality, against a critique of the 'no differential treatment' ideal and the 'per se' type of theories which claim that certain characteristics of individuals, when used as a basis for classifications, necessarily render a classification discriminatory. The main lesson of my critique of 'per se' theories is that any test of non-discrimination which ignores legislative purpose, and the relationship between classification and purpose, is doomed to fail. But relevance-based tests yield a circularity which results from the temptation of implying a classification's purpose from the terms of the classification itself. This danger can be overcome by heightening the level of scrutiny applied to the purpose, and to the fit between the classification and the purpose. If we demand that the government's purpose in legislating be of sufficient importance, and not merely permissible, we restrict the range of purposes which can figure in any justification of the legislation, thus reducing the possibility of manufacturing purposes from the terms of the classification. If, in addition, we demand a narrow tailoring of the classification to the purpose, so that the classification must be a necessary means to the achievement of the important purpose, we increase the likelihood that the purpose which will match perfectly the classification under challenge will be the same purpose that the legislators actually had in mind, and not a purpose conjured up ex post facto.

The heightening of the level of scrutiny of the purpose, and of the relationship between the classification and the purpose, has some important ramifications: it expresses a high degree of suspicion that discrimination might be at work behind a given classification, it abandons the presumption of legislative validity, and it results in little tolerance for the over- and under-inclusiveness of classifications from the point of view of their rationales. In sum, it is likely to result in an invalidation of the classification. Hence, we need some good reasons for heightening the level of scrutiny of the legislation, and these reasons must be embedded in a general theory of what renders a classification discriminatory. Such a theory can be reached by a method of 'reflective equilibrium', that is, by reflecting upon the common evils of those discriminations which we consider intuitively to be particularly invidious. An intuitively justified answer to this question seems to be that a classification is tainted as discriminatory by certain wrongful motives for legislation, in particular, if the legislation is based on prejudice, hostility, and stereotyping.

But it is not easy to ascertain those motives directly, so we need some more 'objective' indicia of suspect nature of the classification; those indicia, again, can be gathered in by thinking about the common traits of undoubtedly invidious discriminations. Three such indicia seem to justify a high level of suspicion that discrimination might be at work: when legislatively imposed burdens fall upon a group which has had a disproportionately low impact upon the adoption of legislation, when they are imposed upon a group traditionally disadvantaged and discriminated against, and when they stigmatize a burdened group as inferior—intellectually, morally, or otherwise. These three indicia, whilst not *sufficient* to support a finding of discrimination, seem to comprise a reasonably workable set of factors which should normally trigger higher than usual suspicion, and therefore, a stricter than usual scrutiny of classification, helping us to detect discrimination.

4

Social Equality (I): The Contours of Social Equality

Legal philosophers debate various meanings and applications of equality understood as a value internal to a legal system: as a property of a fair application of the settled law, or as a norm determining when legal rules are discriminatory in the pejorative sense of this adjective, that is when the law itself violates the requirement of legal equality. *Political* theorists, in turn, are more concerned about equality in the political processes and, in particular, in various processes of deliberation and collective decision-making, for example as reflected in various decision-making rules, such as majority rule or consensus. But surely there is a broader application of equality as well, the equality *tout court,* more general than, and prior to, such 'special' equalities. Only once we have established what such equality should consist in, shall we be able to proceed with discussions as to whether it is proper for the law and for the political decision-making system to approximate such equality. But this broader equality—which we can here call simply '*social* equality'—is not easy to describe and specify.

I will attempt such a description in this and in the following chapter. In the present chapter, I will explore the contours of 'social' equality by discussing, first, a conventional distinction—that between an 'individualized' and a 'collective' concept of social equality—and by showing why, in my view, this distinction is misleading and unhelpful (Part 1). In the remainder of this chapter I will consider the status of a distinction between 'natural' and 'social' differences between people, in a broader theory of social equality. These considerations prepare, in an important way, for the next chapter where I will discuss, in some detail, a particular approach to social equality demanding that it should be concerned with removing those inequalities which result from luck (or, more generally, factors which are morally arbitrary) while preserving those which can be traced back to individual decisions and choices. This idea is sometimes presented as an attempt to undo the negative consequences of 'natural and social lottery' (Part 2 of the current chapter). Before 'luck egalitarianism' can be considered on its own terms, one needs to tackle a certain important ambiguity about what types of factors which are 'arbitrary from a moral point of view' can be legitimately recognized as *improperly* affecting individual positions, and thus subject to nullification or neutralization, under the ideal of social equality. This ambiguity relates to a claim that differences related to 'natural' attributes (such as talents or skills) are significantly different from the differences related to 'social' characteristics (such as the wealth of a family into which one is born), with the consequence that the latter differences should be nullified but the former not, even though both are outside the reach of an agent's choice. It is often presented either as a 'self-ownership' thesis or a thesis about a simple 'extension' of a right of a person over her own body (Part 3). The outcome of either of these conceptions would be that 'natural' attributes are in such a close relationship to individual identities that we cannot hope to redistribute the resources based on 'natural' attributes without interfering with, or disturbing, in an objectionable way, individual identities. This view, I will claim, is based on some implausible presuppositions, which I will discuss and criticize in Part 4, about the relationship of an individual 'self' with the social position of a person, and in Part 5, about the consequences of 'pooling' the benefits which derive from personal talents.

If my argument is correct, there is no reason to draw a distinction between two types of factors which are 'morally arbitrary' if they trigger social inequalities: those which attach to 'natural' attributes, and those resulting from 'social' situations. But is the whole aspiration to neutralize the factors based on bad luck, identified as 'morally arbitrary', defensible in the first place? This question will be addressed in the subsequent chapter.

1. Social Equality: Individualized and Collective

There are basically two answers, both deriving from an egalitarian perspective, to the question about the nature of the parameters of social equality. The first concept of equality, which we can call here an individualized one, considers the relationship between particular properties (P1, P2, etc) of individuals and the amount of socially distributed goods (G1, G2 etc) that these individuals control. The point is to identify the properties which must *not* trigger *unequal* amounts of social goods. According to this approach equality will be achieved whenever, notwithstanding the fact that two individuals have an unequal amount of P1 (for instance, family status as judged by prevailing social standards), they will still have an equal amount of G1 (for instance, salary). So it is important, right at the outset, to indicate the strong caveat that an individualized concept of equality does not require that people have exactly the same amount of a particular good, *simpliciter*; rather, it urges that some facts or factors must not lead to unequal distribution of some resources (with the task of identifying those facts/factors and those resources relegated to a substantive conception of individualized equality). A second conception of equality, which may be referred to as collective, looks at the overall social structure and attributes the property of equality to society as a whole. According to a number of popular formulae, such equality may require that there are no settled hierarchies, or relations of domination, or oppression, or exploitation. Each of these four formulae (and there may be more) means something different and will result in a different substantive conception of equality. But what matters here is that the collective approach seems to be significantly different from the individualized one. Thus, before we proceed, we need to have a better grasp of the stakes underlying the choice (if a choice has to be made) between an individualized and a collective conception of equality, whatever further properties of the latter may be developed.

Starting with the individualized concept, a number of observations can be made. First, it looks like a purely *negative* concept: the way it has been formulated here implies at the outset that equality has been achieved when there is no correlation between unequal amounts of Ps and the amount of Gs. For instance, you and I may come from families which enjoy radically different social standings, but if it is not correlated to our incomes (or educational opportunity etc), the conditions for equality are met. The negative character of this feature is, however, illusory: what matters is that notwithstanding unequal P there is an equal G: equality in G is an affirmative, positive feature, even though it is found against the background of unequal P. It is the disconnection of G from P, added to the ascertainment of the equality of G, which is of relevance. What is crucial, however, is that we do not limit ourselves simply to the determination of equality in G: this is neither here nor there from the point of view of the concept of individualized equality. I may *happen to have* the same salary as you, and this may be described, trivially, as equality but no one would seriously think of such equality as an interesting candidate for an attractive moral *ideal* of equality: this could be just an incidental sameness. Such sameness starts qualifying as a (putatively) attractive ideal when we can establish that notwithstanding a number of unequal characteristics, we still both have access to equal amounts of social goods.

Secondly, there is an immediate ambiguity in postulating that unequal P should not *trigger* unequal G. Is such equality violated only when there is improper *causation* between P and G, or simply when there is a *correlation*? Without going into the details of the argument one should note that a stronger condition, that of non-causation, should be adopted. If correlation is understood in a weak sense, coming close to the simultaneous presence (ie high amount of P coexisting with high amount of G in a comparison between two individuals) then the resulting ideal of equality would be absurd. For instance, you could come from a highly respected family and I from a family of ill repute, and in addition I may have very little money because I just hate hard work for reasons (let us assume *arguendo*) that have nothing to do with my family background; to find the situation as violating a concept of equality would be nonsensical. So, there is a need for a relation of causation. But what sort of causation may it be? Not a very exigent one, for sure. The tighter the test for causation we establish, the less likely we will find a violation of the principle of equality, and the more toothless the ideal of equality will be. If only a direct, strict connection chain is posited in the P→G relationship so as to establish that unequal G is caused by unequal P, then a great deal of inequalities in G will persist without triggering our equality-based concern. This much seems to be obvious.

But a mere 'coexistence' of unequal P and unequal G, with no requirement of causation, may lead to absurd results as well. Suppose you and I have drastically unequal skills to perform a particular professional task, and it is also the case that you and I obtain unequal salaries. Is this difference in salaries a violation of the principle of equality? Not necessarily. Indeed, we usually think of individualized equality as requiring that morally irrelevant factors should not trigger unequal positions in life. But what we consider being relevant or not is a matter of a broader theory of justice. It does not derive from the principle of equality as such. If someone holds that inequality of skills must not count as a decisive factor in the determination of salaries, then the situation described earlier will indeed be deemed unequal. But this is a controversial and not widely accepted approach. If one adopts a substantive conception of justice according to which skills should play an important role in the determination of pay, then the coexistence of unequal P (skills) and G (pay) will not strike us as producing inequality. There will be inequality only if we determine that there is some other P applying both to you and me which indeed is unequal and which our theory disqualifies from producing unequal results, and then we ascertain that this unequal P has triggered an unequal G. So this is the third observation that needs to be made: the very fact of the mutual coexistence between unequal P and unequal G cannot in itself serve as an indication of inequality because inequality in G could be caused by inequality in some other P which, according to our theory of justice, mandates unequal distribution of G.

So much for a schematic outline of equality in an individualized sense which can also be described as equality in distribution.[1] As is clear, it requires a rigorous application of a principle according to which inequalities in some desired goods should not be tolerated when they result from certain characteristics of individuals, which are considered, in this instance, as morally arbitrary. The other conception of social equality—referred to as collective—is quite different. It applies to society as a whole rather than to particular individuals: it is a property of a given social structure or social relations. Looking at what any two individuals receive in function of this or that property of these individuals is insufficient to assess whether social equality has been achieved. One way of construing equality in this sense is a requirement, popularized by recent republican writings, of the absence of any domination among citizens (or members of any other relevant unit within which equality is postulated). Non-domination

[1] Ronald Dworkin uses the term of 'distributional equality'; Ronald Dworkin 'What Is Equality? Part 1: Equality of Welfare' *Philosophy & Public Affairs* (1981) 10: 185–246 at 185 (referred to as 'Equality of Welfare').

has been mainly postulated as a requirement of republican *freedom* but, for our purposes, we can adapt it as an egalitarian postulate. It demands that no one be subject to the possibility of an arbitrary interference by other people: non-domination occurs when people 'live among others and when ... no other has the capacity to interfere on an arbitrary basis in their choices'.[2] And while, as I said, the ideal of non-domination has been developed, by the most influential contemporary republican philosopher Philip Pettit, as an interpretation for a plausible ideal of freedom, it is also directly linked to equality. Indeed, Pettit explains that the republican principle of non-domination is required to support 'structural egalitarianism' because maximizing the ideal of non-domination demands that people enjoy this ideal with equal intensity.[3]

There are other ways of construing a collective notion of equality. One way is to say, with Elizabeth Anderson, that the 'point' of equality is 'to abolish oppression—that is, forms of social relationship by which some people dominate, exploit, marginalize, demean, and inflict violence upon others', and positively, that equality expresses people's urge 'to live together in a democratic community, as opposed to a hierarchical one'.[4] Another is to say with Samuel Scheffler that the nature of our concern with equality as a value is expressed in equal political citizenship: it is encapsulated in the reasons why 'it is important to us ... to live in a society in which citizens relate to one another as equals'.[5] Inegalitarian societies, Scheffler explains, compromise human flourishing and exert 'a stifling effect on human freedom and inhibit the possibilities of human exchange'.[6] Or, in David Miller's formulation of 'social equality' (which corresponds to what I call here a collective one), 'Wherever there is social equality, people feel that each member of the community enjoys an equal standing with all the rest that overrides members' unequal ratings along particular dimensions. This is expressed in the way people interact: ... they shake hands rather than bow ... '.[7]

What does it mean to say that the collective concept of equality describes a property of social relations rather than an individualized property? One should be careful not to confuse different possible implications of this distinction. One meaning would be obviously false: this would be a suggestion that in the first sense equality as such resides in something specific to an individual, while in the second it derives from a social relation. However, both individualized and collective notions of equality are about social relations; equality is a relational concept *par excellence*, and it cannot be ascertained without drawing comparisons

[2] Philip Pettit *Republicanism: A Theory of Freedom and Government* (Oxford: Clarendon Press, 1997) 67.

[3] ibid at 110–17.

[4] Elizabeth Anderson 'What Is the Point of Equality?' *Ethics* (1999) 109: 287–337 at 313.

[5] Samuel Scheffler 'Choice, Circumstance, and the Value of Equality' *Politics, Philosophy & Economics* (2005) 4: 5–28 at 18.

[6] ibid at 19.

[7] David Miller *Principles of Social Justice* (Cambridge, Mass: Harvard University Press, 1999) 239.

between individuals. This partly resonates with a question, once discussed in theories of justice, whether justice is necessarily a comparative virtue.[8] Saying that a person A is equal is semantic nonsense; the difference between individualized and collective concepts of equality cannot reside in a relational versus non-relational character of the ideal. On the other hand, there is a temptation to say that the difference derives from the identity of the beneficiaries of the moral ideal of equality: according to the first conception, the beneficiaries are the individuals, while in the latter sense, it is society (or any other group within which equality is being ascertained). But this distinction, although not preposterous, is very dubious because it would force us to say that under the second (collective) notion of equality, it is an ideal whose benefits do not trickle down to specific individuals but remain, so to speak, at the level of the group. And yet, any social ideal which were to establish that it cannot encompass any particular goods that could be applied to individuals, taken one by one, would be extremely unconvincing: why would anyone be attracted to an ideal which cannot identify any good effects reducible to individual benefits? And it would be inaccurate, and unfair, to attribute to the proponents of a collective concept a view that the worth of equality cannot be translated into something that is of value to particular individuals.

This point deserves to be dwelled upon. Indeed, according to a number of interpretations, equality is a puzzling, perhaps a disturbing value, precisely because it is claimed that equality is *that* sort of ideal: it is about an (alleged) good for the group that cannot be reduced to any meaningful good for the individuals. Such an argument serves to defeat equality as a good in itself, and to show that it is a confused ideal. Joseph Raz claims that, if equality were to be the only moral or political principle then it would have the following absurd consequence: 'The only intrinsic goods and ills such principles admit of are relational ones. If they constitute the entire foundation of morality then the happiness of a person does not matter except if there are other happy people',[9] which is evidently absurd. This can be construed as meaning that *if* equality were the only matter of value then nothing good or bad about individual people would matter, because goodness or badness would reside only in relational properties. But this 'if' is a huge one, and Raz's point only serves to reveal the absurdity of reducing all morality to the single value of equality. It would be absurd indeed, and it is hard to think of anyone espousing such an eccentric philosophy. Such a philosophy would indeed imply that we should be indifferent between equality in happiness and equality in suffering, or between equality achieved by giving deprived people extra goods and equality achieved by removing such goods from those fortunate enough to behold them. But granted that we accept Raz's point, and that we use equality as

[8] See Joel Feinberg 'Noncomparative Justice' in his *Rights, Justice, and the Bounds of Liberty* (Dordrecht: D. Reidel, 1985) (Princeton: Princeton University Press, 1980) 265–305; Phillip Montague 'Comparative and Non-Comparative Justice', *Philosophical Quarterly* (1980) 30: 131–40; Wojciech Sadurski *Giving Desert Its Due* at 14–23.

[9] Joseph Raz *The Morality of Freedom* at 235.

a value necessarily combined with a number of other values that are not reducible to equality: that suffering is bad and happiness is good, for example. Can it not be shown that equality, even used in tandem with another value, is in itself a confused value because it refers to what is good *between* people and not *for and about* people? As Denis McKerlie claims, equality (according to a number of interpretations, which he dubs 'teleological') 'asks us to see as having value something that is in an important sense divorced from benefits for people. Achieving equality does not necessarily mean improving the quality of any life'.[10]

This, let us emphasize, is a conceptually *different* question from that which is often raised together with it, namely whether it is worth achieving equality even if it means taking away something from some people without giving anything extra to the others. This second question, which may be called a levelling-down question, is often adduced to underline the absurdity of egalitarian principles: such a regime of equality would imply accepting as a moral gain, as McKerlie argues, that 'we reduce inequality in a way that harms some people and helps no one', and in particular, that 'the better-off person [is] simply reduced to the level of the worse-off person'.[11] In the words of Raz, 'instead of achieving equality by giving the benefit to those who lack it one can equally (in so far as egalitarian principles are concerned) achieve it by denying the benefit to those who have it'.[12] Indeed, both Raz and McKerlie connect the levelling-down problem with the alleged absurdity of identifying value in relational qualities only. But these are conceptually two separate questions. The levelling-down issue would become a thorny problem for egalitarians only if equality were to be conceived as the *only* value (which is absurd), or if it were so powerful as to trump the disutility of taking away from the better off (which is question begging). But if we combine equality with a number of other moral principles which are not reducible to equality, such an absurd consequence is avoided: we will always be compelled to weigh the good of more equal relations against the bad of removing some goods from those who already have them.[13] But the 'relational' problem is a different one. It is that, as McKerlie correctly observes, there is indeed something deeply troubling about espousing a moral value which does not identify any particular good for the individuals, but whose goodness resides only in relations between people. It is very hard for us to visualize a moral good which, strictly speaking, does not benefit anyone.

So, if the collective conception of equality, described earlier, is to avoid clashing with our intuitive moral sensitivity, it must be shown not to display such characteristics: it must be shown to bring with it the values which are meaningful to

[10] Denis McKerlie 'Equality' *Ethics* (1996) 106: 274–96 at 285.

[11] ibid at 286.

[12] Raz *The Morality of Freedom* at 227.

[13] I take it that it is Cohen's position; see GA Cohen 'Incentives, Inequality, and Community' in G Peterson (ed) *The Tanner Lectures on Human Values* vol 13 (Salt Lake City: University of Utah Press, 1992) 263–329 at 267–8.

particular individuals, taken one by one, and not just to social entities. This can be demonstrated only by exploring the avowed *rationale* of those who posit collective notions of equality as an attractive moral ideal, and by assessing whether this rationale can be translated into goods that are meaningful to particular people, taken individually. Consider Pettit's ideal of non-domination: is it an ideal which can be attributed meaningfully only to a group and not to individual members? Obviously this is not the case. Non-domination is directly related to the values which individuals have good reasons to try to achieve in the course of their individual lives: as Pettit puts it, it is 'the sort of thing that anyone will desire for themselves and, generalizing to the case of others, will admit as desirable for anyone'.[14] Likewise with the ideal espoused by Anderson: to live in a society of democratic equality means 'that one is entitled to participate, that others recognize an obligation to listen respectfully and respond to one's arguments, that no one need bow and scrape before others or represent themselves as inferior to others as a condition of having their claim heard'.[15] And similarly with Scheffler, the way he describes the reasons for valuing equality is unambiguously coined in terms of individual values: the values of human flourishing, of personal freedom, of conditions for self-respect, and of interpersonal communication. '[T]o live in society as an equal among equals is a good thing in its own right'[16] rather than being instrumental to other aims—and it is obvious that this intrinsic goodness is described purely in light of the conditions for an individual good.

The critique of egalitarianism as applying to relations rather than individuals is therefore easily countered when we assess the meaning of this ideal through the only prism which is accurate in the interpretation of moral values, that is, through the prism of the moral good which prompts us to postulate a given ideal in the first place. Once we translate the question: 'who is the proper holder of the attribute of equality: individuals or a social group?' into the question: 'who are the beneficiaries of the values carried by the ideal of equality: individuals or (only) a social group?', the meaninglessness of claiming that equality cannot be attributed to individuals but only to the social group as an entity, becomes obvious. Consequently, this cannot be used as a basis to establish the distinction between the individualized and the collective conceptions of social equality.

So where does this difference reside? To answer, it may be helpful to explore the arguments of those who criticize individualized conceptions of equality from the point of view of collective equality. One approach to individualized equality (not the only one, but a particularly influential one lately) is so-called luck-egalitarianism: the idea that equality can be conceived as an ideal whose aim is to eliminate the impact of luck (or bad fortune) on our social positions, which (it is claimed) would have the result of creating a state of more equality than if these

[14] Pettit *Republicanism* at 82.
[15] Anderson 'What Is the Point of Equality?' at 313 (reference omitted).
[16] Scheffler 'Choice, Circumstance, and the Value of Equality' at 19.

bad-fortune factors were operative. Luck-egalitarianism can therefore be easily translated into what was referred to here as individualized equality: it claims that some types of properties of individuals (P) must not trigger unequal distribution of certain goods (G). In this case, properties P which are disqualified from triggering unequal amounts of good G are those which can be properly described as fortuitous, morally arbitrary, or as being beyond any effective control for an individual concerned.

This version of individualized equality has been subjected to strong criticisms from the point of view of a collective notion of equality. (Note that I am not concerned, at this point, about any possible critiques of luck egalitarianism, and they are legion; I am only interested in those critiques which can be properly seen as warranted by the values foundational to *collective* equality as such, as epitomized by the ideal of non-domination, or non-subordination, or non-exploitation etc—for my only purpose at this point is to see what exactly is at stake in the distinction between individualized and collective ideals of equality.) The most representative critiques are those presented by Anderson and Scheffler. They are important for our purposes here because both are offered explicitly and deliberately as the refutation, from the perspective of collective equality, of luck egalitarianism. Scheffler criticizes luck egalitarianism (which he calls a 'responsibility-based conception of equality') for its excessive, as he claims, focus on questions of distribution, and because of its assumption (unjustified, according to him) that 'an egalitarian conception of justice is one that seeks to distribute something equally'. Thus, in the search for a 'currency' of egalitarian distribution, the theorists espousing that conception 'have made little attempt to situate the distributive principles they favor within a broader conception of the nature of egalitarian social relationships'.[17] Similarly, Anderson rebukes luck egalitarians for conceiving of equality as a 'pattern of distribution' rather than as 'relational', and of thus losing sight of the main objectives enshrined in egalitarian concerns, namely oppression and exploitation.[18] According to these authors, by pursuing the aim of compensating individuals for undeserved bad luck, the egalitarians espousing this ideal have 'lost sight of the distinctively political aims of egalitarianism'.[19]

Both Anderson and Scheffler have advanced a number of very specific, important critiques of luck egalitarianism, and they will be discussed at some length in the next chapter, but at this point what matters is only their rejection of the distribution-oriented concept of equality, on the basis of a relational, ergo collective concept of equality. Why should anyone find these two approaches antithetical? To start with, it is clear that there are many symmetries and mutual dependencies between both concepts of equality. There are many instances when individualized equality is a condition for the implementation of a collective ideal of equality. An

17 Scheffler 'Choice, Circumstance, and the Value of Equality' at 20.
18 Anderson 'What Is the Point of Equality?' at 313.
19 ibid at 288.

obvious example, which springs to mind, is that of equal distribution of votes. Equal distribution of the weight of each citizen's vote (hence, an implementation of an individualized notion of equality, implying here that certain P, such as education, wealth, or IQ, cannot serve as rationale for an unequal allocation of a specific G, in this instance a voting right) is a condition of the sort of equality of citizenship, and of non-subordination, that Scheffler and Anderson have in mind when they defend their collective (my word, not theirs) ideals of equality. It is, of course, only a necessary and not a sufficient condition. But it is clear that any differentiation in the weight of votes in pursuit of factors such as those mentioned above would be offensive to the ideal of equal citizenship by creating a class of people stigmatized as citizens belonging to an inferior category: 'Once the status of citizenship is extended to all competent adults, it becomes essential that every member of the political community is treated equally, and this is given material expression in equality of voting rights'.[20] The example may be extended. A great number of inequalities (from the perspective of a plausible individualized notion of equality) violate the conditions of equality in a collective sense: unequal access to education leads to the possibility of manipulation and exploitation of those confined to lower educational levels; drastically unequal wealth status leads to marginalization and class subordination etc. Some violations of the very ideal of luck egalitarianism, towards which Scheffler and Anderson are so critical from the perspective of collective notions of equality, will clearly undermine the possibilities for a non-hierarchical society. For example, if 'bad luck'—in the form of being born with a socially stigmatized family status—is not neutralized in the process of allocation of desired goods, a person will be confined to a marginalized and subordinated social category, and the conditions for a plausible collective notion of equality will therefore be undermined.

So we can see that some individualized strictures of equality condition the implementation of a collective egalitarian ideal. But there is also a reverse interdependence. A collective ideal of equality, that of a society where dominating structures do not pervade relations among individuals, is a condition for the implementation of any plausible individualized ideal of equality. This can be shown, again, with an ideal promoted by luck egalitarianism. It demands that people are not disadvantaged in the distribution of socially valued goods by factors which are a matter of 'brute luck'—that is, for which individuals cannot be held accountable. This ideal makes sense only against the background of egalitarian assumptions in a larger sense, which are 'collective' in their nature. This larger picture must include some assumptions as to the categories of social goods which should be distributed, and thus make some hypotheses as to the distinction between the spheres of life for which we should be held accountable individually and the sphere within which we have some duties of solidarity towards our fellow human beings. It must also include some moral ideas as to why it is wrong

[20] Miller *Principles of Social Justice* at 238.

(from the point of view of fundamentally egalitarian motives) to let other people endure conditions resulting from social misfortunes. It must therefore identify what counts merely as a 'natural' distribution of certain goods (eg an earthquake occurring in one part of the country, rather than another) as opposed to the social consequences of such facts (eg the failure to compensate for social disadvantages arising from a natural distribution). Furthermore, concerning in particular luck egalitarianism, this broader picture must include the ideal of establishing a free person's accountability for his/her actions: by drawing a line between 'option luck' (the consequences of deliberately undertaken risks) and 'brute luck' (fortuitous consequences not resulting from any deliberate gamble), the theory posits the importance of letting people choose, in light of consequences known beforehand, and therefore lead a style of life characterized by a degree of risk-taking that matches a person's psychological predispositions. Overall, luck egalitarianism is based on a particular view about society as a whole, a society in which there is a certain morally attractive balance between the areas of people's responsibility for their own actions (including for the choice of an acceptable degree of luck in one's life) and, on the other hand, common responsibility for redressing other people's misfortunes which cannot be traced to any deliberate choice or action taken by those people. In such a society, the ideal of equality takes into account the choices people make but not the factors which are fully outside their control. A society which displays such a balance is, naturally, a society with a very limited tolerance for interpersonal oppression, exploitation, and subordination.

One way in which the mutual synergy between the individualized and collective conceptions of equality may be depicted is by underlining that the collective approaches necessarily underdetermine our rules for egalitarian distribution, and that individualized notions may serve to fill the gaps resulting from this underdetermination. A plausible principle of collective equality, that of not allowing social inequalities to create permanently subordinate classes, fails to specify exactly what the differences in incomes should be, and at which point the disparity breaks down social cohesion and creates intolerable dependency. Individualized social equality may determine these more specific rules by identifying the factors, which may (within the limits dictated by collective notions) or may not trigger inequalities. This can be so, similarly, when we are uncertain as to the role various morally relevant factors may have played in a particular individual performance—when we do not know what the relevant desert, as assessed according to the effort, the contribution, or any other morally relevant factor, should be. A conception of individualized equality may provide such a default principle, which would respond to such circumstances of uncertainty.[21]

The picture which emerges from this discussion is that there is continuity rather than a clash between individualized and collective notions of social equality. Individualized ideals cannot be implemented without a pervasive spirit of

[21] Similarly Miller *ibid at* 234–5.

egalitarian social relations postulated by collective ideals, and in turn these collective ideals are made possible through the implementation of morally plausible ideals of individualized equality. Contrary to the critics of individualized ideals who formulate their objections on the basis of collective ideals, there is a fundamental congruence, and the individualized ideals seem to be more precise, specific concretizations of vaguer ideals, ie the collective ones. Why should one believe otherwise?

There are two explanations for this startling contrast drawn by proponents of collective ideals. The first is that the language used by proponents of individual equality conceptions—in particular by 'luck egalitarians'—is often misleading in its anti-collective orientation. In a canonical text of luck egalitarianism—the original Dworkin's two-part article on equality—which sparked the whole luck-egalitarian literature, Dworkin went to quite some lengths to emphasize that, according to his theory on equality of resources, 'equality is in principle a matter of individual rather than group position'.[22] He went on to describe what he meant by this: 'the theory supposes that equality defines a relation among citizens that is individualized for each, and therefore can be seen to set entitlements as much from the point of view of each person as that of anyone else in the community'.[23] I am not sure to what extent this particular statement weighed on the antipathy expressed by Anderson or by Scheffler against individualized conceptions of equality (as none of them refers specifically to this citation) but the tone of Dworkin's words may have led critics to the conclusion that luck egalitarianism has no potential for any structural reform. This would be a mistake, though. This explanation proffered by Dworkin is made in a specific context in which he draws a distinction between his own theory and that of John Rawls, as encapsulated in the difference principle. Dworkin argues that 'equality of resources' focuses on entitlements of an individual qua individual as opposed to the difference principle which is concerned with individuals, insofar as they are representative of groups. In this, but only this sense, his theory is individual-oriented, while Rawls's difference principle may be seen to be postulating 'equality between groups',[24] since individuals are conceptualized right at the outset, at the stage of the construction of the original position, as representatives of groups. But, obviously, the consequence would not be that the conception of equality of resources or, for that matter, any other interpretation of luck egalitarianism, is not concerned about structural dimensions of equality and differences throughout society.

My second hypothesis is that the most vocal critics of recent versions of individualized ideals of equality, ie Scheffler and Anderson, confuse social equality with a conceptually distinct ideal of democratic self-government. (Again, I wish to emphasize that I do not address at this point their more specific objections

[22] Ronald Dworkin 'What Is Equality? Part 2: Equality of Resources' *Philosophy & Public Affairs* (1981) 10: 283–345 at 340 (referred to as 'Equality of Resources').

[23] ibid at 340–1.

[24] ibid at 341.

against luck egalitarianism, to which I will return in the next chapter, but am only concerned with their fundamental rebuttal of individualized notions of equality as such: their critique of luck egalitarianism is, at this point, of interest to me as an exemplification of a collective versus individualized equality confrontation.) This comes across rather clearly in both critiques. Scheffler argues that 'an egalitarian scheme of distributive justice is best understood as one that tries to provide answers' to questions such as 'what forms of political authority are compatible with a society of equals, what regime of rights and freedoms such a society requires, and how compatibly with a commitment to egalitarian membership and individuals' differing aims, values, identifications and group affiliations can best be accommodated'.[25] Anderson formulates her critique in terms of 'the point' of equality: in her view, 'the point' is not to neutralize the effects of bad luck for individuals, but rather to remove oppression. She calls it 'democratic equality', and explains that it 'regards two people as equal when each accepts the obligation to justify their actions by principles acceptable to the other, and in which they take mutual consultation, reciprocation, and recognition for granted'.[26] This formula, it should be emphasized, is being offered as a better *alternative* to equality of fortune according to which 'two people [are] equal so long as they enjoy equal amounts of some distributable good—income, resources, opportunity for welfare, and so forth'.[27] It seems, however, that Anderson's preferred formula is not another, more comprehensive understanding of social equality but rather a parallel ideal, that of democracy, and more specifically, a deliberative version of it, according to which people are equally required to justify their proposed actions, by referring to standards acceptable to others. This impression is further strengthened when Anderson goes on to discuss the interconnection between freedom and (her understanding of) equality: the way she presents it, is by arguing that freedom flourishes in truly equal relationships, and the two ideals are thus coextensive: 'equals are not subject to arbitrary violence or physical coercion by others. Choice unconstrained by arbitrary physical coercion is one of the fundamental conditions of freedom. Equals are not marginalized by others' etc.[28] This may all be true but the co-extensiveness of freedom and 'equality' is achieved here through a very specific notion of equality: democracy is indeed equal freedom, and thus, trivially, it is true that equality of freedom reconciles equality with freedom in just this way. But the conflict cannot be put away so easily; what we want to know is how various aspects of social equality (equality in the access to various other desired goods, not just political influence) can coexist with, and sometimes even be conditioned by, restraints upon individual freedom, and indeed upon the scope of democratic decisions. If we pose the question in such a

[25] Scheffler 'Choice, Circumstance, and the Value of Equality' at 20.
[26] Anderson 'What Is the Point of Equality?' at 313.
[27] ibid.
[28] ibid at 315.

way, equality is not simply reducible to equal political influence in a deliberative version of democracy.

We should therefore keep these ideals separate: both are important, but not identical. In Chapter 2, I insisted on the separation of the political from the social realm: we are justified in insisting that there be equal influence on collective decisions, *and also* on equality in the distribution of social goods (when no plausible grounds for unequal distributions prevail), but these are different concerns, both conceptually and normatively.[29] No advantage is gained from merging them into one aggregate ideal because it prevents us from considering trade-offs, when equal citizenship may lead to objectionably unequal distributions, or when equal distributions are best secured by departures from the ideal of equal voting rights. This is just one other extension of the conceptual and normative separation between democracy and justice.

But Scheffler and Anderson may try to say something else when they reject a version of individual equality in the name of a collective one: they may be trying to contend that the whole aim of the great egalitarian movement ('the point of equality', to use the preferred vocabulary of Anderson) has been to restructure society in a more egalitarian spirit, rather than to ensure equality in distribution of specific goods and opportunities—with less domination and hierarchy, and with more mutual recognition of people as equals, capable of deliberating at equal levels, and recognizing each other as equally worthy fellow citizens. In this light, call it a social-theoretic interpretation, the 'point' of equality is badly distorted (the argument goes) when we try to assess the 'currency' of egalitarian justice, raising questions about what it means to distribute goods to people equally, even though they have unequal endowments, aspirations, initial resources. This interpretation is clearly suggested by both authors who indicate repeatedly how dismayed they are by the equality-of-fortune approach: we should be thinking about societal hierarchies, we are told, rather than about whether 'the state [should] support lazy, able-bodied surfers who are unwilling to work', or 'subsidize extremely costly religious ceremonies that its citizens feel bound to perform', or 'compensate people for being temperamentally gloomy', etc.[30] But if *this* is an interpretation of the 'point' of equality, ie the best interpretation we can give of the movements and strands of thought which we intuitively recognize as egalitarian, then it is a strangely faulty one. For in the human thinking on equality, the problems of 'distributional' equality, that is, of equality in *who* gets *what* under *which* circumstances, have been as (if not more) prominent as the problem of the elimination of hierarchy. In fact, the idea that the latter can be seen as *replacing* the former in our egalitarian motives seems to be puzzling in itself. At this stage,

[29] See pp 74–7; see also Robert E Goodin 'Democracy, Justice and Impartiality' in Keith Dowding, Robert E Goodin, and Carol Pateman (eds) *Justice and Democracy: Essays for Brian Barry* (Cambridge: Cambridge University Press, 2004) 97–111.

[30] Anderson 'What Is the Point of Equality?' at 287.

this may sound like a mere assertion, not an argument, but all I wish to contend is that the idea of continuity between distributional and collective equality seems to reflect well our intuitive thinking about equality. Whether it withstands a critical analytical scrutiny is another matter, to be pursued further in the next chapter.

2. 'Natural and Social Lottery'

It is commonplace, at least within the left-leaning branch of liberalism taking its cue from John Rawls's theory of justice, to argue that socially generated inequalities, ie those attributable to differences in wealth inheritance, family station, upbringing, and various other fortuitous social circumstances, are arbitrary from a moral point of view. We cannot, morally speaking, claim any credit for benefiting from circumstances which we have not brought about, or have affected, through our conscious or our deliberate actions. That much is often accepted as a moral truth so obvious as not requiring any further defence. But then, arguably, it should be equally obvious that 'natural' inequalities, that is, those attributed solely to our inborn superior natural abilities, skills, and talents, are morally arbitrary, too. Their beneficial effect on our life opportunities is as 'undeserved' as that of social circumstances. What implications does this analogy between social and natural inequalities bear for a theory of justice?

There are, roughly, three possible responses to the above observation. The first response is to admit the equal moral arbitrariness of natural and social inequalities, but to deny the validity of any redistributive conclusions stemming from them. This is a classical conservative position: 'undeserved' deprivations are just bad luck, regardless of whether they can be attributed to social arrangements or to natural differences. It is not a proper purpose for a legal system to counter the adverse effects of luck in general. This argument, expressed for example in an article by Richard Epstein, captures well a widespread conservative conventional wisdom, 'in general the effort to use coercion to counter the adverse effects of bad luck tends only to make matters worse'.[31] 'Life is not fair', proclaims Milton Friedman[32] and a legion of free-market conservatives with him. Significantly, Friedman actually uses the analogy between natural and social inequalities in order to assert the inevitability of undeserved social inequalities, on the basis of their equal moral status with natural ones: 'The inheritance of property can be interfered with more readily than the inheritance of talent. But from an ethical point of view, is there any difference between the two? Yet many people resent the inheritance of property but not the inheritance of talent'.[33]

[31] RA Epstein 'Luck' *Social Philosophy & Policy* (1988) 6: 17–38 at 17.
[32] M Friedman *Free to Choose* (Harmondsworth: Penguin Books, 1980) 168.
[33] ibid.

The second response is a mirror image of the first one: it also asserts the equal moral status of natural and social inequalities, but argues, on this basis, for social efforts aimed at nullifying or at least moderating the effects of both. This time, the strength of the intuition of a duty to redress *social* disadvantages is put forth in the argument about removing the differential benefits of *natural* talents and skills. This is developed in the syllogism of Herbert Spiegelberg: '(1) undeserved discriminations call for redress, (2) all inequalities of birth constitute undeserved discriminations... (3) all inequalities of birth call for redress'.[34] The operative is, of course, the first premise, which is considered as 'self-evident'[35] by Spiegelberg. The same result is reached in Rawls's difference principle which he characterizes as representing 'an agreement to regard the distribution of natural talents as a common asset and to share in the benefits of this distribution whatever it turns out to be'.[36] The intuition about the equivalent arbitrariness of natural and social contingencies was articulated by Rawls explicitly: 'It seems to be one of the fixed points of our considered judgments that no one deserves his place in the distribution of native endowments, any more than one deserves one's initial starting place in society'.[37] The equal moral arbitrariness of natural and social 'lottery' provides the basis for an equally justified redistributive action, according to the egalitarian conceptions of the 'common pool' of benefits, be they deriving from natural or social assets (Rawls), Dworkin's idea of the equality of resources, which is not 'endowment-sensitive',[38] Cohen's egalitarianism, built upon the precept that 'no one should fare worse than others do because of bad brute luck' with the proviso that 'no luck is bruter than that how one is born, raised and circumstanced',[39] or a host of other egalitarian theories.[40]

The third possible response is to *deny* the moral equivalence of natural and social differences. This view originates in an appeal for a reasonable compromise which would capture the middle ground between the heartless conservatism of an outright rejection of any compensation for fortuitous disadvantages and (what may be viewed as) the radicalism of the egalitarian position. The third position may still admit that natural and social inequalities are similarly morally arbitrary but it claims that there are some morally relevant differences between these two types of sources of inequalities. The upshot is that while a society has a duty to remove the benefits arising from undeserved *social* inequalities, no such

[34] H Spiegelberg 'A Defense of Human Equality' *Philosophical Review* (1944) 53: 101–24 at 113.

[35] Or, more precisely, 'at least as selfevident [*sic*] as any other ethical insight', ibid at 114.

[36] Rawls *A Theory of Justice* at 101.

[37] ibid at 104.

[38] Dworkin 'Equality of Resources' at 311 ('we must not allow the distribution of resources at any moment to be endowment-sensitive...).

[39] GA Cohen *Self-ownership, Freedom, and Equality* (Cambridge : Cambridge University Press, 1995) 229 (footnote omitted).

[40] See inter alia Ch Ake 'Justice and Equality' *Philosophy & Public Affairs* (1975) 5: 69–90; H Milne 'Desert, Effort and Equality' *Journal of Applied Philosophy* (1986) 3: 235–43; W Sadurski *Giving Desert Its Due* (Dordrecht: D Reidel, 1985).

duty applies to unequal (even though undeserved) *natural* talents, skills and capacities.

It is this third position that I propose to discuss, criticize, and eventually reject in the remainder of this chapter. I will not rest my case against this third position on the simple observation that the natural and social causes of unequal benefits are so mutually entangled that it is not possible to draw the line between these two categories. To be sure, this observation bears a considerable weight. The benefits that are most likely to be challenged by the egalitarians derive from what we may generally call the productive capacities, ie those capacities which yield income. In a complex industrial society, incomes result from a very complex mix of the use of natural talents and of skills developed through upbringing, education, and training, the latter being *par excellence* social. 'A skill at healing, for example, is acquired through a natural aptitude for study, perseverance in school work, and an investment of hundreds of thousands of dollars worth of society's time and energy'.[41] An attempt to separate what is generated by an individual's initial genetic endowment and what is due to social resources, access to which cannot be credited to an individual's effort, may prove hopeless. The very idea that there are some pre-social, natural abilities, which can be discerned in an individual, while all the social inputs can be screened off, sounds fanciful. But in this chapter no use will be made of this observation. This is mainly because the argument about the practical amalgamation of the two categories of capacities is not sufficient to reject the aspiration for a theory of justice that would draw a distinction between the two, if there are sound moral reasons pointing to their fundamental difference. All that this observation may ultimately prove is that perfect justice is unattainable in practice; it does not undermine the moral attractiveness of the aspiration itself. Most importantly, however, the burden of the argument about how to disentangle the natural from the social factors should rely on those who base their conception on this distinction. This is *not* my position, and for the purposes of scrutinizing the natural/social distinction it is enough to posit, *arguendo*, that such a distinction *is* intelligible.

Before going ahead and reviewing the 'natural/social contingency' analogy, a digression about the concept of natural (or social) 'lottery' is in order. The concept of lottery is used now and then, in particular with regard to natural attributes, talents, and skills, but also with regard to social opportunities to which a person has been born (such as family wealth or connections) to emphasize the lack of responsibility, either in terms of praise or of blame, of a person for her own natural attributes and for the social position at birth. 'Birth itself, as the phrase "accidents of birth" suggests, is something of a *lottery*' says Epstein, himself an opponent of a nullification of luck in natural distribution.[42] Among

[41] A Kernohan 'Capitalism and Self-Ownership' *Social Philosophy & Policy* (1988) 6: 6–76 at 62.

[42] Epstein 'Luck' at 18 (emphasis added).

the proponents of such nullification, Rawls has been the most influential in decrying the situation in which 'distributive shares are decided by the outcome of the natural *lottery*'.[43] Echoing him, Anthony Kronman asserts that: 'It is unfair that people's fate should be determined, to a considerable degree, by a natural *lottery*'.[44] By extension, this concept of '*natural* lottery' is sometimes applied also to the *social* opportunities a person has access to without having 'earned' them in any way, such as by being born into a more or less affluent family etc.[45]

The notion of 'lottery' as applied to these circumstances is of course nothing but a metaphor, and just like any metaphor, it illuminates some aspects and distorts others; it has to be used with caution, and one should be aware of its limitations. In the case of the 'lottery' metaphor, there are two reasons why it inadequately captures the point about the contingency of (and, therefore, the lack of personal responsibility for) the distribution of natural attributes and social opportunities (such as the family into which one is born). The first and most striking reason for this inadequacy is that we usually consider lottery as a matter of 'option luck', whose results are traceable to a choice (even though only a choice to take part in the lottery event)[46] and therefore which should not be subject to any nullification or even modification. Indeed, if the results of a gamble were to be subject to reversal, the whole enterprise of gambling (or lottery) would be pointless.[47] The fundamental *moral* point about respecting the outcomes of such ordinary lotteries is that there is a correspondence of identity between the person who 'plays' the lottery and the person who is its winner or loser. But in the 'natural' lottery there is no such equivalence; the 'player' is impersonal: it is life itself,[48] or 'nature', or God, for those who believe. For this reason, the metaphor of the 'lottery' does not grasp adequately the intentions of those who use it and who wish to emphasize contingency, and therefore call for a nullification of the effects of distribution of natural attributes. The second, and minor point of difference, is that normally, the 'prize' in a lottery is known and determined ex ante, at the point of entrance into a lottery: the stakes are well defined from the outset. (Whether it is a necessary ingredient of any properly so-called 'lottery' is irrelevant here; one can probably find examples of 'lotteries' with undefined stakes: for example, when the prize depends on the number of participants, which in itself is unknown at the beginning as the participation in the lottery may be wide open.)

[43] Rawls *A Theory of Justice* at 74 (emphasis added).

[44] AT Kronman 'Talent Pooling' in JR Pennock and JW Chapman (eds) *Human Rights: Nomos XXIII* (New York: New York University Press, 1981) 58–79 at 76 (emphasis added).

[45] See Rawls *A Theory of Justice* where he says that his favoured interpretation of two principles of justice 'does not weight men's share in the benefits and burdens of social cooperation according to their social fortune or their luck in the natural lottery'. From now on, until the end of this part of the chapter I will be referring to 'natural' lottery only.

[46] For a concept of option luck, distinguished from brute luck, see Dworkin 'Equality of Resources' at 293.

[47] See ibid at 293–5.

[48] Dworkin talks about brute bad luck as 'bad luck that flows not from a gamble deliberately taken but from life itself': Dworkin *Sovereign Virtue* at 341.

In contrast, in the 'natural' lottery the outcome is totally indeterminate at the point in which the 'game' is 'played'.

But, as with all other metaphors, one must not protest too much when depicting the inadequacy of this particular metaphor to capture the intuitions we have when reflecting on the contingent nature of the distribution of natural characteristics. In this context, a serious challenge against the lottery metaphor was expressed by Susan Hurley, and I propose to ponder briefly this challenge because it may be helpful to clarify the conceptual field at stake. Hurley refers to the natural-lottery concept as related to 'constitutive luck', understood as a matter of 'good or bad luck in the form of morally arbitrary natural or social advantages or disadvantages: innate talents or handicaps, advantageous or disadvantageous family situations'.[49] The picture of lottery is misleading, she claims, because, usually, when talking about luck in lottery, we presuppose the continuity of identity over time, and in particular before the lottery is entered into, and at the point in which the results of the lottery are announced: 'Without an identity that is constant across alternatives, we do not have a gamble or lottery but merely different possibilities—some good, some bad—in which different entities exist and different things happen'.[50] This identity-dependence, however, is not present in the case of 'constitutive luck': 'it may be good or bad luck *tout court* that this happened rather than that, but if it is not good or bad luck *for someone*, then it is not the result of a lottery or a gamble. It might be a matter of good luck that the sperm and the egg from which Mozart developed came together, rather than some others. But this does not mean Mozart might have been someone else, and that he was lucky to have been Mozart....'. [51] The lottery argument, in this context, Hurley urges, should be abandoned because the lottery metaphor encourages us to think in an incoherent way: 'there can be no proto-self or possible self or bare self who might-have-existed-as-you or who-might-have-existed-as-someone-else...But the metaphor of a lottery of essential properties may encourage us to think in these incoherent terms'.[52]

Is this objection capable of shattering the ideal of a lottery in the distribution of constitutive attributes? If it were, much of the moral impulse behind the lottery metaphor would have to be eroded. To be sure, we intuitively see an intelligible moral insight in saying: 'X was lucky to have been born to this family, or with all her talents', and also in contending, for instance: 'Y was unlucky to have been born in a place where he could not cultivate his innate skills'. Hurley's objection to the use of a lottery metaphor in these cases is that there was no 'X' or 'Y' before their birth (or their conception, if you like) in the first place: how can we thus talk

[49] SL Hurley *Justice, Luck, and Knowledge* (Cambridge, Mass: Harvard University Press, 2003) 117.

[50] ibid at 119.

[51] ibid at 119–20 (emphasis in original).

[52] ibid at 121. Note that Susan Hurley has more to say against the lottery metaphor, including about the notion of 'chance', see ibid at 123–7, but I focus here only on the argument which I find more devastating to the use of the metaphor in the present context.

of a constitutive good or bad luck in these cases? There was no pre-X who turned out lucky, and no proto-Y who turned out unlucky as a result of the operation of a natural or social lottery.

Note that the force of Hurley's objection rests on the lack of identity of the self, prior and after the event (the event which marks the point at which an imaginary 'lottery' announces its results). So to test how devastating the lack of continuity of identity is to the applicability of the lottery metaphor, consider another case of discontinuity, somewhat different from that explored by Hurley. Think about the following sentence: 'Z was very unlucky to have been on that flight as a result of the rebooking of his ticket: there was an accident, and the plane crashed to the ground killing all passengers'. The use of bad luck in this phrase does not strike us (does not strike *me*, at least) as inappropriate; nor does the analogy with lottery. And yet, there is no continuity between Z before the event and Z after the event (or, after the operation of the lottery): Z has been killed, and *this* event was precisely his bad luck.[53] There is no more post-Z than there was pre-X or pre-Y in our earlier examples. There is a discontinuity of the personal identity in both cases: in the case of Z, the 'lottery'-like event occurred at the finishing point of his life, in the case of X and Y—at the starting points of theirs. (Similarly, think of a 'Russian roulette': isn't the whole point about this macabre enterprise that it is lottery-like, with good or bad luck happening to the player?) This would suggest to me that the applicability of the lottery metaphor is not necessarily identity-dependent in the way Hurley urges: to use her own example, we can indeed think of Mozart having been very lucky to be born with all his talents (to think of him as a winner in a natural lottery) even though there had been no proto-Mozart, waiting to be born, awaiting the gifts that nature may, or may not, endow him with.

This is not to say that the symmetry between luck to have been born (into a particular family, in a particular time...etc) and (bad) luck in dying in a particular way, is perfect. In fact, there is a strong asymmetry between them both: it is more plausible to say (1) that X's life would have been better if she hadn't died in a particular accident than to say that (2) Y's life would have been better if he had been born in a different place or in a different country. The asymmetry stems from the fact that in (1) there is a stable 'she' whose life we consider, while in (2) a 'he' born elsewhere would have been a different person. But this asymmetry is not sufficient, it seems to me, to deny the plausibility of luck-talk in the case of (1). Consider this: we think of a life of a young musical genius and we think, how lucky she was that she was born into a family that could detect and help develop her talents; we think: if she was born into a very poor and musically illiterate family, with no-one else around capable of helping her to buy an instrument and study music, her innate talents would have gone undetected, and that would have

[53] A believer in life after death would probably not need to endorse this reasoning. But then, s/he may not characterize the event as a case of 'bad luck' (by considering the badness of it as having ended Z's live) but only an event altering the mode of existence of Z.

been a waste. Saying this does not strike me as unwarranted even though, strictly speaking, if she were born to a different family, she would indeed have been a different person. We implicitly rely on luck-talk in a counter-factual fashion rather than on a continuity of a person before and after the luck-relevant event. And if the luck-talk just provided (about a musical genius) strikes us as coherent, our theory of luck and lottery should preserve and account for this linguistic usage rather than condemn it as unreasonable.

3. Self-ownership and the 'Extensions' of a Right over One's Body

A good starting point for the critique of the third position, as defined in Part 1, namely on the moral non-equivalence of natural and social factors of inequality, is to reflect on the nature of an individual's relationship to his or her natural capacities. A morally relevant difference between natural and social advantages lies, Alan Goldman claimed, in that the former 'derive from, or rather equate with, the distinctness of physically embodied persons',[54] while the latter do 'not affect the basic identities of persons'.[55] To nullify naturally caused (dis)advantages therefore implies disregarding the separate identities of particular individuals.

It is necessary here to unpack the proposition that there is a strong link between natural attributes and individual identities. This usually comes in two versions: a 'self-ownership' version and a 'bodily integrity' version. The first one proclaims a person's ownership over his or her natural capacities. This conception, described by Robert Nozick as 'self-ownership',[56] derives from Locke: 'every man has a property in his own person; this nobody has any right to but himself. The labour of his body and the work of his hands, we may say, are properly his'.[57] The concept of self-ownership has been given a significant prominence in recent 'left-libertarian' literature in particular, and a good definition has been provided by Magnus Jedenheim-Edling: a person has effective self-ownership when she 'formally owns herself' and in addition 'has access to external resources so that she may exercise her self-ownership rights to a reasonable extent and the means to protect herself from marginalisation imposed by others'.[58] The problem with the 'self-ownership'

[54] AH Goldman 'Real People (Natural Differences and the Scope of Justice)' *Canadian Journal of Philosophy* (1987) 17: 377–94 at 378.

[55] ibid.

[56] R Nozick *Anarchy, State and Utopia* (New York: Basic Books, 1974) 172.

[57] John Locke 'The Second Treatise of Government' (ed) TP Peardon (Indianapolis: Bobbs-Merrill, 1952) 17.

[58] M Jedenheim-Edling 'The Compatibility of Effective Self-Ownership and Joint World Ownership' *Journal of Political Philosophy* (2005) 13: 284–304 at 287. Similarly, Michael Otsuka defines the full right of self-ownership in the following manner: 'a person's right of self-ownership is full if and only if that person possesses, to the greatest extent and stringency compatible with the same possession by others, the... rights "to decide what would become of himself and what he would

concept is that it is, at best, a vague metaphor which requires further elaboration, and at worst, a distortion of the nature of a person's relationship to his or her body and natural capacities. Oddly, the concept of 'self-ownership' at the same time *over-* and *under-*values the nature of this relationship. It *over-*values it, because there are certain typical incidents of property rights which do not apply to one's body or natural talents; we cannot, for instance, alienate or bequeath our talents, nor have them taken in repayment of debts.[59] Furthermore, the metaphor of self-ownership *under-*values what is at stake in our relationship to our bodies and talents. To suggest that we 'own' something presupposes a proprietary relationship between a person and an object separate from that person, and yet many writers would argue that our relationship to our bodies is stronger; our talents and bodies are constitutive of our very identities.[60] For my part, while I do not need to accept the equation of one's body with one's 'self', I would claim that a special protection of one's relationship to one's own body is based on the particular vulnerability of one's body to pain and discomfort. As a result, the wrong consisting in hurting the body is qualitatively different (sometimes greater, sometimes lower) than the harm done to one's property.

GA Cohen took issue with the point just made, ie that the concept of 'self-ownership' is incoherent because it confusedly implies a separation between the person-owner and the self being (allegedly) owned, the point I just characterized as disclosing an under-valuation of the relationship between a person and her body, talents etc. 'Self', Cohen explains, in the concept of 'self-ownership' has 'a purely reflexive significance'[61] and it does not connote 'the ownership of a self'.[62] Thus, according to Cohen, in order to use intelligibly the concept of self-ownership, we do not need to imagine that a person owns a separate entity (in this case, her own self), which would indeed be incoherent. But Cohen's defence of the concept is not quite convincing (even putting aside the fact that other users of the concept may indeed presuppose an ownership of the self in a stronger sense than Cohen does). Consider his defence: '[W]hat is there in the content of the concepts of ownership and personhood that might disqualify the concept of self-ownership? Persons and their powers can be controlled, among others by themselves, and there is surely always an answer to the question, with respect to anything that can be controlled, who has the right to control it? Even if that answer is no one: The thesis of self-ownership says that the answer to all such questions about persons and their powers is: the person herself'.[63]

do, and...reap the benefits of what he did"', Michael Otsuka *Libertarianism Without Inequality* (Oxford: Oxford University Press, 2003) 13, quoting Nozick *Anarchy, State, and Utopia* at 171.

[59] See Kernohan 'Capitalism and Self-Ownership at 63–4. To be sure, we can do these things with the products of our talents but this is a distinct relationship from the one between a person and his or her talents.

[60] See Kernohan 'Capitalism and Self-Ownership' at 62; Goldman 'Real People (Natural Differences and the Scope of Justice)' at 379.

[61] Cohen *Self-ownership, Freedom, and Equality* at 69.

[62] ibid at 211.

[63] ibid at 210, (footnote omitted).

But there is a difference between the notion of self-control (or control over the self) and self-ownership. In the case of control there is a fundamental ambiguity to the word, and I suppose that Cohen's analogy (between ownership and control) exploits this ambiguity. The notion of 'control' may be seen as a factual, quasi-mechanical phenomenon, with the consequence that 'self-control' is indeed a coherent and reflexive relationship which does not heave our concerns about the separation of the subject and the object of control. Self-control means, for example, that I exercise a restraint over my own actions: over my body, the words I utter etc. But 'control' is also a normative phenomenon, whereby to control something is to have some authority over that something. This second meaning is in fact suggested by Cohen himself who refers to 'a *right* to control a person or her powers'. In this second sense, the use of the notion of 'self-control' would amount to a normative claim, according to which people should have an *authority* over their own actions. However, claiming that I have an authority over myself entails a confused use of the word (unless it is a vague metaphor), because the authority of A over B presupposes the separate existence of A and B; in fact a much better way of making a point about 'self-control' in this second, normative sense, is that the authority of *other* people (including a community as a whole) over an individual should be strictly limited, so that people should be able to decide for themselves to the highest possible degree. (The same can be said about the notion of sovereignty: to say that a person should be *sovereign* over herself would be a confused way of making a normative claim that sovereign authorities—whatever they are—should see the scope of their sovereignty narrowly drawn. Indeed, at certain points Cohen does use, to defend the concept of self-ownership, the analogy with sovereignty, when he argues for instance that people can 'claim sovereignty' over parts of their bodies according to the thesis of self-ownership).[64] Now, just as between the two notions of 'control', the concept of 'ownership' is certainly more analogous to the latter, normative, notion rather than to the former, factual. And it shares the defect of that normative notion when it is combined with the reflexive 'self'—of incoherently presupposing the separability of the subject and the object of control, or of ownership.

This is not to deny that both in ordinary language and also in somewhat more precise scholarly parlance, we sometimes use the concept of an 'authority' over oneself. In ordinary language it is no more than a metaphor, a *façon de parler*, which corresponds to what I have just described as self-control in the factual sense: it describes a capacity for restraining one's impulses or desires etc. It cannot fulfill the role the normative notion of 'self-ownership' would require from it. But we can perhaps also talk about 'authority over oneself' in the sense of self-binding or pre-commitment: we impose on ourselves limits as to our future conduct, for example by entering into contracts or by making promises. This phenomenon has, of course, been subjected to a very comprehensive discussion

[64] ibid at 69.

in decision theory.[65] For our purposes it is sufficient to state that, if the phenomenon of 'self-binding', or self-restraint, or pre-commitment, is to be understood as akin to exercising an authority over oneself, this translation (of self-binding into 'authority over oneself') is made possible by an idea of temporally split personal identity: an earlier binding self and a later bound self. We imagine that X in time t-1 is, *for the purposes of this argument*, a different person from X at point t-2, so when X binds herself at t-1 (for instance, by entering into a contract with Y), she 'exercises authority' over X at t-2. This, in fact, is not so counter-intuitive as it may sound at first blush, especially if there is a significant passage of time between t-1 and t-2, if the character and the circumstances of X have somewhat changed etc. But even if t-2 is immediately after t-1 (I have just signed a contract and it started to bind me from that moment), I can visualize myself as another person, over whom myself from before the contract signing exercised authority. This, I would suggest, is the only coherent way of thinking about 'authority over oneself', in a normative sense.

It is important to keep in mind the italicized proviso that this imagery of a discontinuous identity is made only for the purposes of making sense of the notion of the authority over oneself, rather than for general philosophical purposes. For it has a significant cost as well, in particular in eroding the value of our ordinary understandings of autonomy and responsibility. For it makes little sense to think that we are autonomous human beings if every voluntary and deliberate act of self-restraint were to be in fact addressed against *someone else* (after all, it seems to be one of the fundamental prerogatives of an autonomous person that she can burden herself, including by pre-commitments), and also it makes little sense to talk about moral responsibility for one's earlier conduct if this earlier conduct was in fact performed by someone else.[66] So in many moral contexts we actually need an assumption of continuity of personal identity over time. It is only in the specific context of 'authority over oneself' that a temporally split personality may be helpful in understanding why talk about such an 'authority' may at times be coherent.

The upshot is that the introduction of the concept of property or ownership is singularly unhelpful in this debate about natural and social inequalities. Indeed, the only way we can consistently, and without doing violence to the language of property rights, represent the idea of self-ownership is by claiming our ownership over the *products* of our talents and work. This meaning is indicated in the second sentence of the quote from Locke already cited: 'every man has a property in his own person; this nobody has any right to but himself. The labour of his body and

[65] See, in particular, the *oeuvre* by Jon Elster, including *Ulysses and the Sirens* (Cambridge: Cambridge University Press, 1984, revd edn) and *Ulysses Unbound* (Cambridge: Cambridge University Press, 2000).

[66] See, similarly, Joel Feinberg *Harm to Self* (*The Moral Limits of the Criminal Law* vol 3) (New York: Oxford University Press, 1986) 84–5.

the work of his hands, we may say, are properly his'.[67] However, in the context of our discussion, this reveals the circularity of the 'self-ownership' argument. Indeed, whether we have or not a moral right to nullify the results of one's natural talents is precisely the question at stake. The right on which the anti-redistributive argument is based turns out, upon analysis, to be a right whose justification is at the very core of the debate.

And this is confirmed by the conclusions drawn by those 'left-libertarian' writers who cling to the concept of self-ownership and yet deny that 'being rewarded in accordance with one's talents and labour' (whatever it may mean in practice) is necessary to achieve effective self-ownership. As Jedenheim-Edling points out; '[e]ffective self-ownership is not simply a matter of getting paid in proportion to one's contribution; it is also a matter of the nature, amount and quality of resources one has at its disposal'.[68] His example is of producers who are required to pay a certain fixed amount of money in tax: 'how can this be said to affect our effective self-ownership? We may still live our lives, materially speaking, as we see fit; our autonomy is not affected'.[69] This seems like a good, commonsensical answer (though it is not explicitly addressed to him) to Nozick's observation that '[s]eizing the results of someone's labour is equivalent to seizing hours from him and directing him to carry on various activities', and thus giving others part-ownership in that person.[70] Translating the results of labour (expressed in the currency of tax money) into someone's hours of labour/life is a thoroughly question-begging 'translation' and calls for a further argumentation. Apart from anything else, if it were true that coercive taxation (which corresponds always to someone's pre-tax wealth, and can be 'translated' into the hours of labour of the payee) were the equivalent of giving others a partial ownership in a payee (or, in an even more striking formulation of Nozick, '[t]axation of earnings from labour is on a par with forced labour'),[71] then it would have to apply to *any* taxation on income from labour, irrespective of its purpose: not only the taxation aimed at redistributing resources to others, but also taxation in a minimal state (endorsed by Nozick) aimed at the provision of minimal services to which a payee may not consent. As Cohen observes, 'it is impossible to argue that an hour's labour that ends up as part of somebody's welfare payment is like slavery, while an hour's labour that ends up as part of a policeman's salary is not, when focus is on the condition of the putative slave himself'.[72]

The second version of the argument about a strong link between natural attributes and individual identity is different. Rather than self-ownership, it

[67] Locke 'The Second Treatise of Government' at 17

[68] Jedenheim-Edling 'The Compatibility of Effective Self-Ownership and Joint World Ownership' at 294.

[69] ibid at 295.

[70] Nozick *Anarchy, State and Utopia* at 172.

[71] ibid at 169 (footnote omitted).

[72] Cohen *Self-ownership, Freedom, and Equality* at 235.

stipulates as a point of departure the right of individuals to bodily integrity. This argument was coined in an article by Alan Goldman which it is worth referring to here, so as to trace the reasoning developed in the second version of the social/natural distinction. The structure of his argument is as follows: having posited this fundamental, core right to bodily integrity, he further subjects it to subsequent 'extensions', which engender a prohibition over the actions that would nullify the advantages produced by natural advantages.

Before examining these 'extensions', it is important to consider the nature of this basic right of individuals over their own bodies. To play the role it is allocated in Goldman's overall argument, this right must be shown to protect individuals against wrongs other than 'pains or discomforts'.[73] The right in question is not reducible to the right 'not to have one's body violated or used against one's will'.[74] The reason for this proviso is clear: the latter right does not lend itself to the 'extensions' which lead to the anti-redistributive conclusion. Thus, a proponent of this version of the argument must show that there is more to the right to bodily integrity than the right against pains and discomforts engendered by the violation of one's body, or by its use without consent.

This, however, one cannot demonstrate, in my view. The problem with this claim is that it cannot be falsified, for in order to do so we would have to conceive of such violations of the right of a person over his or her body which do not entail any pain or discomfort. I cannot think of such instances; indeed, the wrongness of violations of our bodily integrity seems to lie precisely in the pain and discomfort they cause. The rights over our bodies can most conveniently be derived from the Harm to Others Principle—a principle which does not easily lend itself to the 'extensions' which lead to anti-redistributive conclusions. Indeed, the Millian Principle is compatible with (although does not necessarily entail) a nullification of undeserved natural advantages.[75] The fact that the right to bodily integrity is inseparable from the prima facie right not to be subject to pain and discomfort against our will undermines Goldman's argument at its very outset. 'Only the identification of a person with his body explains the fundamental place of rights to control what happens to it', proclaims Goldman.[76] There is a hint of circularity about this contention, similar to the one depicted earlier with respect to 'self-ownership'. Indeed, in one sense, the 'identification' asserted here is either trivial or untrue. Cutting your finger against your will causes you pain and discomfort; it is wrong because it harms and hurts you. To say that the wrong of it consists in removing part of your identity sounds odd. If we have the right not to have our fingers removed against our will, it is because we value them (the fingers, that is)

[73] Goldman 'Real People (Natural Differences and the Scope of Justice)' at 379.

[74] ibid at 380.

[75] See W Sadurski 'Some Ruminations on the Harm Principle' *Archiv fur Rechts- und Sozialphilosophie* 75 (1989) 459–67.

[76] Goldman 'Real People (Natural Differences and the Scope of Justice)' at 379.

where they presently are; not because they are part of our separate identities. The 'identity' line of argument does not add anything new to what we already know: that it is prima facie wrong coercively to interfere with our bodies. This is what the right of persons over their bodies consists in; but then the right to have our separate identity protected is merely another way of talking about our right to non-interference. So non-interference is not the conclusion deriving from a prior right over the body: they are one and the same.

What is the link to be drawn between the fact that we have our capacities, skills, and talents and the moral claim according to which we should keep the *products* of the use of these capacities, skills, and talents? In Kronman's words, '[a]lthough a person obviously possesses his own attributes, it does not necessarily follow that he is also their owner, with the right to exploit them, within limits, for his own benefits'.[77] That is why writers such as Goldman do not use the 'possession' analogy, preferring to equate an individual with his or her attributes. But, for reasons suggested above with respect to parts of one's body, this equation is suspect. It therefore has to operate through the mediation of one's achievements and products, and not directly. However, adding this extra stage to the reasoning renders the relationship between the factor in question (the products of the use of one's abilities) and the 'self' even more remote than the relation between a part of the body (or the ability itself) and the self.

Through an 'extension' of the basic right to one's body (as an alleged ingredient of one's self), Goldman postulates the right to 'the person's products and accomplishments that further embody the self in its environment'.[78] The products of one's labour, Goldman claims, just as one's 'interpersonal ties', should be viewed as 'an extension of one's self'.[79] Hence, 'nullifying all the effects of natural differences among individuals, in the form of differential rewards or fruits of the exercise of individual capacities, is prohibited on similar grounds to those that disallow an attack on natural differences themselves'.[80]

It is important to note that this argument rests on two premises: (1) individual selves are constituted by, among other things, their social positions, including one's work and the products of one's labour; (2) differential financial rewards for these labours are inherent ingredients of these social positions: take them away, and the social contents of one's self will collapse. Both these premises are necessary elements in showing how an attack on differential rewards can be equated with an attack on individual selves. I will consider these two premises in the next two parts of this chapter.

[77] Kronman 'Talent Pooling' at 65.

[78] Goldman 'Real People (Natural Differences and the Scope of Justice)' at 383.

[79] ibid at 382.

[80] ibid.

4. Self: Thick and Thin

To appreciate the role the concept of 'self' plays in the context of a discussion of the relationship between natural inequalities and social equality, it is useful to turn to 'communitarian' writers, because one of their main contributions to the current discourse on justice was to deplore (what they considered to be) under-theorized or simply erroneous conceptions of the 'self' in liberal analyses. Consistently with the terminology proposed by Michael Sandel, we may talk about a 'situated self', or simply a 'thick' conception of the self, where one's aims in life, social achievements, and interpersonal ties are built into the very concept of self. As Sandel urged, we 'cannot conceive our personhood without reference to our role as citizens, and as participants in a common life'.[81] In opposition to the liberal 'thin' concept of the self, defined by a common rationality and a capacity for autonomous choice, the communitarians claim that certain roles which involve us in a society are constitutive of our very identities, that 'we are partly defined by the communities we inhabit',[82] and that the idea (which they attribute to liberals) of an 'unencumbered self', existing prior to, and independent from, the competing purposes and ends in life, fails to appreciate the degree to which our identities are constituted by the communities in which we live.

Incidentally, it should be recalled that the attack against a 'thin' concept of the self was launched from the communitarian *and* libertarian standpoints alike. Common to them is the charge of incoherence. The 'thinness' of the liberal conception, in its traditional Rawlsian version, is said to consist in the fact that individuals are endowed with two distinguishable moral powers: a capacity for a sense of justice and a capacity for a conception of the good.[83] It is important to note the operative force of the word *capacity*. Although Rawls admits that individuals also have 'at any given time a particular conception of the good that they try to achieve',[84] nevertheless, this 'particular conception' (which, in turn, must build upon specific abilities, assets, and aims of particular persons) is not necessarily constitutive of a person. The communitarian and libertarian critics point out that according to this conception, the self is (in Sandel's words) 'shorn of all contingently-given attributes,... essentially unencumbered,... ultimately thin'.[85] Robert Nozick, for his part, doubts whether any 'coherent conception of

[81] MJ Sandel 'Introduction' in MJ Sandel (ed) *Liberalism and Its Critics* (Oxford: Basil Blackwell 1984) 5.

[82] ibid at 6.

[83] Rawls *A Theory of Justice* at 561.

[84] J Rawls 'Justice as Fairness: Political not Metaphysical' *Philosophy & Public Affairs* (1985) 14: 223–51 at 234.

[85] MJ Sandel *Liberalism and the Limits of Justice* (Cambridge: Cambridge University Press, 1982) 94.

a person' remains after real people, 'thick with their particular traits' are reduced to such 'purified' beings.[86]

What is the specific nature of the charge of incoherence? Although Nozick does not spell it out ('Whether any coherent conception of a person remains... is an open question'),[87] the best interpretation of this objection might probably go as follows. A person, in order to be meaningfully recognized by others as a distinct human entity, and as the same entity which is able to maintain a clear continuity in different points of time and space (as well as to recognize oneself as such), must have some features which distinguish him or her from other individuals. A being which would be merely an open repository of contingent features would lack the grounds of separateness and identity over time: such a being would be perfectly interchangeable with other beings. Neither identification by others, nor self-identification are possible without the backing of descriptive features which can be produced on demand to distinguish the one being referred to.[88] So the alleged 'incoherence' of the thin conception would lie in the fact that in order to ascribe the two fundamental moral powers ('capacities') to a person, we need to identify this 'person' as separate from others and identical in different time-stages: the separateness requirement is necessary in forming one's conception of the good, and the identity condition is presupposed by having a conception of justice which implies consistency and rationality. However, we are able to identify a person as such only through some of this person's distinctive, contingent attributes.

But note that there is a *non sequitur* in the move from the conditions of identification (and reidentification) of a person to the 'thickness' of the self. In order to draw the boundary line between a particular person and the rest of the human universe, all we need to know is that a person has *some* distinctive characteristics, and not necessarily the *particular* characteristics that the person happens to have. A person with a different set of abilities, talents, and skills may still be the same person. The fact that all abilities and skills can be identified only as the attributes of some individuals,[89] does not mean that these individuals are 'constituted' by these abilities and skills. The 'thin' conception of the self must therefore recognize that all abilities are always the attributes of some individuals but it does not mean that these individuals are separate and identical over time *because of* these particular attributes.

Consider now a slightly different version of the charge of incoherence. Consider a liberal (and thin) concept of the self that would posit a bifurcated entity: a person's self would, on the one hand, consist in a capacity for choice of ends in life (forming a conception of the good) and, on the other hand, in the personal

[86] Nozick *Anarchy, State and Utopia* at 228.

[87] ibid.

[88] On the role of individuating attributes in the identification and reidentification of objects in general, see PF Strawson *Individuals: An Essay in Descriptive Metaphysics* (London: Methuen, 1959) 15–38.

[89] See AJ Ayer The *Concept of a Person* (New York: St Martin's Press, 1963) 126.

attributes (such as talents, skills etc) which are viewed merely as means to the attainment of various aims that a person chooses to follow. Such a bifurcation, the argument goes, is necessary to reconcile the notion of an individual identity with the 'talent pooling' when considering natural attributes as a matter of lottery or luck whose effects can henceforth be neutralized by a society. But—and here comes the objection against such a conception—this bifurcation is dubious insofar as our choice of ends is to a large extent determined by our awareness of our own talents, skills, and other natural attributes. Indeed, we do not adopt whatever aims appeal to us independently of our talents and other natural skills: we do not first decide that we wish to pursue a musical career and only then figure out whether we have musical talents or not. And, so would conclude this argument, insofar as our talents predetermine our choices, the division of a self between the ends and the means is incoherent.[90]

This argument has *some* force. It cannot be seen as conclusive, however. For one thing, the choice of ends is only partly determined by the talents we have: we all know anecdotal evidence about persons displaying a clear mismatch between their ambitions and potential. Our choice of aims is largely determined, to be sure, but the determining factors only partly have to do with our inner capacities and talents. They are often based on external examples, role-models equipped with different sets of skills and talents than ours, as well as our choice to develop and cultivate talents of our own, which may happen to be at a level inadequate to match the aims we have set for ourselves. This relative independence of the aims from means thus partly supports the bifurcated conception of the self.

But the second, and perhaps more important point, is that the main purpose of the critique of a bifurcated conception is to show that by 'pooling' the resources generated by special assets (the natural assets which bring about extra resources) we somehow infringe upon the individual identity. This is the context in which this debate is being conducted; the charge is that, if the bifurcation is not successful (and it *cannot* be successful, the argument goes) we cannot think of talent pooling (or the nullification of the effects of natural lottery) as innocent from the point of view of the integrity of the individual self.[91] Such an enterprise would be unobjectionable, the argument goes, if we could imagine the compensatory intervention against talent-pooling as not reaching the real self, which is the domain of the ends, ie if we could see the intervention within the domain of means (natural assets and their effects) as strictly separated from the domain in which the real self resides. This would hold only if the bifurcation thesis were plausible. To the extent that it is not, and insofar as the means determine the ends, bifurcation is illusory, and talent pooling-type activities inevitably corrode individual integrity—the anti-bifurcation thesis proclaims. But if *this* is the true nature of the argument, it needs to be placed fairly and squarely within the context of an

[90] For a version of this argument, see Kronman 'Talent Pooling' 71–6.

[91] See ibid 72–5.

argument focusing explicitly on 'talent pooling', and a discussion on whether or not the nullification of effects of natural abilities can be considered as bearing a destructive effect on individual integrity. This is the point I will address later in this chapter—but here the main conclusion to retain is that it really is not a debate about the conception of the individual self but rather about the consequences of redistributive actions.

This point can be now generalized, and we may return to the 'thick' concept of the self, in the context of this discussion. The question now is: what sense can be made of the 'situated', context-sensitive concept of the self? In some respects, the relationships between a social context and an individual are uncontroversial: human actions, individual desires and preferences, choices one makes, and aims one pursues, are inevitably affected by the social context in a variety of ways. This is true but banal. In order to properly understand individual actions and interpret the meaning of one's choices, we must view these actions and these choices against the background of societal arrangements, opportunities available, and dominant ideologies. However, these causal relationships and epistemological postulates are irrelevant from the point of view of our present theme, for they cannot account for the prohibition of the removal of the products generated by natural assets. What is at stake for our problem in this instance is a proposition, which is neither about causality nor about the method used to study human behaviour, but rather about identity. It is, to use Sandel's terminology, a 'constitutive' conception:[92] it attempts to tell us something about what individuals *are*, and not merely why they act in certain ways.

It is important not to confuse this 'constitutive' conception with (largely uncontroversial) claims about causality or methodology. Some communitarians can be held responsible for having contributed to this confusion, or for exploiting the force of the latter interpretations (causal or methodological) to support the former one (constitutive). Michael Walzer's argument is a case in point. In a passage where he declares his general view about the scope of individual identities, Walzer contends that:

> Men and women take on concrete identities because of the way they conceive and create, and then possess and employ social goods. 'The line between what is me and mine,' wrote William James, 'is very hard to draw.'... [P]eople already stand in a relation to a set of goods; they have a history of transactions, not only with one another but also with the moral and material world in which they live. Without such a history, which begins at birth, they wouldn't be men and women in any recognizable sense...[93]

This passage suggests that Walzer integrates the circumstances of an individual's possessions and transactions *within* his or her identity. Furthermore, the contention about the line between 'me' and 'mine' being difficult to draw seems to

[92] Sandel *Liberalism and the Limits of Justice* at 150.
[93] M Walzer *Spheres of Justice* at 8.

directly suggest that any attempt at removing (a part of) what is 'mine' can be seen as an intrusion into what is 'me'. This is the case, however, only providing that this argument, as well as the context, point to the ontology of the self, and that they assert something about what a person actually is, namely, that what is mine is a constitutive part of me.

A brief attempt at tracing the genesis of this alleged quote from William James may be useful at this point. The maxim which he attributes to James is not exactly what James said, nor what James probably had in mind. The correct quote reads, 'The Empirical Self of each of us is all that he is tempted to call by the name of me. But it is clear that between what a man calls me and what he simply calls mine the line is difficult to draw'.[94] James develops this claim in the context of his psycho-sociological theory of the self, in the sub-chapter entitled 'The Empirical Self or Me'. It is clear that he does not consider this statement as being about the ontology of the self, but rather about the way people tend to perceive themselves, and others, within a society. The quoted sentence is followed, a few lines further, by the following explanation:

> In its widest possible sense, however, a man's Self is the sum total of all that he CAN call his, not only his body and his psychic powers, but his clothes and his house, his wife and children, his ancestors and friends, his reputation and works, his lands and horses, and yacht and bank account.[95]

As a description of the empirical observation showing that people do perceive themselves, and others, through the prism of their worldly possessions and personal or proprietary relations, James's statements are uncontroversial. But there is no obvious leap from this empirical observation to a metaphysical notion about what constitutes an individual identity. (Would it include one's 'lands and horses', 'yacht and bank account'?)

Significantly, Walzer quotes James not directly, but from a study by Snyder and Fromkin on the perceptions of scarcity and uniqueness in a society. They use James's observation about 'me' and 'mine' to support the *empirical* assertion according to which one socially acceptable way to redefine the self as different from others is through the possession of scarce commodities.[96] This observation accompanies their description of their own experiments which show that 'increased valuation accompanies the perception of scarcity'.[97] This sounds eminently convincing: in order to distinguish ourselves from others, we tend to define ourselves through our scarce and valued possessions, and similarly perceive those of our fellow citizens whom we wish to endow with the attributes of

[94] W James *The Principles of Psychology* vol 1 (London: Macmillan, 1910) 291.
[95] ibid at 291 (emphasis in original).
[96] CR Snyder and H Fromkin *Uniqueness: The Human Pursuit of Difference* (New York: Plenum Press, 1980) 108.
[97] ibid.

uniqueness. This is *not* a proposition about the ontology of the self, but about the psychological mechanisms of the symbolic representation of the desire for uniqueness. But this is not the use that Walzer makes of the 'line between what is me and what is mine' dictum: his proposition, indeed, claims to be an ontological account of the human self and its constitutive parts.

Walzer's case is instructive because it suggests that what is allegedly a metaphysical proposition (about the ontology of the self) is in fact derived from some non-metaphysical premises. It is my general argument here that the ontological status of the self in the communitarian criticisms of liberal conceptions of justice is parasitic on some other, non-metaphysical grounds. So again, what meaning could be given to the metaphysical claim, according to which the self is constituted (partly) by the community? How can we represent, meaningfully, the contrast between two opposing metaphysical concepts of individual identity: one which builds community attachments, ends, and relations into the very notion of the human self, and the other which relies on the boundary between the self (understood in a 'thin' way) and the social universe?

The preliminary question is, what is at stake in the choice of one or the other conception? I will argue that the choice is informed by the normative theory of justice one espouses, and does not rest on purely metaphysical grounds. To claim that I am defined by a number of my social roles (as a member of a family, of a church, of a nation) may sound obvious, but then it is equally obvious that (at least in some circumstances) I may cease, through my conscious decision, to occupy these roles: we divorce our spouses, convert to other faiths, emigrate from our countries. My identity is at least equally defined by my current attachments as by my capacity to abandon them. If I do revise or abandon these commitments, has my identity *eo ipso* changed? Am I someone else, a different person, in any meaningful sense? To answer affirmatively would be merely a *façon de parler* which would not add anything new to the suggestion that I altered some of my significant relations with my social environment. To say that I am now a different person, in the sense that I am someone else, is odd and redundant in this context.[98] I am different in some respects and identical in others, but this is just another way of stating the obvious, that is, that some of my important attributes have changed. It is not as if I ceased to exist and then re-emerged as someone different. Alternatively, we may say that, as regards the 'constitution' of my identity, I am now a former spouse, church-member, citizen of the country I left, and that my identity is (partly) constituted by these former attachments. But then, it is hard to ascertain in what sense these characteristics define my identity as opposed to merely describing my attributes, past or present. If I am 'defined' by a particular social role, but at the same time I am free to modify and ultimately abandon

[98] For a similar critique of arguments according to which, for the purposes of a discussion on paternalism, different stages of the same self may be treated as different persons, see J Feinberg *The Moral Limits of the Criminal Law* vol 3: *Harm to Self* (Oxford University Press: New York, 1986) 81–7.

this role, the independent weight of this role in constituting my identity seems to be nil. To represent my current and past attributes and roles as components of my identity seems to be a slightly pompous and quite unnecessary way of describing those features of my social characteristics which an observer may consider significant.

What is the function of substituting the 'description of a person' with an assessment of the social components of a person's identity? Consider these arguments developed by Sandel against the 'deontological ethic', which postulates that we view ourselves as independent selves, independent in the sense that 'our identity is never tied to our aims and attachments':

> [W]e cannot regard ourselves as independent in this way without great cost to those loyalties and convictions whose moral force consists partly in the fact that living by them is inseparable from understanding ourselves as the particular persons we are—as members of this family or community or nation or people, as bearers of this history, as sons and daughters of this revolution, as citizens of this republic. Allegiances such as these are more than values I happen to have or aims I 'espouse at any given time'.... They allow that to some I owe more than justice requires or even permits, not by reason of agreements I have made but instead in virtue of those more or less enduring attachments and commitments which taken together partly define the person I am.[99]

This quote, I believe, reveals the real grounds for Sandel's insistence on the social components of individual identity. This is an argument relying on issues of commitments, loyalties, and obligations, which go beyond the ones based on typically liberal grounds, that is, the ones based on fairness, reciprocity, or consent. Whether one agrees with Sandel on the merits of his claim or not, the very beginning of the quote indicates that the social identity of individuals is parasitic upon the normative views about the stringency of individual commitments and loyalties to their communities. '[W]e cannot regard ourselves as independent in this way without great cost to those loyalties and convictions...'; this suggests that the moral price incurred by adopting an un-situated concept of the self is unacceptable to Sandel. The duties we owe to our families, communities, or nations, to our history, traditions, and republics, come first; the situated self is merely an expository device of conveying this message to the readers. It therefore has nothing to do with the ontology of an individual identity but it is just another way of expressing the idea that our commitments go far beyond those made voluntarily by ourselves as free and independent agents. And, in turn, the individualistic concept of the non-situated self is instrumental to the political philosophy which celebrates the supreme value of the free choice and the relative independence of individuals from communal ties. As John Gray admitted, the liberal political philosophy must construct an individualistic conception of the person 'not because of any metaphysical doctrine about personhood...but

[99] Sandel *Liberalism and the Limits of Justice* at 179.

because we need political principles that abstract from political attachments to specific moral communities'.[100] The experience of modern, pluralistic societies displays the continuous revision of communal ties, and frequent transfers from one community to another; furthermore, we belong to a plurality of communities at the same time. As a result, '[w]e conceive the person as an un-situated or unencumbered individual, defined not by communal attachments but by autonomous choice'.[101]

In reality, of course, we are *both* free agents *and* situated in our communities; we choose our attachments *and* they are immersed in our history and traditions; we are involved in social practices and we often challenge them—at times we even reject them entirely. The dilemma of life in modern societies is to combine commitments and their continuous alteration. Sometimes we are faced with the quandary of having to choose between loyalty to the community and the requirements of our independent critical morality, which may lead to the questioning of the values of this community. The language of 'situated selves' suggests the presumptive priority of loyalty over this questioning; the language of a free, unencumbered self emphasizes the importance of independence and criticism. This is a choice between two moralities, not between two ontologies of the self. And if the notion of the 'self' is but a proxy for a moral claim about the stringency of individual commitments and loyalties, it cannot lend support to these propositions.

5. Common Pool of Natural Abilities?

It is time to recall our main theme: the removal of the benefits generated through the exercise of natural capacities. The first premise of the argument which I proposed to explore was that individual selves are constituted by, among other things, social positions, including one's work and the products of one's labour. This I discussed in the preceding part where I concluded that 'the constitution of the individual self' thesis is derived from judgments about the obligation of, and towards, other individuals. The concept of the 'self' is only as good as the judgment from which it is derived. It will not convince those who do not accept the underlying communitarian set of political judgments.

Let us assume, for the sake of the argument, that a 'thick' conception of the individual self is plausible. There still remains the second premise of the argument against nullifying the differential products of natural abilities: that differential *rewards* belong to that sphere of individual identity which cannot be nullified

[100] J Gray 'Contractarian Method, Private Property, and the Market Economy' in JW Chapman and JR Pennock (eds) *Markets and Justice: Nomos XXXI* (New York: New York University Press, 1989) 39.

[101] ibid.

without risking a violation of the human self. This is the point we mentioned when discussing the 'bifurcated' conception of the self as divided into the inviolable sphere of aims and the sphere of natural assets (and rewards consequent upon these assets) which can safely be interfered with. We have observed, it may be recalled, that the objections to such an alleged 'bifurcation' are in effect not about the most plausible picture of the self, but rather about whether the taxation upon the products of one's talents and labour are an intolerable infringement of individual integrity. Even if, as Alan Goldman claims, 'one's work, the products of one's labour [can be viewed] as an extension of one's self',[102] the question is what actually constitutes 'the products of one's labour' in the sense which retains a close link with one's self, whatever way it is understood. One can immediately think of, say, paintings created by an artist, books written by a scholar, software programs developed by a computer expert, or watches made by a watchmaker. These products of our labour indicate to the outside world something about us: about our skills, interests, capacities. If anything, they are part of a description (or, as some would claim, of a definition) of ourselves. But to rebut the nullifying attempts made by egalitarians with respect to these differences is to attack a man of straw. It is not an inference from Rawls's difference principle, or from similar egalitarian constructs, that we should pool these fruits of one's labour into a bundle of communal assets.

An obvious candidate for pooling is the market return generated by various products of one's abilities; in other words, money. This is why the egalitarians influenced by Rawls see the fiscal policies (including taxation and welfare spending) as the most adequate devices for the redistribution from the more to the less fortunate. As Kronman concludes, 'what pooling requires is a system of forced transfers (a tax system) that will counterbalance the effect of the initial and arbitrary distribution of talents among individuals'.[103] These 'transfers' do not aim at the products of the abilities (let alone the abilities themselves).

Consider this challenge that Nozick addressed to Rawls, after having quoted the latter:

> No one deserves his greater natural capacity nor merits a more favorable starting point in society. But it does not follow that one should eliminate these distinctions. There is another way to deal with them. The basic structure can be arranged so that these contingencies work for the good of the least fortunate.[104]

And Nozick retorts:

> And if there weren't 'another way to deal with them'? Would it then follow that one should eliminate these distinctions? What exactly would be contemplated in the case of natural assets? If people's assets and talents couldn't be harnessed to serve others, would something be done to remove these exceptional assets and talents...?[105]

102 Goldman 'Real People (Natural Differences and the Scope of Justice)' at 382.
103 Kronman 'Talent Pooling' at 66.
104 Rawls *A Theory of Justice* at 102.
105 Nozick *Anarchy, State and Utopia* at 229.

But the response from Nozick, while admittedly rhetorically powerful, ignores the fact that it is *always* possible to think of a scheme of taxation which would redistribute some of the gains generated by higher skills, talents, or opportunities. The scheme may be very imperfect, as we will have formidable difficulties with measuring the contributing factors of someone's income or wealth (to what extent their monetary advantages over others are due to factors which are morally arbitrary?). But this is a *different* difficulty from the one implied by Nozick about a hypothetical impossibility of 'dealing with' exceptional talents and skills. So the image of a 'removal' of some exceptional talents is inappropriate here. As Kronman observes: 'it does not follow from the fact that we cannot redistribute talents themselves that we should not require the well endowed to share the benefit of their talent by making a compensation payment to those who have been less fortunate in the natural lottery'.[106]

The presumption, which we are considering now, would have, so as to play a role in the overall argument, to equate an individual's work and achievements with the dollar value he or she commands. This sounds like a bizarre claim, for at least two sets of reasons. First, in most cases (although not all), the product of one's labour (hence, the monetary value one's labour commands) is the combination of one's labour with worldly resources. It does not always have to occur that way; we may think of examples when someone generates income based purely on his own labour without any material resources being added to it. (Michael Otsuka gives an example of performing a song and dance for a paying audience, though even then some non-trivial material resources may be needed, such as a special dress, audio equipment etc; when pressed to give an example of a pure non-worldly-resources income-generating activity, Otsuka imagines the highly artificial example of a person whose hair can be woven into clothing.)[107] But these are arguably non-typical cases: more often than not we combine our labour with things, and then the question of the rights of *others* over those 'things' arises. From the perspective of 'self-ownership', the argument has been made that, in order to equate one's monetary gains with one's work and achievement in the cases where worldly resources are mixed with labour, one would need to assume that 'one's right of ownership over worldly resources that one uses in order to earn income is as full as one's right of ownership over oneself'.[108] But, whether one uses the language of 'self-ownership' or not, the presumption is hardly plausible. The thought that our ownership of external things grants us the exclusive control over these things, without any regard to how such use affects others, is just one of many possible conceptions of what a right to private ownership *should* involve, and a particularly controversial one at that. It seems intuitively persuasive that the others-regarding constraints upon the use of external resources (generated

[106] Kronman 'Talent Pooling' at 66.
[107] Otsuka *Libertarianism Without Inequality* at 18.
[108] ibid at 20 (footnote omitted).

by rightful ownership) should be more extensive than the others-regarding constraints upon the use of our body.[109] At a minimum, the constraints trace the thin restriction imposed by Locke (and famously interpreted by Nozick)[110] upon the power to appropriate natural resources, that is, that enough and as good be left for others. But, the 'enough and as good' proviso has lent itself to differing interpretations, and a minimalist interpretation provided by Nozick (who viewed it as based on a comparison of the appropriation-based externalities with the non-use or non-appropriation of a given resource) has been countered by alternative interpretations.[111] The choice of a proper interpretation is a matter of competing philosophies of justice and cannot be made solely on the basis of an inquiry into the proper meaning of ownership over resources.

Secondly, and this caveat applies even to those cases where monetary gain is a result of 'pure' labour, with no inclusion of material things, the monetary value of labour is shaped, among other things, by factors totally external to one's capacities and which are often unpredictable, such as the intensity and proximity of competition in a given field. To be sure, one can try to draw a link between one's praiseworthy talents and those external factors (by saying, for example, that the talent of a person consists, among other things, in properly determining which types of her efforts, under the current conjuncture of competition with others etc, will lead to the highest returns) but this would be highly convoluted and artificial. In the end, there is much that is fortuitous in the income that one's efforts and talents can command. And if this is the case, it is implausible to claim that an income generated by the products of ones abilities can be identified with these products themselves as the expressions of individual selves.

Conclusions

In this chapter I have considered the main contours of the notion of social equality. I first defended the approach to social equality based on distributional, or individualized, ideals against the claims that such ideals distort 'the point' about equality, and that such individualized approaches diminish the moral and political seriousness of traditional egalitarian ideals. I have contended that an opposition between individualized and more 'collective' approaches (which typically focus on non-domination, non-exploitation, and non-discrimination) is both misleading and unhelpful.

[109] 'It is an intelligible presumption that I alone am entitled to decide about the use of this arm, and to benefit from its use, simply because it is my arm.... But there is not comparable presumptive normative tie between any person and any part or portion of the external world', Cohen *Self-ownership, Freedom, and Equality* at 70–1.

[110] Nozick *Anarchy, State and Utopia* at 174–82.

[111] See eg Otsuka *Libertarianism Without Inequality* at 22–30; Cohen *Self-ownership, Freedom, and Equality* at 74–90.

One influential version of such an 'individualized' approach is a conception, notably made famous in recent decades by John Rawls, which claims that equality calls for the eradication of those inequalities which result from 'morally arbitrary' factors. These factors may roughly belong to 'natural' and 'social' categories, and I have discussed the claim that these two categories should have a different moral status in a theory of social equality: that the inequalities based on former factors must not be removed, even if they are as 'morally arbitrary' as social factors. But in the argument against the nullification of the rewards generated by natural abilities (as opposed to those attributable to social disadvantages) I depicted the circularity of the reasoning with regard to the relationship between social rewards and the individual self. To say that a product of one's own work is a part of the human self and that '[t]he fruits of one's own labor are rightly his own',[112] assumes what is in question—how much people should be allowed to keep of what they produce, or of the income their work generates. What is 'his own' should depend on a substantive conception of distributive justice, not on a definitional fiat about what constitutes one's true identity. If the right to keep the fruits of one's labour is the only meaningful way of understanding a metaphor about what constitutes the human self, then it still awaits a substantive justification to compete with the rival principle of the duty to compensate those less fortunate for their undeserved deprivations. In the next chapter I will consider one such rival principle, which has received much scholarly attention in recent years, and which can be labelled 'luck egalitarianism'.

[112] Goldman 'Real People (Natural Differences and the Scope of Justice)' at 382.

5

Social Equality (II): Luck Egalitarianism and Its Limits

In his recent book, Ronald Dworkin summarizes his ideal of 'equal concern' for all citizens, to be afforded by an economic system with the objective of providing all with 'genuinely equal opportunities to design a life according to their own values': 'They have equal opportunities . . . when their wealth and other resources depend on the value and costs of their choices, but *not on their luck*, including their genetic luck in parents and talents'.[1] This nicely captures some very widespread and powerful moral intuitions about justice. Who would claim that it is *fair* to allow bad luck to affect adversely, pervasively, and incurably some crucial aspects of a person's life, if it is in our power to mitigate these tragic effects? This can be seen as a concretization, and pushing a step forward the Rawlsian insight, discussed in the preceding chapter, that equality requires eradication of all those, and only those, inequalities which are triggered by morally arbitrary reasons. But the elegant sentence by Dworkin conceals a great number of difficulties and complexities, which need to be carefully addressed. What should be considered as 'resources', which are to be submitted to equalization through social action? What should count as 'luck', the effects of which need to be nullified? Are talents separable from choices, and if not, how can they appear on two different sides of the line dividing those factors which should and those which should not register among the acceptable social inequalities? And how can we be confident that, once we eradicate those, and only those, inequalities that are consequent upon luck and allow freely those inequalities which stem from decisions and choices, we will see the society significantly more equal than ours?

These questions will be addressed in this chapter. Luck-egalitarianism is often (and with good reason) characterized also as responsibility-based egalitarianism—and therefore I will consider the relationship between 'luck' and 'responsibility' in this general conception of social equality (Part 1). Next, in Part 2, I will discuss, and largely reject, the fundamental equality-based objection to luck egalitarianism: that it is unfaithful to some of our widespread equality-sensitive intuitions, and therefore that luck-egalitarianism is not really egalitarian in a morally attractive

[1] Ronald Dworkin *Is Democracy Possible Here?* (Princeton: Princeton University Press, 2006) 108 (emphasis added).

way. I will then explore the central distinction which characterizes the leading discourse about luck egalitarianism: that between equality of welfare and equality of resources, and try to illuminate its significance by focusing on the status of individual preferences (in particular, preferences which are particularly costly to satisfy) as regards egalitarian distribution (Part 3). I will then move on to consider another distinction: that between 'persons' and 'circumstances' (a distinction said to separate those factors which should and those which should not be allowed to affect a person's economic position) and see how it correlates with the central moral intuition which triggers the whole egalitarian approach, namely that social inequalities should be allowed to reflect the choices people make in the course of their lives (Part 4). If we consistently maintain the centrality of choice for the whole theory, and construct the technical concept of 'resources' accordingly, we may well realize that the gap between 'equality of welfare' and 'equality of resources' is not as wide as academic writings, structured as they are around this dichotomy, would have us believe—or so, at least, I claim in Part 5. The last part addresses head-on the crucial issue lying in the background of this whole discussion: is the aspiration to eliminate systemically the impact of bad luck necessarily, or at least contingently, egalitarian? Many critics have recently suggested that it is not. If they are right, then the term 'luck egalitarianism' would be incoherent. Luckily, this is not the case, as I will argue in Part 6.

1. Luck and Responsibility in 'Luck Egalitarianism'

So far I have been referring to 'luck egalitarianism' only in the broadest terms, using it as a representative example of an individualized approach to equality, as opposed to the collective one. I have therefore disregarded any inner distinctions among various conceptions within the 'luck egalitarianism' family, and any specific objections against this conception; I mentioned only those that are related to its individualized property. But it is now necessary to explore the conception a little further, and assess in more depth some specific critiques raised against the idea of luck-neutralizing conceptions.

To start with, perhaps the very label 'luck egalitarianism' is a misnomer; for one thing, the very concept of 'luck' is ambiguous, as we will see below. Furthermore, there is a substantive problem of relationship between luck-neutralizing and equality (so that the concept 'luck egalitarianism' may be seen as question-begging, since, according to many theorists, and most notably among them Susan Hurley,[2] there is no connection between the attempts to neutralize the impact of luck and any egalitarian motives or consequences of social action).

[2] SL Hurley *Justice, Luck, and Knowledge* (Cambridge, Mass: Harvard University Press, 2003). See also Timothy Hinton 'Must Egalitarians Choose Between Fairness and Respect?' *Philosophy & Public Affairs* (2001) 30: 72–87 at 77–80.

Thirdly, even quite apart from the first two objections, 'luck' figures in the 'luck egalitarianism' label only *negatively*—insofar as egalitarians wish to *eliminate* the impact of luck on the social positions of individuals. It may seem to be more appropriate in describing a conception to use a concept which figures *positively* in a given conception, and perhaps, about responsibility-based (or responsibility-sensitive) egalitarianism, because what connects the family of conceptions which we will discuss is a deliberate and expansive inclusion of the standards of individual responsibility within the matrix of social equality. Individuals should occupy equal positions, insofar as their valued resources, positions, and opportunities are concerned, unless unequal distributions may be plausibly explained by factors which they are responsible for. 'You are responsible for being in an inferior position vis-à-vis others' sounds like a conclusive and morally justified rebuttal to claims of unfairness, under the egalitarian conceptions which I have in mind here.

But is responsibility the mirror image of luck? Can we indeed say that, when we are making distribution dependent on individual responsibility, we are thereby eliminating the impact of luck upon social distribution (or, vice versa, that when we are successfully eliminating all the effects of luck, we will end up with equal distribution, except for inequalities which can be traced back to individual responsibility)? The very way of formulating these two questions suggests immediately that we are facing two distinct problems, and that it would be unhelpful to merge them into one: a conceptual and a substantive question. The *conceptual* question is about whether responsibility is a mirror image of luck, and the response depends naturally on the concepts of responsibility and luck that we adopt. The *substantive* question concerns the relationship between the elimination of luck (once we have defined luck), or responsibility-sensitivity (once we have defined responsibility), to material equality. Is it really the case that once we eliminate luck or make distribution dependent on responsibility, the resultant distribution will be more equal than now, or in the absence of such operations?

Now it is very important to properly ascertain the status of the 'substantive' question, hinging as it does on the understanding of what the descriptor 'more equal' means in this question. For if 'equality' in the 'more equal' concept means equality already coined in luck/responsibility-related terms (so that equality means equal distribution unless an inequality is traced back to free choices) then the question is uninteresting, and therefore the answer becomes trivial and uninteresting because of course, luck egalitarianism would bring more equality *defined in these terms*. So to make this question a real one, we must understand equality—for the purposes of the 'substantive' question in simple, 'patterned', pre-theoretical terms: as more equal distributions compared to today's prevailing distributions, no matter how responsibility and bad luck affect them. But if we pose the question in this way, the immediate question is, why should it matter? After all, luck egalitarians are concerned about equality only insofar as it allows for responsibility-traceable inequalities. The answer is that it may not matter to adherents to luck egalitarianism but it matters a great deal to those external observers who are as yet undecided as to the most attractive conception of equality, and one of the criteria (perhaps, *the* criterion) of what their preferred choice will be, is how much equality it will produce in the real world—that is, equality coined not in terms which are *internal* to the theory, but equality in a pre-theoretical, intuitive sense. (After all, we are interested not only in the coherence or elegance of a theory but also in how well it squares with our moral intuitions.) Furthermore, some luck egalitarians (notably Dworkin) assure us that the implementation of their theory in the real world *will* produce more equality (in the sense of reducing disparities along main indicia of stratification), so any analysis of luck egalitarianism must test this assurance. Because, if luck egalitarians were not interested in producing more equality in the simple (pre-theoretical) sense, they should have characterized their own theory straightforwardly as luck-*neutralization*, and the use of the word *equality* would be an abuse of an otherwise honorific, value-laden term.

Both the conceptual and the substantive questions are important, but they should be considered each at a time, otherwise the risk is for discussions to be led at cross-purposes. I will address the substantive question in Part 6, and at this stage, my only concern lies in the conceptual relationship between 'luck' and 'responsibility': are they mirror images of each other, for the purposes of discussing luck-egalitarianism (or responsibility-egalitarianism)? It depends on how we understand both concepts. To begin with 'responsibility', there are two separate dichotomies in the uses of the term in the present context, which need to be distinguished from each other. (But please note that I am not ruminating here on the various interpretations of 'responsibility' *tout court*, but only about responsibility as actually figuring in the context of luck egalitarianism). A first dichotomy results from the 'defensive' versus 'affirmative' uses of the standards (whatever they are) of responsibility.[3] The *defensive* use is employed whenever egalitarians *challenge* the (by-and-large conservative) responsibility-based anti-egalitarian arguments, for instance those that are aimed at showing that social policies of equality violate the principle of responsibility (eg, by rewarding those who choose not to work hard and penalizing those who have deliberately invested their time, effort, and resources in their own education, business activity, savings etc). Such defensive uses of responsibility are most typically employed when an argument is made (*vide* Rawls)[4] according to which we do not 'deserve' many of the assets which contribute to our superior social positions, and, correspondingly, that those who are worse off are often disadvantaged due to factors for which they are not 'responsible' in any meaningful sense of responsibility. In such arguments, 'responsibility' is deployed to debunk the spurious (as egalitarians believe) appeals to responsibility made by anti-egalitarians. In contrast, *affirmative* uses

[3] For this distinction, see Scheffler 'Choice, Circumstance, and the Value of Equality' at 7–8.

[4] '[S]ince inequalities of birth and natural endowment are *undeserved*, these inequalities are to be somehow compensated for', John Rawls *A Theory of Justice* at 100 (emphasis added, footnote omitted).

of responsibility are applied whenever equality is demanded on the basis that it gives effect to the actual responsibility of individuals for their distributive shares under a proposed scheme of distribution. The deep logic of the argument is just like that of the conservative anti-egalitarians but the conclusion reached is the opposite: once we follow fully the logic of responsibility, goes the argument, we shall obtain egalitarian distribution. So the disagreement between egalitarians and anti-egalitarians *seems* to concern only the predicted empirical consequences of the application of one and the same principle in real life.

This is, however, not the case. Two points can be made which are relevant to the 'defensive' versus 'affirmative' distinction. The first point is that it is counter-intuitive to claim that one may have a defensive conception without there being an affirmative conception in the background. Translate the preceding discussion into that of 'desert': the argument for a 'defensive' use would be that we do not 'deserve' current (dis)advantages (because we cannot be held responsible for many of the factors which affect our advantaged or disadvantaged position). But can we hold the 'we do not deserve it' position without at the same time endorsing a position about what we *would* deserve? In other words, can a defensive use be self-standing, without being supported by an affirmative use? To be sure, we can find it easier to identify breaches of a moral principle (such as the one linking distribution to responsibility) than relate to the positive implementations of that principle, but it does not follow that the negative uses are intelligible without presupposing the positive ones.[5] Statements of the type 'we do not deserve' make sense only insofar as they identify *departures* from the positive ideal and, similarly, the denial of the link between the responsibility of a person and his/her distributive share is intelligible only insofar as there is, at least intuitively, a standard on what responsibility *would* warrant. Both anti-egalitarian conservatives and egalitarians, when they make defensive arguments about responsibility, must be prepared to accept the affirmative contentions as well. So I disagree with Scheffler who argues that '[i]n advancing th[e] "defensive" arguments, egalitarians do not commit themselves to the principle of responsibility. They simply dispute the conservatives' assessment of the implications of that principle'.[6] True, they may not have any explicit theory of a responsibility-equality link because their main immediate concern may be 'defensive' rather than affirmative. But an implicit affirmative articulation must be available; otherwise the anti-conservative responsibility argument has no moorings.

The second point is as follows. It is tempting to say that the only difference between the responsibility-conscious anti-egalitarians and egalitarians lies in the prediction as to how the use of one and the same principle will make a difference in the real world. But this temptation should be resisted because it overlooks

[5] See, similarly, Sidney Hook 'In Defense of "Justice"' in E Kiefer and MK Munitz *Ethics and Social Justice* (Albany: State University of New York Press, 1968) 75–84; see also Hurley at 134–35.

[6] Scheffler 'Choice, Circumstance, and the Value of Equality' at 8.

too much of a genuine moral disagreement, and ends up with a deceptively simplified picture of what is at stake. Suppose there is a disagreement concerning the inequality in the material positions of A and B: A had a first-class education and is now a successful lawyer, while B had only an inferior schooling and is a manual worker; a tax policy is now proposed to reduce after-tax inequality between them. You object to the scheme by saying that such an equalization would ignore the responsibility factor, because it would fail to reflect the differences between the hard work reflected in undertaking education by A; I claim, on the contrary, that the inferior equipment of B as regards the assets that are rewarded by the job market was not due to his free will, effort etc, and therefore that a redistribution will bring the material positions closer in line with the responsibilities of A and B for their current social fates. Is our disagreement about the empirical predictions related to the way the use of one and the same standard will turn out to equalize or differentiate the positions between A and B? Surely not: the standard is not 'the same': the concept of responsibility is used in different ways by you and me, and these differences are reflective of fundamentally divergent moral outlooks about what characteristics and facts about an individual should trigger social benefits and burdens. This is not to say that there is no room for an empirical, or factual, disagreement between me and you: we may disagree about what in fact was under A's and B's control: was B's failure to obtain a better education a matter of his deliberate choice (he preferred to spend more time partying and surfing) or of unavailability of money for tuition? But our disagreements go further than that. To say that B was not responsible for a failure to secure a better education is based (or at least, may be based and is often based) on a particular view about *what*, as a matter of general principle rather than specific and local facts, is under a person's control: are we 'responsible' for (ie do we have control over) our character traits which incline us towards certain actions, or for certain preferences which were imparted to us by our family and friends, and which further affect our choices; or for our religious convictions which constrain our actions etc? To place any such factors on one or the other side of the line dividing those facts for which we are responsible and those for which we are not, requires to have recourse to a broader moral conception which in itself cannot rely upon a prior notion of responsibility. Indeed, a statement of responsibility is a conclusion rather than a basis for this line-drawing. Such a characterization of a particular fact or action is only partly value-insensitive, and as it relies to a certain extent on a moral conception, it cannot, itself, serve as an explanation as to where the principle of responsibility leads in terms of equality or inequality. In our example, the disagreement between you and me about how the principle of responsibility should affect the (re)distribution between A and B cannot be solved by reference to the concept of responsibility alone because this concept already has some further ethical conceptions built into it, and the differences between you and me in terms of endorsement or otherwise of these conceptions will affect our conclusions.

Let me now spell out the second dichotomy, and here I can be briefer. Marc Fleurbaey has observed that we may use the concept of responsibility, in the context of a discourse on equality, in two senses: in the first sense, as in 'someone being responsible for her actions', and in which the distinction between one's choice and involuntary circumstances is central; and in the second sense, to refer to a number of choices, decisions, issues that are someone's 'responsibility'. This second use, Fleurbaey adds, 'does not have anything to do with free will. This is a purely descriptive concept that is used to describe how a society allocates the power of decision to its members, and no particular explanation needs to be given as to how and why specific decisions are made'.[7] This second meaning is independent of any considerations of free will because however strong the factors affecting my decision, an indisputable fact is that I am a decision-maker in a given domain—and so this domain is under my responsibility. 'It involves an idea of authority as well as an idea of obligation or duty'.[8]

Let us call these two notions of responsibility respectively the input and the output responsibility: input responsibility would relate to notions of free will, voluntary actions, and control over the factors leading to a decision or state of affairs, while output responsibility would identify merely who is in charge of choices in a particular domain. How will this distinction affect questions of luck egalitarianism? Input responsibility has an obvious implication. Equality would demand that this type of responsibility leave the resultant inequalities unaffected: equalizing redistribution would have to ignore the inequalities caused by input responsibility. But output responsibility is a different matter: its role would be to distinguish between those areas within which a redistribution aimed at more equality should occur and those within which it should not. It would be akin to a public/private distinction with a proviso that social equality must not apply to the private domain. For instance, even if, according to any plausible conception of input responsibility, I should be compensated for unhappily ending up with a nasty spouse (I had not known of her difficult character which became apparent only after our marriage) or a religion (I had no choice over my religion which was imposed upon me by my authoritarian parents, and now I cannot mobilize enough energy to convert to another faith), the principles of output responsibility would block such a redistribution. It would be only up to me, acting individually, rather than for the society in its redistributive actions, to do something about my unhappy fate in these domains.

We are thus faced with two oppositions within the context of social equality: between 'defensive' and 'affirmative' uses of responsibility, and between input and output responsibility. To assess whether responsibility-based egalitarianism

[7] Mark Fleurbaey 'Freedom with Forgiveness' *Politics, Philosophy & Economics* (2005) 29–67 at 45.

[8] ibid at 45, (reference omitted).

may be properly apprehended, at a conceptual level, as a simple mirror image of luck egalitarianism, we must now clarify the notion of luck. The popular distinction (in addition to that between good and bad luck, of course) is that between 'brute luck' and 'option luck'. Option luck is said to result from some calculated gambles that a person freely undertakes; brute luck cannot be traced to such free decisions. As Ronald Dworkin, who had coined this distinction, observed, the difference between these two forms of luck is a matter of degree, but his explanation for this property of the distinction suggests that it is a matter of degree only insofar as we are uncertain as to the presence of a 'calculation' in the 'calculated gamble': 'If someone develops cancer in the course of a normal life, and there is no particular decision to which we can point as a gamble risking the disease, then we will say that he has suffered brute bad luck. But if he smoked cigarettes heavily then we may prefer to say that he took an unsuccessful gamble'.[9] So the dimension of degree in the continuum ranging between brute and option luck is only a matter of uncertainty as to whether the cancer is a result of a deliberate decision to smoke, and also of our uncertainty as to the extent to which the decision matched the ideal criteria of voluntary choice, with the proviso of full knowledge of the (possible) consequences etc. But, once these uncertainties are dissolved, any luck-effect can be characterized conclusively, so it seems, either as a matter of option or brute luck.

We now have sufficient resources to compare the notions of responsibility with those of luck, in order to assess whether they are the opposite of each other, for the purposes of luck- and responsibility-egalitarianism. We can perhaps simplify the argument by putting aside 'option luck': such luck is obviously *not* a simple opposite of responsibility because we can trace (by definition) the effects of option luck to a decision for which we can hold a person responsible: a decision to gamble, to participate in a lottery, to engage in an activity where the risks are known etc. Both bad and good option luck are outside the concerns of luck-egalitarianism, and indeed one of the tasks of the conception is to screen off option luck from the egalitarian actions of the society. '[W]e have no reason to object.... to a result in which those who decline to gamble have less than some of those who do not... For the effect of redistribution from winners to losers in gambles would be to deprive both of lives they prefer...'.[10] To be sure, luck-egalitarians admit, indeed postulate, interventions aimed at eliminating the worst consequences of option luck but these arguments are made on paternalistic rather than on strictly egalitarian grounds—not on the basis that there is something wrong about a disparity resulting from that sort of 'luck'.[11] The only type of luck which is viewed with concern by luck-egalitarians is therefore brute luck.

[9] Ronald Dworkin 'What Is Equality? Part 2: Equality of Resources' *Philosophy & Public Affairs* (1981)10: 283–345 at 293 (referred to as 'Equality of Resources').

[10] ibid at 294–5.

[11] ibid at 295.

How does *brute* luck match, as an inverse, our various notions of responsibility? Consider the defensive versus affirmative distinction first. At first glance, it is only the affirmative use of responsibility which should be of interest to us: eliminating the influence of brute luck on distribution means retaining only those disparities which are sensitive to that for which we are responsible. But, as I have suggested, we need not be concerned about the affirmative-defensive dichotomy too much because, if I am right, there is continuity between them, and the defensive cannot plausibly stand without the affirmative in the background. Next we have the input/output distinction. Output responsibility is about drawing the line between realms, and in particular, between the domain in which individuals can expect society to reduce their disadvantaged positions vis-à-vis the others, and those where it is only up to them to do something about it. This clearly cannot be seen as the opposite of luck. But then, it is not a matter of equality either. It is a matter of policy and moral choices which must be *prior* to the application of norms of equality, whatever these norms are: those prior choices are about the domain within which society should be responsible for reducing inequalities. These choices cannot be made on the basis of norms of equality themselves; otherwise we would face infinite regress. They may be made on all sorts of grounds: opinions on privacy, autonomy, protection of self-respect, efficiency etc, but not equality itself.

In fact, the matter is more complicated because the domain within which equal distribution should be made is bordered on two sides, so to speak, by *two* different territories: one is the sphere of the private (where inequalities are not subject to distribution, for example resources for family happiness or religious salvation) and another, the domain where we deliberately want to keep certain resources as public goods in a technical sense of the word, ie not subject to distribution in accordance with equality or with any other standard. We may want to keep certain goods under collective ownership (roads, some essential natural resources etc) and immunize them from distribution which would result in these goods being enjoyed privately, on a user-pays basis.[12] And we of course need some theory to justify the boundary between collective and private ownership, just as we need some theory to justify the boundary between the domain open and that closed to egalitarian interventions.

Now the very idea of output responsibility, as suggested (without using the word output) by Fleurbaey, is at first glance, an odd one because it rests on a metaphorical notion of responsibility so as to exploit a moral connotation of the word, without relying on the moral sources of this connotation, namely, its relationship to free will. Free will is operative in input responsibility (as an analytical truth, we can trace what we are responsible for to the exercise of our free will), but irrelevant to output responsibility (what is our responsibility, in the output-responsibility sense, is not determined by what is affected by our free will: free

[12] See Eric Rakowski *Equal Justice* (Oxford: Oxford University Press, 1991) 66.

will is neither here nor there in the delimitation of domains, as dictated by the output responsibility conception).[13] A line-drawing (or domains-distinguishing) function of this sort of responsibility must have some moral rationale, after all; as pointed out earlier, it may be based on privacy, autonomy, efficiency etc. We may, for example, believe that to make a social judgment about inferiority in a particular domain (as a prelude to a decision about compensation) is such a grave violation of the person's conditions of self-respect that any gains in terms of equality will be morally insignificant: to make a judgment about a person's ugliness (to trigger a redistributive decision, eg in terms of resources for cosmetic surgery) or lack of social skills (as a basis for psychological services) would be intolerable, for reasons other than equality, because it would further undermine the person's self-esteem, his sense of self-respect etc. So, not all socially valued goods should appear on the radar of social equality, and we need a general conception about the parameters—the boundaries—of social equality before we set about determining the standards operating within that domain.

It is perhaps illusory to hope that we can keep some domains fully immunized from the intrusions of free will exercised in other spheres. For if we draw the borderline between the private and the public, and announce that in the former no equality of whatever sort is to be socially promoted, we are liable to a charge of moral hypocrisy: the boundaries between the private and the public are porous, and a person left fully to her own devices in the private sphere may justifiably complain that her opportunities in the public sphere are compromised by her disadvantages in (what was defined as) the private one. (For instance, we may contend very plausibly that the differences in the ability to engage in interpersonal contacts are totally a private matter, and so we have no duty to undergo a process of social compensation for deficiencies in this ability. However, if one's low capacities in this domain affect adversely one's employment opportunities, then what is essentially a private resource translates into a social disadvantage, and the claim for compensation—through, for instance, publicly supported training and counseling services—is no longer implausible). Thus, to confine something safely to the private, we must be able to show that it will not affect outcomes in the public, and consequently that it will not constitute the sort of 'bad brute luck', which is disallowed under responsibility-based views of equality. To this, but only to this extent, output responsibility must take some account of input responsibility.

This is a proviso which limits, but does not eliminate, the use of output responsibility in egalitarian theories. Beyond this, output responsibility is something prior and external to social equality aspirations. Input responsibility—responsibility linked to choice, control, and free will—is, in contrast, central to social equality, insofar as it views as its mission to eliminate the impact of bad brute luck on human fortunes. The upshot of this conceptual reflection is, therefore, that yes,

[13] See Marc Fleurbaey 'Equal Opportunity or Equal Social Outcome?' *Economics & Philosophy* (1995) 11: 25–55 at 51.

luck egalitarianism and responsibility egalitarianism may be seen as coextensive, with luck and responsibility perceived as the direct inverse of each other, under the condition that we understand luck in the sense of brute luck, and responsibility as input responsibility, when affirmative and defensive uses of responsibility are seen as mutually self-supporting.

2. Luck Egalitarianism and Moral Intuitions about Equality

The main proposition of luck egalitarianism is that only those unequal outcomes are justified which are caused by the factors for which a person can be held responsible in a meaningful rather than purely tautological sense of responsibility.[14] More specifically, it claims that those inequalities which can be fully, or primarily, traced back to bad brute luck, should be eliminated. Bad brute luck can be defined in various ways but the most usual way of giving it a more specific meaning is by identifying it with those aspects of a person's circumstances which are not chosen, and yet which affect her position of inferiority in the access to socially valued goods. The line to be drawn between the unchosen circumstances (the effects of which must be neutralized) and the person's choices (the results of which should be unaffected, even if they are unequal for different persons) is the object of one of the fundamental controversies within the strand of luck egalitarianism, and will be discussed shortly. Another side of the coin—usually afforded much less attention in the writings of the main proponents of luck egalitarianism—is that compensation for these undeserved inferiorities is derived exclusively from resources held by those who are more fortunate, which are themselves undeserved, ie cannot be attributed to choices but only to circumstance.

Luck egalitarianism thus provides a response to those detractors of egalitarian redistributions who claim that egalitarians condone taking goods away from the deserving—ie from those who have earned their prosperous positions through their own effort, superior abilities and knowledge, smart choices, and risk-taking. Egalitarians respond that only those superior goods will be taken away (through redistributive transfers) which can be traced back to facts and features for which a person cannot be held responsible—or, to be more precise, which cannot be described as a person's choices. No one who worked hard, for instance, to earn his current superior position vis-à-vis the one who has chosen to live a life of leisure will be penalized for that choice. So the principle of responsibility (or luck neutralization) figures on both sides of the redistributive equation. Generally, luck egalitarianism can be described as postulating the principle of social equality,

[14] The tautological understanding would define the factors for which a person can be held responsible as those which can justifiably figure in the reasons given for an unequal outcome; see Scheffler 'Choice, Circumstance, and the Value of Equality' at 9.

while being at the same time sensitive to the actual choices people make in and about their lives.

One immediate observation which may perhaps be provoked by this description, is: it may be a principle of justice all right, but why call it a principle of *equality*? The idea that no one should be advantaged or disadvantaged by arbitrary factors seems to be a reasonably good candidate for a universal concept of justice,[15] with various specific theories about what constitutes arbitrariness giving rise to differing conceptions of social justice. The idea that we cannot claim any credit for the factors which are morally arbitrary—those that are outside our control—seems like one among many conceptions of justice, and it may be (so the argument goes) debated precisely in these terms: as a theory of justice, plausible though no doubt controversial. But why consider it under a rubric of social *equality*, and why characterize those who espouse this theory as luck egalitarians, rather than luck-*neutralization* theorists of justice? After all, nothing on the face of the theory suggests, in a self-evident manner, that the implementation of luck neutralization will bring about equality, ie *more* equality, either in comparison with alternative conceptions (and much depends here on what specific theories we use as comparators for this purpose) or in comparison with the real-life status quo. Two responses seem available here.

First, it can be contended that luck egalitarianism is indisputably egalitarian by virtue of using social equality as a default position: unless inequalities can be clearly traced to facts and factors for which we can hold people responsible, equal distribution is required. In this understanding, responsibility-related factors are modifiers of the basic standard—which is that of equality. (Equality of *what?* is of course an obvious question here but this we can postpone to a further discussion; as long as a theory demands equality of *something*, it deserves being called egalitarian). The strength of this response is uncertain. In a situation where responsibility-traceable inequalities are massive, the modifier may devour the norm. This connects with a second possible response. It can be argued that, if we apply properly the standard of responsibility to real-life distribution, we will end up with much less inequality than there is in real life now and, therefore, that if the social reality of today is to be taken as a baseline, the theory will bring about egalitarian reforms. This response would have to rely on the contention that (1) much of today's inequality is traceable to facts and factors for which people cannot properly be held responsible, and also that (2) the additional *inequalities* produced by the implementation of the theory of luck egalitarianism compared with real life, would be fewer than equalities produced as a result of (1). As one can see, these are contingent judgments. I will suggest, however, that while contingent, they are eminently plausible. Much will depend here, of course, on what particular

[15] As it is often articulated, see eg GA Cohen 'Where the Action Is: On the Site of Distributive Justice' *Philosophy & Public Affairs* (1997) 26: 3–30 especially at 12 (referred to as 'Distributive Justice'). See, generally, Wojciech Sadurski *Giving Desert Its Due: Social Justice and Legal Theory* (Dordrecht: D Reidel, 1985) especially Ch 5.

facts and factors we take to be under a person's effective control, so that they will need to be considered as part of a person's choice rather than her circumstances. The broader the range of such facts considered as being under a person's control, the less egalitarian the theory will be in its practical consequences. As I have suggested above, the disagreement about which factors to consider morally arbitrary in this sense (in the sense of being traceable to a person's choice) is not merely an empirical disagreement but touches upon moral judgments which themselves cannot be derived from the rule of equality. In this sense, the egalitarian character of luck egalitarianism is both contingent and parasitic upon prior, non-egalitarian principles. But it does not follow that it is a mistake to call it egalitarian: we must just be clear about the relative thinness of this property.

Before going further in specifying the contents of the theory (and in particular, addressing the 'equality of *what*?' question), I should consider some of the important critiques which have been levelled against this theory, as described up to this point. Among these critiques, I will put aside those which I have already discussed above, in Chapter 4, where I was interested in the criticisms against an individualized theory of equality levelled from the standpoint of a collective conception, and where I considered luck egalitarianism only as representative of a broader family of individualized theories of equality. The critiques considered then were not necessarily specific to luck egalitarianism as such. Here is the place to consider some of these more specific criticisms. In particular, I am interested in two related criticisms, formulated usually from the standpoint of intuitive judgments of justice: that not all inequalities based on unchosen factors are ipso facto illegitimate (or, to put it from a positive angle, that some inequalities traceable to factors for which individuals cannot be held responsible are legitimate) and, on the other hand, that not all inequalities traceable to choice are acceptable (or that some inequalities based on factors for which persons may plausibly be held responsible need to be eliminated under the principles of social equality). These two objections taken together would render luck- or responsibility egalitarianism effectively void.

Before considering these two objections in turn, let us observe that they are not correlates of each other: that the acceptance of the one does not necessarily commit us to the other. For someone may accept that some inequalities unrelated to choice may be legitimate but consider that all inequalities traceable to choice are legitimate: such a person would simply expand the range of legitimate inequalities beyond the choice principle. Choice, under that theory, would be a sufficient but not a necessary condition legitimating a given inequality. On the other hand, someone may accept that there are many inequalities traceable to choice which must be eliminated, and at the same time claim that all inequalities unrelated to choice should be eliminated too: such a person would expand the range of morally required equalities beyond the choice principle. These are both plausible, internally non-contradictory positions: each of them rejects the premises of luck egalitarianism—although from the opposite moral perspectives. For this reason, both objections to luck egalitarianism need to be considered in turn.

Let us consider first an objection which, I think, is less detrimental to luck egalitarianism, namely that in our intuitively accepted moral positions we consider as legitimate some inequalities which are based on 'unchosen' factors, and which we cannot trace back to individual responsibility in any meaningful sense of the term. As Samuel Scheffler suggests, 'many people regard material inequalities deriving from differences of talent and ability as acceptable within limits'. This proves, for him, that 'any version of the principle of responsibility that is strong enough to support a luck-egalitarian conception of distributive justice is bound to be controversial'.[16] And he further observes that 'few people endorse a blanket policy of refusing to reward unchosen talents or traits of character'.[17] It seems to me that here we face a problem of under-justification of a moral principle by referring to an intuitive judgment of justice. Would the intuitions to which Scheffler appeals pass the standard of being 'fixed points' in a serious reflective-equilibrium type of moral exercise: would they rank as such unquestionable moral convictions that general principles must be tailored to match them? I have my doubts. 'Many people regard...'—but not *all*; 'few people endorse...'—but some *do*. I have no doubt that Scheffler's reconstruction of conventional thinking will resonate with many people's actual views, but perhaps they are not as widespread, as settled, and as fundamental as to undermine a contrary intuition, namely that those inequalities which are based on morally arbitrary factors are unjust, and that anything which is beyond our power to choose or modify is morally arbitrary. This doubt is reinforced by the evidence Scheffler provided for his point. Directly following this, Scheffler goes on: 'in their personal lives, for example, few people have a general policy of refusing to praise their friends and acquaintances for anything other than effort or hard work. Such a policy would also be liable to strike us as strange and moralistic'.[18] And so it would, but it does not necessarily prove the point that in the domain of *social* equality an equivalent 'general policy' would be inappropriate. Our private lives, and more particularly our actions of praising our friends and acquaintances for their achievements, are not a good model for social equality within a domain where socially valued goods are being distributed by collective means. This has been discussed above, when the choices regarding the domain of social equality were characterized as being prior to, and independent of, judgments of standards of equality. We express praise for people often without any morally good reasons; further, we often congratulate people for actions or achievements where there is obviously no moral ingredient (consider congratulating someone on winning in the lottery[19] or, in a different way, congratulating someone for buying a new house or

[16] Scheffler 'Choice, Circumstance, and the Value of Equality' at 10.

[17] ibid at 15.

[18] ibid.

[19] Perhaps, in line with the theory of 'option luck' such congratulation may be seen as based on a congratulation of a wise gamble or of wise risk-taking, but I do not think that, as a matter of psychology, this is what congratulation for a win on the lottery boils down to.

a new car: arguably, a trite praise from the standpoint of any plausible theory of justice). Neither do we believe that the choosing of friends, partners, and spouses should be done on non-arbitrary grounds, and that everyone should get a friend or a spouse he deserves, according to a meaningful responsibility principle. The question of grades, literary prizes, sporting awards etc is more complicated: these are much less private domains, and we clearly do accept such rewards based on largely unchosen factors. No one would wish for an equalizing of luck-related factors in such a way as to grant those rewards only on a basis which can be traced to a person's choice. But here, I suggest, this unwillingness can be accounted for by several explanations which do not necessarily affect the responsibility-inequality moral link: (1) the impossibility to discern with any plausibility the chosen ingredients (choice) and disentangle them from the unchosen ones (such as inborn talent); (2) the fact that much of the purpose in the acts of grading, prize-giving etc is related to an incentive for future enterprises rather than expression of praise for its own sake; (3) the fact that literary prizes and sporting awards etc are not seen as a matter of dispensing justice, but rather as part of a certain rule-governed entertainment (*sensu largo*) and so cannot serve as a model for the rules of social equality in the general domains, where the distribution of socially valued goods takes place. In sum, the general tenor of my response to the argument according to which intuitively we do not question all inequalities based on factors for which people are not responsible, is to express a doubt as to the strength and the scope of applicability of this intuition qua a ground for a moral argument.

The second objection is more challenging to luck egalitarianism: it is that not all inequalities based on free choice—on the factors for which a person can be held responsible—are morally acceptable, and that a theory of equality which postulates such a tolerance for choice-based inequalities is cruelly and implausibly unforgiving. As Elizabeth Anderson puts it: 'the reasons luck egalitarians offer for refusing to come to the aid of the victims of bad option luck express a failure to treat these unfortunates with equal respect and concern'.[20] Timothy Hinton echoes Anderson's concern:

> Negligent accident victims, or those who choose not to buy catastrophe insurance, and in general people whose calculated gambles have severe outcome surely have some claim on us in justice for help. How could it be consistent with treating them as our equals to force such people to bear the entire costs of their poor choices or their bad behaviour?[21]

In a similar vein, and appealing to widespread intuitive judgments, Scheffler observes: 'most people do not have a blanket policy of refusing assistance to anyone who has made a mistake or a poor decision. Such a policy would strike us as harsh, unforgiving, insensitive to context, and unduly moralistic'.[22]

[20] Anderson 'What Is the Point of Equality?' at 295.

[21] Timothy Hinton 'Choice and Luck in Recent Egalitarian Thought' *Philosophical Papers* (2002) 31: 145–167 at 165 (referred to as 'Choice and Luck').

[22] Scheffler 'Choice, Circumstance, and the Value of Equality' at 15.

This second objection is, I must admit, more serious, and it may well point to a feature of the theory which may be truly embarrassing to the proponents of luck equality. And yet, I am not convinced as to how successful the objection is. Consider two sets of parameters, which usually accompany the 'parades of horribles'—the arguments about the harsh and unforgiving (and thus, intuitively unacceptable) consequences of legitimating choice-based inequalities. The first set of parameters is about the degree of *probability* of negative consequences resulting from a choice; the second is a qualitative assessment of the *nature* of those negative consequences: about the absolute badness of the consequences. As to the first one, it is perhaps telling that, almost each time the critics of luck egalitarianism (such as those just quoted above) decry the harshness of the theory, they refer to the examples of *option* luck: of a gamble that turned bad. And yet this is not the only example of choice-based inferiority. Another case is that of a *certainty* of the consequences: suppose I know for sure that if I do not spend more time studying I will be unable to secure a well-paid job. No gamble here: I deliberately choose a life of leisure now to forsake a higher economic position in the future. Is it necessarily harsh and unforgiving to have my choice reflected in the distributive scheme in such a way? I do not think so. Hence, much of the persuasiveness of the 'harsh and unforgiving' critique depends on whether we are talking about option luck (gamble) or certainty. In real life, of course, our decisions are almost always taken in conditions of relative uncertainty, and there is a spectrum of decisions whose consequences can be predicted with a differing degree of certainty: at one end of the spectrum, we have gambles and lotteries, on the other, decisions such as the one about 'more leisure, less income'. The more we approach the former end, the more persuasive the 'harsh and unforgiving' critique is. This prompts us to wonder why this is the case. Perhaps there is a certain moral wisdom in the intuition that the choice to gamble is not equally morally weighty as the choice to accept the consequences which will follow it for sure (with the weight of the consequences being equal). This wisdom may suggest to us that the decision to gamble involves a lesser responsibility than a decision whose consequences are certain, and this variable responsibility may well be accepted by luck-egalitarians and built into their theory. In this way, a victim of bad option luck is less responsible for his predicament than a 'victim' of a decision whose negative consequences are certain. The maxim *volenti non fit iniuria* may well apply to the latter but not to the former case, and so a luck egalitarian may, consistently with the spirit of the conception espoused, mandate a degree of redistribution for the victims of bad option luck.

The second set of parameters applies to the absolute badness of the consequences. Not every inferior position is equally bad, and for instance allowing an uninsured negligent driver to die (one of the favourite examples of critics of the harshness of luck egalitarianism)[23] is much worse than getting less income based

[23] Anderson 'What Is the Point of Equality?' 295–6; Hinton 'Choice and Luck' at 165.

on one's lower educational standard. The critics of luck egalitarianism exploit the moral horror of the examples where there is an absolute (as opposed to comparative) badness of the consequences of bad decisions or where bad option luck is enormous. But our intuitive response to cases of less dramatic inequalities is markedly different: we do not think that it is a denial of equal respect for victims of their own choices if they will have to suffer lower incomes, but still well above the threshold of living with dignity, if that is what they have knowingly decided to embark upon. We simply hold people to their deliberate choices, assuming that in their own minds they have made rational calculations of trade-offs between certain pleasures and gratifications (eg less effort when studying) versus certain negative consequences in the future (lower income).

This shows that luck egalitarianism, in order to have its moral plausibility rescued in the face of 'harsh and unforgiving' critiques, must be accompanied by a safety net: it must accept that no one will be allowed to fall below a certain minimum, no matter what his choices were. The question is not whether luck-egalitarians do in fact allow for such safety net: they do (in his foundational text on luck equality, Dworkin made an express allowance for such interventions, either on paternalistic grounds or on the grounds of 'a theory of *political* equality').[24] The question is rather, can such safety-net measures be harmonized with the general spirit of luck egalitarianism? The burden would be on the critics to show that they *cannot* be, and I fail to find the arguments which would support such an eccentric position. As one of the critics of luck egalitarianism admits himself: 'few luck egalitarians present the luck-egalitarian principle as an absolute requirement or as constituting the whole of political morality; most acknowledge that the principle needs to be supplemented or qualified in various respects'.[25] The proviso that there will be a safety net against the harsh consequences of one's choices may well be such a 'supplement' or 'qualification', and it may plausibly be calibrated along the lines suggested (as I have just claimed) by our moral intuitions, as a function of the degree of certainty of negative consequences arising from our decisions, and the absolute badness of such consequences. It is true that the rationale for such a safety net cannot be found in the logic of luck egalitarianism itself; after all, it is a qualification to, rather than an implication of, the principle. In this way, the theory loses its architectural elegance, but this 'loss' matches our intuitive moral judgments, and should be accepted.

The only reason for finding the 'harsh and unforgiving' critique of luck egalitarianism devastating would be if it could be shown that the safety net principles are *incompatible* with the theory of luck egalitarianism. This is the argument made by Elizabeth Anderson who, after having listed all the nefarious consequences of abandoning the imprudent (the victims of bad option luck) to their own misfortune, recognizes that luck egalitarians resort to paternalistic devices in order to

[24] Dworkin 'Equality of Resources' at 295 (emphasis added).

[25] Scheffler 'Choice, Circumstance, and the Value of Equality' at 16.

escape such implications of their theory: 'Luck egalitarians do entertain modifications of their harsh system, but only on paternalistic grounds'. Anderson goes on: 'In adopting mandatory social insurance schemes for the reasons they offer, luck egalitarians are effectively telling citizens that they are too stupid to run their lives, so Big Brother will have to tell them what to do. It is hard to see how citizens could be expected to accept such reasoning and still retain their self-respect'.[26]

Anderson is right in saying that luck-egalitarians probably have to resort to some form of paternalism in order to justify a safety net: to exclude certain risk-taking, or certain decisions whose consequences are truly awful for the decision-makers. As such, paternalism is a troubling but not an incurably implausible position. There is no need here to rehearse various arguments about paternalism *tout court* because the only question which we face concerns whether the paternalism implicit in safety nets is *necessarily* at odds with the reasons provided for luck egalitarianism in the first place. We already know that paternalism is a modifier of (rather than a simple consequence of) luck egalitarianism and therefore has to resort to *different* rationales than those underlying luck-egalitarianism; it would be embarrassing to luck egalitarians only if those rationales were incompatible with luck-egalitarianism's rationale. Only then would the paternalistic qualification not be credible enough to allay our concerns about 'harsh and unforgiving' consequences of luck egalitarianism.

Although Anderson suggests that the arguments for paternalistic laws 'move us away from equality of fortune',[27] it is hard to find the support for such a suggestion. Such support cannot be found in the proposition (quoted above) that paternalism, as reflected in 'mandatory social insurance schemes', violates citizens' self-respect. Whether such schemes are offensive to individual self-respect is entirely question-begging: insofar as paternalism aims plausibly at protecting us from our own thoughtlessness, lack of imagination, and defective knowledge, no necessary denial of self-respect is involved. After all, Anderson herself admits that '[s]elf-respecting people can endorse some paternalistic laws as simply protecting themselves from their own thoughtlessness'.[28] And it is clear that to label a regulation paternalistic is not equivalent to condemning it: there may be laws which protect people against the effects of their own stupidity or weakness of will and yet which do not necessarily treat them with disrespect.

What criterion may be used to distinguish between an objectionable and a tolerable paternalism? The main yardstick should be, I suppose, whether a limitation of freedom for the sake of the agent herself expresses a fundamental disrespect for her own sincerely held values. As Isaiah Berlin had suggested, what is wrong with paternalism is that it is 'an insult to my conception of myself as a human being, determined to make my own life in accordance with my own (not

[26] Anderson 'What Is the Point of Equality?' at 301.
[27] ibid at 301.
[28] ibid at 301.

necessarily rational or benevolent) purposes'.[29] But not every version of paternalism *sensu largo* (that is, where a person's liberty is restricted for her own sake) is at the same time such an objectionable paternalism *sensu stricto*, which conveys the sort of insult that Berlin was writing about. If a paternalistic (*sensu largo*) restriction follows our views about the risks which we would all consider too dangerous to take, under the stricter understanding of paternalism there is nothing particularly objectionable or insulting in it. So, for example, if the range of transfers and redistributions follows correctly a hypothetical insurance scheme designed by Dworkin (by providing insurance, at public expense) against misfortunes which we all would have found reasonable to insure ourselves against, there is no necessary objectionable paternalistic defect in it. Hence our actual values are not being overridden: it is not the case that Big Brother tells us: 'You may like to take such a risk, but we will not allow you'. Instead, we are forced to behave in accordance with the values which we actually espouse, but which we tend to disregard sometimes in our conduct.

One should not underestimate the hazard of such reasoning: there is an underlying danger of hypocrisy when we tell people what their 'real' values are, when not reflected in their actual behaviour. So the availability for such a non-objectionable paternalistic argument depends on the accuracy of the detection of actual values held by the people to whom it applies. And there will always be dissenters who will genuinely not identify themselves with a socially dominant judgment of unreasonableness concerning certain types of risks. To *them*, such a safety net regulation will be paternalistic in an objectionable way. But the legitimacy of such a regulation will crucially depend on how small such a group will be, and therefore how well the safety net will reflect the dominant judgment about unacceptable risks against which we should all be insured.

To be sure, there are perhaps also some possibilities of non-paternalistic rationale for mandatory social insurance schemes: one can say, for instance, that such schemes protect those prudent among us who do not want (and find it unfair) to pick up the bill for the careless risk-takers. As one knows from the literature on paternalism, it is almost always possible to identify some third-party interests protected by what seems, at first glance, to be a paternalistic restriction.[30] The tendency to resort quickly to such rationales should, however, be resisted, because as we also gather from the literature on paternalism, such third-party rationales are often ex post facto rationalizations for regulations which are *predominantly* motivated by paternalistic motives. In my opinion, rather than conjuring up a third-party rationale for what is primarily motivated by the aim of protecting the person compelled to participate in a mandatory insurance scheme (or, more precisely, to participate in the redistributive scheme which mimics such an ideal

[29] Isaiah Berlin *Four Essays on Liberty* (Oxford: Oxford University Press, 1969) 157.

[30] See Joel Feinberg *Harm to Self* 16–23; Gerald Dworkin 'Paternalism: Some Second Thoughts' in Rolf Sartorius (ed) *Paternalism* (Minneapolis: University of Minnesota Press, 1983) 105–12 at 109.

insurance scheme), it is more candid to 'bite the bullet', to admit that safety-net devices added to the luck egalitarian scheme have a paternalistic character, and then try to see whether they are objectionable in a way which makes them incompatible with the basic premises behind luck egalitarianism.

What is odd is that some of the critics of luck egalitarianism—who argue that it reflects an insulting sort of paternalism whenever it resorts to safety-net devices supplementing the main scheme of choice-based redistribution—are at the same time opting for an objectivist assessment of personal values, hence an approach which favours rather than dismisses paternalistic interventions. Elizabeth Anderson, in a classic article, where she framed the objection of a paternalism against luck egalitarians' approach to the victims of bad option luck, insists also that 'democratic equality' (her own position of choice) urges that 'the weight that a citizen's claim has on others depends solely on the content of her interest and not on the importance she places on it in her own conception of the good'.[31] But if we can disregard the subjective rankings of various particular interests that people pursue, the reasons to be hostile to paternalism seem to evaporate because then there is no way that a person can object that her *own* values, properly internally ranked, have been replaced by the values of the legislators. Here is an example provided by Anderson to illustrate her point: '*From a public point of view*, it is more disrespectful to deny a person in a wheelchair access to public schools than it is to deny her access to an amusement park ride that only accommodates the walking. This is true even if she'd rather go through the Fun House than learn how to read'.[32] She draws this example not to decry paternalism in luck egalitarianism but to criticize Arneson's subjectivist approach which would merge expensive tastes and disabilities into one category of expensive preferences. I think that Anderson has a point against Arneson, but the collateral damage of her own critique is that she disarms the paternalism-related weapons against luck egalitarianism. Because her own example, provided above, *is* paternalistic, although not necessarily in an objectionable way. Assume that nearly all of us agree that it is much more important to access schools than amusement parks, and that this ranking is shared by the disabled persons themselves, so that the specific preference for an amusement park in precedence of the school described in the passage from Arneson can be reasonably seen as a sort of aberration, perhaps resulting from weakness of will or ignorance. In that case, a social decision which facilitates the disabled person's access to schools in precedence to amusement parks is not paternalistic in an objectionable way. After all, Anderson herself argues, when introducing the amusement park example: 'Some deprivations of capabilities express greater disrespect than others, in *ways any reasonable person can recognize*'.[33] The italicized words here and in the previous quotation from

[31] Anderson 'What Is the Point of Equality?' at 332 (footnote omitted).
[32] ibid at 332 (emphasis added).
[33] Anderson 'What Is the Point of Equality?' at 332 (emphasis added).

Anderson indicate precisely what renders the safety-net regulations, added to the luck egalitarian scheme, non-paternalistic (or not paternalistic in the objectionable sense of the word). If 'any reasonable person can recognize' that falling below a minimum threshold of decent life is unacceptable, and if this 'public point of view' is decisive for accepting the range of bad option luck which cannot be tolerated, one wonders how an argument about the insult represented by a safety net to the self-respect of the victims of bad option luck can be consistently upheld.

3. Equality of Resources, of Welfare, and the Status of Preferences

Much of the discussion within contemporary egalitarian theory—perhaps *most* of the discussion within today's egalitarianism—oscillates around the contrast between two theorems formulated by Dworkin in his classic articles on equality: equality of welfare (EoW) and equality of resources (EoR).[34] Dworkin himself famously rejected EoW and endorsed EoR as a correct interpretation of the general egalitarian ideal, and both his critics and followers consolidated the centrality of the distinction.

In a piece written well after his original refutation of EoW, and on the occasion of criticizing Amartya Sen's capability-oriented approach,[35] Dworkin looked back at the distinction at the heart of his own theory, and summarized his unease about the idea of redistributing opportunities in such a way as to equalize people's capacities to achieve various desirable states of affairs. The problem about such an approach stems from the fact that:

> [w]hat makes it impossible for most people to achieve happiness, self-respect, and a decent role in community life is a lack of resources – largely impersonal resources, including education, but also, in many cases, personal ones. So we are tempted to say that what we aim to achieve, by redistributing resources and creating opportunities, is an improvement in people's ability to secure these important goods.[36]

This temptation, Dworkin goes on to say, should nevertheless be resisted, for reasons which encapsulate his own approach to 'EoW v EoR' problems:

> [T]here is . . . a danger in putting the matter that way – the danger of sliding into the fallacy of supposing that our ultimate political goal is not simply to make people equal

[34] Ronald Dworkin 'What Is Equality? Part 1: Equality of Welfare' and Ronald Dworkin 'What Is Equality? Part 2: Equality of Resources' *Philosophy & Public Affairs* (1981)10: 283–345 (referred to as 'Equality of Resources'), reprinted also as chs 1 and 2 of Ronald Dworkin *Sovereign Virtue* (Cambridge, Mass: Harvard University Press, 2000).

[35] Chapter 7 of *Sovereign Virtue*, where the discussion of Amartya Sen is carried on, was written originally for that book, published in 2000; the original articles on equality were published in *Philosophy & Public Affairs* in 1981.

[36] Dworkin *Sovereign Virtue* at 302.

in the resources they need to achieve happiness, self-respect, and like desiderata, which is an attractive and compelling goal, but to make them equal in their overall capacity to achieve these goals, whatever ambitions, projects, tastes, dispositions, convictions, and attitudes they might have, which is the false goal of equal welfare or well-being.[37]

The fundamental point he makes in this context is that the ideal of EoW would necessarily be insensitive towards the distinction between the impersonal and personal assets which people have, and consequently would commit us to equalizing the personal assets (such as ambitions, tastes etc), a prospect Dworkin characterizes as 'frightening'.[38] A related point is that it would be unfair because it would disregard people's choices, as reflected in their 'projects, tastes, dispositions' etc. These are two separate points. But before looking at them, it is useful to realize that, at first glance, the EoW ideal is intuitively more compelling and attractive than EoR. After all, there is nothing inherently good and valuable about resources; what makes them good and valuable is how instrumental they are towards our welfare (understood in a broad sense of the word); consequently, there is nothing inherently fair in equality of resources. What makes such equality fair is the degree to which it contributes to equality of that which is meaningful to people. Welfare is meaningful; bare resources are not. To focus on resources (and consequently, on equality of resources) would seem to be confusing the means with the ends.

This is the intuitive reason why EoW would be, initially, a more attractive interpretation of the general ideal of equality. The most damning criticism of this interpretation is, as we have just seen, that it would be insensitive to the choices people actually make, *and* to the distinction between impersonal resources and the personal ones. These are clearly two *separate* objections because there may be some personal resources which cannot be traced back to any human choice, in a meaningful sense, and hence placing them beyond the bounds of equalization (or neutralization) is morally question-begging: if choice is the main criterion, distribution should nullify the effects of at least some personal assets; if, in turn, the main dividing line (between those assets which should be equalized and those which should not) is between the personal and impersonal assets, then distribution will remain insensitive towards (ie will keep intact) some differential assets which are not chosen. Dworkin, as we have seen, merges these two yardsticks into one when he seems to object to equalizing all personal resources, and at the same time warns against equalizing the assets in a way insensitive towards ambitions, projects etc. But we need to choose between one or the other yardstick whenever they do not coincide. I will return to this point in Part 4.

This criticism of EoW is traditionally presented in the literature (again, Dworkin has led the way)[39] through the lens of the problem of 'expensive tastes'

[37] ibid at 302.

[38] ibid at 303.

[39] Dworkin 'Equality of Welfare' 228–40.

(or 'expensive preferences'): one thoughtful scholar explicitly draws the connection between the 'expensive tastes problem' and the (alleged) insensitivity of the EoW ideal to 'the distinction between preferences or needs people have chosen, cultivated, or preserved, and those they have not'.[40] Dworkin's original argument went as follows: in order to achieve the same level of welfare for all, those individuals whose tastes require more resources to attain equal satisfaction, would have to be provided with more resources. This, however, is counter-intuitive: why should we, as a matter of promoting equality, provide money for champagne to those who require it to achieve the same level of welfare as we, ordinary mortals, get after drinking mineral water? Ergo: EoW is a confused ideal. This has been taken as a conclusive argument by a great number of writers sympathetic to Dworkin's strategy. As Eric Rakowski pointed out: 'Egalitarian welfarism would require that the allotment of someone who cultivated expensive tastes—for flashy cars, posh restaurants, designer clothes—be increased, in order to reestablish parity of welfare, even though everyone else's stock of resources would have to fall to repair the deficit he created. By contrast, those whose predilections are more cheaply satisfied would receive smaller shares'.[41] It is sufficient to describe such an implication of EoW to discredit the ideal seemingly beyond redemption.

Dworkin considered, at some length, a possible defence of EoW against the expensive tastes–based objection, namely, that we need not compensate for extra tastes because, and insofar as, they have resulted from a conscious decision of a person to acquire and/or cultivate them. Against this defence Dworkin observed that the very decision to cultivate these expensive tastes must have been based on some beliefs which were *not* (or were not traceable to) voluntary choices. The decision about what sort of life to live is 'rarely if ever voluntary all the way down'[42] and so we cannot rely on the voluntary nature of acquisition/cultivation of expensive tastes in screening off such choice from measuring welfare for the purposes of the EoW ideal. So there is no clear distinction between 'expensive tastes that are deliberately cultivated and other aspects of personality or person, such as native desires or socially imposed tastes, that affect people's welfare'.[43] And if no such distinction is available to us, and at the same time compensation for the former is wildly counter-intuitive, then we must not compensate for the latter either, and if the differences in 'native desires or socially imposed tastes' cannot figure in the differential distribution of resources to people, what is left of EoW? This seems to be the main argument against EoW, as launched by Dworkin.

[40] Rakowski *Equal Justice* 41.

[41] ibid at 41.

[42] Dworkin 'Equality of Welfare' at 233. This has been a very stable point in Dworkin's thinking about equality: he has reiterated the same point in a piece written much later; see *Sovereign Virtue* at 289. In the context of responding to Cohen's critique, he argues that someone with an expensive taste, say for champagne, 'cultivated refined tastes because... he thought such tastes appropriate to him: he had, we might say, a taste for refined tastes', which is not traceable to choice.

[43] Dworkin 'Equality of Welfare' at 232.

It is important to be clear about the structure of the argument and about its aspiration. The aspiration is to discredit the ideal of EoW, and this aim has been successfully attained, in my view. But the structure of the argument reveals a *non sequitur* which is significant to our thinking about the role of the personal/impersonal distinction and its connections with the voluntary/involuntary assets of individuals. The general argument, summarized above, can be presented schematically as follows: (1) compensating for (ie distributing resources in a way sensitive to) expensive tastes is absurd; (2) expensive tastes are indistinguishable from other aspects of personality which affect the degree to which we attain our welfare—at least not distinguishable in terms of their voluntary character; hence: (3) compensating for *any* of our personal assets in order to equalize welfare is absurd. I think that the premise (1) is unimpeachable. Asking others to subsidize my expensive tastes strikes us immediately as unfair. At this point, the goal of undermining EoW has been already accomplished because at least *some* individual characteristics which affect our attainment of welfare can be characterized as expensive tastes. The problem is with point (2), and if it is faulty, then (3) does not follow.

The problem about (2) is that while we may indeed acquire expensive taste in a non-voluntary way, it is not the case that we are unable to get rid of them through our own conscious action, once we realize that they are a hindrance to attaining a satisfactory level of well-being.[44] The case of the champagne-lover is a good (even though extreme) example: it may well be that someone's taste for champagne has been implanted through non-voluntary mechanisms (family, upbringing, social pressure etc) but it is not the case that we are unable to do anything about it once we ascertain that having it hinders us in achieving a proper level of satisfaction in life.[45] It is, in this sense, different from many other personal attributes which are not so easily cast aside. Perhaps a simple test should be: would we consider ourselves better off if we did not have a particular attribute (which rendered our achievement more costly) in the first place? A positive answer to such a counterfactual question may be a sign that it is not really possible to put the attribute aside and thus that it is not voluntary in a morally relevant sense: why would we have persisted with having an attribute if it renders us worse off and yet can be cast aside? It would be plainly irrational. A negative answer would be a sign that the attribute may be seen as voluntary in a thin but morally relevant sense: we value this attribute and consider it as part of our accomplished life, even though it makes our achievement of satisfaction more costly. (Consider a fundamental

[44] For a similar argument about voluntariness of preferences, see Richard J Arneson 'Equality and Equal Opportunity for Welfare' *Philosophical Studies* (1989) 56: 77–93 at 79–80.

[45] Note that it is a different, and a more modest, argument than a contention, made by Susan Hurley, that the very concept of responsibility for certain choices need not presuppose that we can be responsible for everything that has led to those choices (a conception which she calls a regression conception of responsibility, and which she rejects); consequently, 'We can agree that someone did not control and was not responsible for his constitution, but still think he was responsible for certain choices that flow from his constitution'; SL Hurley *Justice, Luck, and Knowledge* at 113–14.

difference, precisely in these terms, between a disability and an expensive taste!) But since we value it, and consider that discarding it is a loss, we need to 'pay' for it, and so surrender the right to claim compensation. Now my view is that expensive tastes belong to this latter category: we normally do not consider that we would have been better off if we did not have them in the first place, and we do not consider them on a par with handicaps.[46] Rather, we tend to be proud of them, to cherish them, and find that overall we are better (or more interesting, or more accomplished) human beings for having them. They are not something that we just happen to have and would prefer not to have: a champagne- or opera-lover does not consider her expensive tastes to be afflictions without which she would have been a better human being. So by surrendering them she would agree to a loss rather than a removal of a costly handicap. In this sense these tastes are 'discardable': if by having to satisfy my taste for champagne, or opera, I make a moral decision not to discard these costly preferences, by making this choice I surrender the right to claim compensation from society, many members of which do not need to pay so much for the attainment of a comparable level of satisfaction.

Note that the aim of my argument is not to resuscitate the ideal of EoW but rather to show that the argument against EoW should not bear collateral damage in the form of linking 'expensive tastes' with all other personal attributes, merely on the basis of (an alleged) equal involuntariness of both categories of personal attributes. The aim is to disconnect the personal/impersonal distinction from the question of choice. Why would it matter? I will return to the dividing line between personal and impersonal factors in Part 4 below, but at this point it is important to emphasize that our main concern is with the grounds of those disadvantages for which society as a whole has a duty to compensate an individual, as opposed to those which can be (morally speaking) left to individual self-help. The whole debate about EoR versus EoW is precisely about that: what should be equalized, or in other words, what factors of (or leading to) inequality must be compensated for? This can be translated into the language of 'subsidy': as resources are limited, when should we subsidize our fellow beings, in a relevant justice-community, for their disadvantages? In a statement which is suitable for a general proposition nicely encapsulating those intuitions which may serve as our fixed point in the argument about the relationship between expensive tastes and a duty to equalize

[46] Another possibility would be to distinguish, within the category of expensive tastes, between those that are traceable to a person's choice (hence, for which we can hold a person responsible) and those that are not. This was Cohen's approach; see GA Cohen 'On the Currency of Egalitarian Justice' *Ethics* (1989) 99: 906–44 at 923 (referred to as 'Currency'). But this is equivalent to denying any significance to the 'expensive tastes problem' and merely having this 'problem' superseded by a straightforward appeal to individual choice. In the end, I prefer a general characterization of 'expensive tastes' as typically traceable to choice, in a way described in the main text. Cohen's distinctions within the expensive tastes category (see ibid at 923–4) are just not convincing, as Dworkin has persuasively shown; see *Sovereign Virtue* at 288–9. And Cohen's proposition that involuntary expensive tastes should be compensated for, hence subsidized by others, for the sake of overall equality (see 'Currency' at 923), seems deeply counter-intuitive.

resources/welfare, Eric Rakowski argues that: 'Unless people's desires...were forced upon them by their upbringing or other manner of conditioning to which they were involuntarily subject, and *unless they disapprove of those desires and wish to be rid of them*, the costs of satisfying their wishes, or the frustration of leaving them unsatisfied, are of no concern to others who do not choose to make them their concern. Justice leaves these matters to private decisions, to be made against the backdrop of a just distribution of resources determined...on other grounds'.[47] The italicized words resonate with the proviso which I have just suggested in the previous paragraph: we can have a commonsensical test for which costly preferences can be considered 'voluntary', so that redistributive egalitarian transfers should disregard them, and their existence may thus well be reproduced in the final distribution, without any infringement of social equality.

A comment about the contrast between 'expensive tastes' and disabilities is in order.[48] I have argued above that the main difference, from the point of view of equality-related social obligations, is that—while both expensive tastes and disabilities add extra costs to the attainment of a level of satisfaction by an individual—the former (expensive tastes) can be seen as 'voluntary' only if it means that a person would not consider discarding them as a gain, but the latter (disabilities) cannot be seen in that way because a person normally would consider himself to be better off without them. Hence, there are duties of compensation under a conception of social equality stemming from the latter but not from the former personal predicament. For this reason, the attempt to draw a moral analogy, as in the work of Richard Arneson,[49] strikes me as deeply counter-intuitive. In Arneson's theory, the analogy is drawn, because he needs a strategy to defend the welfarist ideal (even though in a modified version, as equal opportunity for welfare, with a subjectivist standard for welfare) but *this* strategy seems to be a non-starter.[50] Elizabeth Anderson has convincingly criticized Arneson for analogizing expensive tastes with disabilities, but she went further and claimed that the whole argument according to which disabilities call for compensation under the ideal of equality is baseless. Anderson claims to 'take seriously what the

[47] Rakowski *Equal Justice* at 64 (emphasis added).

[48] On this contrast, see also Dworkin 'Equality of Resources' at 300–4, and *Sovereign Virtue* at 293.

[49] See Richard J Arneson 'Liberalism, Distributive Subjectivism, and Equal Opportunity for Welfare' *Philosophy & Public Affairs* (1990) 9: 158–91 at 187–8 (referred to as 'Liberalism').

[50] Whether the attribution to Arneson of a position that 'disabilities are just another kind of involuntarily expensive taste', Elizabeth Anderson 'What Is the Point of Equality?', is fair is another matter. It is true that he claims that his own preferred theory (which he dubs 'distributive subjectivism') would 'involve[...] a generalization from th[e] particular example involving physical handicap to all other expensive preferences that individuals are not plausibly regarded as bearing any personal responsibility for'; Arneson 'Liberalism' at 187. But later in the same article, he speculates that perhaps there is a viable perfectionist theory which would allow us to make objectively valid judgments about worthwhile human life as a result of which we could distinguish between expensive extravagant tastes and expensive preferences due to physical handicaps; see ibid at 190–3. For the purpose of the argument in the main text, I presuppose (but am not fully convinced) that Anderson's attribution of the no-distinction view to Arneson is correct.

disabled are actually complaining about': 'They do not ask that they be compensated for the disability itself. Rather, they ask that the social disadvantages others impose on them for having the disability be removed'. As one example of such call for a removal of social disadvantage, she demands 'that the disabled have good enough access to public accommodations that they can function as equals in civil society'.[51] No one could take issue with such a claim; the question is, what is the point of characterizing it as a 'removal of social disadvantage imposed by others' rather than a compensation for a disability with the aim of equalizing the conditions of the functioning of a society? The former characterization strikes me as convoluted and counter-intuitive: to say that, by failing to provide special measures for the mobility of the disabled we are 'imposing' disadvantages on them may be a useful rhetorical device to mobilize public opinion but seems to miss the point that our failure to act (to compensate for disability) may be equally reprehensible as a positive 'imposition of disadvantage' on the disabled.

Now the whole point of this distinction (which by now may strike a reader as meaningless) is that the language of compensation, but not the language of removal of the disability, can be aligned with the general theme of luck egalitarianism. This is why: the language of compensation for a disability (aimed at social equality) is perfectly at ease with the central place of choice/responsibility-sensitive equality. Consider the starting point of the present reasoning: it aimed at drawing a meaningful distinction between expensive tastes and disabilities. The distinction can be drawn, I have suggested, on the basis of a test which reflects the thin standard of voluntariness; can we discard an attribute, and would we feel a sense of loss once we did? So if the dissimilarity between expensive tastes and disabilities is indeed based on this test of voluntariness, the claim for compensation for disabilities is perfectly compatible with (indeed, mandated by) choice-sensitive equality. Any strategy aimed at defying the dissimilarity (hence, affirming the analogy), as in Arneson, is detrimental to this aim. But so is any strategy aimed at showing that disabilities do not trigger claims for compensation (but rather claims for the removal of disadvantages imposed by others), as in Anderson. And it is now clear why she has a stake in rebutting the disability-compensation thesis: she is a vocal critic of choice-sensitive equality in either of its forms. So to square the duty of extra measures for the disabled with the rejection of choice-sensitive equality, she needs to propose a totally different characterization of the former, and she offers the 'removal of disadvantages' characterization. But it is unconvincing (for the reasons suggested above) and this is an additional reason making her challenge to luck egalitarianism seem ineffective.

Another attempt radically to disconnect the question of 'expensive tastes' from egalitarianism is by confining them *en bloc* to a private sphere, and to explain our lack of obligation to compensate precisely by their private status rather than by their involuntary (in the sense suggested above) character. This is the strategy favoured by Marc

[51] Anderson 'What is the Point of Equality?' at 334.

Fleurbaey. Responding directly to Dworkin's argument (and using Dworkin's invented character, Louis, as an instance of a person with expensive tastes), Fleurbaey says: 'It is not because Louis has chosen to cultivate a taste for plovers' eggs and ancient claret that he will not receive a subsidy, but rather because he has been given by the institutions, a personal autonomy over his tastes and the satisfaction of these tastes. The reasons why he develops such tastes are not to be scrutinized, unless they interfere with social outcomes (for instance, not to be threatened or manipulated would probably be a social outcome)'.[52] But this strikes me as question-begging: our decision to consider that something is within a private sphere is a *result* rather than a basis of our judgment about whether we have a duty to compensate for the absence of assets which impair our satisfaction. The line between the private and the public sphere is contingent, and part of the contingency is our judgment about people's responsibility for the factors which affect their satisfaction in life. Suppose Albert is deeply miserable because his loneliness is due to psychological characteristics which make him unable to cope: should we necessarily deny him subsidized resources to obtain psychological support merely on the basis that his suffering is in the private sphere? Compare that case with Barbara's choice of a lonely life as a deliberate decision as to the best allocation of her resources (founding a family would reduce her financial means and her freedom to travel): when she subsequently occasionally gets troubled about her lonely life, are we not less concerned about compensation that would be due to her than in the case of Albert? If so, the 'privatization' of a given matter already takes on board the judgments about individual choices/responsibility.

This is, indirectly, confirmed by the very language Fleurbaey uses: when he talks about Louis's lack of claim for compensation he talks about the 'autonomy' he has over his tastes: is not this autonomy a sphere in which free choice operates? Albert's predicament is less autonomous than that of Barbara: this is because autonomy delineates a sphere in which (among other things) our free choice reigns. And where there is no choice, the autonomy claim is empty. So Fleurbaey is right that, when considering status of expensive tastes under a conception of social equality, the *reasons* why a person develops these tastes are irrelevant; what *is* relevant is that she *develops* them, rather than getting stuck with them, in a way which impairs her level of satisfaction in life.

4. Persons, Circumstances, and Talents in Luck Egalitarianism

The problem of expensive tastes is important not only per se but mainly because it is a useful angle from which to consider the central issue for luck egalitarianism,

[52] Fleurbaey 'Equal Opportunity or Equal Social Outcome?' at 52 (footnote omitted).

namely, what it is about a person that is to count as a basis for a compensable bad luck and what (even if it amounts to, or produces, inequalities among people) should be left intact, without infringing the ideal of equality. As we saw, for Dworkin the absurdity of subsidizing expensive tastes was a platform from which to launch an assault on the ideal of EoW. For some of Dworkin's critics, notably for GA Cohen, the same presupposition (about the absurdity of subsidizing expensive tastes, at least those which are unchosen) was not so much the reason for rejecting EoW, but rather a proof that some choice-based inequalities are acceptable under a broader ideal of equality (however labelled). The difference between these two positions within the luck-egalitarianism theory stems from the different answers given to a more fundamental question: towards what factors should social equalitarian redistribution be sensitive; or in other words, what it is about human beings that should be subject to equalization? This is the question to which we now turn.

Dworkin, both in his original exposition of the argument and in his later response to critics, insisted on the centrality of the distinction between 'persons' (including their talents and abilities) and 'circumstances' (where circumstances include also ambitions and tastes): the differential impact of the latter should be neutralized, but the consequences of the former should be left intact. This was initially encapsulated in the general formula according to which distribution should be ambition-sensitive but endowment-insensitive, and the goal of redistribution should be to neutralize the effects of differential talents but to preserve the effects of choices.[53] In an article which was the first important response to Dworkin from within the luck-egalitarian theory, Cohen agreed with Dworkin in rejecting EoW but criticized Dworkin's 'cut' and suggested that it should be 'relocated'. Noting that Dworkin would compensate for shortfalls in capacities but not for shortfalls traceable to tastes and preferences, Cohen suggested that involuntary expensive tastes should also be compensated if we were to stick to the centrality of the choice/luck distinction.[54] Numerous critiques, comments, and suggestions for other 'relocation of the cut' followed.

It is important to be clear about what the discussion is about. The disagreement (as exemplified by the first round of the debate between Dworkin and Cohen) has sometimes been presented as concerning the following alternative: either the 'persons/circumstances' distinction is fundamental (as in Dworkin) or the choice/luck distinction is fundamental (as in Cohen).[55] But this is not so. At least in his more recent restatement of his own position, Dworkin clearly implies that both distinctions are coextensive but that the chance/choice distinction is primary. The former distinction (persons/circumstances) emerges when he says,

[53] Dworkin 'Equality of Resources' at 312–14.

[54] Cohen 'Currency' at 918–23.

[55] This interpretation can probably be read into Hinton 'Choice and Luck' *Philosophical Papers* (2002) 31: 145–67 at 148–62 and Scheffler 'Choice, Circumstance, and the Value of Equality'.

for instance, that 'a political community should aim to erase or mitigate differences between people in their personal resources... but should not aim to mitigate or compensate for differences in personality'.[56] As an example of compensable personal resources, he gives that of physical handicaps or other reasons accounting for the inability to earn a satisfactory income; as an example of aspects of personality (which must not be subject to mitigation or compensation), he gives that of people's tastes and ambitions. So here the persons/circumstances distinction seems central. But almost immediately after this passage, Dworkin reaffirms as a general principle the proposition that 'individuals should be relieved of consequential responsibility for those unfortunate features of their situation that are brute bad luck, but not from those that should be seen as flowing from their own choices'.[57] So for both Dworkin and Cohen (and their respective supporters) the choice/luck distinction is central. The debate is about where exactly to draw the line. For Cohen the distinction between ambitions and talents drawn by Dworkin is unfounded: if talents are unchosen (and therefore subject to redistributive responses) so are ambitions, or at least some. So at least when we can show that certain ambitions, tastes, preferences etc are involuntary and yet costly, according to Cohen social redistribution should mitigate resultant inequalities. And, in effect, we should subsidize them. For Dworkin, in turn, any distinction *within* the category of preferences, between those which are involuntary and those which are chosen, is suspect, and all preferences (tastes, ambitions) should be linked to the 'persons' side of the 'persons/circumstances' division, and thus not compensable.

But now note a puzzling incoherence in Dworkin. On the one hand, he claims that the choice/chance distinction is primary; the role of equality is to respect choice, but mitigate chance. On the other hand, he claims that preferences (ambitions) belong to personality and must not be mitigated even though they are unchosen: the distinction between chosen and unchosen (expensive) preferences is dubbed by him as 'illusory'.[58] How can we reconcile one with the other? In sum, we have three propositions here: (1) choice is to be respected by equality-promoting measures, and its results left intact, while chance must be mitigated; (2) personality must be respected, but personal resources (circumstances) should be corrected; (3) preferences and ambitions are unchosen. We can have (1) + (2) (choice becomes part of personality, while personal resources are unchosen and can be corrected), or (1) + (3) (results of differential preferences should be mitigated because they belong to chance, *vide* Cohen), or (2) + (3) (same), but how can we have (1) + (2) + (3)? How can we consider preferences to be unchosen, hence part of luck, and yet belong to personality and so not be subject to mitigation

[56] Dworkin *Sovereign Virtue* at 286.
[57] ibid at 287.
[58] ibid at 289.

through equality measures? To put it even more crudely, how can preferences be within the realm of individual responsibility and yet unchosen?

As may be clear from my earlier argument, I believe that it is point (3) which is the weak link here, and which infects Dworkin's conception with incoherence. We need to revisit the point about preferences being unchosen. For Dworkin, this thesis was a part of a larger strategy to show that non-respectable expensive tastes (such as for champagne) cannot be distinguished from more respectable expensive proclivities (such as for photography), by arguing that both can be claimed not to be totally traceable to choice. But to agree that they are both equally unchosen seems to throw the baby out with the bathwater; we may rather say that they are both equally subject to the individual decision to drop them (regardless of how a person came to have them in the first place), and therefore that we are sufficiently responsible for them to place them on the choice side of the choice/chance divide. (This strategy would not be perhaps convenient for Dworkin in the context of his argument against Cohen, which is precisely the context in which he employed it, but we do not need to be concerned about this specific polemical purpose here.) Apart from showing the way out of the incoherence just noted in the previous paragraph, such a characterization would have the benefit of achieving a better resonance with our intuitive judgments about people being 'responsible' for the preferences they have, at least insofar as these preferences require (as they usually do) access to scarce social resources. Or would it?

There is possibly a way of defending a decision to place preferences on the non-compensable side of the divide, even if they are not under a person's control: it would be to say that we *identify* with them to such a high degree that they deserve to be respected and not subjected to any compensatory actions. This idea is perhaps present, although not made explicit, in Dworkin, when he elaborates on the way in which we are associated, as individuals, with our tastes and preferences: we do not consider them as being a matter of choice, similar to a choice of a shirt from a drawer or a dish from a menu. Dworkin goes on:

> We . . . do not count the fact that we have reached some particular moral or ethical conclusion as a matter of good or bad luck. That would be to treat ourselves as *dissociated from our personalities rather than identified with them*—to treat ourselves as victims bombarded by random mental radiation. We think of ourselves differently—as moral and ethical agents who have struggled our way to the convictions we now find inescapable. It would strike us as bizarre for someone to say that he should be pitied, or compensated by his fellow citizens, because he had the bad luck to have decided that he should help his friends in need, or that Mozart is more intriguing than hip-hop, or that a life well lived includes foreign travel.[59]

I think that as a matter of moral psychology Dworkin has a point—although it is questionable whether he can merge into one and the same category some moral

[59] ibid at 290 (emphasis added).

convictions (the duty to help one's friends) on the one hand, and aesthetic or life-style preferences (Mozart, foreign travel) on the other. While the core argument (in the first three sentences) exploits a convincing theme that fundamental moral convictions are not a matter of choice or good or bad luck, the extension of this intuition to preferences guiding our consumption choices (where the real burden of possible compensation for expensive tastes lies) is suspicious. But this is not the main problem about the argument with which I am now concerned. From our point of view, what is significant is how this argument may support Dworkin's surprising (as I have suggested) categorization of preferences as part of personalities, which are not compensable even though they are unchosen. The argument may be precisely as I have suggested in the previous paragraph, that it is due to a strong identification which we have with them, and that they cannot be 'dissociated from our personalities'. But there is something strange about this argument. It seems to abandon the yardstick of choice (as something to which compensatory changes should be insensitive) and adopt the yardstick of 'identification': even though the preferences are as unchosen as external circumstances, we must not compensate for the former while we have to compensate for the latter, presumably only because we cannot identify a personality within circumstances. But then, why should we treat preferences and talents so differently? After all, if we cannot dissociate ourselves from our preferences, neither can we distance ourselves in such a way from our talents. If anything, we identify ourselves even more *strongly* with our talents and capacities than with our preferences and convictions.[60] And yet, talents are on the pole of compensable assets (a point to which I will return below). So identification may not be, after all, a strong yardstick either. Which, come to think of it, is not surprising: why would a decision about which individual assets should be compensable be in any way related to the fact that we identify with them or not? We may see our identity strongly related to a particular disability which very much should trigger social compensation, and on the other hand we can discern aspects of 'circumstances', which, even though they affect our welfare adversely, do not give rise to any compensatory claims. So 'identification' is neither here nor there from the point of view of the division between those factors which should be mitigated through a social equality policy and those which should not.[61]

The general observation that Dworkin operates with an eccentric notion of individual responsibility (what a person can be deemed to be responsible for), which does not coincide with the notion of choice (what is under a person's control), can be seen as the basis of a major theoretical division within the luck-egalitarian theory: almost all influential critics of Dworkin from within the luck-egalitarian stream, including Cohen, Roemer, and Arneson,[62] have objected

[60] See Hurley at 140.

[61] For a similar conclusion, see also Scheffler at 11.

[62] Cohen 'Currency' at 916–35; Arneson 'Equality' at 78–82; John E Roemer 'Equality and Responsibility' *Boston Review* 20 (April–May 1995) <http://bostonreview.net/BR20.2/roemer.html>.

to the cut being drawn between personal goals and ambitions on the one hand, and resources and circumstances on the other, and postulated, in various ways, division lines more faithful to the cut between factors within and outside a person's control. This latter division, as has been observed,[63] cuts across the persons/circumstances division: there may be some personal goals which are outside a person's control, and there may be some aspects of human circumstances which, at least to some extent, are traceable to human will and choice. This emerges most starkly if one considers the matter of human talents and abilities (understood here as one category), in comparison with human desires, preferences, and ambitions (*ditto*).

But before I turn to this question, just one final observation about what I called an 'eccentric' notion of responsibility used by Dworkin, where what we are responsible for does not coincide with what is under our effective control. Indeed, there are points at which Dworkin uses the concept of responsibility—which is not merely eccentric but plainly ambiguous—and this ambiguity is then exploited to draw a surprising (as I believe) conclusion about our preferences being at the same time unchosen and not grounding compensation. In responding to the critics of such a construction, Dworkin contended:

> The critics [of the idea that preferences are part of the personality and as such should not be the basis of compensation] could not just appeal to a supposed normative principle holding that people should never he held responsible, *in any sense of responsibility*, for what they have not deliberately chosen. That principle would be contradicted not only by our practice of taking consequential responsibility for our convictions, but by much else in ethical and moral experience besides, including, for example, the obligations and responsibilities most people believe they have toward their political community, their parents and their siblings.[64]

The italicized words are revealing because the 'normative principle' to which Dworkin refers in the first sentence works with one sense of responsibility but not with the other. If 'responsibility' means 'what people have a responsibility to do' then the principle is probably unimpeachable: most of us believe, as a matter of substantive moral principle, that we are responsible also for things which are not traceable to our choice, as the example referred to at the end of the quoted passage suggests: we have moral obligations towards our country, parents, and siblings even though no choice or action of ours can be cited as the ground of this obligation. This responsibility-as-obligation merely points at a moral truth that our deliberate commitments, choices, and voluntary actions are not the only possible bases of our moral obligations (consider our moral obligation to help a stranger—a victim of an accident which we have not caused and where we just happened to find ourselves). This corresponds to, what in Part 1 of this chapter, I called an 'output responsibility': this notion of responsibility is parasitic upon

[63] Fleurbaey 'Equal Opportunity' at 26–7.

[64] Dworkin *Sovereign Virtue* at 294 (emphasis added, footnote omitted).

some prior grounds upon which we may, legitimately, place on certain persons certain obligations towards others. But what these prior grounds are is not explained by the notion of responsibility (in the output responsibility sense), and whether the only grounds upon which we may make people so obliged are those which can be traced to their own free and voluntary choices is precisely one of those substantive moral issues to which a theory of such prior grounds must respond. (And, as already said, it would be a rather eccentric theory which restricted all our personal obligations to the ones traceable to our choices.)

But there is an altogether different sense of 'responsibility', as in 'what we can be held responsible for', that is, moral responsibility for facts or actions which can be cited as a reason for blame or praise, punishment or reward: call it responsibility-as-control. This is what in Part 1 we called an input responsibility: the sort of responsibility which is not a conclusion but a moral ground of holding people responsible for certain facts or events. And here, in contrast to 'output responsibility', it should be observed that free will and choice are central. I take it to be one of the firm moral convictions implicit in common morality that we cannot be held responsible for something over which we had no control: that we cannot be blamed or praised, in a moral sense, for that over which we exercised no control at all. This, some would say, is a controversial idea, and can be negated by various examples when law holds us responsible for events even though they cannot be attributed to any will or even negligence on our part: take all those cases where civil or criminal laws provide for strict liability. But, in my view, this is where law parts company with common morality, and the fact that normally legal cases of strict liability are so controversial and trigger so much unease and concern is evidence that here morality provides very weak, if any, support for such legal rules. In cases of input responsibility, the existence of free will, choice, and control are crucial. Perhaps the case of a duty to help the stranger whom we come across on the road is a good test of how these two senses of responsibility can be distinguished. We can plausibly say: 'You are responsible for helping the stranger', in the sense of output responsibility, which is the conclusion of a prior moral conception which does not make our free choice the single decisive factor for placing output responsibility on someone (for the fact, that this stranger happened to be there and is in danger cannot be traced to our choice). We cannot, of course, in the language of input responsibility, hold you responsible for the predicament of the stranger (his situation not being traceable to your choice) but we can, still in the language of input responsibility, blame you for not helping, because the decision to help or not to help was under your control, and you exercised your choice.

So, going back to the status of preferences and convictions in Dworkin's scheme, if we indeed had no control over the way our convictions were formed (the idea I reject) then we cannot be held responsible for those convictions, just as we cannot be held responsible for our native talents and abilities. And if we cannot be held responsible for either, under the general choice/chance division, as long as it is held to be fundamental for luck egalitarianism, both should give rise to compensation, insofar as they impede our pursuit of valued aims. Again, to restate my general position, I do not believe that we should indeed propose compensatory measures for expensive preferences, but this is not because we identify with them particularly intimately but rather because we are 'responsible' for them in the thin sense of exerting control over them, as suggested above.[65] So we do not need to exploit the ambiguous notion of 'responsibility', as Dworkin does, and appeal to responsibility-as-obligation in affirming our responsibility for our preferences and convictions because we can appeal to a non-ambiguous notion of responsibility-as-control in showing why we have no claims for compensation resulting from our expensive tastes and preferences.

This is not to deny that we may face, in real life, many truly troubling, borderline cases in which convictions are largely unchosen, or result from unchosen commitments, even under the relaxed test for voluntariness suggested above, and yet it would be counter-intuitive to consider them as a ground of compensation under any attractive conception of social equality. In such cases, we could not benefit from characterizing them as 'voluntary' because arguably they are not voluntary even in the thin sense of the word; the fact that social equality must be insensitive to them would seem to undermine the centrality of the chance/choice distinction. So we need to reconcile the rejection of compensation for expensive convictions with the fact that they are unchosen. Cohen raised this issue and suggested the following exception to the general rule of compensation for unchosen factors: if a disadvantage is 'intrinsically connected' to a commitment based on unchosen beliefs, then no compensation is called for because 'the bearer [of those commitments] would not choose to be without them'.[66] The paradigm case is that of religious convictions which may be very burdensome and costly, and yet which cannot be traced to a 'choice of religion', because 'people often no more choose to acquire a particular religion than they do to speak a particular language: in most cases, both come with upbringing'.[67] This is a questionable statement: even if we do not acquire a religion in a voluntary way, part of our religious maturity surely rests on constant decisions to retain one's faith (or change it, as the case may be), and even a failure to examine one's own faith can be plausibly represented as a

[65] See also this description by Rakowski: 'Virtually everyone has a vast range of desires—some cheap to satisfy, others dear—the satisfaction of which gives them greater or lesser pleasure or welfare. People may choose to strengthen some desires or weaken others out of moral or religious conviction, affection, self-interest, or other concern, but in each case they do so in the knowledge of possible costs, both material and experiential, of cultivating or preserving various preferences or hankerings. Those costs are a fact of life....To the extent that people elect to expose themselves to, preserve, or suppress certain desires, the more or less expensive preferences they develop are beyond the bounds of justice: no correction need or should be made for them', *Equal Justice* at 57–58. I could hardly find a better expression of my own views about the voluntary character of preferences, and their status under social equality.

[66] Cohen 'Currency' at 937.

[67] ibid at 936.

choice.[68] But let us assume, *arguendo*, that religious commitments are by and large unchosen. Compensation for such convictions would be wildly implausible, and Cohen's solution in the test: 'Would a person choose to be without these convictions?' seems like a reasonable revision of the general luck→compensation rule. It suggests some sort of responsibility for commitments, and for the impact of those commitments on one's welfare. It is also in line with the thin notion of choice/responsibility suggested here.

What *is* strange about Cohen's proposal, however, is the suggestion that if certain costly effects are only indirectly (rather than intrinsically) related to underlying commitments, so that we can imagine a person wishing to be rid of these costly effects without at the same time undermining his commitments, then society owes such a person compensation.[69] His example is of a pilgrim who deserves compensation for the costs of his pilgrimage: 'I do not think that it is strange for a lame or poor person to request the cost of transport for a pilgrimage mandated by his religious conviction'.[70] Cohen uses this as a case relevantly distinguishable from the 'intrinsic costs of commitments' (which do not trigger a duty of compensation), and he later reasserts: 'I see no glaring oddity in a believer's claim that, since all should be equally able to worship as they will, his own worship, because it requires what happens to be expensive, warrants public subsidy'.[71] And yet it *is* odd because the line separating those religiously-based costly commitments which require subsidy from those which do not, is drawn on two separate criteria which do not seem to point in the same direction. The first criterion is whether the connection between underlying commitments and costly actions is intrinsic or not: if it is not, the believer has a good claim for compensation. Considering that Cohen conceded earlier that religious commitments per se were usually not voluntary, the argument should simply be the other way round, in order to keep coherence with the fundamental choice/chance distinction: something that is intrinsically related to unchosen commitments seems to warrant a better case for compensation than something that is only indirectly or contingently related. The second criterion is that of a counterfactual regret: would a person prefer to be without those costly consequences, assuming that no underlying commitments would be undermined? If yes, compensation is owed; if not, it is not owed. This sounds like the thin notion of choice proposed earlier in this chapter, but in the specific context of Cohen's example I fail to see how it can be employed here. If a person would prefer to do without some costly consequences (such as a pilgrimage) of his commitments, and yet has to 'suffer' them because otherwise the underlying commitments will be undermined, then it seems to be a proof that the link between commitments and costly efforts is intrinsic. And the example of the pilgrimage just proves this point. To support Cohen's argument,

[68] For a critique of Cohen on that score, see Rakowski *Equal Justice* at 62.

[69] For a similar critique, see Rakowski *Equal Justice* at 60.

[70] Cohen 'Currency' at 936.

[71] ibid at 938 (footnote omitted).

we would need to think of a religiously-driven action which is not intrinsic to religious commitments, and which a believer would rather not suffer. If we can imagine such cases, then clearly they indicate caprice on the part of the believer: why should *that* be compensated by society at large?

We can now confront the question of the status of talents: why should talents be seen as belonging to the pole of 'chance' so as to be compensable, contrary to preferences? 'We want to develop a scheme of redistribution, so far as we are able, that will neutralize the effects of differential talents....'[72] This goal is perfectly in line with the status of talents as being the means to our success in life—our resources—which are largely independent of our will and choice. Of course, '[t]alents are nurtured and developed, not discovered full-blown, and people choose which talents to develop in response to their beliefs about what sort of person it is best to be'.[73] Hence, the dramatic practical question is, are we able to disentangle the native ingredient from the layer which is due to a conscious effort aimed at development, cultivation, and improvement of genetically or socially determined capacity? (For the purposes of this argument, we can consider social and natural luck jointly, as being something that a person equally cannot claim any desert for. I have considered and rejected a proposal to de-link social from natural contingencies in Chapter 4.) As Dworkin has observed: 'it is no more possible to erase all differences in wealth that derive from inequality in talent without also erasing some of those that derive from choice than it was for Shylock to take his pound of flesh without drawing a drop of blood'.[74] Marc Fleurbaey referred to it as the scepticism about 'separability': the separability thesis claims that trade-offs between external resources and internal talents are independent of human will, so that we can compensate for inferior talents with extra resources without offending the principle that equality should be insensitive towards choices people make. Such separability is rarely available to us in the real world.[75]

Whether we can disentangle the native from the choice-based factors, so as to make distribution endowment-insensitive but ambition-sensitive, is a practical matter which I am going to put aside here. I wish only to note that there have been some more or less ingenious attempts to construct a matrix which would reflect the native ingredient in a person's success, and attempt to establish a process of redistribution, which would take this ingredient into account. Some time ago, Jan Tinbergen advanced a proposal of a capability tax: taxes, Tinbergen argued, should be based on the innate capabilities of individuals rather than on their incomes, so that we would not tax marginal efforts made by individuals. Accordingly, such 'capability taxes' based on complex tests of innate abilities would result in all additional income obtained from extra effort remaining with

72 Dworkin 'Equality of Resources' at 312–13.
73 ibid at 313.
74 Dworkin *Sovereign Virtue* at 341.
75 Fleurbaey 'Equal Opportunity' at 30–1.

individuals.[76] This would be one way (arguably a crude one, because it would not factor into the tax many other luck-based assets) of disentangling choice-based factors from luck-based ones. Note that this seems like one way of giving effect to Rawls's idea of a common pool of natural assets, as corresponding to the difference principle. As Rawls argued: 'We see... that the difference principle represents, in effect, an agreement to regard the distribution of natural talents as a common asset and to share in the benefits of this distribution whatever it turns out to be'.[77] While the wording is misleading and gave rise to the charge that the common-pool idea 'does not take seriously the distinction between persons',[78] it is clear that the 'common pool' is constituted by the social advantages accruing to natural assets, not to assets themselves. Such a common pool is a metaphorical way of expressing the idea that luck-based assets (such as talents) should not affect a person's position in social distribution.

Anthony Kronman wisely observed that 'as a practical matter, talent pooling represents nothing more than a system of taxation'.[79] How can such taxation be designed? Perhaps Tinbergen's proposal may be used as one such method. In any event, my aim here is not to inquire into how accurate and feasible such mechanisms may be. Perhaps they are not feasible at all, and luck egalitarianism must consequently be confined to the category of those ideas which just cannot ever be put into practice. What I wish to emphasize is what follows from the earlier discussion of preferences: if talents are to be associated with the pole of compensable factors, then it cannot be that they belong to 'circumstances' rather than 'persons', and so the 'persons/circumstances' distinction cannot be seen as central for the purposes of luck egalitarianism. 'My talents are mine in just the way that my values and convictions are mine.... They are part of what makes me *me*'.[80] And if this identity-constituting character of talents is not sufficient to overcome the social obligation to compensate for the consequences of inferior talents (indeed, it is irrelevant to the goal of compensation), then it is hard to see why any identity-constituting characteristic should be relevant to any other factors people may possess, such as their convictions, preferences, and desires.

5. Resources and Welfare: Shortening the Gap

A person's position in society is influenced mainly by three sets of factors: (1) material goods and opportunities (which can be called external resources), (2) personal talents, skills, capacities, and other characteristics, including strength and beauty (which may be called personal assets), and (3) individual choices,

[76] Jan Tinbergen *Income Differences* (Amsterdam: North-Holland Publishing, 1975) 63.
[77] Rawls *Theory of Justice* at 101.
[78] Robert Nozick *Anarchy, State, and Utopia* at 228.
[79] Anthony T Kronman 'Talent Pooling' at 66.
[80] Hinton 'Choice and Luck' at 152.

decisions, efforts, and acts of will (which may generically be called choices). Luck cuts across all three categories, although in an uneven way. Many external resources represent something we are born into; personal assets are largely, although not solely, determined by native determinants; choices are partly affected by predispositions, which are in turn partly genetically determined. (There is also a lot of luck operating besides these three sets of categories, but social equality is mainly concerned with these three.) EoR attempts to bring about rough equality in (1) + (2) across the population,[81] and hopes in doing so to neutralize the impact of luck upon our social positions. More specifically, it attempts to make a final distribution sensitive only to inequalities resulting from (3), and more accurately, from this aspect of (3) which is luck-independent, or which can only be traced to human decision and choices discounted by the degree to which those choices have been affected by chance.

If this is a correct statement of the ideal of EoR then the fundamental question which emerges is, are the two aspirations of EoR in line with each other, that is equalization of (1) + (2) and luck-neutralization? Is it necessarily, or even contingently, true that if we attempt to correct luck (so that the outcome is luck-independent), we will achieve an equalitarian state of affairs, in any meaningful sense of equality? But before I address this big question (in Part 6), a note on EoR versus EoW is in order. As our earlier discussion of the status of talents suggested, talents are seen as part of overall resources for the purposes of the EoR ideal: (1) and (2) are viewed jointly as things to be equalized. '[A] person's resources include personal resources such as health and physical capacity as well as impersonal or transferable resources such as money, and... though different batteries of techniques are required to correct or mitigate inequalities in these two major domains of resource, both must command the attention of egalitarians'.[82] This suggests an eccentric, or a stipulative, understanding of 'resources' which in turn implies a shorter gap between the ideals of EoR and EoW, than the abstract statement of the opposition would suggest. On the part of EoW conception, there is hardly anyone who would advocate equality of *welfare* in its pure and unadulterated form: it would be both perverse and unattainable (and also deeply counter-intuitive) if the aim of society were to achieve equality in the sense of well-being, or satisfaction, or any other positive subjective state of affairs, among individuals. This much has been well demonstrated by Dworkin and a legion of other authors. So the so-called welfarist proponents of luck equalitarianism refer to equality of

[81] 'Rough equality' is an imprecise wording; at some points, EoR proponents establish a much higher test, for example that the transfers and redistributions should be such that 'no further transfer would leave [people's] shares of the total resources more equal'; Dworkin 'Equality of Welfare' at 186. But this seems to be, in practice, a very strict test, which would require a comparison of a given distribution with all other possible distributions of total resources. Let us settle here for 'rough equality' as a more practicable and lenient standard.

[82] Dworkin *Sovereign Virtue* at 300.

opportunity for welfare,[83] or equal *access* to advantage,[84] etc—ideals which largely depart from EoW *tout court*. One other, obvious, reason why EoW *tout court* is an unacceptable ideal for any luck-egalitarian, is that much of the Inequality among persons issues from (or is traceable to) individual choices:[85] Insofar as it is, EoW would stand in direct contradiction with the main reason for adopting luck egalitarianism in the first place, which is to respect individual choices and hold people accountable for them.

On the other hand, however, EoR does not mean equality of *resources* in the standard or conventional sense of the word. For, once we include personal assets (such as talents, skills etc) into a category of resources to be equalized, we commit ourselves to some very significant implications which can be detected by comparing these 'resources' with more conventionally understood resources. Two differences are of particular relevance.

First, personal assets are not subject to redistribution or equalization in the same way as external resources are. We cannot shift and transfer among people human intelligence, beauty, or energy. What we can do is compensate with other resources the relative deficit of some of these, compared with a social norm, say, with an average. But because these assets are incommensurable with external resources, any such compensatory move risks a high degree of indeterminacy. Alternatively, we can downplay the significance of any of these features for social distribution of other goods and opportunities. This, however, carries a risk of creating perverse counter-incentives against the cultivation and display of some of the characteristics which are socially beneficial.

The second feature is that personal assets are not really resources per se: they are only good within a particular specific context. There is nothing particularly bad about someone being less intelligent than the average unless he attempts to obtain a job where intelligence is required: otherwise he may be a perfectly contented person. There is nothing particularly bad about a person not fitting the conventional standards of physical beauty unless it becomes a hindrance in her professional or personal life: an ugly university professor may never think of this feature as being a disadvantage, and objectively speaking, it may not be a hindrance at all. In this way, personal assets are different from material resources, such as money, which is an all-purpose good. Well, nearly: money cannot buy you happiness, as the saying goes, but it can nevertheless do a great number of good things for you, in a broad range of contexts.

This second characteristic of personal assets suggests that they cannot be simply factored into a larger aggregate set of 'resources' in a way which would enable us to compare the sets of resources belonging to particular persons throughout society: personal assets (or, rather, their deficits) will count only if they actually

83 See Arneson 'Equality'.
84 See Cohen 'Currency'.
85 See Arneson 'Equality' at 83–4.

are an obstacle in a person's life. Unless they do, they have no chance of being registered on our radars for the purpose of social equality. (Perhaps the cases of obvious physical disabilities are an exception to this proposition.) They will register only if we know what the person's aims are, and how a putative deficit of assets (intelligence, beauty, strength) may be a hindrance in the accomplishment of these aims, so that it requires social compensation (because, under the first characteristic, we cannot simply 'add' this asset to a disadvantaged person). Disadvantage regarding personal assets will always be aims-relative.

But note that once we have adopted this position, the distance between EoR and EoW has narrowed quite significantly. This is because some aspects of welfare have been incorporated into 'resources' as a result of the extension of the category of resources to include personal assets, such as talents, skills, and capacities. These aspects of welfare which I have in mind are precisely about the relevance of a given 'raw' asset (intelligence, strength etc) to the aims a person has in her life. While we have brought into the picture the perspective of aims, and how we are equipped to achieve these aims, this scrutiny operates similarly to the scrutiny applied to the question of determining how a person is *capable* of achieving satisfaction in her life, which is a typically welfarist perspective. To be sure, it is not about how equally people actually do achieve satisfaction, which would be an unadulterated EoW ideal. The ideal is absurd because a great number of factors which stand between us and the achievement of our aims may have to do with factors which cannot or should not be socially equalized.[86] We do not want to, or cannot, make people equally cheerful, positive in their outlooks, successful in finding great life partners etc—and all these, and many other, factors affect people's level of well-being or satisfaction in life. But then, as already said, no one seriously postulates an unadulterated ideal of EoW.

This is not to deny that EoR (with the element of welfare included within it, as described above) and EoW (with the revisions emphasizing the *opportunity* for welfare, or access to advantage etc) are different ideals. Even with the necessary qualifications just suggested, there still remain significant differences between the consequences of adopting the ideal as described by Dworkin, on the one hand, and Arneson on the other, to give just two examples of protagonists in the debates within luck egalitarianism. The identification of talents as resources will lead to consequences which are unfair to the more talented, claims Arneson,[87] while Dworkin rebuts this charge.[88] I will not go into this, and other,

[86] For an eloquent depiction of the consequences of such an ideal, see Dworkin *Sovereign Virtue* at 302: 'Of course, it is good when people are happy, think well of themselves, and are thought well of by others. The idea that people should be *equal* in their capacities to achieve these desirable states of affairs, however, is barely coherent and certainly bizarre—why would that be *good*?—and the idea that government should take steps to bring about that equality—can you imagine what steps those would be?—is frightening'.

[87] Arneson 'Equality' at 89.

[88] To be more precise, Dworkin recognizes that under EoR the more talented have no claims to the benefits of their superior talents, but does not find it unfair; under his 'envy test' (which

controversies within the luck-egalitarian school of thought. All that I want to emphasize is that the gap between the opposing ideals of EoR and EoW is narrower than the proponents of these ideals sometimes lead us to believe.[89]

6. How Egalitarian is Luck Egalitarianism?

Now is the time to face the most fundamental issue about luck egalitarianism: isn't it really an oxymoron? Is luck equalization an *egalitarian* theory? According to some critics, there is nothing inherently, or even contingently, egalitarian about the pursuit of the aim of neutralizing the impact of luck, chance, and other factors under human control, upon our social positions.

As always, it is important to be careful about the status of the question. Much of the criticism of luck egalitarianism is launched from the position of what may be called a collective notion of equality: luck egalitarianism is accused of being not really egalitarian, because it focuses on individualized equality and disregards the phenomena which should truly be a matter of concern for egalitarians, eg hegemony, domination, exploitation.[90] As I have suggested in the previous chapter, the charge is unfair, and the distinction between individualized and collective notions of equality overdrawn, but that charge is quite different from the point which I am concerned with now. That other charge was not accusing luck egalitarianism of being inegalitarian under its own criteria of equality but rather that it operates through a wrong matrix of equality: that it is looking at the wrong places so as to locate social equality. The point which I am going to discuss now is different: it is rather whether luck egalitarianism is egalitarian in *any* plausible sense, ie can the pursuit of the aim of neutralizing luck be seen as leading to more equality (including in the individualized sense of the word) in society? This is seen as self-evident by luck egalitarians: luck neutralization and the achievement of more equality are seen as co-extensive. In fact, this co-extensiveness is the constitutive feature of luck egalitarianism.

Perhaps the most devastating critique of luck egalitarianism is that there is no reason to believe that if we indeed succeed in eliminating the impact of chance (or of 'morally arbitrary' factors) then we will end up with a more egalitarian distribution than before: eliminating luck may bring all sorts of distributions, and if luck egalitarians do not object to luck-affected *equality* (and why should they? they are egalitarians, after all!) then in fact they are not concerned about the impact of luck but about inequality as such; luck would play no independent role

proclaims that equality is accomplished when no one envies another's set of total resources) neither penalization for talent nor benefits for superior talent are allowed; 'Equality of Resources' at 312.

[89] For an emphasis on the depth of the gap between these ideals, see Dworkin *Sovereign Virtue* at 303.

[90] See, in particular, Anderson 'What Is the Point of Equality?' and Scheffler 'Choice, Circumstance, and the Value of Equality'.

in their argument. Here an argument by Dennis McKerlie is instructive because it is made in the context of a critique of the argument 'intended to derive the importance of equality from . . . the value of preventing morally arbitrary factors from determining the quality of people's lives'.[91] Consider his example: in a particular society with a competitive economy, people's positions are affected by all sorts of morally arbitrary factors (natural abilities, family backgrounds etc), and yet 'coincidentally the factors cancel one another out and the result is distributive equality'. According to McKerlie, people with egalitarian sympathies would not find such an equal distribution objectionable even though, in this special case, the emergence of equality does not mean 'that the influence of morally arbitrary factors has been eliminated'.[92]

McKerlie follows up this train of thought with another example which, as he claims, 'makes the same point'. Suppose that there is only one person in the world, and his good position in the world has been secured by the use of predominantly native assets. Would we find such a situation morally troubling? Surely not, responds McKerlie. 'The example involves one life being influenced by morally arbitrary factors, but we do not object because it does not involve inequality between different people'.[93] From this, McKerlie concludes that we do not object to the influence of morally arbitrary facts on our life per se but only to the fact that such factors are responsible for inequalities among people; in effect, it is inequality (of a certain kind) per se which is objectionable, and not the fact that it was caused by morally arbitrary factors.

This is a *non sequitur*. The argument can be seen as proceeding in the following way. (1) We do not object to the fact that a single life has been affected (positively) by luck (as the second example, of a single person in the world, shows). (2) We object when some forms of inequality are created by the impact of morally arbitrary factors. (3) It is not the impact of luck, but the fact of a certain inequality which is the cause of our concern; hence, luck (or morally arbitrary factors, more generally) plays no independent role in our condemnation of the state of affairs. The premise (1) is persuasive: few of us resent that someone's position in life, viewed independently of the position of other persons, and especially when it is a good position, has been affected by luck and other choice-independent factors. Some luck egalitarians admit so much explicitly,[94] but even those who do not would probably be surprised if such a bizarre view were to be attributed to them. But (1) cannot be added to (2) in order to produce (3) because (2) is about a totally different moral case: it is about the comparative positions of different people, in a context of the inevitable scarcity of resources, where the distribution of at least some resources (which are part of a set of total resources which people have) is a

[91] Denis McKerlie 'Equality' at 279.
[92] ibid at 279.
[93] ibid at 280.
[94] See eg Arneson 'Equality' at 80.

zero-sum game. So the complaint about (2) is not a mere aggregate of individual complaints of the type (1) in a real society where there is a plurality of individuals; it is an altogether different moral concern. When faced with the distribution of scarce resources among people, we look for the kind of factors which affect individual shares, and the fact that someone's *comparative* share has been affected by morally fortuitous circumstances, combined with the fact that it is lower than that of others is an independent ground for moral concern. It may be challenged on its merits but it cannot be shown to play no independent role in the equality argument.

But this does not fully respond to another aspect of McKerlie's argument, as reflected in his first example, namely that if luck may happen to lead to *equality* (rather than to inequality) and if luck egalitarians would not object to that outcome (and why should they?) then they are not really serious about luck equalization but about equality per se. This leads us to a different objection to luck egalitarianism than the one just considered; now it is not about whether luck elimination plays any independent role in luck egalitarianism but rather about whether luck elimination will indeed lead to more equality? If McKerlie's first example is plausible, and therefore if we can visualize luck-affected equalities as plausibly as luck-affected inequalities, then indeed perhaps luck egalitarianism is an oxymoron? Interestingly, some luck egalitarians entertain such a hypothesis. Richard Arneson, in a recent article speculated: 'it could happen by sheer chance that the operation of... a market economy over time yields outcomes that satisfy whatever egalitarian or other principles of distributive justice are deemed morally required'. From this he draws a conclusion: 'when the operation of a market economy yields outcomes that fail to satisfy those justice norms, what is wrong is not that chance factors are bringing about the outcome. What is wrong is that justice norms are not satisfied'.[95] So what is left of *luck* egalitarianism after such an admission?

There are two ways in which we can understand a claim which is, rightly or falsely (this will come as an upshot of this argument) attributed to luck egalitarians, about the connection between neutralizing luck and bringing about more social equality: a strong (necessary) and a weak (contingent) interpretation. The strong interpretation of the claim is that, whenever the impact of luck upon people's positions is neutralized, the resulting situation will necessarily and inevitably be more equal than before such a neutralizing action.[96] This strong claim seems almost certainly wrong because unprovable. McKerlie's and Arneson's examples just quoted are irrefutable: if it were the case that chance factors happened to produce an *equal* distribution of whatever goods we consider, then an action to eliminate the impact of chance would inevitably lead to less equality, not more.

[95] ibid at 80.

[96] Has any 'luck egalitarian' ever sincerely endorsed such a position? For an exegesis of some leading luck egalitarians, and a conclusion that they have not, see Kasper Lippert-Rasmussen 'Hurley on Egalitarianism and the Luck-Neutralizing Aim' *Politics, Philosophy & Economics* (2005) 4: 249–65 at 255.

Consider this somewhat grotesque example: you and I are greatly unequal in our material goods in a way which (*arguendo*) largely corresponds to our unequal efforts, choices, and responsibility, so at a time t-1 the distribution is sensitive to choices but largely insensitive to endowments. Then comes a flood or another natural disaster which effectively makes us equal: your palatial house and my modest hut have both been destroyed: we are now, at t-2, equal because of bad luck. Any attempt to neutralize the impact of luck, at t-3, would have the form of bringing more inequality between us.

Now observe something peculiar about this example. The description of 'inequality' at t-1 and t-3, and of equality at t-2, corresponds to our conventional, pre-theoretical understandings of (in)equality. However, under Dworkin's EoR conception we would have to say that, under some additional assumptions, our respective positions were equal at t-1. For *if* all the causes of our unequal positions at t-1 were solely traceable to our choices, effort, and will, and if the impact of our native abilities upon our position (including indirectly, via their impact on our industriousness, effort etc) had already been properly neutralized (and this assumption is necessary to make the example work), then we were at t-1 equal in our resources. The aggregate sets of our personal and impersonal resources at t-1 were, ex hypothesi, equal; it is just that the material segments of our total resource sets were vastly unequal but this (again, ex hypothesi) was because of our choices. The bad luck in the form of a natural disaster at t-2 has upset this initial correspondence between our choices and our outcomes (hence, it has upset the choice-sensitivity of the distribution) and, assuming that nothing new happened about our relative wills, a reintroduction of the prior choice-sensitivity of distribution would re-establish equality rather than inequality.

But I do not wish to protest too much. I am unable to provide evidence for the argument that luck neutralization will necessarily and always bring about more equality. It may happen that in some, highly artificial, examples it could be shown that the elimination of the impact of luck may do nothing to reduce inequality, or even bring about more inequality. While I confess that I cannot think of such examples in real life, I cannot refute the proposition *in abstracto*. Rather, I prefer to focus on a weak interpretation of the luck neutralization/equality connection. Under this interpretation, it is a very plausible although a contingent proposition that, in the world as we know it, systematic neutralization of the impact of luck will, more often than not, lead to more equal outcomes than before, or than in the absence of, such a luck-neutralizing campaign.

What are the 'contingencies' upon which the contingent judgment about 'luck neutralization/equality' rests? Most importantly, it presupposes as correct the view that much of the inequality in the social life of societies which we know today can be traced directly or indirectly to factors which are morally arbitrary: factors for which people cannot be held responsible and which present themselves to people as bad luck, in the case of those in inferior social positions. This is a partly empirical and partly conceptual question. The conceptual part of it is about which factors we characterize as morally arbitrary in the requisite sense: in the sense that their occurrence in a person, and the degree to which they occur in particular individuals, is a matter of brute chance. (The fact that it is a conceptual aspect does not mean that it is a purely analytical question, independent of our perception of psychological and social reality. But in the end, the proof that certain categories of factors, taken *in abstracto*, are outside our control, is impossible and so here we inevitably appeal to moral judgments about what it is proper to hold people responsible for; the judgments not reducible to judgments of equality because then the whole construction would be circular.) The broader the range of such factors, the more egalitarian the potential of luck neutralization will be. The empirical part of it is about the actual social diagnosis as to what extent observable inequalities are indeed caused by such morally arbitrary factors. While it is an empirical question, the view that a great number of inequalities in our society are due to factors outside our control seems so massively confirmed that the egalitarian potential of luck neutralization seems self-evident, even though contingent in the way described above.

But this is not the end of the contingencies involved. What about the actual *equalities* that have been produced by luck? After all, as Susan Hurley points out, '[e]qualities can be just as much a matter of luck as inequalities'.[97] Once we eliminate these equalities, shall we not in the process cancel out all the removals of *inequalities* under the luck neutralization principle, and perhaps in the balance bring even more inequality than before? It sounds like a plausible proposition: if we accept a luck-neutralizing principle that (1) all inequalities that are a matter of luck should be eliminated, then we must also be committed to the principle that (2) all equalities that are a matter of luck should be eliminated; otherwise luck neutralization does not play any role in the argument. Here we must be careful about what count as inequalities or equalities for the purposes of these propositions. As with the earlier example natural disaster bringing about an (alleged) equality, it is easy to commit a conceptual failure and read equality only on the basis of one part of the total set of resources (if we adopt Dworkin's version of luck egalitarianism). Such a *pars pro toto* mistake is easily committed because, in our conventional observations, we consider only the easily observable aspects of total resources (such as wealth) and naturally disregard those which relate to personal assets, such as personal abilities and skills, and even less observably, these aspects of abilities and skills which are directly traceable to native endowments. But if we did the right calculation of resources, under Dworkin's matrix, the category falling under (2) (ie resources which people have equally, but which result from luck) would be extremely thin. For remember that the resources we have in mind in this category are only those which are 'productive' (in the sense that they are useful in the pursuit of human aims), and it is hard to think of a sizeable category of resources which are at the same time equally distributed and a result of chance.

[97] Hurley *Justice, Luck, and Knowledge* at 151–2.

In any event, under a contingent (weak) interpretation of the luck neutralization/equality connection, we would need strongly to believe that the category of luck-affected *inequalities* (1) is much more sizeable than the category of luck-affected equalities (2), so that luck neutralizations under (1) and (2) will not cancel each other out. Even under a conventional understanding of equality (that is, not as in Dworkin, where the relevant resources which count in the equality calculus, include both personal and impersonal assets), hence, under an understanding where only impersonal assets are relevant to define a person's relative position in society, it is probably quite obvious that equalizing effects under (1) will greatly outweigh any possible inegalitarian effects under (2). However, I do not propose to even begin providing the evidence for such a prediction. All I wanted to do is to suggest the way in which such a proof would have to be conducted (the sort of evidence which would have to be considered) in order to render 'luck egalitarianism' an internally coherent term.

Conclusions

This chapter explored the intellectual resources of the seemingly most attractive—from the point of view of this author—conception of social equality, namely of 'luck egalitarianism': an idea that equality is attained when a person's position depends on her choices and the exercise of free will rather than on bad luck in finding herself with fewer assets than others enjoy, although through no fault of her own. The moral attractiveness of this idea can be traced back to a powerful insight articulated, among other philosophers, by John Rawls. It argues that a good society should minimize the impact of 'morally arbitrary' factors upon a person's position; an insight so convincing that it borders, under some understandings, upon tautology, since the 'moral arbitrariness' is identified with that which should not affect our stations in life. But there is, of course, a non-tautological interpretation of this insight available to us which places a premium on those factors which can be associated with our exercise of free will.

In this way, 'luck egalitarianism' is an attempt to build individual responsibility into the conception of social equality. But can 'bad luck' be seen as a simple inverse of the exercise of 'responsibility', so that the operation of bad luck excludes personal responsibility? Much depends on the interpretation of both these terms. 'Responsibility', I argued, can be understood in an 'input' or an 'output' sense: 'input responsibility' is centrally linked to choice, control, and free will, while 'output responsibility' is not; rather, it is about drawing the lines between the domains of individual responsibility based on various moral grounds, including, but not being limited to, the effects of individual choices and decisions. In turn, 'luck' can be understood as 'brute' or 'option' luck, and it is only the former which figures in 'luck egalitarianism' as a cause for equalization, although the 'bad option' luck can give rise to moral duties of compensation under some plausible paternalistic principles. In conclusion, it is 'input responsibility' and 'brute bad luck' which are direct opposites, from a luck-egalitarian perspective.

The attractiveness of luck egalitarianism should be tested against some of our strongly held moral convictions, two of which seem to contradict the hold that luck egalitarianism may have on our intuitive morality: that not all 'undeserved' inequalities (ie not traceable to our free choice) are bad and should be eradicated, and that some 'deserved' inequalities (for instance, traceable to 'option luck') should be eliminated. These two moral objections to luck egalitarianism are independent of each other, and do not prove to be devastating. The first appeals mainly to those inequalities which belong to the domains normally outside the operation of *social* equality: there are many inequalities which do not strike us as wrong because they are in the domain where no duty of redistribution, egalitarian or otherwise, is appropriate (for instance, in private lives). The second objection, that accepting choice-related inequalities may sometimes be unduly harsh and reveals an unforgiving attitude, can be best handled by additional principles, which should—under a comprehensive ideal of justice—modify and supplement luck egalitarianism, including paternalistic principles of rescuing people from the particularly dramatic consequences of their own choices. While these extra principles do not appeal to the logic of luck egalitarianism, they are not incompatible with that ideal.

A central issue in the discourse of luck egalitarianism is raised by the question about the status of individual preferences or tastes. Where do they belong in the divide between those factors which are 'unchosen' (which come as bad brute luck) and those which are traceable to our choices? At first blush, they seem to belong, largely, to the latter category, but the matter reveals its complexity when we translate the unchosen/chosen factors into another dichotomy, that between impersonal circumstances and personal assets. This 'translation' is imperfect for there may be factors which are at the same time 'personal' and 'unchosen', and individual preferences which seem to belong precisely to that category: this may be embarrassing to someone who claims (as Dworkin does) that a plausible conception of equality should make a distribution insensitive towards 'circumstances' but sensitive to individual factors, such as choices. A long debate about the status of 'expensive tastes', the satisfaction of which is costly and yet—intuitively—the existence of which should not warrant special societal compensation, responds to that problem. In my view, the solution lies in a certain ambiguity or vagueness in finding that personal 'preferences' or 'tastes' are unchosen. While in a certain sense (in the sense of the formation of these preferences) this may often be true, it is not necessarily true in a thinner notion of what is 'chosen'. This thinner test, which is all we need to place safely the preferences in the category of factors which are under our control, refers to whether we can, in the process of exercises of our free choice, get rid of them when we ascertain that their satisfaction imposes prohibitive costs on ourselves or on society. This test should be connected with a counterfactual test: would we consider ourselves worse off, as human beings, if we did not have those preferences in the first place. An affirmative answer to this question suggests that there are *assets* which, therefore, do not warrant a social duty of compensation. A negative answer (that is, that we would rather not have these preferences at all) implies that they are more like handicaps or afflictions, and therefore should figure in the overall calculus on the side of compensable bad brute luck.

Following Ronald Dworkin, the discussion of luck egalitarianism is often located within the framework of two models of equality: equality of welfare and equality of resources. The above discussion of luck egalitarianism suggests, however, that the gap between these two models is in fact narrower than the arguments often assume. Hence it can be said that neither is equality of welfare understood in an unqualified way (no one could seriously postulate equalizing welfare *simpliciter* for the implications would be obviously absurd, hence, the plausible models are of equality of opportunities for, or access to, welfare), nor is equality of resources understood with the conventional 'resources' in mind. In order to qualify as a model exhibiting luck egalitarianism, equality of resources must construe resources holistically, both as impersonal (external) and personal resources, such as talents. And yet talents can be properly seen as assets only if we consider them in connection with specific aims people have in life: they are resources only insofar as they are instrumental to particular life-plans. Once we recognize them as such, and providing that they must be included in the broader category of resources the equality of which we want to maximize, the divide between the model of equality of welfare and that of resources is less dramatic than often thought because these resources play a similar moral role as the opportunities for welfare in the more welfarist models of equality.

But how egalitarian is luck egalitarianism? The question admittedly sounds odd, so it is important to understand it not by reference to the standards of equality internal to luck egalitarianism (that only those inequalities are scandalous which cannot be traced to our choices), in which case the answer would be uninteresting because tautological, but rather by reference to intuitive and pre-theoretical ideals by which we judge equality and inequality in social reality. Would the implementation of luck egalitarianism make a difference in the real world, by making it more egalitarian in these simple, pre-theoretical terms? Critics of luck egalitarianism ask a good question: if luck neutralization is the operational ideal, then why should we expect that equality will be the result? After all, they say, it may well be that some real equalities result from the operation of luck, then we will need (under luck neutralization ideal) to eliminate them too, so the egalitarian effects of eliminating luck-related inequalities may be cancelled out by the inegalitarian effects of eliminating luck-related equalities. In response, I claimed by the end of this chapter, that such a calculus is very deeply improbable, and that, while the egalitarian effect of luck neutralization is only contingent rather than inherent, it is also probable that there is no reason to deny the luck neutralization ideal the dignity of being a genuinely egalitarian one.

which, therefore, do not warrant a social duty of compensation. A negative answer (that is, if we would rather not have these preferences at all) implies that they are more like handicaps or afflictions, and therefore should figure in the overall calculus on the side of compensable *brute luck*.

Following Ronald Dworkin, the discussion of luck egalitarianism is often located within the framework of two models of equality: equality of welfare and equality of resources. The above discussion of luck egalitarianism suggests, however, that the gap between these two models is in fact narrower than the [illegible]

6
Conclusion

This book has had two aspirations: one was less and the other more ambitious. A (perhaps) less ambitious set of objectives was to elucidate and clarify the plausible and morally attractive conceptions of equality in three domains: political, legal, and social. I hope that I have been able to provide some reasons for accepting certain conceptions which are controversial enough to be interesting and sufficiently well supported by the arguments to be prima facie plausible: not compelling, of course, but not outright nonsensical either. In doing so, I relied upon certain accounts in contemporary legal, political, and social philosophy, and rejected others. My aspiration was less to show the originality of my undertaking and more to find a degree of fit with some widespread convictions, never consensual, to be sure, but certainly prominent in a democratic culture.

On *political* equality, I argued in Chapter 2 that its moral contours can be best gauged by inquiring into the rationales for, and also objections against, the principle of majority rule which constitutes an irreducible core of the democratic process. The fact that occasionally the democratic process may result in outcomes which strike us as violating conceptions of substantive equality does not automatically undermine its egalitarian credentials. A democratic (majoritarian) process relies upon some strong substantive egalitarian values which can be described as equality of political opportunity, and which support a number of our strongly held and widely spread political intuitions, for instance about the relative insensitivity of democratic elections to the varying intensity of individual political preferences, or about the inadmissibility of vote trading etc. Strong, substantive moral premises which are revealed by these, and other, moral intuitions, privilege a democratic political system in contrast to its political competitors. They also help explain why the occasional recourse to unanimity or a qualified majority rule should be seen as exceptions to a norm, or even an aberration. Equality of political opportunity also informs a number of principles regarding political deliberation, at pre-decision stages of the process. So the overall idea behind Chapter 2 is that we adopt a democratic rule for reasons that are profoundly egalitarian. And this substantive equality behind the process affords a detachment of the procedural concerns from those about outcomes; if only because the recognition of which outcomes are substantively equal will encounter much more disagreement, in a pluralistic society, than a conclusion based on standards of equality within the process.

On *legal* equality, I argued in Chapter 3 that we need a test for non-discrimination which takes note of the purpose of a given classification, and—most crucially—of the relationship between the classification and the purpose. This means that some popular candidates for a working (or relatively neutral) test of non-discrimination such as the hostility to any legal classification whatsoever, or a 'per se' standard (under which the classification is tainted as discriminatory by the very use of certain, prohibited, criteria of classification) must be rejected. But the test of relevance is not self-evident, either, and we need to make a crucial choice about what level of scrutiny has to be applied, that is, how tight a fit between the classification and the purpose we should demand. The tighter the fit required, the more likely it is that we will deem a classification to be discriminatory. So we need some good reason for the suspicion, triggering a close match between the classification and its (permissible) purposes, and these good reasons should be provided by a reflection, in a 'reflective equilibrium' mode, about the moral and political evils which are displayed by those classifications which, as our strongly held convictions suggest to us, are discriminatory (that is, which are not just a legislative error in means-ends calculus, but are morally iniquitous). I have argued that there are, at least, three such evils: that legislatively imposed burdens fall upon a group which has had a disproportionately low say in the adoption of the legislation, that they are imposed upon a group already disadvantaged in many ways, and that they improperly stigmatize a burdened group as morally or intellectually inferior. The presence of these indicia in a legal act under scrutiny may justify our suspicion that a classification is triggered by wrong motives, such as dislike, ignorance, hatred, stereotyping etc. This cannot be seen as a conclusive proof of discrimination (people will always disagree about what motives can be reasonably attributed to legislators) but at least we may be justified in subjecting the legislation to a more rigorous than usual test of scrutinizing the relationship between the classification and the avowed purpose of the law.

Finally, when it comes to *social* equality, discussed in Chapters 4 and 5, here I have defended an 'individualized' (or distributional) approach to social equality, against the charge that viewing social equality in an 'individualized' perspective (who is getting what and why, compared with others) somehow trivializes the 'point of equality' as recognized by those who are concerned with removing the structures of domination and oppression. I followed the well-known Rawlsian insight that equality demands the removal of those inequalities which result from morally arbitrary factors, and I defended the position that, in the category of the 'morally arbitrary', the natural and social categories have equal status, notwithstanding the protests by some libertarians and communitarians alike. Having thus cleared the conceptual field, I introduced and defended my preferred conception of social equality, known as 'luck egalitarianism', namely that those inequalities which result from the exercise of a person's choices should be maintained, while those which can be traced to the circumstances outside a person's control—to a person's bad brute luck—should be eradicated. The attractiveness of this conception, I believe, is largely due to the fact that it tries to take seriously a person's responsibility for her choices while retaining an overall egalitarian impact of the ideal. It is immune, in my view, to the popular twin objections that some inequalities traceable to individual choices should nevertheless be eradicated, and that some inequalities traceable to circumstances outside our control are acceptable. The former argument is rebutted by an appeal to non-objectionable forms of paternalism which are at least not inconsistent with luck egalitarianism; the latter—by pointing out that those non-objectionable inequalities traceable to circumstances outside our control normally belong to the domain where social equality should not reign in the first place. The problematic and controversial status of individual preferences—where do they belong in the divide between circumstances and choices—can, I believe, be addressed by arguing realistically that, while not 'chosen' in a pedantic sense of the word, their continued existence is under a person's control. Additionally, if one does not consider them as afflictions or handicaps which make our life more difficult, the intuitive conviction that expensive tastes should not give rise to claims of compensation under social equality can well be squared with the divide between persons and circumstances (or between choices and morally arbitrary factors) that the theory erects. However, the theory, as I understand it, fits uneasily the conventional distinction between 'equality of welfare' and 'equality of resources', largely because the distinction is never as stark as often suggested: equality of welfare *simpliciter* (rather than equality of opportunity of welfare) is too absurd an ideal to be seriously postulated by anyone, and 'equality of resources' uses the term 'resources' in a non-conventional sense, which also includes personal assets, but only those which are directly instrumental towards achievement of our specific aims and life-plans. With these modifications, the distinction is less pronounced, and perhaps less useful, than often thought. In the end, what really matters to preserve the moral attractiveness of the theory of luck egalitarianism is whether it is egalitarian in a simple, pre-theoretical way, that is to say, by comparison with the actual inequalities in today's societies as we know them. Would an implementation of the ideal bring about more equality than we see in our social world? While admittedly the operative principle is that of luck neutralization (that is, of eradication of the consequences of bad brute luck), the occasional inegalitarian impact of the eradication of *equality*-producing luck would no doubt be more than offset by the egalitarian effect of eradicating *inequality*-producing luck. There is nothing analytically obvious about this proposition but it is an eminently plausible (although a contingent) prediction.

So much for a rough summary of my main conclusions about the three domains of equality studied in this book. Are these three domains as self-contained and separate from each other as this summary may suggest? The boundaries between the three domains of equality are, of course, to some degree, arbitrary and conventional, but not fully so. In Chapter 2 I claimed that the boundary between *political* and *social* equality is significant and worth preserving. Equality of opportunity in the political process of collective decision-making is an important value in itself (which people may plausibly appreciate for its own sake) and should not be seen as entirely parasitic on equality in the distribution of other (other, that is, than political influence) social goods. This corresponds to some persuasive moral intuitions, for instance: we value equal participation in a political process (or equal political opportunity) not only as an instrument of protecting equally our interests or values in the outcomes of political decisions, we also value it because it is, per se, an important facet of equal citizenship. This is not to deny the importance of an instrumental function of equal political opportunity, but this instrumental link does not exhaust the value of equal political opportunity. So, to the degree that equal political opportunity does not collapse into the equality of outcomes of collective decisions, political equality has a value which is independent of social equality, and the boundary between the political and the social in our thinking about equality is worth preserving.

In turn, the boundary between *legal* and *political* equality exists to the extent to which political equality is discerned in the democratic *process* (although it is justified by referring to values which are *not* themselves procedural), while legal equality is perceived through the indicia which are only partly procedural (the indicium of political under-representation in the law-making process) and partly outcome-oriented (the indicia of freezing the pattern of disadvantage and of stigma). The existence of these outcome-related indicia of discrimination implies that legal equality does not fully collapse into political equality. We presume that the stigmatizing effect of a legal classification may be prima facie evidence of its discriminatory character (something, at least, that warrants a high suspicion in subjecting this classification to a proper scrutiny of relevance to a justified legislative purpose), although we know very well that a majoritarian political process often results in decisions and laws insensitive towards traditionally disfavoured groups.

Finally, the boundary between *legal* and *social* equality is even more porous: the indicium of freezing the pattern of disadvantage builds upon a conception of social disadvantages which must be informed by a theory of social justice that also, eventually, determines the chosen conception of social equality. The same may be said about the indicium of 'stigma': not every 'stigma' counts as an improper judgment even if it inflicts a burden on a stigmatized group. To 'stigmatize' paedophiles or tax evaders does not strike us as problematic enough to warrant a special suspicion of discrimination involved in anti-paedophile or anti-tax-evader laws; not unless the sanctions are disproportionate to the misdeeds. Perhaps we would need a different word to describe an unjustified or unwarranted stigma, but the problem is not that easily solved by a semantic invention. What matters is that the indicium of stigma in our scheme must follow an antecedent, substantive theory of justice which will allow us to distinguish between unjustified and justified cases of negative social judgments addressed against a particular category. And in this sense, the wall of separation between legal and social equality crumbles.

As I said at the outset of this concluding chapter, this book has two aspirations. Up to now in this concluding chapter I have sketched out how I attempted to discharge the 'less ambitious' task: that of describing attractive substantive conceptions of political, legal, and social equality. My more ambitious project was to tie up these analyses with that of legitimacy, and to see how equality in these domains supports the legitimacy of the state and its law towards citizens. The motto for this aspiration, which informed my project, was—allow me to restate it—the proposition announced by Ronald Dworkin: 'A legitimate government must treat all those over whom it claims dominion not just with a measure of concern but with *equal* concern'.[1] Where do I stand, in concluding this book, in respect of exploring this connection?

Not surprisingly, this aspiration resulted in a less satisfactory realization. The overall conclusion of Chapters 1 and 2, combined, is that substantive values which give moral sense to the democratic process are thoroughly egalitarian, and that it is these values which endow democracy with legitimacy. But this conclusion should not disappoint those who lament the weaknesses of a 'merely procedural' democracy. For one thing, there is nothing 'mere' in democratic procedures: they are founded on substantively (and controversially) powerful values. Moreover, I argued for a concept of legitimacy which does not necessarily lead to an unconditional duty of obedience to a legitimate law. This may be seen by some as a semantic gambit, but there is more to it: I argued that it is impossible to combine the justification, legitimacy, and the duty of obedience in one argument. My preference is for a thinner concept of legitimacy: one in which justification endows the law with legitimacy, with the claims supporting the duty to obey requiring separate argument. So to say that a law is legitimate, in the sense of justification, does not necessarily lead to a prescription that it must be obeyed by everyone, and our moral intuitions about the need to preserve a scope for civil disobedience by those greatly upset by a legitimately enacted law support rather than detract from this conclusion. And if we want to preserve the possibility of reconciling the statement that the law is legitimate and that it can be, on occasions, disobeyed on moral grounds, we have one more reason to adopt a concept of legitimacy which does not incorporate substantive moral criteria of the outcome into the criteria of legitimacy of law.

The upshot of Chapter 2 is, again, that a 'merely procedural' democracy endows the outcomes with legitimacy precisely because democratic procedures are supported by substantive, egalitarian, legitimacy-conferring values. This is the legitimating work done by *political* equality. But what about the tests for non-discrimination

[1] Ronald Dworkin *Is Democracy Possible Here?* (Princeton: Princeton University Press, 2006) 97 (emphasis in original).

developed in Chapter 3: is a law which fails under a heightened scrutiny of means-ends relationship *eo ipso* illegitimate? It depends. It may well be that such law has been enacted in a way which is inconsistent with democratic procedures, and in that case it clearly fails to meet the legitimacy threshold. But over and above this threshold the judgments of illegitimacy become more and more controversial, in so far as they rely increasingly on our judgments of justice and are less capable of being a part of a working theory of discrimination—a 'working theory' in the sense that people who are on the opposite sides of a substantive moral disagreement may still agree about what is discriminatory or not. The upshot of Chapter 3 is that such a working theory *is* available to us—to a degree; namely, to the degree to which the 'indicia' coined in Chapter 3 can be identified in a value-neutral way. But even within *this* range, a challenge to a discriminatory law on the basis of its illegitimacy, provided that all procedural rules of the process have been respected, is problematic. This is because the equality inherent in the process of majority rule endows the outcome with the modicum of legitimacy which requires a duty, on the part of citizens, to grant it at least some minimal respect, even if they disagree with the substance of the law (including when this disagreement is articulated in terms of substantive discrimination).

The seemingly negative impact of this conclusion upon the moral intuition, encapsulated in the citation from Dworkin at the outset of the Introduction and repeated a moment ago in this concluding chapter ('A legitimate government must treat all those over whom it claims dominion not just with a measure of concern but with *equal* concern'), may be mitigated by two sets of considerations. First, one important conclusion from Chapter 1 is that the legitimacy of the law, at least within the understanding of legitimacy proposed here, does not imply our duty to unconditionally obey it. So by calling for a basic respect for the law produced through a democratic process, we are not precluding a justified civil disobedience against a law which is offensive in its content. Secondly, legitimacy as understood here is not an all-or-nothing affair but a matter of degree.[2] A democratic pedigree confers a fundamental legitimacy, at a threshold level, upon the law, but above this level, the finding of substantive equality in the law, under the standards of non-discrimination proposed in Chapter 3, adds greatly to its degree of legitimacy.

What about *social* equality? Again, just as in the case of legal equality understood in a substantive, thick sense, proposed in Chapter 3, social equality, whose standards are discussed in Chapters 4 and 5, has only an indirect connection with legitimacy, at its threshold level. A system departing from luck egalitarianism is not *eo ipso* illegitimate: indeed, no political system we know in the world would be legitimate under such a standard. But neither is the standard of luck egalitarianism irrelevant to the legitimacy of the political system altogether. It may be used (and should be used, in the case of those convinced by luck egalitarianism

[2] See similarly, Dworkin *Is Democracy Possible Here?* at 97.

standards) to describe the aspirations of reaching for *more* legitimacy, beyond the threshold point.

The varying degrees to which the three dimensions of equality are connected with legitimacy (as its preconditions) can be studied by looking at them from the point of view of how 'controversial' they are, in terms of widespread moral and political intuitions in a pluralistic, democratic society. This is because the test for legitimacy must attempt at being reasonably non-controversial, in the sense of not starkly flying in the face of conventional moral and political thinking. After all, the function of legitimacy is to identify such grounds upon which we may hope to muster people's respect for a law with which they may, sometimes substantively, disagree. Otherwise, the whole discourse of legitimacy would simply collapse into a discourse of justice, and its specificity vis-à-vis substantive justice would be lost. And yet, it is an underlying aspiration of the arguments about legitimacy that they attempt to ascertain the sources of compliance with, or at least respect for, the law which are more universal, more ecumenical, less controversial, than the sources of endorsement of a given law or policy as substantively just.

Viewed in this way, the three dimensions of equality studied in this book display a varying degree of 'controversialness'. Political equality as revealed by majority rule is, I take it, the least controversial of all. This is not to say that it musters an unconditional acceptance in a society—no idea commands universal consensus in a political sphere—but rather that (as I suggested in the opening passages of Chapter 2) we can invoke a great number of practices, both political and non-political, in which we simply assume, in an unreflective way, that the decision of a majority should be seen, in cases of disagreement as to the substance of a decision to be taken, as the decision of a group. Any exceptions to this rule are seen as precisely that: exceptions which require a special and compelling argument, in the absence of which they are seen as an aberration. This is not to say that the special interpretation of 'equality of political opportunity' as coined by the end of Chapter 2, is equally uncontroversial: far from it. In the process of moving from a simple majority rule to the richer interpretation of equality of political opportunity I may have committed mistakes of inference, or added some additional values and ideals which would taint the end result with features which may be objectionable to some. But this is not the case with the basic principle of majority rule, and in this sense, political equality, as revealed through the operation of majority rule, is a platform which may unite people who otherwise endorse widely different and often opposing conceptions of justice. It thus lends itself to being properly viewed as a condition of legitimacy.

To a lesser degree this is the case with a conception of legal equality, as developed in this book. At least one important indicium of discrimination, that the law which imposes special burdens on a particular group, has been brought about in a way which had not given that group a sufficient hearing in the legislative process, strikes a chord which is easily recognizable to many, no matter what their conceptions of justice are. It resonates with some intuitively widespread and compelling principles of natural justice, of allowing stakeholders in the decision to have their say etc. This insight was, for instance, behind a judicial and jurisprudential doctrine popular for a time in American constitutional law and constitutional theory, that when a law adversely affects some 'discrete and insular minorities' then it warrants a special scrutiny of such a law by a judicial body because the belief that the majoritarian process has worked fairly is the least justified in such circumstances.[3] But two other basic indicia of non-discrimination proposed in Chapter 3 build upon some more substantive, and hence more controversial, judgments of justice. What constitutes an objectionable stigma is an outcome rather than a premise of a substantive judgment of justice (as already indicated in this concluding chapter), and similarly, what constitutes an additional burden imposed upon a by-and-large socially burdened group is a judgment which also, to a large extent, relies upon substantive judgments of justice.

Even more so, the standards of luck egalitarianism—our preferred conception of social equality—are controversial and widely contested. I believe they are right—otherwise I would not have defended them here—but I am not sure how they can be described as sufficiently non-controversial or self-evident as to be assigned a role of engines of legitimacy of the law. Perhaps a very general statement such as 'the factors outside our control should not affect the differences among individuals' may muster a large degree of consensus, although I am not so sure since many will insist along the lines of the 'life is not fair'[4] dictum that there is nothing particularly unfair about benefits accruing upon superior native intelligence, innate skills and talents, good luck of being born in a wealthier family or benefiting from inheritance etc. All these differential and yet 'undeserved' rewards seem to enjoy a relatively high degree of understanding and do not incite great objections. But even if the initial stage of the reasoning were consensually approved, at each subsequent stage of the argument leading to a developed luck-egalitarian conception, as explored in Chapter 5, there will be theoretical steps and moral judgments which will strike many people as controversial or question-begging, including about the borderline between the 'natural' and the 'social' factors, the interdependencies of the innate talents and the choice-dependent cultivation of those talents, the degree to which expensive tastes are subject to control and management by a person etc. So, while any exponent of luck egalitarianism—including myself—has good reasons to applaud any moves in social policy which give effect to the precepts of this conception, a depiction of its implementation as a condition of recognizing the legitimacy of the state seems to be wildly unreasonable. Once the threshold of legitimacy is met, the

[3] See *United States v Carolene Products* 304 US 144, 152–3 n 4 (1838); JH Ely *Democracy and Distrust* (Cambridge, Mass: Harvard University Press, 1980) *passim*; Wojciech Sadurski *Moral Pluralism and Legal Neutrality* (Dordrecht: Kluwer, 1990) 133–48.

[4] M Friedman *Free to Choose* (Harmondsworth: Penguin Books, 1980) 168.

luck-egalitarian social policy will add to the quantity of legitimacy of the state (remember, legitimacy is a matter of degree), but this is the only way in which the connection between social equality and legitimacy can be plausibly depicted. This, arguably, is the limited extent to which social equality supports the state's legitimacy, but then legitimacy is only one of a number of values in a constellation of democratic ideals.

Bibliography

Ackerman, Bruce A, *Social Justice in a Liberal State,* (New Haven: Yale University Press, 1980).

—— *We the People: Foundations,* (Cambridge, Mass: Harvard University Press, 1991).

Ake, Christopher, 'Justice and Equality', (1975) 5 *Philosophy & Public Affairs,* 69–90.

Alexy, Robert, *A Theory of Constitutional Rights* (translated by Julian Rivers); (New York: Oxford University Press, 2002).

—— 'Constitutional Rights, Balancing, and Rationality', (2003) 16 *Ratio Juris,* 131–40.

Anderson, Elizabeth, 'What Is the Point of Equality?' (1991) 109 *Ethics* 287–337.

Arneson, Richard J, 'Liberalism, Distributive Subjectivism, and Equal Opportunity for Welfare', (1990) 9 *Philosophy & Public Affairs,* 158–91.

—— 'Equality and Equal Opportunity for Welfare', (1998) 56 *Philosophical Studies,* 77–93.

—— 'Luck and Equality—II', (2001) 75 *Proceedings of the Aristotelian Society,* 73–90.

Ayer, AJ, *The Concept of a Person,* (New York: St. Martin's Press, 1963).

Baer, Judith A, *Equality Under the Constitution,* (Ithaca: Cornell University Press, 1983).

Balkin, JM, 'Agreements with Hell and Other Objects of Our Faith', (1997) 65 *Fordham Law Rev,* 1703–1738.

Beitz, Charles, *Political Equality,* (Princeton: Princeton University Press, 1989).

Berlin, Isaiah, *Four Essays on Liberty,* (Oxford: Oxford University Press, 1969).

Bickel, Alexander, *The Morality of Consent,* (New Haven, Yale University Press, 1975).

Brennan, Geoffrey and Lomasky, Loren E, 'Large Numbers, Small Costs: The Uneasy Foundation of Democratic Rule', in Geoffrey Brennan & Loren E Lomasky, eds, *Politics and Process: New Essays in Democratic Thought,* (Cambridge: Cambridge University Press, 1989), 42–59.

Brest, Paul, *Processes of Constitutional Decision-Making,* (Boston: Little, Brown & Co, 1975).

Brighouse, Harry, 'Egalitarianism and Equal Availability of Political Influence', (1996) 2 *Journal of Political Philosophy,* 118–41.

Buchanan, James M and Tullock, Gordon, *The Calculus of Consent,* (Ann Arbor: University of Michigan Press, 1965).

Buchanan, James M, *The Limits of Liberty,* (Chicago: The University of Chicago Press, 1975).

—— 'Contractarian presuppositions and democratic governance', in Geoffrey Brennan & Loren E Lomasky, eds, *Politics and Process: New Essays in Democratic Thought,* (Cambridge: Cambridge University Press, 1989), 174–82.

Burt, Robert A, *The Constitution in Conflict,* (Cambridge, Mass: Harvard University Press, 1992).

Campbell, Tom, 'Unlawful Discrimination', in Wojciech Sadurski, ed, *Ethical Dimensions of Legal Theroy,* (Amsterdam: Rodopi, 1991), 153–70.

Christiano, Thomas, *The Rule of the Many: Fundamental Issues in Democratic Theory*, (Boulder: Westview Press, 1996).

—— 'The Authority of Democracy', (2004) 12 *Journal of Political Philosophy*, 266–90.

Cohen, GA, 'On the Currency of Egalitarian Justice', (1989) 99 *Ethics* 906–44.

—— 'Incentives, Inequality, and Community', in G Peterson, ed, *The Tanner Lectures on Human Values*, vol. 13, (Salt Lake City: University of Utah Press, 1992), 263–329.

—— *Self-ownership, Freedom, and Equality*, (Cambridge: Cambridge University Press, 1995).

—— 'Where the Action Is: On the Site of Distributive Justice', (1997) 26 *Philosophy & Public Affairs*, 3–30.

Cohen, Joshua, 'Deliberation and Democratic Legitimacy', in David Estlund, ed, *Democracy*, (Oxford: Blackwell, 2002).

Dahl, Robert A, 'Procedural Democracy', in Peter Laslett & James Fishkin, eds, *Philosophy, Politics and Society*, Fifth Series, (Oxford: Basil Blackwell, 1979), 97–133.

Dijk, P van, and van Hoof, GJH, *Theory and Practice of the European Convention on Human Rights*, 3rd ed, (The Hague: Kluwer Law International, 1998).

Dunn, John, *Setting the People Free: The Story of Democracy*, (London: Atlantic Books, 2005).

Dworkin, Gerald, 'Paternalism: Some Second Thoughts', in Rolf Sartorius, ed, *Paternalism*, (Minneapolis: University of Minnesota Press, 1983), 105–12.

Dworkin, Ronald, 'What Is Equality? Part 1: Equality of Welfare', (1981) 10 *Philosophy & Public Affairs*, 185–246.

—— 'What Is Equality? Part 2: Equality of Resources', (1981) 10 *Philosophy & Public Affairs*, 283–345.

—— *A Matter of Principle*, (Cambridge, Mass: Harvard University Press, 1985).

—— *Law's Empire*, (London: Fontana, 1986).

—— *Sovereign Virtue: The Theory and Practice of Equality*, (Cambridge, Mass: Harvard University Press, 2000).

—— 'Thirty Years On (Book Review of *The Practice of Principle* by Jules Coleman)', (2002) 115 *Harv L. Rev.*, 1655–89.

—— 'Hart's Postscript and the Character of Political Philosophy', (2004) 24 *OJLS*, 1–37.

—— *Justice in Robes*, (Cambridge, Mass: Harvard University Press, 2005).

—— *Is Democracy Possible Here?* (Princeton: Princeton University Press, 2006).

Eisgruber, Christopher L, *Constitutional Self-Government*, (Cambridge, Mass: Harvard University Press, 2001).

Elster, Jon, *Ulysses and the Sirens*, rev'd ed, (Cambridge: Cambridge University Press, 1984).

—— *Ulysses Unbound*, (Cambridge: Cambridge University Press, 2000).

Ely, John Hart, 'Constitutionality of Reverse Racial Discrimination', (1974) 41 *U. Chi. L. Rev.*, 723–41.

—— *Democracy and Distrust*, (Cambridge, Mass: Harvard University Press, 1980).

Epstein, Richard A, 'Luck', (1988) 6 *Social Philosophy & Policy*, 17–38.

—— 'Affirmative Action for the Next Millenium', (1998) 43 *Loyola L.Rev.*, 503.

Estlund, David, 'Political Quality', in David Estlund, ed, *Democracy,* (Oxford: Basil Blackwell, 2002) 175–212.
Fallon, Richard H Jr, 'The Supreme Court, 1996 Term—Foreword: Implementing the Constitution', (1997) 111 *Harv. L. Rev.*, 54–152.
Feinberg, Joel, *Rights, Justice, and the Bounds of Liberty*, (Princeton: Princeton University Press, 1980).
—— *The Moral Limits of the Criminal Law, Harm to Self,* vol 3 (New York: Oxford University Press, 1986).
Finnis, John, *Natural Law and Natural Rights,* (Oxford: Oxford University Press, 1980).
Fishkin, James S, 'In quest of the social contract', in Geoffrey Brennan & Loren E Lomasky, eds., *Politics and Process: New Essays in Democratic Thought,* (Cambridge: Cambridge University Press 1989), 183–93.
—— *The Dialogue of Justice,* (New Haven: Yale University Press, 1992).
Fleurbaey, Mark, 'Equal Opportunity or Equal Social Outcome?', (1995) 11 *Economics & Philosophy*, 25–55.
—— 'Freedom with Forgiveness', (2005) 4 *Politics, Philosophy & Economics*, 29–67.
Friedman, M, *Free to Choose*, (Harmondsworth: Penguin Books, 1980).
Fuller, Lon L, *The Morality of Law,* (New Haven: Yale University Press, 1977) (1st edn 1969).
Gallie, WB, 'Essentially Contested Concepts', (1956) 56 *Proceedings of Aristotelian Society*, 167–98.
Galston, William, *Liberal Purposes,* (New York: Cambridge University Press, 1991).
Goffman, Erving, *Stigma,* (New York: Simon & Schuster, 1963).
Goldman, AH, 'Real People (Natural Differences and the Scope of Justice)', (1987) 17 *Canadian Journal of Philosophy*, 377–94.
Goldsworthy, Jeffrey, 'Originalism in Constitutional Interpretation', (1997) 25 *Federal L. Rev.*, 1–50.
Goodin, Robert E, 'Democracy, Justice and Impartiality', in Keith Dowding, Robert Goodin & Carol Pateman, eds., *Justice and Democracy: Essays for Brian Barry,* (Cambridge University Press: Cambridge, 2004), 97–111.
Gray, John, 'Contractarian Method, Private Property, and the Market Economy', in JW Chapman & JR Pennock, eds; *Markets and Justice*: *Nomos XXXI,* (1989) (New York University Press, 1989), 13–58.
Gray, Tim, *Freedom*, (London: Macmillan, 1991).
Greenawalt, Kent, *Conflicts of Law and Morality,* (New York: Oxford University Press, 1987).
Gutmann, Amy, and Thompson, Dennis, *Democracy and Disagreement*, (Cambridge, Mass: Harvard University Press, 1996).
Habermas, Jürgen, *The Inclusion of the Other: Studies in Political Theory*, (Cambridge, Mass: MIT Press, 1998).
—— 'Civil Disobedience: Litmus Test for the Democratic Constitutional State', (1985) 30 *Berkeley Journal of Sociology*, 95–116.
Haksar, Vinit, *Liberty, Equality, and Perfectionism*, (New York: Oxford Univeristy Press, 1979).
Hamlin, Alan, 'Constitutional Political Economy: The Political Philosophy of *Homo Economicus*?', (1995) 3 *Journal of Political Philosophy*, 280–303.
Hart, HLA, *The Concept of Law,* (Oxford: Oxford University Press, 1961).

Hart, HLA, *Law, Liberty, and Morality,* (Oxford: Oxford University Press, 1963).
Hayek, Friedrich A, *The Constitution of Liberty,* (Chicago: Henry Regnery, 1960).
Hershovitz, Scott, 'Legitimacy, Democracy, and Razian Authority', (2003) 9 *Legal Theory,* 201–20.
Hinton, Timothy, 'Must Egalitarians Choose Between Fairness and Respect?', (2001) 30 *Philosophy & Public Affairs,* 72–87.
—— 'Choice and Luck in Recent Egalitarian Thought', (2002) 31 *Philosophical Papers,* 145–67.
Hook, Sidney, 'In Defense of "Justice"', in E Kiefer & MK Munitz, *Ethics and Social Justice,* (Albany: State University of New York Press, 1968), 75–84.
Hurley, SL, *Justice, Luck, and Knowledge,* (Cambridge, Mass: Harvard University Press, 2003).
James, W, *The Principles of Psychology,* vol 1, (London: Macmillan, 1910).
Jedenheim-Edling, M, 'The Compatibility of Effective Self-Ownership and Joint World Ownership', (2005) 13 *Journal of Political Philosophy,* 284–304.
Jones, Peter, 'Political Equality and Majority Rule', in David Miller & Larry Siedentop, eds, *The Nature of Political Theory,* (Oxford: Oxford University Press, 1983).
Kay, Richard S, 'American Constitutionalism', in Larry Alexander, ed, *Constitutionalism: Philosophical Foundations,* (Cambridge: Cambridge University Press, 1998), 16–63.
Kelsen, Hans, 'On the Essence and Value of Democracy', in Arthur J Jacobson & Bernhard Schlink, eds; translated by Belinda Cooper; *Weimar: A Jurisprudence of Crisis,* (Berkeley: University of California Press, 2000), 84–109.
Kennedy, Duncan, 'Form and Substance in Private Law Adjudication', (1976) 89 *Harv.L. Rev.,* 1685–778.
Kernohan, A, 'Capitalism and Self-Ownership', (1988) 6 *Social Philosophy & Policy,* 60–76.
Knight, Jack and Johnson, James, 'What Sort of Equality Does Deliberative Democracy Require?', in James Bohman & William Rehg, eds, *Deliberative Democracy: Essays on Reason and Politics,* (Cambridge, Mass: MIT Press, 1997), 279–319.
Kronman, AT, 'Talent Pooling', in JR Pennock & JW Chapman, eds, *Human Rights: Nomos XXIII,* (New York: New York University Press, 1981), 58–79.
Ladenson, Robert, 'In Defense of a Hobbesian Conception of Law' in Joseph Raz, ed, *Authority,* (New York: New York University Press, 1990), 36–7.
Locke, John, *The Second Treatise of Government,* ed, TP Peardon (Indianapolis: Bobbs-Merrill, 1952).
Marmor, Andrei, 'Authority, Equality and Democracy', (2005) 18 *Ratio Juris,* 315–45.
May, Kenneth O, 'A Set of Independent Necessary and Sufficient Conditions for Simple Majority Decision', (1952) 20 *Econometrica,* 680–4.
Mayo, Henry B, *An Introduction to Democratic Theory,* (New York: Oxford University Press, 1960).
McKerlie, Denis, 'Equality', (1996) 106 *Ethics,* 274–96.
Michelman, Frank I, 'The Supreme Court, 1968 Term—Foreword: On Protecting the Poor Through the Fourteenth Amendment', (1969) 83 *Harv. L. Rev.,* 7–60.
Miller, David, *Principles of Social Justice,* (Cambridge, Mass: Harvard University Press, 1999).
Milne, H, 'Desert, Effort and Equality', (1986) 3 *Journal of Applied Philosophy,* 235–43.
Montague, Phillip, 'Comparative and Non-Comparative Justice', (1980) 30 *Philosophical Quarterly,* 131–40.

Mowbray, Alastair, *Cases and Materials on the European Convention of Human Rights*, (London: Butterworths, 2001).

Mueller, Dennis C, 'Democracy: the Public Choice Approach', in Geoffrey Brennan & Loren E Lomasky, eds, *Politics and Process: New Essays in Democratic Thought*, (Cambridge: Cambridge University Press, 1989), 78–96.

Nino, Carlos Santiago, *The Ethics of Human Rights* (Oxford: Oxford University Press, 1991).

Note, 'Developments in the Law: Equal Protection', (1969) 82 *Harv. L. Rev.*, 1065–192.

Note, 'Legislative Purpose, Rationality, and Equal Protection', (1972) 81 *Yale L.J.*, 112–34.

Note, 'Toward a Redefinition of Sexual Equality', (1981) 95 *Harv. L.Rev.*, 487–509.

Nozick, Robert, *Anarchy, State and Utopia*, (New York: Basic Books, 1974).

Offe, Claus, '"Homogeneity" and Constitutional Democracy: Coping with Identity Conflicts through Group Rights', (1998) 6 *Journal of Political Philosophy*, 113–14.

Ortiz, David R, 'The Democratic Paradox of Campaign Finance Reform', (1998) 50 *Stanford Law Review*, 893–914.

Otsuka, Michael, *Libertarianism Without Inequality*, (Oxford: Oxford University Press, 2003).

Parijs, Philippe van, 'Justice and Democracy: Are they Incompatible?', (1996) 4 *Journal of Political. Philosophy*, 101–17.

Perelman, Chaim, *Justice, Law, and Argument: Essays on Moral and Legal Reasoning*, (Dordrecht: D Reidel, 1980).

Perry, Michael J, 'What Is "Constitution"? and Other Fundamental Questions', in Larry Alexander, ed, *Constitutionalism: Philosophical Foundations*, (Cambridge: Cambridge University Press, 1998).

Pettit, Philip, *Republicanism: A Theory of Freedom and Government*, (Oxford: Clarendon Press, 1997).

Post, Richard C, 'The Supreme Court, 2002 Term—Foreword: Fashioning the Legal Constitution: Culture, Courts, and the Law', (2003) 117 *Harv. L. Rev.*, 4–112.

Radin, Margaret Jane, 'Justice and the Market Domain', in John W Chapman and J Roland Pennock, eds, *Markets and Justice: Nomos XXXI*, (New York: New York University Press, 1989), 165–97.

Radin, Margaret Jane, 'Market-Inalienability', (1987) 100 *Harv. L. Rev.*, 1849–937.

Rakowski, Eric, *Equal Justice*, (Oxford: Oxford University Press, 1991).

Rasmussen, Kasper-Lippert, 'Hurley on Egalitarianism and the Luck-Neutralizing Aim', (2005) 4 *Politics, Philosophy & Economics*, 249–65.

Rawls, John, *A Theory of Justice*, (Oxford: Oxford University Press, 1971).

—— 'Justice as Fairness: Political not Metaphysical', (1984) 14 *Philosophy & Public Affairs*, 223–25.

—— *Political Liberalism*, (New York: Columbia University Press, 1993).

—— *The Law of the Peoples*, (Cambridge, Mass: Harvard University Press, 1999).

Raz, Joseph, *The Authority of Law*, (Oxford: Oxford University Press, 1979).

—— *The Morality of Freedom*, (Oxford: Oxford University Press, 1986).

—— *Ethics in the Public Domain*, (Oxford: Oxford University Press, 1994).

—— 'On the Authority and Interpretation of Constitutions: Some Preliminaries', in Larry Alexander, ed, *Constitutionalism: Philosophical Foundations*, (Cambridge: Cambridge University Press, 1998), 152–93.

Risse, Mathias, 'Arguing for Majority Rule', (2004) 12 *Journal of Political Philosophy*, 41–64.

Roemer, John E, 'Equality and Responsibility', (1995) 20 *Boston Review* (April-May).

Rousseau, Jean-Jacques, 'Of the Social Contract', in *Rousseau: The Social Contract and Other Later Political Writings*, edited and translated by Victor Gourevitch, (Cambridge: Cambridge University Press, 1997).

Sadurski, Wojciech, 'Social Justice and Legal Justice', (1984) 3 *Law and Philosophy*, 329–54.

—— *Giving Desert Its Due*, (Dordrecht: D. Reidel, 1985).

—— 'Gerhardy v Brown v the Concept of Discrimination: Reflections on the Landmark Case that Wasn't', (1986) 11 *Sydney L. Rev.*, 5–43.

—— 'Judicial Protection of Minorities: The Lessons of Footnote Four', *Anglo-Amer. L.Rev.* (1988) 17, 163–81.

—— 'Some Ruminations on the Harm Principle', (1989) 75 *Archiv für Rechts- und Sozialphilosophie*, 459–67.

—— *Moral Pluralism and Legal Neutrality*, (Dordrecht: Kluwer, 1990).

—— 'Natural and Social Lottery, and Concepts of the Self', (1990) 9 *Law and Philosophy*, 157–75.

—— *Freedom of Speech and Its Limits*, (Dordrecht: Kluwer, 1999).

—— 'Judicial Review and the Protection of Constitutional Rights', (2002) 22 *OJLS*, 275–99.

—— *Rights before Courts: A Study of Constitutional Courts in Postcommunist States of Central and Eastern Europe*, (Dordrecht: Springer, 2005).

Sandalow, Terrance, 'Racial Preferences in Higher Education: Political Responsibility and the Judicial Role', (1975) 42 *U. Chi. L. Rev.*, 653–703.

Sandel, Michael J, *Liberalism and Its Critics* (Oxford: Basil Blackwell, 1984).

—— 'Freedom of Conscience or Freedom of Choice?', in JD Hunter & O Guinness, eds, *Articles of Faith, Articles of Peace: The Religion Liberty Clauses and the American Public Philosophy* (Washington: Brookings Institution, 1990), 74–92.

Scalia, Antonin, *A Matter of Interpretation,* (Princeton: Princeton University Press, 1997).

Schauer, Frederick, *Playing by the Rules,* (New York: Oxford University Press, 1991).

Scheffler, Samuel, 'Choice, Circumstance, and the Value of Equality', (2005) 4 *Politics, Philosophy & Economics*, 5–28.

Shapiro, Ian, *The State of Democratic Theory,* (Princeton: Princeton University Press, 2003).

Siedentop, Larry, *Democracy in Europe,* (London: Allen Lane, 2000).

Simmons, John A, 'Justification and Legitimacy', (1999) 109 *Ethics,* 739–71.

Skelly Wright, J, 'Color-Blind Theories and Color Conscious Remedies', (1980) 47 *U. Chi. L. Rev.*, 213–45.

Smith, JC, *Legal Obligation*, (London: The Athlone Press, 1976).

Snyder, CR and Fromkin, H, *Uniqueness: The Human Pursuit of Difference,* (New York: Plenum Press, 1980).

Sowell, Thomas, *Affirmative Action Around the World: A Comparative Study,* (New Haven: Yale University Press, 2004).

Spann, Girardeau A, 'The Dark Side of Grutter', (2004) 21 *Constitutional Commentary*, 221–50.

Spiegelberg, Herbert, 'A Defence of Human Equality', (1944) 53 *Philosophical Review*, 101–24.

Still, Jonathan, 'Political Equality and Election Systems', (1981) 91 *Ethics*, 375–94.

Strawson, PF, *Individuals: An Essay in Descriptive Metaphysics,* (London: Methuen, 1959).

Sullivan, Kathleen, 'The Supreme Court, 1991 Term—Foreword: The Justices of Rules and Standards', (1992) 106 *Harv. L. Rev.*, 22–123.

Tinbergen, Jan, *Income Differences* (Amsterdam: North-Holland Publishing, 1975).

Waldron, Jeremy, *Liberal Rights,* (New York: Cambridge University Press, 1993).

Waldron, Jeremy, 'Precommitment and Disagreement', in Larry Alexander, ed, *Constitutionalism: Philosophical Foundations,* (Cambridge: Cambridge University Press, 1998), 271–99.

Waldron, Jeremy, *God, Locke, and Equality: Christian Foundations in Locke's Political Thought,* (Cambridge: Cambridge University Press, 2002).

Waldron, Jeremy, 'Is the Rule of Law an Essentially Contested Concept (in Florida)?', (2002) 21 *Law and Philosophy*, 137–64.

Waldron, Jeremy, 'Legal and Political Philosophy', in Jules Coleman & Scott Shapiro, eds, *The Oxford Handbook of Jurisprudence and Philosophy of Law,* (Oxford: Oxford University Press, 2002), 352–81.

Waldron, Jeremy, 'The Core of the Case Against Judicial Review', (2006) 115 *Yale Law Journal*, 1346–406.

Walzer, Michael, *Spheres of Justice*, (Oxford: Basil Blackwell, 1983).

Williams, Bernard, AO, 'The Idea of Equality' in Hugo A. Bedau, ed, *Justice and Equality,* (New Jersey: Prentice-Hall, 1971).

Index

Lightning Source UK Ltd.
Milton Keynes UK
UKOW06n1447131215

3620UKLV00021B/158/P